From Untouch

Essays on the Amb

ELEANOR ZELLIOT

MANOHAR
2005

First published 1992
Second revised edition 1996
Reprinted 1998
Third edition 2001
Reprinted 2005

ISBN 81-7304-143-1

Published by
Ajay Kumar Jain for
Manohar Publishers & Distributors
4753/23 Ansari Road, Daryaganj
New Delhi 110 002

Typeset by
A J Software Publishing Co. Pvt. Ltd.
New Delhi 110 005

Printed at
Print Perfect
New Delhi 110 064

Distributed in South Asia by
FOUNDATION
B●●KS
4381/4, Ansari Road
Daryaganj, New Delhi 110 002
and its branches at Mumbai, Hyderabad,
Bangalore, Chennai, Kolkata

Introduction to the Third Edition

Just last year I was asked by some highly educated followers of Dr. Ambedkar if I was going to do a book called "From Untouchable to Buddhist", since this group resented the term "Dalit" as negative, even demeaning. I replied that I could not, since not all Dalits were Buddhist, and that the term Dalit was not only to be interpreted as "the oppressed", but also as "the proud, the defiant". As long as there is a group or groups, chiefly Untouchable and in some cases Backward Castes or Scheduled Castes, who are the victims of caste oppression, there must be a term to describe them and the literature they create to tell their stories. The rejection of "dalit" by those who are able to take their destinies in their own hands is understandable, and in many ways a good sign, a sign of progress. But the title of the Human Rights Watch report, *Broken People: Caste Violence against India's Untouchables*, by Smita Narula (1999) also reflects a reality, a translation of *dalit* in one of its meanings as "ground down, broken". The reader of my essays will find much that is positive, much that is hopeful. Both realities—oppression and a dynamic movement against oppression—must be kept in mind. When Martin Macwan won the Kennedy award for his work on the Dalit Human Rights Campaign, he said, "To me Dalit is not a caste, but a moral position . . . one who respects all humans as equal is a Dalit."

Some Notes on New Approaches, New Books

The release of Jabbar Patel's feature film, *Dr. Ambedkar*, in India has brought the life of Ambedkar in a very positive way into this media, video tape of which is not available. However a cassette of the music is available. Equally innovative is a new website, "Ambedkar.org" which contains dozens of articles about Dalits, including Ramchandra Guha's "Gandhi's Ambedkar" which suggests that in some ways Ambedkar is now the only all-India pre-Independence hero. Also available on the web is a 26 page bibliography prepared by Simon Charsley and his group at Glascow: *www.gla.ac.uk/Acad/Anthropology/Sisc.htm*. The *Dalit International Newsletter* (P.O. Box 932. Waterford CT 06385) is now in its fifth year of bringing thoughtful articles about Dalit developments. An important development for me is the publication of Gail Omvedt's translation of Vasant Moon's Marathi autobiography, *Vasti* (Hindi bustee or slum locality). It will be released in 2001 by Rowman and Littlefield as *Growing Up Untouchable in India* with my introduction, the first Dalit autobiography to be published in the U.S. and a very vibrant story which reflects the complexity of the Dalit concept.

What follows is a list of some of the most important or unusual of the many new books on Dalits or Untouchables. Note that many of them are from Europeans, and published in the West:

Bandyopadhyay, Sekhar. *Caste, Protest and Identity in Colonial India: The Namasudras of Bengal, 1872-1947.* London: Curzon, 1997.

Chaarsley, Simon R. and G.K. Karanth, eds. *Challenging Untouchability: Dalit Initiative and Experience from Karnataka.* New Delhi: Sage, 1998.

Deliege, Robert. *The Untouchable of India.* Tr. from the French by Nora Scott. Oxford and New York: Berg, 1999.

————. *The World of the "Untouchables": Paraiyars of Tamil Nadu.* Tr. from the French by David Phillips. Delhi: Oxford University Press, 1997.

Dube, Saurabh. *Untouchable Pasts: Religion, Identity and Power among a Central Indian Community, 1780-1950.* Albany: State University of New York, 1998.

Dube, Siddharth. *In the Land of Poverty: Memoirs of an Indian Family, 1947-1997.* London: Zed Books, 1998.

Jogdand, P.G., ed., *New Economic Policy and Dalits.* Jaipur: Rawat, 2000.

Kotani, H., ed., *Caste System, Untouchability and the Depressed.* New Delhi: Manohar, 1997.

Mendelsohn, Oliver and Marika Vicziany. *The Untouchables: Subordination, Poverty and the State in Modern India.* Cambridge: Cambridge University Press, 1998.

Nagaraj, D.R. *The Flaming Feet: A Study of the Dalit Movement.* Bangalore, South Forum Press, 1993.

Prasad, Vijay. *Untouchable Freedom: A Social History of a Dalit Community.* New Delhi: Oxford University Press, 2000.

Shourie, Arun. *Worshipping False Gods: Ambedkar and the facts which have been erased.* New Delhi: ASA Publications, 1997. (I do not recommend this dreadful book except as an example of what truly bad history is and how far a biased caste Hindu will go to try to discredit Ambedkar.)

Viramma, Josiane and Jean-Luc Racine. *Viramma, Life of an Untouchable.* Tr. from the French by Will Hobson. London: Verso, 1997.

Webster, John C.B. *Religion and Dalit Liberation: An Examination of Perspectives.* New Delhi: Manohar, 1999.

Eleanor Zelliot

Introduction to the Second Edition
A BIBLIOGRAPHIC ESSAY

My use of the title *From Untouchable to Dalit* was to indicate the idea that the Untouchables of India had themselves chosen a new identity, that of "dalit"—ground down, oppressed—to indicate their lack of belief in being polluting, their sense that their condition was the fault of the caste system, and their inclusion in the Ambedkar movement of all those subordinated by their religious, social and economic status. The word is now current among all those who subscribe to these beliefs, although "harijan" is still current among Gandhians and many high castes and "Scheduled Castes" is the legal term for Untouchables. I have used the term, aware that not all Dalits are comfortable with it, to indicate the vitality and innovation of the Ambedkar movement.

In the short space of time since this book was published in 1992 there have been some new developments in the Ambedkar movement and a great many new publications. Dr. Babasaheb Ambedkar continues to be ever more important, although almost forty years have passed since his death in 1956. What is even more interesting, however, is that there continue to be innovations in the religious, social, political, educational worlds that he attempted to change.

For the first time, the Dalit movement of western India has been thoroughly analyzed. Gail Omvedt has taken the upper Deccan—Maharashtra, Andhra and Karnataka, the Marathi, Telugu and Kannada speaking areas—as her field, and brought into play geographic and pre-historic factors as well as history and sociological analysis. In my mind, it is the most creative Marxism since D.D. Kosambi. Omvedt explains why the Phule-Ambedkar movement has been omitted or marginalized in most histories of modern India: caste was seen as subsumed in class by Marxist and leftist historians (who dominate the field); the nationalist movement was idealized as inclusive of all India by nationalist historians, who saw pre-Independence history "only in terms of political opposition to a foreign power" (Omvedt 1994:16). She analyzes Ambedkarism with a keen sense of Ambedkar's own total grounding in Indian reality. Her title, *Dalits and the Democratic Revolution,* indicates her understanding of the democratic vision of Dr. Ambedkar, even as he struggled with varied economic and political ideologies. While there are many biographies of Dr. Ambedkar, none (including my own unpublished 1969 Ph.D. thesis) have probed Ambedkar's writings as thoroughly or analyzed Ambedkar's political and economic choices and his responses as carefully or docu-mented his rejection of caste and Brahmanism and "Nehruvian secularism" (Omvedt 1994:242) as well. Her work has been facilitation by the series of *Writings and Speeches of Dr. Babasaheb Ambedkar,* edited by Vasant Moon and published by the Government of Maharashtra. These volumes, soon to number seventeen, allow a close study of all Ambedkar's thought.

Another new sociological analysis by M.S. Gore (1993) has been made possible by the accessibility of the Ambedkar volumes and the republication of Ambedkar's Marathi editorials by Ratnakar Ganvir. Using Robert K. Merton's theory of the sociology of knowledge, Gore first sets Ambedkar's thought in a universal paradigm and then sets that ideology in a chronological historic perspective. Gore's note on his late consciousness of the importance of Ambedkar is touching, and his study is set both in the context of his earlier devotion to Nehru and Gandhi and his more recent studies of the non-Brahman movement (1989) and Maharshi Shinde (1990) and in his policy of using Ambedkar's own writings rather than involvement with the movement and its participants.

Dalit Literature

Another new area of publication is that of Dalit literature. The first comprehensive anthology of Dalit writing was published just as the first edition of this book appeared and so escaped mention. Arjun Dangle's *Poisoned Bread* (1992) would be more complete if it had included work by Gangadhar Pantawane and Raja Dhale, to name a few omissions, but it does have an extensive selection of poetry, short stories, autobiographies and essays. The first three genre have been published separately in very attractive paperback editions as, respectively, *No Entry for the New Sun, Homeless in My Land,* and *A Corpse in the Well.* I find the collection a little more pessimistic and dark in tone than I find the Dalit movement itself, but I am most grateful to Arjun Dangle and Priya Adarkar of Orient Longman for this first large collection. For other new material, see my publications listed on p. xx and Dharwadker (1994) in the Bibliography of this Introduction. The first English translation of Dalit theater, Datta Bhagat's

"Routes and Escape Routes," which was a very successful TV play, appeared in 1994. Another first is a new Dalit journal in English begun by Kashinath Ranveer of the English Department at Dr. Babasaheb Ambedkar Marathwada University. He has titled it *The Downtrodden India: A Journal of Dalit and Bahujan Studies*, and the first issue appeared early last year. I think *Subordinate India* would be a better title, encompassing both Dalit and Bahujan (the majority, the masses) and carrying an undercurrent of insubordination and revolt. Ranveer studied Black women writers at Yale under a Fulbright fellowship.

The growth in Dalit literature seems to be in an ever widening circle of Dalit writers, not only women but now various adivasi and nomadic groups. Women poets Hira Bansode, Jyoti Lanjewar and Surekha Bhagat have published books. The initial circle of Marathi poets has expanded to include Gujarati and Kannada writers. All these poets appear in the Marathi journal *Asmitadarsh* (mirror of identity), the Dalit literary journal edited by Gangadhar Pantawane, which celebrated its twenty-fifth year with great fanfare in December 1992.

The 1994 annual conference of Asmitadarsh illustrates just how closely tied Dalit literature is with Dalit reality. On January 14 the long battle for the re-naming of Marathwada University in Aurangabad was won, and Dr. Babasaheb Ambedkar Marathwada University became a fact. On January 15, as the Asmitadarsh conference was meeting in one part of the city of Chandrapur, watching a Dalit play by Premanand Gajbhiye at two in the morning, the Library of Dr. Ambedkar College in another part of Chandrapur was torched and completely destroyed. No one, of course, claims responsibility.

The Innovations of Women

One of the most interesting new event is the first Dalit Women's Solidarity Conference which brought Buddhist, Christian, Muslim and Hindu women together in Bangalore in March of this year. A few men and some high caste Hindu women were also present, and Vimal Thorat of Indira Gandhi National Open University in Delhi tells me that she asked the high caste women there why they did not protest atrocities on Dalit women. This seems to be the first all-India conference of Dalit women, and the leadership was drawn from several states. The literature on Dalit women is growing but does not reveal all the stages of their life or their progress. Older studies of Bhangi women in the North (this level of women not directly represented in the conferences) are by Mary Chatterjee (1981) and Malavika Karlekar (1982). Karlekar told me that she could not do further studies after the women asked her, "What good does your study do for our lives?" A question which does indicate some awakening.

An interesting collection of biographies of Dalit women in Maharashtra, many of them Buddhist but none educated, is Sumitra Bhave's *Pan on Fire* (1988). Gabriele Dietrich's chapter on Dalit women (1992) is excellent for the Tamil world. Women in the Ambedkar movement were the subject of a Marathi book by Meenakshi Moon and Urmila Pawar, and a condensation of their findings appeared in English in 1992. There is a fascinating account by Kumud Paude of her difficult path to becoming a teacher of Sanskrit in Arjun Dangle's collection (1992).

It seems to me significant that the first really inspiring film on Dr. Ambedkar is feature film produced by a Dalit woman, Dr. P. Padmavathi of Andhra. Leaving her clinic in the hands of her pediatrician husband, she worked for seven years to make *Dr. Ambedkar,* and her hope is that it can be released with Marathi and Hindi dubbing, with English sub-titles added to the original Telugu version. Her Ambedkar is tirelessly dedicated to knowledge, to the welfare of all Dalits, including women.

Economic Problems

The new economic policy of India, stressing market economy and private industry, has created great apprehension among those whose path into any kind of economic opportunity has been through reservations. One thousand Scheduled Caste and Scheduled Tribe officers attended a forum on "The New Economic Policy and Its Implication for Scheduled Castes and Scheduled Tribes" sponsored by the Indian Social Institute on April 16, 1994. I am told that Manmohan Singh, Finance Minister and chief policy maker, listened for two hours and spoke for one. At a July 1994 meeting, Ram Vilas Paswan, a bright light of the Janata Dal and a popular Scheduled Caste leader from Bihar, asked for reservations in the private sector as well as the filling of government reserved posts, especially those high positions in which Dalits are still grossly under-represented. One wonders if India will try "Affirmative Action" in its new market economy even as it struggles to enter the world market.

Dr. Ambedkar's economic thought is receiving new attention in India, just as is Gandhi's idea of decentralization. Omvedt (1994) discusses Ambedkar's ideas, and the most recent of several full length studies is Narendra Jadhav's (1993.) For a study of one city's Scheduled Caste entrepreneurs see S.M. Dahiwale (1989).

The Political Field

There has been a remarkable new development in politics. Kanshi Ram, a Ramdasi from the Punjab, highly educated and a former high level government servant, formed the Bahujan Samaj Party, which in concert with the Samajwadi Party of Mulayam Singh Yadav won the vast province of Uttar Pradesh from the right wing Hindu control of the Bharatiya Janata Party last year. With a controversial Dalit woman, Mayawati, as his right hand, Kanshi Ram attempted to keep Dalit and Muslim voters in an alliance with the "Other Backward Castes" led by Mulayam Singh. Most press releases indicate constant friction, but an article in the prestigious Economic and Political Weekly by Anil Nauriya bears the title: "Dalit-Intermediate Caste Alliance: A Call to Greatness" (XXXIX:27, 2 July, 1994:1640-1643).

Kanshi Ram has a small but widespread following in Maharashtra. Prakash Ambedkar, Ambedkar's grandson and the head of the Republican Party, continues to have strong support especially in the Northern areas of Maharashtra, and he has made some new electoral alliances. The Party has little elected strength at the state level, more at the local Panchayat level. Politics, like Buddhism, is an area of some pessimism among Dalits, but there is probably no more than there is elite Indian pessimism about politics in general.

Ram Vilas Paswan of Bihar, a star in the short lived Janata Party rule of V.P. Singh (1989-1990), is still active, but no longer the dominant national figure. Kanshi Ram and Ram Vilas Paswan both base their political message in the image of Dr. Ambedkar. Politics is ever changing; the only constant is the inspiration of Ambedkar.

More material continues to come out on "Mandal," the extension of reservations to the Other Backward Castes, the level just above Dalit. One of the best short pieces on Mandal is by Mihir Desai, "A Justification of Reservations and Affirmative Action for Backward Castes in India," in the South Asia Bulletin XI (1991):110-130, a journal easily available in America. A recent phenomenon, however, has not been at all studied, and that is the inclusion of a Scheduled Caste or Tribe person in every educational institution which gets funds from the Government of India. This means a Dalit in every academic department, and there are stories of success and failure from both sides. Some Dalits feel mistreated; some high castes feel that "merit" has been ignored. Would that some sociologist would take up this study and see if it has had the profoundly beneficial effect that "Affirmative Action" has had in my own College.

Buddhism

The progress of the Buddhist conversion movement is difficult to access. It has now been almost forty years since Babasaheb Ambedkar took *diksha* at Nagpur, and I think it is fair to say that many serious Buddhists are concerned that there still is not a bhikhu in every locality or that some who converted still follow Hindu practices, or that Buddhism has not developed the kind of festivals that make Hinduism such a participatory religion. But the outside observer does see change: there are more and more viharas, complete with images of the Buddha and Babasaheb Ambedkar, many of them in slum areas. There are now perhaps a dozen Buddhist nuns as well as several dozen Marathi speaking bhikhus. Literally hundreds of Maharashtrian Buddhists go to the Vipassana meditation retreats offered by the growing movement of Goenka, who now has a permanent center at Igatpuri. The Trailokya Bauddh Mahasangha Sahayaka Gana begun by the Venerable Sangarakshita as the Indian branch of the Friends of the Western Buddhist order is steadily adding new centers and new dharmacharis—dharmachari rather than bhikhu since the order stresses lay leadership rather than a sangha of monks. At latest count, the TBMSG maintained hostels and dhamma work at ten towns in Maharashtra as well as in Goa, Ahmedabad, Agra and Hastinapur. There is a beautiful center of extensive work at Dapodi near Pune and a retreat center in Nagpur, and across from the two thousand year old Buddhist caves at Karla is a retreat center for today's Buddhists.

The enormous stupa which marks the conversion spot at the Diksha Bhumi (conversion spot) in Nagpur is still being built but is impressive even in its unfinished state. The training center of the late Venerable Anand Kausalyayan at that place continues, and a branch at Kampti has been established. There were recent mass conversions at Patna in Bihar (under the care of Meiku Ram, Inspector General of Police) in December 1994 and at Bhopal by the Bauddh Maha Sangha based in Bombay in May 1994. A Japanese bhikshu, Surai Sasai, who lived for years in Nagpur, leads a continuous protest of the Hindu domination of Bodh Gaya, the place of the Buddha's enlightenment, and a number of Maharashtrian Buddhists join him and the Nagpur leader L.S. Rokde. One of the first Maharashtrians to become a bhikhu, the Venerable Sumedh, has written his biography, *Mi pahilele Bodhisatva Dr. Babasaheb Ambedkar* (Bombay: Kapilvastu Prakashan, 1994) and continues to serve at Wadala, a hostel and center of the Peoples Education Society founded by Ambedkar in Bombay. Perhaps the outsider sees more change and progress than the Buddhist inside the movement is aware of. But it is still true that change comes through individual action. No great over-arching organization seems possible, but there are noble efforts. The All India Boudha Dhamma Parishad was held in Nanded in January 1994 with perhaps ten thousand people and eighty bhikhus in attendance. The organizer of this sixth conference was Dr. S.P. Gaikwad, a long-time worker for Buddhism in Maharashtra, who invited the Venerable Shasan Rashmi, general secretary of the All India Bhikku Sangh, to inaugurate the conference.

The Christian Dalit Movement

Another new area of thought and action is that of the Christian Church in India. Not only have remarkable publications on "Dalit Christians" and "Dalit Theology" poured out, but the Church has also fostered new writing on Scheduled Castes in general and sponsored conferences in which scholars, Dalits and other interested folk as well as Christians participate. There seem to be two thrusts to this movement—one is the acknowledge- ment of the fact that there are Dalit Christians, a matter of shame for the Christian Church, and that the Church must not only recognize their needs but form a theology that encompasses all and even recognizes their Dalit creativity. The other is that the Church in India is wholly Indian as well as international, and must participate in solutions to India's problems. The suffering of Christian Dalits in a 1991 attack on Dalits at Chundure in Guntur District brought home this fact. The Indian Social Institute in New Delhi, led by Christians, has become an extraordinarily active and effective force in many Dalit matters.

The book on Dalit Theology edited by M.E. Prabhakar (1988) was noted in the first edition of this volume. New material appears in the Bibliography after this Introduction. See James Massey, V. Devasahayam (1992), John C.B. Webster (1992), Dr. K. Wilson (1982), Walter Fernandes (1981), Arvind P. Nirmal (1989), T.S. Wilkinson (1972) and the September 1990 issue of *Religion and Society* (XXXVII:3) on Dalit Ideology, especially the article by Dr. A.M. Abraham Ayrookuzhiel.

Gandhi and Ambedkar

Studies of Gandhi and Ambedkar seem to be increasingly important. And even as there is a revival of interest in Gandhi among the Subaltern group of historians, there is a current of understanding of Ambedkar's opposition among other writers. Dileep Padgaonkar, editor of the *Times of India*, titled his editorial "Ambedkar and Gandhi: An Antagonism of Profound Significance (14 April 1990) and concluded that cynicism has replaced Gandhi's "smoldering moral zeal" and Ambedkar's "intensely secular humanist mission." Other writers are less pessimistic. Among the most interesting of the new material not listed among the books and articles at the end of my Gandhi and Ambedkar article in this volume is work by Harish Doshi (1986) and Ravinder Kumar (1989). Bhikhu Parekh does not discuss Ambedkar but indicates the basis of Ambedkar's criticism of Gandhi: Gandhi "undermined the moral basis of untouchability but not its economic and political roots" (p. 209). It should be added that Ambedkar's followers have won the battle to ban Gandhi's term Harijan in all government pronouncements in Maharashtra and Madhya Pradesh. I have nothing to add to my early article on the leadership of the two except to say that a Gandhian voice crying out against the atrocities committed on Dalits would be very welcome.

Collections and New Studies

The centenary year (celebrated from 1991 to 1992) of Ambedkar's birth saw numerous seminars and collections of articles. One of these, edited by A.K. Narain and the most prolific writer in English on Ambedkar and Buddhism, D.C. Ahir, (1994) contains new work by three Western scholars: the first easily available work on new Buddhist art by Gary Tartakov, an analysis of three responses to Buddhism by Timothy Fitzgerald, and Christopher Queen's essay on Ambedkar's Buddhism from a classical perspective. (I must add here that I find Fitzgerald's work interesting as the first work by a Western trained anthropologist, but deficient in that it ignores the many efforts of Buddhists in urban centers.) K.N. Kadam has also included some new writers in his collection (1993), including Lokmitra, the able and energetic head of the work of the Friends of the Western Buddhist Order in India.

Other collections are those edited by S.N. Chaudhary (1988), K.L. Bhatia (1994) and Sudarshan Agarwal (1991), the latter containing articles written chiefly by members of parliament and government officers, and an elaborate two volume set from the Government of India (1992).

New studies by individuals include Lata Murugkar (1991) on Dalit Panthers) and Jayashree Gokhale (1993) on the radicalization of the movement; R.C. Prasad (1993), the first book on Ambedkar published by a normally traditional Hindu press; the review of social movement literature by Ghanshyam Shah (1990), whose work is always thorough and innovative;

the first study by a Russian, E.S. Yurlova (1990); two studies of the movement by those who are part of it: Pralhad Gangaram Jogdand (1991) and R.K. Kshirsagar (994); Nirupama Prakash's competent analysis (1989); and a new life of Ambedkar by the prolific D.C. Ahir (1990); and Sukhadeo Thorat's unusual study of Ambedkar's 1942-46 Development of Water Resources.

New Interests

My interests lately have turned to a field which is not now fashionable, and that is a critical analysis of India's culture as Great/Little tradition or as a hierarchy acceptable to all. Building on the slightest suggestion in R.K. Khare's *The Untouchable as Himself* (1985), I wonder if there isn't an Indic tradition, something apart from and underlying great and little, Brahmanic or Untouchable, something from which an egalitarian impulse as well a hierarchical framework can spring. In my mind, the Mahabharata (in part) is Indic. Buddhism and Jainism are Indic, as are the great numbers of creation myths of Untouchables which differ vastly from the Great Tradition of karma (see Robert Deliege 1993). Ramanujan's folk tales are Indic, as is the egalitarian Mahanubhav sect in Maharashtra. Ambedkar's passionate devotion to India in spite of his intense criticism of some Indian institutions rests on this Indic sub-stratum. I find hints of the development of this unformed idea of mine in Robert Deliege (1992) and the work of Jonathan Parry.

Related to this interest is a study of the religion of Dalits. I am working on editing a book on Untouchable bhakti saints, with articles by different scholars on Nandanar, Tiruppan Alvar and Ravidas, and my own work on Cokhamela and his family. And in pursuing this I have found many references to Untouchable saints, from the Mahar Gopal Baba Yervalkar who has seven samadhis, including a grand one in the Maharwada in the holy town of Pandharpur, and a Chambhar woman saint simply called "Santbai". Studies of the Telugu and Tamil oral traditions indicate Untouchables have participated in creating and preserving the common culture of societies. As a historian I must follow my own bent of study of the meaning of religion as it affects history, but I hope that the students of the history of religion, the anthropologists and the sociologists, will probe even further this fascinating field.

Pune, August 1994   Eleanor Zelliot

REFERENCES

Agarwal, Sudarshan, editor. *Dr. B.R. Ambedkar: The Man and His Message: A Commemorative Volume.* New Delhi: Prentice-Hall of India, 1991.

Ahir, D.C. *Life of Dr. Ambedkar.* Delhi: BR Publishing, 1990.

Ambedkar, Dr. B.R. *Dr. Babasaheb Ambedkar: Writings and Speeches,* edited by Vasant Moon. Bombay: Department of Education, Government of Maharashtra, 1989—. Thirteen volumes of seventeen projected volumes, the last an index, were published by 1994.

Bhagat, Datta. "Routes and Escape-Routes" (*Wata pal wata*), translated by Maya Pandit, in *Yatra: Writings from the Indian Subcontinent Vol. III.* Guest editor Satish Alekar. General Editor Alok Bhalla. New Delhi: Indus (Harper Collins), 1994.

Bhatia, K.L. *Dr. B.R. Ambedkar: Social Justice and the Indian Constitution,* New Delhi: Deep and Deep, 1994.

Bhave, Sumitra. *Pan on Fire: Eight Dalit Women Tell Their Story,* translated by Gauri Deshpande. New Delhi: Indian Social Institute, 1988.

Chaudhary, S.N., editor. *Changing Status of Depressed Castes in Contemporary India: Essays in Honour of Professor S.C. Dube.* Delhi: Daya Publishing House, 1988.

Dahiwale, S.M. *Emerging Entrepreneurship among the Scheduled Castes of Contemporary India: A Study of Kolhapur City.* New Delhi: Concept, 1989.

Dangle, Arjun, editor. *Poisoned Bread: Translations from Modern Marathi Dalit Literature.* Hyderabad and Bombay: Orient Longman, 1992.

Deliege, Robert. "Replication and Consensus: Untouchability, Caste and Ideology in India" in *Man,* n.s. 27 (1992):155-173.

————. "The Myth of Origin of the Indian Untouchables, in *Man,* n.s. 28 (1993):533-549.

Devasahayam, V., editor. *Dalits and Women: Quest for Humanity.* Madras: The Gurukul Summer Institute, 1992.

Dharwadker, Vinay. "Dalit Poetry in Marathi" in *World Literature Today* 68 (Spring 1994):319-324.

Dietrich, Gabriele. *Reflections on the Women's Movement in India: Religion, Ecology, Development.* New Delhi: Horizon India Books, 1992.

Doshi, Harish, "Gandhi and Ambedkar on the Removal of Untouchability," in *Reservation Policy, Programmes and Issues, edited* by Vimal P. Shah and Binod C. Agrawal. Jaipur: Rawat Publications, 1986.

Fernandes, Walter. *Caste and Conversion Movements.* New Delhi: Indian Social Institute, 1981.

Gokhale, Jayashree. *From Concessions to Confrontation: The Politics of an Indian Untouchable Community.* Bombay: Popular Prakashan, 1993

Gore, M.S. *Non-Brahman Movement in Maharashtra.* New Delhi: Segment Book Distributors, 1989.

————. *Vitthal Ramji Shinde*. Bombay: Tata Institute of Social Sciences, 1990.

————. *The Social Context of an Ideology: Ambedkar's Political and Social Thought*. New Delhi: Sage Publications, 1993.

Government of India, Publications Division. *Ambedkar and Social Justice*. New Delhi, 1992.

Jadhav, Narendra. *Dr. Ambedkar's Economic Thought and Philosophy*. Bombay: Popular Prakashan, 1993.

Jogdand, Pralhad Gangaram. *Dalit Movement in Maharashtra*. New Delhi: Kanak Publications, 1991.

Kadam, K.N. *Dr. Ambedkar and the Significance of His Movements: A Chronology* Bombay: Popular Prakashan.

Karlekar, Malavika. *Poverty and Women's Work: A Study of Sweeper Women in Delhi*. Delhi: Vikas, 1982.

Kshirsagar, R.K. *Dalit Movement and Its Leaders 1857-1956*. New Delhi: M.D. Publishers, 1994.

Kumar, Ravinder. "Gandhi, Ambedkar and the Poona Pact, 1932," in his *The Making of a Nation: Essays in Indian History and Politics*. New Delhi: Manohar, 1989.

Massey, James, editor. *Indigenous People: Dalits. Dalit Issues in Today's Theological Debate*. Delhi: ISPCK, 1994.

Moon, Meenakshi and Urmila Pawar. "We Made History Too: Women in the Early Untouchable Liberation Movement," in *South Asia Bulletin* 9:2 (1989):68-71.

Murugkar, Lata. *Dalit Panther Movement in Maharashtra: A Sociological Appraisal*. Bombay: Popular Prakashan, 1991.

Narain, A.K. and D.C. Ahir, editors. *Dr. Ambedkar, Buddhism and Social Change*. Delhi: B.R. Publishing Corporation, 1993.

Nirmal, Arvind P., ed. *Toward a Common Dalit Ideology*. Madras: Gurukul Lutheran Theological College and Research Institute, 1990.

Omvedt, Gail. *Dalits and the Democratic Revolution: Dr. Ambedkar and the Dalit Movement in Colonial India*. New Delhi: Sage Publications, 1994.

Parekh, Bhikhu. *Discourse on Untouchability*. New Delhi: Sage Publications, 1989.

Prakash, Nirupama. *Scheduled Castes: Socio-Economic Changes*. Allahabad: Chugh, 1989.

Prasad, R.C. *Preface to Ambedkarism*. Delhi: Motilal Banarsidass, 1993.

Searle-Chatterjee, Mary. *Reversible Sex Roles: The Special Case of the Benares Sweepers*. (Women in Development). Oxford: Pergamon Press, 1981.

Shah, Ghanshyam. *Social Movements in India: A Review of the Literature*. New Delhi: Sage Publications, 1990.

Singh, K.S. *The Scheduled Castes*, vol. II of *The People of India* (Anthropological Survey of India), Delhi: Oxford University Press, 1993.

Thorat, Sukhadeo (Central Water Commission). *Ambedkar's Contribution to Water Resource Development*. New Delhi, 1993.

Webster, John C.B. *A History of the Dalit Christians of India.* Lewiston, N.Y.:
    Edwin Mellen, 1992. There is also an Indian edition: *The Dalit Christians:
    A History.* Delhi: ISPCK, 1992.

Wilkinson, T.S. and M.M. Thomas. *Ambedkar and the Neo-Buddhist Movement.*
    Madras: Christian Literature Society, 1972.

Wilson, Dr. K. *The Twice Alienated: Culture of Dalit Christians.* Hyderabad:
    Booklinks Corporation, 1982.

Yurlova, E.S. *Scheduled Castes in India.* New Delhi: *Patriot*, 1990.

Introduction to the First Edition

I began my study of Dr. B.R. (Babasaheb) Ambedkar and his movement when I was a graduate student preparing for my Ph.D. thesis. I read all I could for a year and then in 1963-65 spent a year and a half in India under the auspices of the American Institute of Indian Studies, gathering material on Dr. Ambedkar. The study of a low caste movement was then a rather novel thing for a historian. Most modern historians had worked on the nationalist movement or the British period or the revolt of 1857. Social history was beginning to be recognized as a necessary field, and in the 1960s studies of the Dravidian movement, a Saraswat caste and a Kayastha caste were published by American historians. My study, however, took me further into the field (most people who met me thought I was an anthropologist since historians did not go to villages) and it also took me further back into the history of Maharashtra, trying to find the roots of this most unusual movement among the Untouchables.

Although I have published in other areas, namely, the Bhakti movement, Maharashtrian intellectual history, and maps on many historical subjects for the *South Asia Historical Atlas*, my life has continued to be dominated by Babasaheb Ambedkar and his movement. No other Western scholar has studied the movement as a whole, although Owen Lynch, as an anthropologist, has written on the Jatava movement in Agra which was greatly influenced by Ambedkar. And so as a reluctant "expert", I have responded to requests for articles over these twenty-six years, trying to make sure that volumes on caste and politics, religion and politics, Indian political thought and Indian leadership contained material on this historically important movement. The new wave of encyclopaedias on Asian history and world religion, the new edition of *Sources of the Indian Tradition* also recognized the need, for the first time, to include untouchability and Ambedkar as entries, and I have diligently responded to these requests. With my teaching and this constant necessity to produce meaningful articles came another factor—the continuous growth and change of Ambedkar's movement. There were new developments and publications in the field of Buddhist conversion; the Dalit Panthers arose as a new force; the movement began to produce literature of such quantity and quality that Dalit Sahitya became a prominent part of the Marathi literary scene, and spread to the neighboring states of Gujarat and Karnataka. With this constant need to be aware of new trends in the movement, with the continued pressure to write short articles, I was unable to turn my 1969 Ph.D. thesis "Dr. B.R. Ambedkar and the Mahar Movement" into a published book. I hope to do that yet, although I will not use the word Mahar, since that limits the movement.

In the meantime, I have edited a selection of my articles to make those widely scattered publications more available to those interested, especially in India. There are many faults in this collection. For one thing, I am an incurable optimist, and that tone predominates. I find Gandhian influence at times helpful, when many of Ambedkar's followers would diagree with me. I find the Buddhist movement still innovative in terms of literature and institutions, when others might feel it has lost its momentum and some of its idealism. I find the politicization of Ambedkar's followers important, although the Party he founded is riven with splits and without national or state political power. I find the fact that no one leader has come to replace Ambedkar a natural phenomenon, rather than a lacuna to be mourned.

A fault in this volume is that it is often repetitive. I have tried to remove what I could without rendering an article unable to stand on its own. There is also a lack of theory which may trouble the social scientists, and a lack of comparison with other movements, in India and in America. I have often done this in speech, but since my articles were all written in response to requests, and no one requested such topics, those comparisons remain in my head. I have also not dealt specifically with the increasing violence in India against ex-Untouchables and Dalits. I have suggested that when the lower castes reject their traditional duties and attitudes, there is retaliation in areas where they are vulnerable, but the reader will have to turn elsewhere for a thorough coverage of the current scene.

In technical matters, references have been somewhat standardized, but the anthropological system of internal references has been allowed to stand in those articles in which it was used. Some errors and unclear passages have been corrected. Substantive additions have been enclosed in square brackets. An attempt to bring the reader more up-to-date with recent material is made in Addendums at the end of some chapters and after Sections II and III on religion and politics, respectively. And finally, after much thought I have abandoned diacritical marks, and have even allowed varied spellings, such as Cokhamela and Chokhamela, Gaekwad and Gaikwad, to stand.

These essays go out to the reader, as does all my work, with thanks to all the people of Maharashtra who shared their knowledge, their spirit and their love for Babasaheb Ambedkar with me. They number in the hundreds, but among them a few must be singled out for their constant and indispensable help: the late Professor S.D. Gaikwad, K.N. Kadam of Yeravada, Vasant and Meenakshi Moon of Nagpur and Bombay, and Sudhir and Pushpa Waghmare of Pune. I alone, however, am responsible for both fact and interpretation in my writing.

December, 1991   Eleanor Zelliot

Articles on the Ambedkar movement and other relevant material by Eleanor Zelliot which do not appear in this volume

"Background of the Mahar Buddhist Conversion", in Robert Sakai ed., *Studies on Asia*, 1966 (Lincoln: University of Nebraska, 1966).

"Dalit Sahitya—The Historical Background", together with a translation of *Maran Swast hot ahe* (Death is getting cheaper) by Baburao Bagul, in *Vagartha*, 12 (1976).

"Introduction to Dalit Poems" With Gail Omvedt, in *Bulletin of Con-cerned Asian Scholars*, 10:3 (1978).

"The Indian Rediscovery of Buddism, 1855-1956", in A.K. Narain, ed., *Studies in Pali and Buddhism*, A Memorial volume in Honour of Bhikku Jagdish Kashyap (New Delhi: D.K. Publishers, 1979).

"An Historical View of the Maharashtrian Intellectual and Social Change", in Yogendra K. Malik ed., *South Asian Intellectuals and Social Change: A Study of the Role of Vernacular-Speaking Intellec-tuals* (Columbia, Mo: South Asia Books and New Delhi: Heritage Publishers, 1982).

"The Political Thought of Dr. B.R. Ambedkar", in Thomas Pantham and Kenneth L. Deutsch eds., *Contemporary Indian Political Thought* (Delhi: Sage Publications, 1986).

"Dr. B.R. Ambedkar" and "Marathi Religions", entries in *Encyclopaedia of Religion*, Chief Editor, Mircea Eliade (New York: Macmillan, 1986). The religion article was co-authored by Anne Feldhaus.

"Four Radical Saints of Maharashtra", in Milton Israel and N.K. Wagle eds., *Religion and Society in Maharashtra* (Toronto: Centre for South Asian Studies, University of Toronto, 1987).

"Untouchability", "Dr. B.R. Ambedkar", "Republican Party", entries in

Encyclopaedia of Asian History, Ainslee Embree, Chief Editor (New York: Charles Scribners Sons, 1988).

"Dr. B.R. Ambedkar: Selections from his Writings and Speeches" in the revised edition of Stephen Hay, ed., *Sources of Indian Civilization* (New York: Columbia University Press, 1988). (Please note: the spelling Bhim Rao Ambedkar in this selection is an error.)

The Experience of Hinduism: Essays on Religion in Maharashtra, Eleanor Zelliot and Maxine Berntsen, eds. (Albany: State Uni-versity of New York Press, 1988).

"Congess and the Untouchables", in Stanley Wolpert and Richard Sisson eds., *Congress and Indian Nationalism* (Berkeley: University of California Press, 1988).

"Buddhist Women of the Contemporary Maharashtrian Conversion Movement", in Jose Cabezon, ed., *Buddhism, Sexuality and Gender.* (Albany: SUNY Press, 1992).

An Anthology of Dalit Literature (Poetry) edited by Mulk Raj Anand and Eleanor Zelliot. (New Delhi: Gyan, 1992).

"Dr. Ambedkar through Western Eyes" in K.N. Kadam, ed., *Dr. B.R. Ambedkar: The Emancipator of the Oppressed.* (Bombay: Popular Prakashan, 1993).

"Stri Dalit Sahitya" (The literature of Dalit Women) in *The Downtrodden India* I:1 (1994) (Aurangabad) and *Images of Women* (papers from the Fifth Maharashtra Conference, Arizona), Albany: SUNY Press, (forthcoming).

"The New Buddhist Poetry" in A.K. Narain and D.C. Ahir, eds. (Delhi: B.R. Publishing Corporation, 1994). *Dr. Ambedkar, Buddhism and Social Change.*

"Cokhamela: Piety and Protest", in David Lorenzen, ed, *Bhakti Religion in North India.* (Albany: SUNY Press, forthcoming).

"The Dalit Community of Pune", to be translated into Marathi for *Pune: eka sanskritik sanchitace sarvagin darshan,* Aroon Tikekar, ed. (forthcoming).

"Dalit—New Perspectives on India's Ex-Untouchables", in *India Briefing 1991.* New York: The Asia Society, 1991.

Contents

Introduction to the Third Edition   v
Introduction to the Second Edition   vii
Introduction to the First Edition   xix

I. BACKGROUND

1. Chokhamela and Eknath: Two Bhakti Modes of
   Legitimacy for Modern Change   3
2. The Nineteenth Century Background of the
   Mahar and Non-Brahman Movements in Maharashtra   33

II. POLITICS

1. The Leadership of Babasaheb Ambedkar   53
2. The American Experience of Dr. B.R. Ambedkar   79
3. Learning the Use of Political Means: The Mahars
   of Maharashtra   86
4. Buddhism and Politics in Maharashtra   126
5. Gandhi and Ambedkar : A Study in Leadership   150

   Addendum to Part II   179

III. RELIGION

1. The Revival of Buddhism in India   187
2. Religion and Legitimization in the Mahar Movement   197
3. The Psychological Dimension of the Buddhist
   Conversion   218
4. Tradition and Innovation in Contemporary Indian
   Buddhism : Activities and Observances   222
5. Buddhist Sects in Contemporary India: Identity
   and Organization   235
6. The Buddhist Literature of Modern Maharashtra   249

   Addendum to Part III   262

IV. Dalit Literature

1. Dalit -- New Cultural Context for an
    Old Marathi Word   267
2. India's Ex-Untouchables: New Past,
    New Future and the New Poetry   293
3. The Folklore of Pride: Three Components
    of Contemporary Dalit Belief   317

    Addendum to Part IV   331

Select Bibliography (see also Addendum to Sections II, III,
IV and each chapter of I)   335

Index   341

BACKGROUND

Chokhamela and Eknath:
Two Bhakti Modes of Legitimacy for
Modern Change*

Chokhamela, a thirteenth-fourteenth century Maharashtrian *sant*[1] in the Bhakti tradition, and Eknath, a sixteenth century *sant*, are both revered figures in the *warkari sampradaya*,[2] the tradition of pilgrimage to Pandharpur which marks the important Bhakti movement in the Marathi-speaking area. The lives of both are known by legend; their songs are sung by devotees on the pilgrimage and in *bhajan* sessions. Chokhamela was a Mahar, the only important Bhakti figure in Maharashtra from an Untouchable caste. Eknath was a Brahman from the holy city of Paithan who wrote about Chokhamela, ate with Mahars, allowed Untouchables into his *bhajan* sessions, and wrote poems in the persona of a Mahar who was wiser in spiritual matters than the Brahmans.

Both, then, offer models for contemporary change in regard to untouchability: even though an Untouchable, Chokhamela, achieved sanctity and a place among the Bhakti pantheon of *sants*; Eknath, even though a Brahman from a distinguished, scholarly family, showed by his actions that there was equality among the true Bhaktas. This paper will explore the thought and the actions of both Bhakti figures in an attempt to determine their basic social and religious ideas, and then note the contemporary attempts to legitimize change through reference to these earlier religious figures.

Chokhamela was born in the second half of the thirteenth century,

*This article was first published in the *Journal of Asian and African Studies*, XIV, 3 & 4 (July-October 1980), an issue which also appeared as a book, *Tradition and Modernity in Bhakti Movements*, edited by Jayant Lele (Leiden: E.J. Brill, 1981). A few corrections have been made. Any additional material is indicated by square brackets. The addendum includes information on major new works in the field.

probably about the time that Dnyaneshwar, who is considered the founder of the Bhakti sect in Maharashtra, was born. He died in 1338 in Mangalvedhe, a town in Sholapur district, not far from Pandharpur. Chokhamela and his family seem to have followed the traditional village duties of a Mahar. The legend of his birth involves his parents' carrying mangoes to Pandharpur on the orders of the village headman, a duty expected of the Mahar village servant who was at the beck and call of the *patil*. On their journey, God Vitthal (or Vithoba), worshipped as the central divinity by the *warkari sampradaya*, disguised as a Brahman, begged for a fruit from the woman. He tasted it, found it sour and returned it to her. She tucked it into the folds of her sari and delivered the other mangoes to the priests at Pandharpur. When the fruit was counted and one was found missing, she pulled the half-bitten mango from her sari only to find that it had become a lovely child--Chokhamela.[3]

The legend of Chokhamela's death also involves traditional Mahar work and God's grace. He and other Mahars were called to repair the wall at Mangalvedhe--another traditional Mahar duty. As they worked on it, it collapsed, burying them. Namdev, a Bhakti *sant* from the *shimpi*, or tailor community who was Chokhamela's most devoted friend, went to the village to claim Chokhamela's body. He found the bones that murmured "Vitthal, Vitthal" and took them to Pandharpur, where they were buried near the steps of the temple.[4]

The legends, of course, can do no more than suggest that Chokhamela and his family were thoroughly and uncomplainingly involved in the traditional work of the Mahar caste, with divine intervention only to allow that work to proceed more smoothly. In even the lowliest of duties, that of dragging dead cattle out of the village, the God Vitthal appeared to help Chokhamela.[5] There is no evidence to suggest that Chokhamela ever protested the traditional limits of Mahar village work.

The internal evidence of Chokhamela's *abhangas* (Bhakti songs) suggests some protest, however, about the concept of untouchability, even though the greater number reveal only the traditional devotion and piety of the *bhakta*. The printed collection of Chokhamela's *abhangas* with which I have worked contains 211 songs,[6] some of them obviously spurious since the names of later *sants* appear in them. The collection was prepared for popular use, and no substantive scholarly work has been done on the manuscripts [allegedly] held at Pandharpur. It seems to me, however, that an authentic voice does come through these songs, however corrupt the text may be.

All but thirty-two of Chokhamela's over two hundred songs could

have been written by any of the *sants*. They are simple, direct, without
reference to his caste, such as this one:

> Why do you need a mirror
>   to see the bangles on your wrist?
> Have faith in the Name of Vitthal.
> You don't need to think about ritual;
> Chant the Name of Vitthal.
> The path of the Yogi is filled with clutter;
>   the chant is free;
>   do it first.
>
> Chokha says: there is bliss in the company
>   of the saints;
> chant the Name every night, every day.
>
> > *Abhanga 4*

The *abhangas* which do refer to untouchability, however, reveal
that Chokhamela was probably profoundly troubled by his despised
place in society. At times he was accepting, at times rebellious.[7]

> If You had to give me this birth,
>   why give me birth at all?
> You cast me away to be born; you were cruel.
> Where were You at the time of my birth?
> Who did You help then?
> Chokha says: O Lord, O Keshava, don't let me go.
>
> > *Abhanga 6*

> O God, my caste is low; how can I serve You?
> Everyone tells me to go away; how can I see you?
> When I touch anyone, they take offense.
> Chokhamela wants Your mercy.
>
> > *Abhanga 76*

> The only impurity is in the five elements.
> There is only one substance in the world.
> Then who is pure and who is impure?
> The cause of pollution is the creation of the body.
> In the beginning, at the end, there is nothing but
>   pollution.

No one knows anyone who was born pure.
Chokha says, in wonder, who is pure?

Abhanga 11

One *abhanga* seems to relate to one of the legends about Chokhamela,
a legend of rejection in the temple and acceptance by God which is also
commonly told about other Untouchable Bhakti *sants* in other traditions.
In the Marathi version, Chokhamela sits on the banks of the Bhima river
behind the temple after having been driven away by the temple priests,
the Badve. Vitthal himself comes to comfort him, and Chokhamela
offers him curd. A priest following Chokhamela overhears him address
his companion as "Vithoba", an affectionate name for God Vitthal, and
slaps his face. When he returns to the temple, the priest finds the image
of Vitthal with a swollen cheek and curd spilt on his garment.[8] The
abhanga which follows leaves out the miraculous, but indicates the
Badve's interference with Chokhamela's attempts to worship Vithoba.

Run, run, Vithu, don't come slowly.
I am beaten by the Badve for some transgression:
They ask: "How can you wear the garland of Vithoba?"
They abuse me and curse me: "Why have you polluted God?"

I am Your dog by Your door; don't let me go without mercy.
O Lord of the wheel, You are the creator of our lives.

I, Chokha, hands clasped, beg You, O God,
Don't be angry with my importuning.

Abhanga 5

However, Chokhamela more often than importuning God simply
uses the symbols of his Mahar-ness to reinforce the idea of his devotion
to Vitthal as well as to weave his own tradition, his own work, into the
life of the devotee. In the following *abhanga*, the word *call* in the last line
is a translation of *daundi*, which means the proclamation the village
Mahar servant makes in the centre of the village to call people together
for an announcement:

Clap hands, raise flags,
    take the road to Pandhari.[9]

The marketplace of Pandhari, the marketplace of joy!
There pilgrims meet in ecstasy,
So many flags they cannot be counted!
The banks of the Bhima resound with joyous shouts.
Let unbelievers come;
     let them go back pure.
Chokhamela gives this *call* from his heart.

Abhanga 54

Chokhamela even uses the customary right of the Mahar to receive any discarded food as a way to worship Vitthal. In this *abhanga*, he also uses the customary address of a Mahar to a superior, *johar*, as a salutation to Vitthal, here addressed as *May-Bap* (Mother and Father).

Johar, May-Bap, Johar.
Iam the Mahar of Your Mahars.
I am so hungry I have come for Your leavings.
I am full of hopes; I am the slave of Your slaves.
Chokha says: I have brought a bowl for Your
     left-over food.

Abhanga 71

In contrast to his *abhanga* on impurity, Chokhamela in another *abhanga* accepts his low status as his *karma*, the result of bad action in a previous life. [The reference to Nila in the following *abhanga* is probably to King Nila who fought against the Pandavas in the Mahabharata war, but there are many puranic and epic figures named Nila. At any rate, the meaning is clear.]

Pure Chokhamela, always chanting the name.
I am a Mahar without a caste, Nila in a previous birth.
He showed disrespect to Krishna; so my birth as a Mahar.
Chokha says: this impurity is the fruit of our past.

Abhanga 4

The ultimate reconciliation Chokhamela seems to have made was to consider himself fully an Untouchable in the eyes of men, without hope of acceptance as anything but impure, but just as fully a beloved of God. The most popular of all his *abhangas* raises his own defect of body (or caste) into a universalized concept: even the ugly, the deformed, the outwardly unacceptable, can be holy. Iravati Karve, in her narration of a pilgrimage to Pandharpur,[10] tells that the Brahman group in which she was traveling sang this song by the Untouchable Bhakta Chokhamela:

Cane is crooked, but its juice isn't crooked,
Why be fooled by outward appearance?

The bow is crooked, but the arrow isn't crooked,
Why be fooled by outward appearance?

The river is twisting, but its water isn't crooked,
Why be fooled by outward appearance?

Chokha is ugly, but his feelings aren't ugly,
Why be fooled by outward appearance?

Abhanga 52

Protest and question though he did, it would seem that Chokhamela lived in his traditional role as a Mahar and with its traditional limitations. The spirit of most of the *abhangas* is delight in the Lord, delivery from life's suffering through devotion. Even though agony is there, the central message is that Chokha, even though a Mahar, could experience the grace of God.

With the growth of nationlism and the awakening of interest in Maharashtra's past, the Bhakti movement, still very much alive, came to serve a new purpose. Mahadeo Govind Ranade, a Brahman, a judge and a member of the reformist religious group, the Prarthana Samaj, as well as a leading nationalist, wrote in 1900 of the historic importance of the Bhakti movement:

. . . like the Protestant Reformation in Europe in the sixteenth century, there was a Religious, Social and Literary Revival and Reformation in India, but notably in the Deccan in fifteenth and sixteenth centuries. This Religious Revival was not Brahmanical in its orthodoxy; it was heterodox in its spirit of protest against forms and ceremonies and class distinctions based on birth, and ethical in its preference of a pure heart, and of the law of love, to all other acquired merits and good works. This Religious Revival was the work also of the people, of the masses, and not of the classes. At its head were Saints and Prophets, Poets and Philosophers, who sprang chiefly from the lower orders of society--tailors, carpenters, potters, gardeners, shop-keepers, barbers, and even *mahars*--more often than Brahmans.[11]

Ranade's interpretation of the Bhakti movement served as legitimization for modern ideas of social justice, but his interpretation has been disputed. One reprint of Ranade's *Rise of the Maratha Power* includes a disclaimer in the introduction by R.V. Oturkar:

It must further be emphasized, as Professor G.B. Sardar has done, that while the saints in Maharashtra released the people from the thralldom of rituals they did not raise a revolt against Chaturvarna [the four Classes] and the Caste system. Their revolt was more or less of a conceptual character, severely confined to the field of religious thinking...[12]

The supposed equality of the Bhakti movement continues to be a much used concept, however, chiefly by those not directly involved in the political or religious aspects of the contemporary attempt of ex-Untouchables to gain equality. W.B. Patwardhan, as quoted by R.D. Ranade in *Pathways to God in Marathi Literature*, stated what still is probably the general popular impression:

The gates of the Bhakti school were ever open. Whoever entered was hailed as a brother--nay more--was honored as a saint. . . . All separatism tendencies vanished . . . all were equal. . . . For five successive centuries, Maharashtra was the abode of that noblest and truest of all Democracies, the Democracy of the Bhakti school.[13]

This conception was echoed as recently as 1964 by the then Supreme Court Justice, P.B. Gajendragadkar, as he inaugurated the canopy he had presented for the main temple at Pandharpur. He called for a spirit of equality and brotherhood in Maharashtra today of the same sort that the *warkari* tradition had taught. And he claimed that he called for equality and brotherhood with the same intensity that Chokhamela had cried out his grievances at the feet of Vithoba.[14]

In the 1930s, when the Mahar movement for religious rights was at its height, the message of Pandharpur was invoked to call for a lessening of the practice of untouchability by C.B. Agarwal:

> One of the greatest reformers in Maharashtra was Dnyaneshwar. According to the Shastras the Harijans were debarred from hearing or reading the sacred Vedas. . . . Dnyaneshwar opened the gates of Vedic spiritualism to the Hindu masses including the Harijans . . . We have only to read the writing of Chokha Mela, the untouchable Saint and follower of Dnyaneshwar, to get an idea of the tremendous joy he felt. . . . Certainly those persons who Dnyaneshwar thought good enough to share our spiritual heritage cannot be unworthy of our touch.[15]

In the first third of this century, Mahars themselves seem not to have called for social justice in the name of the Bhakti saints as did the higher caste reformers, but to invoke the name of Chokhamela as their claim to a place in past religious life and past greatness. Apart from Chokhamela[16] and some legends of a hero in the days of the Muslims Sultanates,[17] there was little in the Mahar past that could serve the necessary purpose of legitimizing their worth. And so many new efforts to improve their position in society carried the name of Chokhamela. A night school run by Mahars in Poona intermittently from about 1912 to 1933 was called the Chokhamela Vidhyawardah Mandal. A hostel started in 1914 in Nagpur by an educated Mahar, G.A. Gawai, was called the Chokhamela Hostel, and the Government Hostel now in Nagpur continues with that name. There was a Chokhamela Reform Society in Vidarbha in the early 1920s which asked for a new temple which would be open to all. According to a ballad written about the Mahar-led *satyagraha* in Poona in 1929, Untouchables attempted to climb the holy hill to the Parvati temple singing the names of Lord Shankar, Shivaji Maharaj (the seventeenth century Maratha king), Dr. Ambedkar (by that time the most important leader of the Mahar movement) and Chokhamela.

The best known early leader of the Mahars in the Vidarbha area was Kisan Fagu Bansode, whose work in the 1920s and early 1930s stressed attempts to claim religious rights. Even though the Bhakti movement did not have a strong history in the area, Bansode made pilgrimages to Pandharpur, collected Chokhamela's *abhangas*, wrote a play on Chokhamela's life, and created at least one poem invoking the image of Chokhamela to encourage bravery:

Why do you endure curses?

Chokha went into the temple resolutely,
Why do you, ashamed, stay far off?
You are the descendants of Chokha.
Why do you fear to enter the temple?

Brace yourself like a wrestler, come,
Together let us conquer pollution.[18]

With the rise of Dr. Ambedkar as the leader of the Mahars, however, the use of Chokhamela's name dwindled in importance. Being Western educated, Dr. Ambedkar was, from the beginning, more confident of political means to raise status and effect improvements than of religiously oriented methods. His first newspaper, *Muknayak* (the voice of the dumb), begun in 1920, carried under its title an *abhanga* by Tukaram in which the poet reminded men that the shy, the dumb, the bashful, were never noticed. While Ambedkar occasionally quoted Tukaram or Dnyaneshwar, he did not speak of the piety of Chokhamela as an example to Mahars, even in the days when he encouraged Untouchables to enter temples, put on the sacred thread, hold Vedic ritual weddings, and join in the public Ganpati festival.

In 1929, Ambedkar presided over a meeting at Trymbak, a pilgrim centre at the source of the Godavari river, which discussed the building of a temple there in the name of Chokhamela. The meeting decided, after discussion, that a "real memorial consisted in devoting themselves with unflagging energy to the removal of the blot of untouchability".[19] In 1932, Ambedkar elaborated on the ineffectiveness of religious piety:

The appearance of Tulsi leaves around your neck will not relieve you from the clutches of the money-lenders. Because you sing songs of Rama, you will not get a concession in rent from the landlords. You will not get salaries at the end of the month because you make pilgrimages every year to Pandharpur.[20]

Ambedkar's family were followers of the Kabir and Ramananda Bhakti sects, but his wife's led her to a devotion to Pandharpur. She wanted to make a pilgrimage there, but Ambedkar would not allow her to go because she would have been allowed no farther into the temple than the *samadhi* of Chokhamela at the foot of the temple steps.

Ambedkar's biographer reports that he consoled his wife with these words:

> What of that Pandharpur which prevents its devotees from seeing the image of God? By our own virtuous life, selfless service and spotless sacrifice in the cause of downtrodden humanity we would create another Pandharpur.[21]

In the 1936 speech to the Mahar Conference that called for Untouchables to leave Hinduism and convert to another religion, Ambedkar told his audience:

> If someone asks you what your caste is, you say that you are a *Chokhamela* or *Harijan*; but you do not say you are a *Mahar*. Nobody changes his name unless there is need for it. But there is no meaning in adopting a name like *Chokhamela* or *Harijan*. The stench of the old name will stick to the new and you will be forced to change your name continually. Then why not change it permanently?[22]

The permanent change was not to come until 1956, when Ambedkar converted to Buddhism, followed in the next months by over three million people, most of them former Untouchables. The reasons for a group as united, as educationally eager, and as politicized as the Mahars to opt for Buddhism instead of Chokhamela and the Bhakti *panth* are clear. The Bhakti movement in the twentieth century was without any social protest or social reform content, with a few exceptions such as saint Gadge Maharaj.[23] Even more to the point, Chokhamela had accepted his place in the village hierarchy, while the twentieth century Mahars saw no option but to leave what they then saw as servility, a part and parcel of untouchability. Chokhamela had accepted the concept of sins in past lives resulting in low birth, but most twentieth century ex-Untouchables reject this rationale.[24] Chokhamela had found joy in equality with other *bhaktas* and in God's eyes; the new generation wanted equality in social and political matters.

Buddhism offered scriptural justification for worth achieved by mind and action, not by birth. And since Ambedkar's interpretation of the history of the Untouchables was one in which they had been Buddhists, who were isolated and denigrated once Hinduism regained its authority, there was now a glorious past of great accomplishments to reinforce current ideas of their potential as a worthy and creative people. The change seemed swift, but the ground had been well prepared. In 1955, Dr. Ambedkar had been invited to come to Dehu Road, a small town near Pune, where some Untouchables who had made some money through their employment at a local ammunition depot wanted him to dedicate a temple to Chokhamela. Ambedkar agreed to come only if he could dedicate the temple to the Buddha, and since Ambedkar's ideology, not Chokhamela's, had become important, his suggestion was accepted. On Chiristmas Day, 1955, he arrived with a Buddha image and a Buddhist monk to make the Dehu Road temple the first Buddhist structure of the coming conversion movement. Less than a year later, when crowds gathered in Nagpur for the actual conversion day, local newspapers reported that the scene seemed like "another Pandharpur."

Although there is still pride in Chokhamela, interest in the Bhakti sect among educated Buddhists is primarily academic: efforts to find Chokhamela's authentic *abhangas* and to trace the influence of Buddhism on the development of the Bhaki ideology. In contrast, the Chambhars of Maharashtra, a smaller ex-Untouchable caste which works with leather, did not join Ambedkar's movement en masse and continue to celebrate the Chamar *sant* of the Hindi-belt, Rai-das or Ravidas [or Rohidas], as their patron saint. The doors of the temple at Pandharpur are now open to all, forced open after Independence by a Brahman socialist, Sane Guruji, who sat fasting in the temple doorway. A *Samadhi* (memorial) of Chokhamela marks his burial place at the foot of the temple stairs. The Mahars who traditionally tend it have not converted to Buddhism, and there are still a few Mahar *warkaris* who find great meaning in their Bhakti faith. But for the caste as a whole, Chokhamela's life and message cannot serve as a model for the kind of change they have come to feel is theirs by right.

The background of Shri Eknath Maharaj (c. 1533-1599) was completely different from that of Chokhamela. He belonged to a Brahman family of considerable fame, living in the "Benares" of the Marathi-speaking area, Paithan. His great grandfather, Bhanudas, was a Bhakta and a poet, credited with bringing back the image of Vitthal from the state of Vijayanagar, after it had been taken there to reinforce the Vijayanagara King's piety--or dominance. The scholarly learning which surrounded Eknath by virtue of his family and his birthplace was reinforced by worldly knowledge. Paithan had been an ancient capital and in the sixteenth century was a trading centre of great importance, producing exquisite silk saris known as Paithani.

The political world around Eknath was also dissimilar to the four-teenth century world in which Chokhamela lived. Chokhamela was probably a very young man when Alla-ud-din Khilji stormed Devagiri (modern Daulatabad) in 1296, bringing the creative energy of the Yadava period to an end. His time period also witnessed the raids of Muhammad Tughlaq, who shifted his capital to Daulatabad in 1327, but Chokhamela died before the stable Bahmani kingdom was created in 1347. One senses little of the political life around Chokhamela from either his *abhangas* or the legends about him. Mangalvedhe seems to have been a backwater, unaffected by the to-ing and fro-ing of armies.

Eknath lived at the time of the Ahmadnagar Sultanate. Its influence can be seen in the number of Persian words which Eknath used in his writings, in the Muslim terms for administration which he wove into the poetry which used obligations to government as an analogy for debts to God. He was in contact with many Muslims, a fact verified by his use of Muslim holy men as figures in his dramatic poems and by his inclusion of Hindustani in those poems. An even more telling fact is that Eknath's own guru, Janardan Swami, was both an acknowledged holy man and the keeper of the Daulatabad fort! At one time, according to legend, Eknath even took Janardan's place at the head of the Muslim ruler's army when the fort was attacked and Janardan was deep in meditation.

Eknath's massive volume of work shows all these influences: his Brahmanical training, his interest in scholarship, his tradition of devotion to the Pandharpur Bhakti sect, his knowledge of a very heterogeneous world in a religious centre and market city crossed by several trade routes. He was in the unusual position of living in a highly orthodox and closed Brahmanical world and yet being in contact with the foreign, the non-Sanskritic, indeed all manner of men. His devotion to the lowly, his insistence on using Marathi instead of Sanskrit, his unorthodox behavior in performing charitable acts for all men, meant that he was often ostracized and lived under the threat of excommunication. But in part because of the grace of the God of Pandharpur, in part because he never challenged the right of Brahman privileges for other Brahmans, he lived his life fairly peacefully in Paithan and took samadhi there; his home is now a temple which serves as a pilgrimage centre even today.

Eknath's scholarly work does not concern us here, except for its primary purpose of bringing the highest of philosophical thought and moral teaching to the people of his area through the common language,

Marathi. One of the basic texts of the Bhakti devotees is the "Eknathi
Bhagavata", a translation of the eleventh book of the *Bhagavata Purana*
from Sanskrit to Marathi.[25] Unlike those parts of the *Bhagavata Purana*
which tell of the love between Krishna and the Gopis and are popular in
the Northern Bhakti tradition, this expresses a stern morality. Eknath also
began a Marathi version of the *Ramayana*, commented on the Vedantic
philosophy of the ninth chapter of the second book of the *Bhagavata
Purana*, corrected the 250 year old text of the *Dnyaneshwari* (the foundation stone of the Bhakti movement), and produced a number of philosophical works. He is also credited with some four thousand *abhangas*,
but these never achieved the poetic intensity of the more popular
abhangas of Tukaram.

But Eknath is not only the most scholarly and prolific of all the *sants*
in the Marathi Bhakti tradition, he is also the most conscious of the
presence of Untouchables in society and of their spiritual capabilities.
His most unusual contribution to the "performance genre"[26] of Bhakti
literature are some three hundred *bharuds*, drama poems meant to be
acted out, and of these almost fifty are written as if an Untouchable were
the author. Forty-seven *bharuds* seem to come from the mouths of Mahar
men or women; one is written in the name of a Mang, one of the three
important Maharashtrian Untouchable castes.

The *bharud* form has been used by a number of poets, both in
Karnataka and Maharashtra. It requires a symbol or a metaphor to carry
the message of the poem; this can be not only a particular caste, but a dog,
a Muslim fakir, a wandering acrobat, an unhappy wife, a demi-god, a
prostitute, a game, a bird, a notification of debt collection--a symbol
drawn from almost any aspect of ordinary life. Eknath's *bharuds* contain
references to Vedantic philosophy and stories from the Epics and the
Puranas, but their importance here is as a reflection of Eknath's omni-
scient eye and his all-encompassing compassion. No orthodox Brahman,
no peasant appears in his *bharuds*; instead they reflect the non-Sanskritic
street life he must have seen in the busy town of Paithan.

The poems in which the Mahar is the speaker are Johar poems,
beginning with the greeting used by Mahars to their superiors. Most are
very different from the poems of Chokhamela; in Eknath's *bharuds*, the
Mahar not only preaches to others about morality, the necessity for a guru
and the company of the *sants*, but also of the calamity of rebirth that is
inevitable for those who do not take the Bhakti path, and of the false lives
of the pseudo-pious.

There are many ways to interpret these Johar poems. Eknath can be

seen as the Mahar of the Lord, one who does His work faithfully and with
devotion. Some poems suggest that the life of the Mahar is so difficult it
stands for the hardship of constant rebirth. The fact that the Johar poems
are often harsh and vulgar indicates that Eknath may have taken on this
voice in order to preach a fundamentalist kind of Bhakti--the certainty of
rebirth for non-devotees being a sort of hell-fire and damnation threat.
What is clear, however, is that Eknath has closely observed the work of
the Mahar, and seems to try to put himself into the Mahar's skin. These
poems also indicate a deep belief that the faith of the true Bhakta is true
wisdom, and that the devout Mahar can speak with clarity and truth about
the evils of the world and its people.

The following *bharud* shows the Mahar in his typical role: doing
anything that is necessary, begging for food, sweeping, announcing
officials--the official in this case is the God Rama:

> Johar, May-Bap, Johar.
> My Johar to all the Saints.
> I am the Mahar of Ayodhya City,
> Of Ramji Baba's court, ki ji May-Bap.

> Ramji Baba's work is the
> rule of Ayodhya city;
> There this lowly servant's work
> is to do all the good, all the bad.

> I wake early in the morning
> and ask Sita for food.
> I sweep the court and
> throw the dirt outside.

> When Ramji Baba comes to Council
> I go ahead to announce him.
> In truth, Eka Janardan
> Offers Johar, ki ji May-Bap.[27]

Bharud 3864

The Mahar in the next *bharud* also belongs to Rama, but his name is
Atmanak (*atma*, meaning soul, and *nak*, the suffix to their names used by
Mahars until the beginning of this century).[28] The poem is addressed to
the *patil*, the headman of a village which is used as a metaphor for the

human body. Each being must live through eighty-four hundred thousand lives, each time dying painfully and being beaten by the Lord of Death before being born again. Only the true Bhakta is not reborn. The "ki ji May-Bap" at the end of each stanza is literally, "O mother and father", or "O master", but has been retained in its Marathi rhythmic form.

Johar, May-Bap, Johar.
I am sun-born Rama's Mahar.
My name--Atmanak Mahar.
I do all the work of the Lord, ki ji May-Bap.

What will remain in the broken hut?
Your feet will fall into the trap of bones.
If you hide your face, you'll lose your honor.
Then what's the use of living? ki ji May-Bap.

Ruin is drawing near.
Eighty-four hundred thousand creditors—
watchmen of the Lord of Death [are coming]—
and they will beat you and beat you, ki ji May-Bap.

Johar, Honorable Patil.
Are you pleased with the Darbar?
Today they have come to tell you
The balance of your debt is due, ki ji May-Bap.

The due date comes near.
A warning must be given.
So many have been beaten and taken away.
I am speaking the truth, am I not? ki ji May-Bap.

Leave your body-village?
Shave your head, change your name?
Leave the house and stay in the temple?
Better keep your staff in your hand! ki ji May-Bap.

Eka-Janardan Mahar [says]
Johar to the Company of Saints.
They have felt the endless treadmill
of Births and Deaths, ki ji May-Bap[29]

Bharud 3877

In the following *abhanga*, which is full of puns and of the typical shouts or calls of certain religious performances, which the audience undoubtedly shouted in unison, Eknath's Mahar criticizes all religious fakery. The exclamations have been left in Marathi, since, like ''Bravo'' or ''Whoo-pee'', they carry a tenor and a sense of occasion which cannot be translated.

> Johar, May-Bap, Johar.
> Good guru Janardan's Mahar says
> Listen attentively to a thought
> about the Age of Kali, ki ji May-Bap.
>
> Among the four chief Ages
> the Age of Kali is the best
> Good deeds should be done, praise to God sung,
> the Name should be remembered.[30]
>
> Perform the nine kinds of Bhakti;
> Then you will miss the cycle of 84 hundred thousand lives.
> Believe in what I say
> or you will be trapped!
>
> There should be an altar of basil by the door.
> You should worship the uninvited guest.
> Take shelter with the saints.
> This is the sign of Bhakti.
>
> Wear the tulsi beads around your neck,
> put the mark of sandal on your forehead.
> Chanting the Names should be the
> garland of the mouth.
>
> Observe the fast of the eleventh day,
> keep vigil all night.
> On the twelfth day eat sweets, drink milk
> with respect and love.
>
> These are the signs of Vaishnava Bhakti.
> I have told you all the marks.
> He who does not know the secret
> follows the non-religious way.

There are eighteen kinds of castes.[31]
I will tell you what they think.
Listen carefully, without doubt;
don't be angry.

We are Brahmans, they say,
But they don't bathe, pray to the sun, read the Vedas.
They perform impure deeds by chanting
to kill and bind, fascinate and hold.

They say, in this world we have attained the end,
but they are far from even the means.
They are involved with other women,
kulululu, ki ji May-Bap.

I have become a Sannyasi, they say,
but the six enemies are in their hearts.[32]
Their minds, night and day, are on
Other people's money, other people's food. . . .

He became a Fakir for the sake of his stomach.
His life was spent saying Allah, Allah.
He wore "faultlessness" like a garment,
calling *haydosh haydosh*. . . .[33]

They say, "We have become Lingayats".
Yet they do not worship Shiva.
They beg for the sake of their stomachs.
They blow the conch: *bham, bham, bham*. . . .

They say, "we have become saints"
They put on garlands, sandal paste.
Taking a lamp in their hands,
They cry *udo udo*. . . .[34]

They do kirtan for the sake of their stomachs.[35]
They teach the "meaning of all" to the people.
They cheat their ignorant devotees.
They do not know the secret of kirtan. . . .

Do the one kind of Bhakti.
Don't wait for anything else.
Good and bad come in their own way.
They are the proof of past deeds.

As in the mind of a faithful wife,
The final measure is the husband's,
So to understand the causes and the remedies,
Take the Lord as Measure....[36]

Bharud 3891

Many of the Johar *bharuds* are repetitious; many concern themselves with officials and different aspects of life in the village; many use the complex numerology of the initiate: the five elements, the six great enemies, the nine doors to the body, etc. Throughout, however, the Mahar preaches, and Eknath deliberately uses him as both metaphor and actual Untouchable, indicating several times that the Mahar as Mahar should be listened to:

A Mahar speaks--so you turn away in arrogance.
But you should do what is good for you!
O you men! Don't close your eyes!

Bharud 3880

One of the most popular *bharuds* is a conversation between a Mahar and a Brahman, in which the Mahar teaches the arrogant Brahman about the formless God and the grace of the Saints.[37] This might seem to be bolder than it actually is, since another amusing dialogue takes place between a Brahman and a dog, with the same sort of authority given the dog. It is clear that Eknath's basic message is that even a dog, or a Mahar, can share God's grace. Or is it? The very daring of this sort of dialogue must have fascinated Eknath's audiences, and the device is still striking today, when the *bhajan* members, sometimes in costume, act out the *bharud*.

Brahman: Come here, doggie, come here.
             Don't pollute me--
             just take your food.

Dog: Give it to me, give it.

	The pollution is in you-- pull your robe back.
Brahman:	Now this dog has gotten arrogant! . . .[38] Look, I'll let you die without food.
Dog:	So what! Everything is nectar!
Brahman:	You have only one home-- What will you eat in the morning!
Dog:	Where will you yourself be tomorrow?
Brahman:	Where did you get this wisdom?
Dog:	It is the great gift of my guru.
Brahman:	What! You have a guru?
Dog:	He is in everybody.
Brahman:	But we call you a dog!
Dog:	You're fooled by ignorance.
Brahman:	Call a Brahman ignorant?
Dog:	If you are so great, why do you die? The devotees of God are immortal!
Brahman:	How do you know that? I would like to become immortal!
Dog:	Then why don't you? Don't even look at caste or lineage.
Brahman:	How did you come by this knowledge?
Eka Janardan:	I learned it by the grace of the guru.

Bharud 3792

The whole Maharashtrian Bhakti tradition, and probably the Bhakti tradition everywhere, makes it clear that there is no caste distinction in the sight of God. Dnyaneshwar, the founder of the Bhakti sect in the Marathi speaking area, put this very plainly in his commentary on the *Bhagavad Gita*, the *Dnyaneshwari*:

There is a distinction between the Khaira and the Chandana trees only so long as they are not put into fire; but as soon as they are put inside it, they become one with it, and the distinction between them vanishes. Similarly, the Kshatriya, the Vaisyas, the Sudras and Women are so called only as long as they have not reached Me. But having reached Me, they cease to be distinguished; as salt becomes one with the ocean, even so they become one with Me.[39]

Eknath put it in simple, colorful terms, using the names of Non-Brahman *sants* from both Maharashtra and Northern India:

God baked pots with Gora,
drove cattle with Chokha,
cut grass with Savata Mali,
wove garments with Kabir,
colored hide with Ravidas,
sold meat with butcher Sajana,
melted gold with Narahari,
carried cow-dung with Janabai
and even became the Mahar messenger of Damaji.[40]

The concept of living according to caste in non-religious aspects, however, was not challenged. Each caste was expected to do its duty; even the corrupted Brahman, according to Eknath, was to be shown respect. Birth in a low caste was in accord with past deeds, and the only way out was a life of devotion and duty which would obviate the necessity of rebirth. Eknath's message was by no means one of social protest; his basic views on caste and the position of Brahmans were quite orthodox. But his vision of God's presence in all humanity and his compassion lifted his orthodoxy into the kind of creative approach shown in the above *bharuds* and from time to time, according to legend, into most unorthodox action.

Mahipati, the eighteenth century biographer of all the *sants*, tells many legends of Eknath's compassion, the following being one of them.

On the day of the worship of ancestors, Eknath invited Brahmans to his house for the feast. An Untouchable sweeper and his wife working in the alley smelled the food, but told each other they could never have such a splendid feast, and on this holy occasion even the food left on the plates would be buried, not given to them. Eknath overheard them and went out to invite all the Untouchables in the town to the feast, serving them himself. The Paithan Brahmans were furious and excommunicated Eknath. But Lord Krishna, who was working in Eknath's house as a menial Brahman, known as Shri Khandya, said, "Serve a feast to the ancestors anyway". And so the ancestors came, and the local Brahmans saw the splendid heavenly Brahmans eating the feast at Eknath's house. Added to this, Eknath cured a leper even as he was performing the penance imposed on him for this deed by the Brahmans, and so they said to him, "You are indeed the avatar of Vishnu."[41]

A long story in Mahipati's *Bhaktalilamrta* tells of Eknath dining with a pious Bhakta, Ranya Mahar, and his wife. Ranya had been a worshipper of Vishnu, but through some fault was reborn as a Mahar. He sat outside Eknath's *kirtans*, swept a path to his bath, etc. Ranya Mahar's pious wife wanted Eknath to come to their house to eat, and Eknath accepted, quoting this verse from the *Bhagavata Purana* (VII:9:10):

A dog-eating outcaste, who has made an offering to God of his mind, his words, his actions, his property and his very life, is to be considered far superior to a Brahman, who, although gifted with the twelve characteristics of a Brahman, has turned away from the feet of God. The former purifies his whole family, not so the latter puffed up with pride.

Hearing the Sanskrit verse, the Paithan Brahmans were enraged. "Why do you repeat a sloka to this unmentionable?" Eknath replied, "I am convinced that he has the right to philosophic knowledge. By his reverent devotion he has made the Supreme Brahma, existing in the form of Shri Hari, subject to him." Eknath submitted himself to the penance imposed by the Brahmans, but even as he stood penitentially in the river, he again accepted Ranya Mahar's invitation to dine at his home. He went to the Mahar quarters for dinner, but as the Brahmans went to check on him, they also saw him eating at his own home. God Vitthal had taken Eknath's form and eaten at the house of Ranya Mahar.[42]

Eknath and his wife also took in a starving Mahar thief after he was let out of the jail, and kept him in their house for many days, converting him from a life of crime to that of piety by their kindness.[43]

A legend that still has power because it involves the all-important matter of touch concerns Eknath's pity for a small boy, left crying on the hot sands on the banks of Godavari river during the summer heat. He picked him up and carried him to the hovel the child pointed out to him, realizing only when he saw the child's mother that he held a Mahar boy. He put the boy down at his home, returned to the river and bathed with all his clothes on. None of the Brahmans saw him, but the deed became known, according to God's plan. A learned Brahman with leprosy was told by God that Eknath had performed an act of special goodness. If Eknath would give that good deed to the Brahman, he would become whole. Hearing this, Eknath smiled, put a little water in the leper's hand, and the leper's body became beautiful.[44]

It is Eknath's generosity, his liberality of spirit, his imagination, his kindness that is moving, not his piety. It is these qualities that make him an important figure in contemporary times, and it is the actions stemming from his all-encompassing compassion that offer a model for modern day elite reformers.

Eknath's compassion does not have much appeal to the ex-Untouchables themselves. A couplet reading "I am the bastard Mahar, son of the Lord",[45] may be moving to a Brahman, but not to a Mahar. I have found no reference to Eknath in any of the writings of the early Mahar movement, and none during the period since the Buddhist conversion, nor is there much interest in Eknath's vision of humanity. That vision seems to bear some similarity to that of Mahatma Gandhi, whose views on caste were only somewhat less orthodox and whose humanitarianism was closely linked with charity. Gandhi's vision and methods have been rejected by most of those drawn into the more radical Ambedkar movement.

Indeed, some Dalit[46] poets reject the Bhakti idea as totally useless. In a very avant-garde poem, Namdeo Dhasel speaks of "Crumpled-paper Pandurang-dindi goes on singing, winding, the sweet notes flute", and in the next line speaks of prostitutes on Juhu beach. The image of procession to Pandharpur is mocked as unreal, while the life of the city poor is a reality the Pandharpur pilgrims do not see.[47] Daya Pawar also picked up this theme of neglect of humans in pursuit of the divine [or the pious care of animals] in a poem called "Pay" (legs or feet), in which the theme is that those born from the feet of the primordial being, the Shudras, are at the bottom of a crushing pyramid of castes. The poem ends with the pyramid being sanctified, but the sanctifying water is given to a thirsty donkey: "The pitchers of Ganges water come and are poured into the mouth of a donkey".[48] The original legend of the Ganges water given to a thirsty donkey is the one told of Eknath.

But for the elite reformer, the wise and scholarly Brahman whose compassion allows him to rise above caste distinctions is a powerful image. One of the most interesting and effective ways in which the figure of Eknath was used in a modern context was in the film on his life produced by the Prabhat Film Company in Poona. Using traditional Maharashtrian themes as the basis for very popular movies, this young, highly intellectual and socially committed group of the film makers produced a number of excellent films during a "Golden Age" of Marathi films in the late 1930s and early 1940s. The film on Eknath was called *Dharmatma* (the soul of righteousness). In it, the miraculous events of Eknath's legendary life were downplayed to allow a more realistic picture of a good and pious householder who loved and cared for everyone. Some of Eknath's *abhangas* and *bharuds* were sung in the film in the context of anyone at all being able to give the message of Bhakti. And one of the most dramatic high points of the movie was the scene in which Eknath goes to the Maharwada and eats in the house of Ranya Mahar!

A recent pamphlet for children, *Don mahan sant* (Two Great Saints) by Datta J. Kulkarni (Pune: Aragade Kulkarni Prakashan, 1968), illustrates another possible use of Eknath as a model for social consciousness. The two saints are Gadge Maharaj, the twentieth century wandering holy man whose social teachings on the evils of drinking, practicing untouchability, and putting ritual above social good were extremely strong and effective, and the sixteenth century *sant*, Eknath. The washerman Gadge Maharaj, rough, unlearned, homeless and completely unorthodox, and the pious Brahman Eknath are unlikely companions. Linking them is an effective device for legitimizing modern reformist social attitudes.

Of all the *sants*, only Eknath could have served as legitimacy for protesting orthodoxy in the incident of the 1977 Marathi Literary Conference in Pune. The Marathi Sahitya Sammelan is not only the literary event of the year, but one of the most prestigious gatherings in all Maharashtra. To be elected President is a recognition not only of literary worth but of real presence on the Maharashtrian scene. When a man known for his conservative views and his religious orthodoxy, P.B.

Bhave, was elected President over liberal candidates, there was a charge that the election committee was fixed, and the radical student groups of Pune disrupted the last day of the Conference with a demonstration. The shout of the procession which prevented the Conference President from speaking was: "Eknath carried a Mahar child on his shoulder, but all you Brahmans want is power".[49]

The popular Sunday edition of the Pune newspaper, *Sakal*, picked up this theme in its edition of 25 March 1979, with an article entitled "On the banks of the Godavari Eknath showed the light of equality", illustrated by a picture of the *sant* in full Brahman regalia with a dark child in his arms. [A number of recent popular pamphlets picture Eknath in this pose].

It should be emphasized that the living Bhakti sect in Maharashtra today is not a force for change. The *warkaris* themselves, those who actually wear the tulsi beads, go on pilgrimage to Pandharpur, eschew liquor and meat in order to live pious lives, have not initiated any sort of social reform campaign. They continue to make the distinctions between equality in the sight of God and equality in daily life that the *sants* made through the centuries. In her essay on the Pandharpur pilgrimage, Iravati Karve wonders that the songs sung so vigorously preach equality of all the Bhaktas, and the pilgrims preserve caste groups in the procession as they are singing them.[50]

However, it is equally clear that the Bhakti Movement and its literature is still a reservoir of living ideas.[51] The lives of the poets of Pandharpur are known to everyone, even the children, and there is material in this common pool of regional ethos which can serve many purposes.

There is a possibility that Chokhamela will be revived, not as a "sanskritizing process" in the usual Srinivasian sense of upward mobility within the caste system,[52] but as "sanskritization" in the broader sense of participation in the recognized higher intellectual culture. The current interest in Chokhamela and his family may be academic, but the result may be new editions of his *abhangas* and those of his family, perhaps some theater, perhaps some use of the legends about him in poetry, as well as several Ph.D. theses. After all, Chokhamela represents a clear and important participation of Untouchables in the past culture of the area and although he no longer serves a model for emulation, he may well become once again a theme of inspiration as a creative figure from the past

The figure of Eknath also has a real but limited appeal. What wa unusual about him was his observant eye, his enormous ability to se things as they were and to act according to human need. The idea that one so scholarly and so wise could be so quick to understand the life around him and so human is a forceful idea. The message, however, seems limited to those who are "scholarly and wise"--to the intellectuals and the elite. But interpreted with imagination and skill, the figure of Eknath can become an enabling force; his synthesis of the worldly and the spiritual has the capacity to be understood today. The future importance of Eknath as a social force depends largely on the ability of the educated elite who emulate him to affect the social tenor of life today.

Notes

1. *Sant* can easily be translated "saint". I have kept the Marathi word, however, because it is used only for the saints in the Bhakti tradition, not for all holy men.

2. *Warkari sampradaya* "Tradition of the pilgrims". The finest study in English of this tradition as a whole is G.A. Deleury's *The Cult of Vithoba* (Poona: Deccan College Postgraduate and Research Institute, 1961). I have tended to use the term "Bhakti movement" in this paper rather than the usual Marathi designation or Deleury's term in order to stress the continuity of the line of *sants,* who wrote their poetry over a five hundred-year period, and in order to link the movement with Bhakti traditions in other language areas.

3. *Chokhamela abhang gatha.* (Collection of Chokhamela's Abhangas.) (Bombay: Balkrishna Lakshman Pathak, 1950), pp. 1-2.

4. See R.D. Ranade, *Pathway to God in Marathi Literature* (Bombay: Bharatiya Vidya Bhavan, 1961; originally published in 1933) for a slightly different version of this legend.

5. Nicol Macnicol, *Psalms of the Maratha Saints* (Calcutta: Association Press and Oxford University Press, 1919), p. 23.

6. The references to Chokhamela's abhangas in this paper are from *Chokhamela abhang gatha* (Bombay: Balkrishna Lakshman Pathak, 1950). A newer collection, *Shrisant Chokhamela Maharaj yanche charitra va abhang gatha,* edited by S.B. Kadam (Bombay: Mandakini S. Kadam, 1969) contains 349 *abhangas.*

7. A.K. Ramanujan has informed me that *Abhangas* 6 and 11 need not refer to untouchability since similar songs appear in the work of caste Hindu *sants* in the South. However, since some of Chokhamela's songs do refer to untouchability, a phenomenon which seems not to appear in the words of other Untouchability *sants,* I think *Abhang* 6 can be interpreted as protesting

his low birth and *Abhang* 11 as protesting the concept of untouchability.

8. See Justin E. Abbott and Narhar R. Godbole's translation of Mahipati's *Bhaktavijaya* (Ch. XXIII, pp. 6-60) in *Stories of Indian Saints* (Poona: Office of the Poet Saints of Maharashtra,1933) for a slightly different version of this legend.

9. Pandhari - Pandharpur.

10. Iravati Karve, "On the Road", *Journal of Asian Studies,* XXII:1 (1962), pp.13-29. The translation of *Abhang* 52 is by Maxine Berntsen. R.D. Ranade translates the "ugly" of the last line as "untouchable". (See Ranade op.cit., p.161). [The usual translation of "feelings" in the last line is "devotion" (*bhav*).]

11. M.G. Ranade, *Rise of the Marathi Power and Other Essays* (Bombay: University of Bombay, 1961, first published in 1900), p. 5.

12. R.V. Oturkar, Introduction to M.G. Ranade, op.cit., pp. vi-vii. The work of G.B. Sarkar to which Oturkar refers has been translated by Kumud Mehta as *The Saint-Poets of Maharashtra (Their Impact on Society)* (New Delhi: Orient Longmans, 1969).

13. R.D.Ranade, *op.cit.*, p.165.

14. *Kesari* (Pune), 27 December 1964.

15. C.B. Agarwal, *The Harijans in Rebellion* (Bombay: Chhotelal Bhugwan-das, 1934), p. 64. "Harijan", i.e., people of God, is Mahatma Gandhi's term.

16. Chokhamela's wife, Soyrabai, his son and brother-in-law, Karmamela and Banka, and his sister, Nirmala, are all considered saints and poets. Their *abhangas* have been collected by S.B. Kadam, *op. cit.*

17. For the legend of the hero Amrutnak, see my article "The Leadership of Babasaheb Ambedkar", in this volume and in B.N. Pandey ed., *Leadership in South Asia* (New Delhi: Vikas, 1977), which analyzes the cultural images of the Mahar past.

18. Kisan Fagu Bansode, *Pradip* (Nagpur: Jagruti Prakashan, no date), p. 48.

19. Dhananjay Keer, *Dr. Ambedkar, Life and Mission* (2nd ed. Bombay: Popular Prakashan, 1962), p.126.

20. *Ibid.*, p. 218.

21. *Ibid.*, p. 247.

22. *The Depressed Classes--a Chronological Documentation* (Kuseong: St. Mary's College, 1930), p. 103.

23. The life of this contemporary *sant* should be studied, since he seems to be the only figure who revived both the idea of castelessness among the Bhakti devotees and the radical actions of the earlier saint-poets. There are a number of popular pamphlets in Marathi on his life, including *Gadge Maharaj* by Amrendra (Bombay: Vora, 1959). [See also a book - length study, *Shri Gadge Maharaj*, by Gopal Nilkanth Dandekar (Bombay: Majestic Book Stall, 1976 and 1982). A *Kirtan* of the radical saint has been translated by Maxine Bernsten for Eleanor Zelliot and Maxine Berntsen

eds., *The Experience of Hinduism* (Albany: State University of New York Press, 1988).]

24. For non-acceptance of re-birth as an explanation for untouchability, see Bernard S. Cohn, "Changing Traditions of a Low Caste", in Milton Singer ed., *Traditional India: Structure and Change* (Philadelphia: The American Folklore Society, 1959); and Pauline Mahar Kolenda, "Religious Anxiety and Hindu Fate", *Journal of Asian Studies*, XXXIII (1964), pp. 71-81.

25. The 23rd chapter of the *"Eknath Bhagavata"* has been translated by Justin E. Abbott as *Bhikshugita: The Mendicant's Song* (Poet-Saints of Maharashtra series No. 3, Poona, 1928). [Hugh van Skyhawk submitted a Ph.D. thesis on Eknath's Bhagavata in 1988 to the University of Heidelberg.]

26. The phrase is from Kunta Narayan Jagdale, "The Use of Symbols in Bharud Literature" (*Journal of the Shrimati Nathibai Damodar Thackersey Women's University*, V, 1975. It is useful in distinguishing Bhakti literature meant to be sung or acted out in a group, such as *abhangas* and *bharuds*, from literature intended to be recited or read.

27. There is no critical edition of Eknath's *bharuds*. The edition I have used is *Shri Eknath Maharaj Yanoya Abhangachi Gatha*, collected and edited by Brahmibhut Shrinanamaharaj Sakhre (Poona: Indira Prakahan, 1952).

28. In other *bharud*s the term 'Vithnak' is used as the name of the Mahar, a combination of the name of God Vithal and the traditional Mahar ending of a name.

29. All Eknath's *bharud*s are signed with a shortened version of his name combined with that of his guru, Janardan. In the Johar *bharud*s, he makes it clear that Eka-Janardan speaks as a Mahar.

30. The *Kaliyug* or Age of Kali is traditionally the worst of the four *yugas*. Here, Eknath calls it the best because it is the age in which Bhakti can lead men to salvation from rebirth. The phrase *karve haribhajan*, literally *"the bhajan to Hari* should be done", is translated "praise to God sung". The *bhajan* is a sort of musical prayer meeting; Hari is a name for Vishnu.

31. There are traditionally eighteen castes in Maharashtra. Eknath uses the words *varna-yati* here, but delineates types of religious figures, not castes, in the stanzas following.

32. The six enemies are hypocrisy, passion, anger, greed, pride and envy. Eknath makes frequent use of this concept in the *bharud*s, either by name or number.

33. "Haydosh" (O friend) is an exclamation used in the processions of the Shiite observance of Mohurram. *Dosh* in Marathi means "fault", and Eknath has combined it with a variant pronunciation of the Persian *dost* here to make a pun.

34. *Udo, Udo*, meaning "awake" or "arise" is exclamation used by the worshipper of the Goddess.

35. *Kirtan*, like *bhajan*, is a group gathering in which *abhangas* are sung, but there is also usually a leader who recites from scripture or gives a sermon.

Eknath's *kirtans* in Paithan were famous far and wide.

36. A number of stanzas have been omitted from this translation. Other religious figures whose hypocrisy is criticized in the *bharud* are Jogis, members of the Mahanubhav sect, Dev Rishis who heal by magic, followers of Khandoba, worshippers of the demi-gods Vetal and Mahishasur and even imperfect Bhaktas.

37. [For a translation of this *bharud*, see Eleanor Zelliot, "Eknath's Bharude: the *Sant* as a link between Cultures", in *The Sants: Studies in a Devotional Tradition of India*, edited by Karine Schomer and W.H. McLeod. Berkeley: Religious Studies Series; Delhi: Motilal Banarsidass, 1987.]

38. The three lines following "Now this dog has gotten arrogant!" are not clear and have been omitted.

39. Quoted in R.D.Ranade, *op.cit.*, p. 88. For a full translation of Dnyaneshwar's classic, see the *Jnaneshvari (Bhavarthadipika)*, translated by V.G. Pradhan and edited by H.M. Lambert, in two volumes (London: George Allen and Unwin, 1967 and 1969). [This translation has been recently reprinted by State University of New York Press, which has also published a translation by Swami Kripananda. Dnyaneshwar's name is often spelled Jnaneshwar.]

40. Adapted from the translation in R.D. Ranade, *op.cit.*, p.177. A similar *abhang* is credited to the great seventeenth century *sant*, Tukaram. The story of Damaji concerns a Bhakta who was a revenue official for the Muslim Sultan of Bedar. He gave away all the storehouses of grain in Mangalvedhe during a great famine, and was arrested by the Sultan for looting his property. God Vitthal, disguised as a Mahar whose traditional duty is to carry taxes to the capital, brought gold to pay for the grain. See *Stories of Indian Saints*, Vol. II, translated by Justin E. Abbott and Narhar R. Godbole from Mahipati's *Bhaktavijaya* (Poona: Office of the Poet Saints of Maharashtra, 1934); Chapter XL, pp. 85-99.

41. See Mahipati's *Bhaktavijaya*. Chapter XLVI, pp. 45-128; English translation as in footnote 40, pp. 176-81.

42. Mahipati's *Bhaktalilamrita*, Chapter XLVI, pp. 138-240; see Justin E. Abbott's translation in *Eknath* (Poet-Saints of Maharashtra No. 2, Poona, 1927), pp. 139-49.

43. *Ibid.*, Chapter XX, pp. 168-203; pp. 166-69 in Abbott's translation.

44. *Ibid.*, Chapter XXII, pp. 124-49; pp. 201-04 in Abbott's translation.

45. *Abhang* 3867:1.

46. *Dalit* means "ground down, broken, depressed". It is the term by which many ex-Untouchables, chiefly those converted to Buddhism, refer to themselves.

47. "Darulate glasat ambar" in *Golpitha*, by Namdeo Dhasal. (Poona: Nilkant Prakashan, 2nd edition, 1975). [A translation of this poem, entitled "Amber/ Sky Alcohols in the Glass", appears in the *Journal of South Asian*

·   *Literature* XVII:1 (Winter, Spring 1982), pp. 97-8.]
48. "Pay" in *Kondwada*, by Daya Pawar. Poona: Magowa Prakashan, 1974.
49. Communication from Gail Omvedt-Patankar.
50. Iravati Karve, *op.cit.*
51. For a comprehensive review of Bhakti literature in the context of all pre-
    modern Marathi literature, see Shankar Gopal Tulpule, *Classical Marathi
    Literature* (Vol. IX, Fasc. 4, in the History of Indian Literature series;
    Wiesbaden: Otto Harrassowitz, 1979).
52. M.N. Srinivas's basic concept of "Sanskritization" is presented in a
    chapter with that title in *Social Change in Modern India* (Berkeley:
    University of California Press, 1966).

Addendum

Note on Transliteration and Meanings

abhanga-- "unbroken, inviolate". The rhyme scheme used for the songs
of the saint-poets. An English plural, *s*, has been added in this essay.
bharud -- a word of uncertain origin and meaning. A drama poem not in
the *abhang* meter. The English plural, *s*, has been added in this essay.
Cokhamela is the proper transliteration for Chokhamela. I have used *ch*
for *c* in order to come slightly nearer to the Marathi pronunciation,
which is not *k* but *ch* for Sanskrit derived words and *ts* for non-
Sanskrit words, such as Chokhamela.

Translation help

Over a period of years, the following friends have helped me with translations: Dr. S.G.Tulpule, Dr. P.N. Joshi, Mr. Jayant Karve, Dr. Pramod
Kale, Mrs. Rekha Damle, Mrs. Hemant Fanse, and the late Mrs. Lalita
Khambadkone. The responsibility for the final version, except in the case
of *Abhanga* 52, translated by Dr. Maxine Berntsen, is my own.

New events, new publications and editions

The Pandharpur pilgrimage of the *warkaris* and other devotees continues
with ever increasing numbers. The only liberal change, however, is the

decision to allow the Raidas *dindi* (group of devotees) in the *palki* (inclusive procession bearing the palanquin of a particular saint, in this case Dnyaneshwar) that begins in Alandi to take a place in back of the sacred horse of Dnyaneshwar rather than in front of the horse. In other words, the *dindi* of Untouchables is now in the same line of march as other caste *dindis*, but in the least prestigious position.

Other relevant works in English on the *warkari sampradaya* and the Pandharpur pilgrimage not mentioned in this essay include a translation of D.B. Mokashi's *Palkhi* by Philip Engblom, with introductory essays by Engblom and Eleanor Zelliot (Albany: New York State University Press, 1987); Charlotte Vaudeville's "Chokhamela, An Untouchable Saint of Maharashtra", in the *South Asian Digest of Regional Writing* 6 (1977): pp. 60-79 and her "Pandharpur, the City of the Saints" in Harry M. Buck and Glenn E. Yocum eds., *Structural Approaches to South Indian Studies* (Chambersburg, Pa.: Wilson Books, 1974); and articles by Jayant Lele, Jayashree B. Gokhale-Turner and Bhalchandra Nemade in the volume in which this essay first appeared. The State University of New York Press has reprinted R.D. Ranade's major study of the Poet-Saints as *Mysticism in Maharashtra* (1983). Motilal Banarsidass has re-printed many of the translations of Mahipati by Justin E. Abbott and N.R. Godbole in the early series entitled "Poet-Saints of Maharashtra". R.C. Dhere and S.G. Tulpule have published major works on the poet-saints in Marathi. Gunther Sontheimer has made a film of the Pandharpur pilgrimage, *Vari.*

I have made a rather different attempt to analyze the tradition of Eknath and Chokhamela together with two other holy figures, Gundam Raul of the thirteenth century and Gadge Maharaj of the twentieth century in Milton Israel and N.K. Wagle eds., *Religion and Society in Maharashtra* (Toronto: Centre for South Asian Studies, University of Toronto, 1987).

My work on Eknath has been supported by a fellowship from the American Institute of Indian Studies.

The Nineteenth Century Background of the Mahar and Non-Brahman Movements in Maharashtra*

Two large and effective protest movements flowered in Maharashtra in the twentieth century. The Non-Brahman movement which grew chiefly among the dominant agricultural castes of the Marathas resulted in a quiet and almost total takeover of the Congress Party in the mid-century decades. The Mahar movement brought that much smaller [and Untouchable] caste into a degree of awareness and unity that enabled them to create a political party; a system of hostels, schools and colleges; and an effective Buddhist conversion movement before the death of its leader, Dr. B.R. Ambedkar, in 1956. The organizational triumphs of these movements in this century were dependent on the democratizing processes of the period of political reforms, 1921-1939, but both had roots reaching back to an apolitical period in the last half of the nineteenth century. This essay is a speculative one, attempting not so much to find *why* these movements began but *what* qualities of the Maharashtrian soil allowed both to come to fruition.

Non-Brahman movements and attempts of Untouchable castes to organize for social and political purposes have occurred in other parts of India. The Non-Brahman movement of Madras actually has a more coherent history and an earlier period of successful political activity than that of Maharashtra.[1] There was also a movement, or a group of movements, among the Untouchables of Madras, although neither this movement nor others among the Ilavas of the Malabar coast, the Chamars of Chhatisgarh area, the Depressed Classes of the Punjab or the Namashudras of Bengal, were as sustained and all-encompassing as that among the Mahars of Maharashtra.[2] The juxtaposition of movements among *both* Non-Brahmans and Untouchables in Maharashtra suggests an assortment of factors conducive to social change. What role these

---

*First published in *The Indian Economic and Social History Review*, VII, 3 (Sept. 1970), pp. 397-415. A few corrections have been made. See also the addendum for new *works* on the subject.

factors played in the rise of the Mahar movement in the nineteenth
century, and the extension of this thesis to the early Non-Brahman
movement, is the subject of this paper. The term "nineteenth century"
in this paper has been stretched to cover the early period of movement,
ending when Dr. Ambedkar's effective and dominant leadership began
in 1920.

The essential factors in the processes by which the Mahar movement
grew were:

1. A leadership released from traditional service [and followers
    with some economic freedom].
2. Grievances understood and felt by both the "elite" members of
    the caste and the masses.
3. Some form of legitimization of the new non-traditional Mahar
    ambition both within the caste and among members of the elite
    in the larger society.
4. A group of "brokers" -- men who could serve as links between
    the caste and the institutions of power in society, or who knew
    how to use modern channels of change.
5. Channels for communication, both within the group and from
    the group to the public.
6. Some form of protection for protesters when the overstepping of
    traditional boundaries brought retaliation.

Without any one of these factors, the Mahar movement would have
taken a different path, or would have narrowed its aims, or would have
remained a minor protest. The first four of these factors will be considered at length, the last two briefly noted. Similar conditions affecting the
Non-Brahman movement will be briefly discussed.[3]

Leadership Released from Traditional Service

The traditional role of the Mahar was, in British official parlance, that of
"inferior village servant". Every village in the Marathi-speaking area
had its *Maharwada*, Mahar quarters somewhat removed from the village
proper. Mahars had no special skill or craft, but performed necessary
duties for the village as watchmen, wall-menders, messengers, removers
of cattle carcasses, servants of any passing government official, aides to
the *patil* (headman) in boundary disputes, tax or police matters. The
Mahar service was hereditary, with those families which inherited the

position filling it in turn. It carried with it a small amount of *watan* land as a badge of public office, and this *watan* land bound the Mahar to his village still more firmly.

Whenever excessive numbers of Mahars or the implementation of a cash economy threw this village role out of balance, Mahars entered other occupations. The coming of British administration also reduced the importance of the Mahar village role as many village functions were removed from local control; however, at the same time, it also opened new fields of occupation. The new freedom from the traditional village service almost invariably brought some social changes. The Khandesh Gazetteer for 1880 defines the traditional Mahar as a "lazy", "unthrifty" but "intelligent" village servant, and notes that other Mahars "make excellent railway gang laborers and have gained almost a monopoly of the unskilled railway labor market...." The implications of the occupational change are also noted:

> Of late between landholders and village Mahars complaints and feuds have grown very common...the railway has done much for the Mahars.... Some of them, gathering capital as petty contractors and moneylenders, show much independence, and manage their business without the help of any high caste clerks. Of late too, they have begun to send their boys to school.[4]

The upward thrust of the Mahars was especially noticeable in the nineteenth century in Vidarbha, the eastern part of the Marathi-speaking region. Here the percentage of Mahars approached nearly twenty per cent of the population, in contrast to three or four per cent along the coast and an average of nine per cent over the entire area. This larger percentage could not be absorbed as village servants and in these eastern parts Mahars were also weavers, petty traders, carpenters and cultivators. A report on the Land Revenue Settlement effected during 1890-1895 in the Nagpur area commented prophetically on the Mahar venture into new fields:

> They turn their hands to anything and everything.... The rise of the Mahar will probably be one of the features of social change in this district during the next fifty or a hundred years. He at present lacks education and a sense of self respect, but these will come and the day may not be far distant when a Mahar will be found among the ranks of the native magistrates.[5]

New occupations and the concomitant upward thrust created a new sort of Mahar and the pioneering leadership for the larger movement came from a group which lacked neither education nor a sense of self-respect. With one exception, this early leadership in the western area came from those Mahars who had entered the British army. From sometime in the late eighteenth century until the last decade of the nineteenth, thousands of Mahars particularly from the Ratnagiri area, the coastal strip south of Bombay, entered the army, and some advanced to high non-commissioned ranks.

Gopal Baba Walangkar, a pensioned soldier from Ratnagiri, began the first Mahar newspaper, attempted to send a petition to the British protesting against the closure of army service to Untouchables, and addressed a plea for better treatment publicly to Hindu leaders. Subhedar (captain) Bahadur Gangaram Krishnajee of Pune was the President of the earliest conference of Mahars, which met in 1903. Subhedar Savadkar, an ex-soldier, was instrumental in securing the cooperation of village Mahars for the historic 1927 Mahar conference, a meeting planned by Dr. Ambedkar and his associates but dependent on Savadkar's work for its local support. Ambedkar himself came from a Ratnagiri family whose men had served in the army for several generations, and he gave credit for the Mahar thrust toward new rights to the education received by army men and their children. While ex-army men formed the new "aristo-cracy" of the western Mahars, one other new English related occupation produced a major leader. Shivram Janba Kamble, organizer of most of the petitions, conferences, night schools, temple and hotel entry move-ments in the Pune area from 1903 to 1930, was a butler in the Masonic Hall in the Pune Cantonment.

Later Mahar elite came from a new breed of primary school teachers, arising sometime after 1920, and from traditional watandar families who made good use of their land or extended their traditional role into governmental supply and contracting work. The early movement was dependent upon those who had freed themselves from economic or psychological subservience to the existing village structure.

Just as Mahar leadership did not come from those still bound in the village system, so the early Non-Brahman leadership did not come from traditional Maratha headmen (*patils*). The Maratha was a farmer, and although the administration of the British in the nineteenth century affected the political structure of his village, it is not clear how much his indebtedness, loss of land or economic situation was affected. It is clear that the *patils* lost much in power and status, and although this created a grievance among Marathas which was widely shared, it did not seem to produce a new movement towards regaining power.

Two events of the same period, the 1870s, illustrate the point of the necessity for non-traditional leadership. The Deccan Riots, the stirring of the peasant masses in the areas around Pune and Ahmadnagar in 1875, *were* led by traditional village leaders. They were directed, however, at the foreign element in the village, the Gujarati or Marwari merchants and moneylenders, not toward the British or the Brahmans, nor were they a precursor of a plea for a change of system. The first Non-Brahman organization, the Satya Shodak Samaj (Truth-seeking Society), was founded in Pune in 1873, just before the Deccan Riots. It is this organization which is seen as the earliest sign of the modern Non-Brahman movement. The group gathered around Jotirao Phule, the founder of the Satya Shodak Samaj, is striking in that it consisted chiefly of non-Marathas and of those urban and not village based. Phule himself was a Mali, a member of a gardening caste whose farming practices adapted well to the new irrigation systems introduced by the British. He was first a school teacher in a Christian school, then ran an agency for molds for types, and finally supported himself well through contracting work for British public enterprises. In later years he returned to the Mali role at a high level by purchasing a 200 acre irrigated farm near Pune.[6]

Phule's associates include other Malis, Krishnarao Pandurang Bhalekar and N.M. Lokhande; two Telugu-speaking Malis, Ramayya Vyankayya Aiyyavaru and P. Rajanna Lingu; V.R. Gholay, a Gawli (cowherd), Eliaya Soloman, probably from the Bene Israeli group of Jews which fit the Teli (oil-presser) caste category; Dhondiram Namdeo Kumbhar (a potter), and Tukaram Tatya Padval, a Bhandari (toddy-tapper).

Biographical information on later Non-Brahman leaders indicates that many were not directly associated with the village. Shahu Maharaj of Kolhapur, who kept the movement alive from the turn of the century until his death in 1923, was obviously above any traditional village ties; Bhaurao Patil, the Jain educator of Satara and the southern districts, was a tutor and a salesman for Kirloskar Brothers industries, although his name indicates a village headman background; Bhaskarrao (B.V.) Jadhav, the first Maratha minister in Bombay under the Montagu-Chelmsford reforms, had been in the administration of Kolhapur State. The early Non-Brahman leadership did not come from those directly affected by the decline of Maratha power. Those who first protested the loss of Maratha status and the omnipresent power of the Brahmans were not from the old Maratha leadership (with the obvious exception of the

Maharaja of Kolhapur), but from a new middle class, urban-based and with some perception of Western organizations.

Grievances Understood by both Elite and·Mass

In both Non-Brahman and Mahar movements, there seems to be a double set of grievances, one a longing look back at past glory, the other a protest at current treatment in the light of current standards and opportunities. In the early Mahar movement there was little sense of past glory, just an occasional reference to pre-Aryan "Lords of the Land", and no sense of pride at all in their current village status, even though early British commentators held their role to be important.

Although Mahar history is not well documented until the modern period, a few indications of protest against the untouchable status are in evidence. The fourteenth century Mahar poet-saint Chokhamela speaks generally of devotion to God, but occasionally a note of anguish enters his poetry. He laments his being turned away from the temple in one poem; he cries out, "O God, who is pure?" in another.[7] Legal evidence indicates later protest of a more practical sort. Mahars in Junnar in the seventeenth century appealed for the privilege of having Brahman priests officiating at their weddings, an appeal which was refused by Aurangzeb on the basis of the preservation of custom. This decision was quoted by the Peshwa's government in the late eighteenth century in support of that government's refusal to allow Mahars in the Konkan a similar request.[8]

In the mid-nineteenth century, a Mahar boy from Dharwar applied for admission to a government school. Upon being refused, he appealed to the Education Department of Bombay Province, and in 1857 to the Government of India at Calcutta, but his petition was not granted on the grounds that opposition from higher castes was too strong.[9]

It is difficult to extrapolate any widespread sense of grievance or ambition from such evidence. In 1890, however, Gopal Baba Walangkar, the retired army leader from Ratnagiri, petitioned "the Shankaracharya and other Hindu leaders" for redress of grievances, and from this point on such grievances are noted often enough that a common sense of deprivation among these Mahars can be surmised. In language "vigorous . . . tho' not always correct", Walangkar listed the disadvantages of the Untouchable: difficulty in getting education, exclusion from *dharmshalas* (pilgrims' and travelers' guest houses), discrimination while traveling, ban on participation in trade, social stigma even when army service pay might allow the Untouchables to better their conditions, revulsion towards the Untouchables because of their handling of dead cattle.[10] Most of these disadvantages were experienced by the non-traditional Mahar. The last note on "revulsion", however, applies both to the Mahar in the new occupation and the village Mahar. Moving out of the traditional Mahar work did not affect the Mahar's ritual status, and resentment of treatment received both in village and town seems to have tied both those who stayed and those who left together. A word used frequently in the movement in the twentieth century indicates this tie: *manuski* (of man, i.e. self respect, humane attitudes) figures so often in Mahar speech-making that it seems to stand for a widely understood emotional grievance.

Among the Marathas, so recently a people of power and prestige, a loss of glory or, in more down-to-earth terms, of authority in the village was combined with resentment of the dominance of the Brahmans. Maureen Patterson reports that documentation for Brahman-Non-Brahman conflict is in evidence from the thirteenth century onward.[11] The movement emerging in an organized form in the nineteenth century built upon this age-old conflict, but was expressed in terms that dealt with the modern world and with the village situation as it existed in the last half of that century.

The early Satya Shodak Samaj movement stressed two things: education for the masses and the reduction of Brahman ritual power. Phule himself was a creative pioneer in education, and he and other Samaj members not only worked in actual educational enterprises but used every channel available to them to urge the Government to take more responsibility for mass education. The most amusing example of this occurred when the Prince of Wales was greeted on his visit to Pune in 1889 with a sign hung from the Din Bandhu Sarvajanik Sabha free school for boys:

Tell Grandma we are a happy nation.
But 19 crores are without education.[12]

The jingle picks up a stress on masses, on the majority, which was common in the Non-Brahman movement. *Bahujan Samaj*, the majority society, was often used as a synonym for Non-Brahman. And education was seen as the way by which members of that majority could enter the elite.

The pledge of the Shodak Samaj reflects its anti-Brahman bias only in its denial of the need for a priest in the relationship of a human being to God:

> All human beings are the children of one God. They are my brothers,
> and I shall always try to act upon this principle. I shall not entertain
> the services of any intermediary at the time of adoring, worshipping
> and meditating upon God and at the time of performing a religious
> ceremony, and I shall always try to induce others to follow the same
> practice. I shall always be loyal to the British Government. I shall not
> neglect to educate my boys and girls . . . [13]

The effort to do away with reliance on Brahman priests was part of
a larger emphasis on reducing the combined ritual-administrative power of
the nineteenth century Brahman. It was the power of the Brahman in both
the secular and ritual worlds that elicited the attack on Brahmans.
The Maharashtra Brahmans' extraordinary ability to take advantage of
the opportunity offered by the British administration and the westernizing
process of the nineteenth century Maharashtra brought them into a position
of dominance beyond that of the Peshwa times.

The link between resentment of Brahmanical power on the part of
the urbanized middle castes and the peasants of the village seems to be
the figure of the *kulkarni*, the village accountant. As the *patil* was
traditionally a Maratha, the village *kulkarni* was traditionally a Brahman. British methods of administration and revenue collection reduced
the power of the *patil*. An official description of the *patils* in mid-century:

> They may be considered as the relics of a brighter era of a national
> prosperity; and they have in most instances profited by the mutabil-
> ity and continual changes of succeeding governments . . . but the
> present change of system has effected a corresponding change in the
> circumstance of the Patel: each individual ryot being alone respon-
> sible for the assessment on his holding, the principal onus is removed
> from the Patel, and he is deprived of uncontrolled action, and shorn
> of a great portion of his dignity. [14]

Resentment was turned not so much against the new system as
against the village figure who seemed to profit by the recent change, the
Brahman *kulkarni*. Phule's words on the usurpation of the *patil's* power by
the *kulkarni* indicate this treatment:

> The Patil of a village, the real head, is in fact a non-entity. The

Kulkarni, the hereditary Brahmin village accountant . . . moulds the Patil according to his wishes. He is the temporal and spiritual advisor of the ryots, sawkar (money-lender) in his necessities and the general referee in all matters.[15]

Anti-*kulkarni* protest can be found at all levels: in the non-Brahman newspapers of the nineteenth century, in petitions to British administrators against the power of Brahman clerks, in poems and polemics. It seems to have served as a symbol for a deep-seated sense of lessened stature and frustration over an inability to deal as well with the new regime as did the Brahmans. It reached its apogee not in the nineteenth century or even in the early days of the political reforms when the Legislative Assembly became the platform for protest against Brahman dominance. In 1948, when a Maharashtrian Brahman assassinated Mahatma Gandhi, almost every village in the *desh* (plains) area of Maharashtra erupted in violence against the Brahmans of that place.

Legitimization

The eventual legitimization for the Mahar movement was the acceptance of a Western (or modern) view of democracy and the equality of man. Before the establishment of this credo with Ambedkar's rise to power, several other forms of justification for the Mahar's protest and claims to rights were put forward. The writing of the earliest modern leader, Gopal Baba Walangkar, reflects two things: the claim of *kshatiryahood* (which was abandoned early, probably because the Marathas pre-empted the field), and the contradictory but more popular claim of dominant status in the area before the advent of the Aryans. This sort of prestige became basic to the movement of Untouchables in South India, where the term Adi-Dravida (original Dravidians) was sought and gained as Census nomenclature. In Maharashtra, however, the concept seems to have been discarded as early as 1910, when Shivram Janba Kamble based his petition to the British on a simple human rights issue.[16] Later, Ambedkar refused to use the pre-Aryan "Lords of the Land" claim, which he felt might result in permanent separation of the Untouchable and the caste Hindu. As political action became the most successful channel to social change, the legitimization of the movement in terms of "liberty, equality and fraternity" sufficed.

Legitimization of the movement in the eyes of the elite took the forms of sympathy, denial of inherent inferiority in the Untouchable, claims that through the Bhakti movement and the saint Chokhamela the Mahar had already proved his worth, and adherence to a belief in equality that had a western base. Maharashtra was especially rich in justification of social change, and the very Brahmans castigated by both Mahar and Maratha provided the public encouragement for their movement upward. A few examples show the range of the nineteenth century and early twentieth century attitudes. They reflect an openness and a radicality which was not widespread, but which was found among very influential men. A poem from the nineteenth century by Krishnaji Keshav Damle (Keshavsut), a Brahman revered as the first modern Marathi poet, illustrates this unusual quality of empathy:

The First Question of the Untouchable Boy

The children of untouchables,
poor, gay, playing on the roadside—
A Brahmin came from far
to the simple kids what should he say:
'O you brats of *Mahars*, move away,
be gone! What are you playing at, you louts?
Run and give way to the Brahmin!'
The boys fled—who would dare stay!
One amongst them did;
the wicked Brahmin brandished his club and shouted,
'Ass! thy shadow must not fall on me,
get thee gone, or else this "Sweet present"!'
The kid too slunk homewards,
musing—
'What if my shadow fell on him,
What's so wrong about it?'
At home he asked the question of his mother.
The poor mother said:
'We are low and they are high,
when you see them, you had better step aside.'
She said so—simply.
How should she know
that highness in this world is built
on sin and glory
on the degradation of others!'[17]

Another quotation indicates a view far ahead of its time. Dr. R.G.

Bhandarkar, the eminent Sanskritist, told the Indian Social Conference in 1895 about a Mahar *haridasa* who had performed a *kirtan* [combined sermon and music] at his house, ending the story thus: "... and I believe from the opportunities I have had of observation, that the despised Mahar possesses a good deal of natural intelligence and is capable of being highly educated. So that to continue to keep him in ignorance is to deprive the country of an appreciable amount of intellectual resources."[18] Quotations which offered support to the Mahar movement can be found in the work of Mahadev Govind Ranade, Gopal Ganesh Agarkar, the novelist Hari Narayan Apte and other eminent figures of the nineteenth and early twentieth centuries. They offered an intellectual climate for change which was not often expressed in action but which encouraged among the Mahars an expectation that their own efforts for a better place in society would have elite support.

In the long run, the same idea of participatory democracy that justified the Mahar movement came to dominate the Non-Brahman movement. However, it took sixty years between the founding of the Satya Shodak Samaj and the realization that democracy could mean majority control. In the intervening period, those in the Non-Brahman movement were, in general, loyal to the British and often battled against increased extensions of the democratic process, such as the granting of the vote to women, on the grounds that such innovations would only increase Brahman power.[19] The concept of *bahujan samaj* -- the majority, however, was present in the movement from the first.

The traditional legitimization for many castes' claim to better status was the attempt to secure Kshatriya status. The Marathas as warriors considered themselves to be Kshatriya and it had taken some effort for the king of the seventeenth century Maratha empire to have himself crowned Chhatrapati Shivaji by a Brahman in true Kshatriya style. But while a number of sacred thread ceremonies are recorded there seems to have been no major attempt to secure a Census listing of the Maratha caste as Kshatriya. In a sense the Marathas needed no such legal bolstering of their claim to power and worth; the memory of Shivaji's empire was not dead. The first Non-Brahman glorification of Shivaji in the modern period seems to have been Mahatma Phule's Shivaji ballads of 1888.[20] The extent of pride in Shivaji in rural areas in the late nineteenth century is not known, but the current knowledge of Shivaji and his accomplishments is so widespread that one must presume either a constant folk memory or a thorough resurrection which met a ready response. One anthropologist's findings indicate that a greater percentage of village residents could correctly identify Shivaji than Nehru in the 1950s.[21]

Shivaji was also essential to the nationalists' image of India. The writings of Mahadev Govind Ranade and Bal Ganghadar Tilak, both Brahmans, reactivated pride in the Maratha past and also offered reinforcement for the Non-Brahman's claim to a greater share of contemporary power. The writing of the elite on the Maharashtrian Bhakti (devotional religion) movement centred on Pandharpur also added legitimacy to the Non-Brahman's concept of his proven worth. While saints from all castes entered into the movement in its period of creativity from the thirteenth through the seventeenth century, the most popular by far was the Shudra Tukaram, a poet-saint of Shivaji's period and, according to some, the spiritual source of his greatness.[22]

The reform associations of the Brahmans contributed to the intellectual justification of the Non-Brahman movement. Western India's religious reform movement, the Prarthana Samaj, allowed its ceremonies to be conducted by Marathas. The Poona Sarvajanik Sabha, a social and political organization which was the most important predecessor of the Indian National Congress in the Maharashtra area, attempted for a time to use Marathas from the landed aristocracy as its figureheads and also took on the presentation of peasant grievances to the Government. Jotirao Phule was extremely critical of both Prarthana Samaj and Sarvajanik Sabha, considering them both to be too much under Brahmanical control to be of any service to Non-Brahmans. Nevertheless, these elite attitudes could be used to justify Non-Brahman aims.

Brokers

While leadership within caste ranks and tacit intellectual approval on the part of the elite was necessary for the development of the Mahar movement, a group of "brokers" -- men who formed links with power sources or who could perform the duties members of the caste were not yet able to undertake -- seems to have been essential. This is especially clear in the early period of Ambedkar's leadership, from 1925 to 1935, when members of the Chandraseniya Kayastha Prabhu (C.K.P.) caste were of great importance in the development of his institutions. The presence of this group, highly educated and yet considered Shudras by the Brahmans, working both from a reformist commitment and in their own self-interest in the twentieth century, has caused me to look for similar "brokers" in the nineteenth. An easily defined group cannot be isolated, but it is clear that a number of individuals participated meaningfully in the earliest stages of movement.

Jotiba Phule himself served as a link between Mahars and the larger society. His schools for Untouchable children in Poona in the 1850s were among the earliest non-missionary efforts on behalf of the Depressed Classes. Vithal Ramji Shinde, himself a Maratha reformer who devoted much of his life to the education of the Depressed Classes, reported that Jotiba Phule, Baba Padmaji and others helped and guided Walangkar in his early effort to petition the British for redress of the ban on Untouchables' recruitment in the army.[23] Shivram Janba Kamble is said to have received help from the Gaikwad of Baroda in his various efforts at securing rights for the Untouchables. Just before Ambedkar came on the scene to represent Untouchables directly, two Mahars were brought before the Secretary of State for India, Edwin Montagu, on his 1917-1918 tour of India. Montagu reports:

Then we had Rai Bahadur Dougre on behalf of the depressed classes. He was a very nice fellow, taking a great interest in the depressed classes. He is a caste Hindu, and he brought along with him two Untouchables, who struck me, although one did not speak English, by their extraordinary intelligence. He thinks that communal representation for them is necessary. . . .[24]

The incident is an illustration of the necessary form of brokerage. Dougre was a Non-Brahman, anxious to serve that cause while aiding the Depressed Classes. While there was much paternalism extended to lower castes and Untouchables in many parts of India, and many instances of this in Bombay province, there was also a form of aid more conducive to the growth of a movement in the depressed group itself. That category of help which I have catalogued as "brokerage" was responsive to the initiative of the depressed group itself, allowed leadership when possible to direct the action taken, and contained a healthy element of self-interest.

In the Non-Brahman movement, reformist Brahmans generally served this role as friends, aids and associates of Mahatma Phule. There is also some indication that at the village level members of the C.K.P. caste quite early took on some responsibility in the Non-Brahman movement. The necessity of "brokers" is clearer in the history of the Mahar movement than in the Non-Brahman. Both movements, however, needed men more literate, more sophisticated, better able to approach the thrones of authority than the men actually of those movements in the nineteenth century. And in Maharashtra at every turn such men quietly performed that service.

Communication and Protection

These two necessities are obvious, and although communication was an all important and interesting development in both movements, perhaps it is sufficient to say here that in Maharashtra the newspaper was the *sine qua non* of any movement. Even before Ambedkar's sophisticated leadership began in 1920, at least four newspapers had emerged from the Mahar movement. And the Non-Brahman movement produced *Din Bandhu* (Brother of the Poor), a Marathi weekly, within four years of the establishment of the Satya Shodak Samaj in 1877.

Especially in the case of the Mahars, a minority in every village, protection for the breaker of tradition was a necessity. The Mahars' own reputation for toughness offered some of this, although here British law also was used as often as possible.

Conclusion

From this set of six "essentials" for the successful growth of a lower caste social protest movement, two comments on the particular quality of the Maharashtrian milieu may be made. There were similar sorts of changes in the late nineteenth and early twentieth centuries all over India--occupational opportunities, reform bodies, democratized legislative processes. Two factors in Maharashtra, however, seem to have enabled the Mahars and the Non-Brahmans to work through these opportunities with peculiar success. One is the basic Maharashtrian social structure; the other the nature of the reformist impulse in that part of western India.

In Maharashtra, as in the South, society consists of three blocks: a small (3 to 4%) group of Brahmans at the top; a great block of Shudra castes; a bottom layer (12%) of Untouchables. While this three tiered system is common to both areas, the differences seem to be in three facts. In Maharashtra, just below the Brahmans at the top of the Shudra block, lies a highly educated and mobile group of small castes, without the numbers to press their own advantage to the full and willing to cooperate with less literate groups in cutting inroads into Brahman power. The Shudras themselves contained a vast caste, the Marathas, land-owning and comparatively free from a landlord system, able to be mobilized with a call to their historic greatness and their contemporary disadvantages. Within the Untouchable block also was a dominant caste, the Mahars, spread throughout the language area, searching for ways to move from their unskilled and decaying position into new areas. The blocks of the Maharashtrian social structure existed before the nineteenth century, and may well have seen other periods of social change. In the nineteenth century, however, their inter-dependence on one another at the village level lessened, and grievances deepened as the Brahmans added increased amounts of secular power to their ritual superiority.

The other great difference lies in the nature of the reform movement in Maharashtra. In contrast to the Arya Samaj in Punjab and the Brahmo Samaj in Bengal, the Prarthana Samaj and the independent reformers in the Maharashtra area stayed within Hinduism. Their program was in some ways more moderate than that of both the Arya Samaj and Brahmo Samaj, but their pronouncements on caste and equality were more radical. While they themselves created no alternate system for those among the lower orders who desired better status, they offered intellectual justification for both Mahars and Non-Brahmans to seek new forms of power. The new energies released in the second half of the nineteenth century by changing circumstances found their own channels to work through.

Notes

1. See Eugene F. Irschick, *Politics and Social Conflict in South India: The Non-Brahman Movement and Tamil Separatism, 1916-29* (Berkeley: University of California Press, 1969) [See Addendum].

2. Although there is much material in censuses and in anthropological studies, there was no historical monograph on an Untouchable caste movement when this essay was written except my Ph.D. thesis, "Dr. Ambedkar and the Mahar Movement" (University of Pennsylvania, 1969). Owen Lynch's study of the Jatavas in Agra, *The Politics of Untouchability* (New York: Columbia University Press, 1969) does cover the history of that segment of the Chamar caste which became related to the Mahar movement in 1940s through Dr. Ambedkar's leadership. [There is now a study of Ad-Dharm in the Punjab in Mark Juergensmeyer's *Religion as Social Vision: The Movement against Untouchability in 20th Century Punjab* (Berkeley: University of California, 1982). The Ilava movement of Narayana Guru has now been

covered in at least a dozen recent books.]

3. The chief sources in English for Non-Brahman history when this essay was written were Dhananjay Keer, *Mahatma Jotirao Phooley* (Bombay: Popular Prakashan, 1964); A.B. Latthe, *Memoirs of His Highness Shri Shahu Chhatrapati Maharaja of Kolhapur*, 2 Vols. (Bombay: The Times Press, 1924); Anjilvel V. Mathew, *Bhaurao Patil* (Satara: Rayat Shikshan Sansta, 1957); and Maureen L.P. Patterson's unpublished M.A. thesis, "A Preliminary Study of the Brahmin versus Non-Brahmin Conflict in Maharashtra" (University of Pennsylvania, 1952). See the Addendum for the flood of recent material.

4. *Gazetteer of the Bombay Presidency.* Vol XII: Khandesh. Compiled by James M. Campbell, William Ramsay and James Pollen (Bombay: Government Press, 1880), pp. 116, 119.

5. *Report of the Land Revenue Settlement of the Nagpur District in the Central Provinces.* Compiled by R.H. Craddock (Nagpur: Government Press, 1899), p. 28.

6. Biographical information on Jotirao Phule has been drawn from Dhananjay Keer's biography, *Mahatma Jotirao Phooley* [For more recent studies, see the *Addendum* to this essay.]

7. *Cokhamela abhang gatha* (Bombay: Balkrishna Lakshaman Pathak, 1950). See *Abhangas* 5 and 11 and the essay on "Chokhamela and Eknath" in this volume.

8. See Hiroshi Fukazawa, "State and Caste System (Jati) in the Eighteenth Century Maratha Kingdom", *Hitotsubashi Journal of Economics,* IX:1 (June 1968), p. 43.

9. See Syed Nurullah and J.P. Naik, *History of Education in India* (Bombay: Macmillan, 1951), pp. 421-22.

10. *Indu Prakash* (Bombay, 5 May 1890), p. 4.

11. Maureen L.P. Patterson, *op.cit.*, p.1. [More recent scholarship suggests that Brahman-Maratha cooperation was more common than competition, but a change in areas of power and dominance would throw caste interdependence into competition.]

12. Dhananjay Keer, *op.cit.*, p. 240. According to Census figures, there were 580 literate males per 1000 among Brahmans, 43 in 1000 among Marathas, and 7 in 1000 among Mahar males in 1901. No significant change in these proportions appeared until the 1931 Census when literate males per 1000 were: Brahman, 788; Maratha, 223; Mahar, 63.

13. *Indian Statutory Commission,* VII. Memorandum submitted by the Government of Bombay (London: H.M.S.O., 1930), pp. 227-28.

14. R.N. Gooddine, *Report on the Village Communities of the Deccan* (Selections from the Records of the Bombay Government, No. IV) (Bombay: Government of Bombay, 1852), p. 15.

15. Quoted in Ravinder Kumar, *Western India in the Nineteenth Century* (London: Routledge & Kegan Paul, 1968), p. 307 from Jotirao Phule's *Gulamgiri* (slavery).

16. The petition is reproduced in H.N. Navalkar, *The Life of Shivram Janba Kamble* (Poona: S.J. Kamble, 1930.)

17. Translated by Prabhakar Machwe in his short biography, *Keshavsut* (New Delhi: Sahitya Akademi, 1966), pp. 45-6.

18. R.G. Bhandarkar, *Collected Works*, Vol II, edited by Narayan Bapuji Utgikar (Poona: Bhandarkar Oriental Institute, 1928), p. 491.

19. *Bombay Legislative Council Debates*, Vol I (1921), pp. 358-61.

20. Dhananjay Keer, *op.cit.*, pp. 100-01.

21. William A. Morrison, "Knowledge of Political Personages held by the Male Villagers of Badlapur", *Sociological Bulletin*, X:2, pp. 1-26 and XII:1, pp. 1-17.

22. The popular view of Tukaram as saint in Shivaji's time is vividly shown in the Marathi film, *Sant Tukaram*, produced by Prabhat Film Company Poona in 1936. [Tukaram's problems with orthodox Brahmans and his eventually winning their approval and Shivaji's devotion are the high points of the film.]

23. Karmavir Vithal Ramji Shinde, *Majhya athavani va anubhav* (My memories and experiences) (Poona: R.B. Andre, 1958), p. 214.

24. Edwin S. Montagu, *An Indian Diary*. Edited by Venetia Montagu (London: William Heinemann, 1930), p. 306.

Addendum

This early essay was an attempt to analyze at the simplest level the common factors at the root of two low caste movements in Maharashtra. At the back of my mind were two questions: why were there Non-Brahman movements in Maharashtra and Madras and nowhere else? Why did Maharashtra produce such an unusual Untouchable movement? The social structure and the dominant place of small Brahman castes in the two states help explain the Non-Brahman movements. For the second question, that concerning the Mahars, one would have to look much more closely at economic factors than I have done here, including the industrial growth of western Bombay Province, and the migration patterns of the Marathi-speakers who supplied the basic manpower. A great deal of literature has been published on the Non-Brahman movement since this essay was written; a study of the Mahar movement in its early phases awaits a more sophisticated effort than mine.

For recent analyses of the Non-Brahman movement, see Gail Omvedt, *Cultural Revolt in a Colonial Society: The Non-Brahman Movement in Western India: 1873 to 1930* (Bombay: Scientific Socialist Education Trust, 1976); Rosalind O'Hanbon, *Caste, Conflict and*

Ideology: Mahatma Jotirao Phule and Low Caste Protest in Nineteenth Century Western India (Cambridge: Cambridge University Press, 1985); J.R. Shinde, *Dynamics of Cultural Revolution: 19th Century Maharashtra* (Delhi: Ajanta, 1985); Kasinath K. Kavlekar, *Non-Brahmin Movement in Southern India: 1873-1949* (Kolhapur: Shivaji University Press, 1979) and M.S. Gore, *Non-Brahman Movement in Maharashtra* (New Delhi: Segment Book Distributors, 1989.)

The role of Maharshi Shinde, the Maratha reformer, has also received recent attention in Shivaprabha Ghugare, *Renaissance in Western India: Karmaveer V.R. Shinde, 1873-1944* (Bombay: Himalaya Publishing House, 1983.) The Gaekwad of Baroda's many reforms are narrated for the first time in a biography by Fatesing Rao Gaekwad, *Sayajirao of Baroda: The Prince and the Man* (Bombay: Popular Prakashan, 1989.)

II

POLITICS

The Leadership of Babasaheb Ambedkar*

During his lifetime, Dr. B.R. Ambedkar (1891-1956) played three roles: that of a caste leader, that of an Untouchable[1] spokesman, and that of national statesman. In his first leadership role, he was guide, guru and decision maker for his own caste, the Mahars of Maharashtra, from the mid-twenties of this century until his death.[2] From the early 1930s onwards he was the chief spokesman of the Untouchables in the eyes of the Government of India, the Untouchable leader who had to be dealt with from the viewpoint of the Indian National Congress, and the individual most responsible for India's policies of compensatory discrimination toward the Scheduled Castes. In his third role, he spoke on all phases on India's development, worked on problems of labor and law as a member of the Government, and even put aside some of his own theories to help create a viable, generally accepted Constitution.

My concern here is with the first of these perspectives, that of Ambedkar as *Babasaheb*, an affectionate term of respect used by the Mahars. This is patently unfair to Ambedkar, who never saw himself as merely a caste leader and who only once called a conference or founded an institution that was meant for Mahars alone.[3] However, Ambedkar's first and chief support was from his own caste, and this massive support is what enabled him to work effectively in larger circles. A narrow approach which examined *how* he led and *why* his caste responded to him with such devotion may point toward an understanding of leadership among other inarticulate, low-status groups in a changing society. Also, a close look at the Mahars at the time Ambedkar rose to leadership among them may point to the factors which produce readiness for change among a depressed people.

I want to look first at myths, legends and heroes, those all-important

*First published in B.N. Pandey ed., *Leadership in South Asia* (New Delhi: Vikas,1977). This essay was translated into Marathi by Vasant Moon and published by Sugava Prakashan in Pune, 1986. Additional notes appear in brackets. Some material duplicated in other essays has been omitted.

cultural images which any sub-group must deny or change if they are to
challenge a dominant culture. Ambedkar's very presence created a new
image. He appeared at a time of incipient changes among the Mahars.
Building on a movement which had just begun, Ambedkar designed,
over the years, an ideology and a program which counteracted negative
self-images, made use of Mahar virtues, and urged the Mahar toward
every channel open to participation in a modernizing democratizing
India. In the end he left the caste with new images and legends, and with
a new history as past and present Buddhists. In the words of an older
Mahar, "He took us to the stars". A stanza from a recent poem is not as
sophisticated as much current Buddhist writing, but it reveals the
awesome place Ambedkar holds in the hearts of his people and the
innovation he represents:

> Lord Beema[4]
>
> The Emancipator-Spartacus
> The Philosopher-Socrates
> The Law-giver-Aristotle
> The Orator-Demosthenes
> The Samson of Intellect
> The Nation's Architect
> The New-epoch Builder
> Lincoln-Lenin-Ambedkar

Myths of Origin and Heroism

The Mahar myths of origin, as do those of other Untouchable castes,
reflect the idea that an innocent, misunderstood or mistaken action
caused their untouchability. Unlike many other myths, however, they
concern not occupation[5] but the eating of forbidden food. A common
myth was a story of four cow-born brothers who were asked by their
mother how they would treat her after she died. Three brothers said they
would worship her; the fourth said he would bear her inside him just as
she had borne him, and he, of course, was the ancestor of the carrion-
eating Mahar. Even a later myth stresses this sin: Mahars were demoted
to untouchability in the seventeenth century by the Peshwa because they
ate anything they could find during the Mahadurga famine.[6] A Marathi
proverb links them with despised outsiders because of this fault: "The
Kanarese is a cheat, the Telugu is a thief, the Mahar is an eater of

forbidden food.''[7]

The eating of carrion was perhaps an inevitable consequence of a traditional duty of the Mahar as village servant, that of dragging carcasses out of the village. He had one other duty which was polluting in nature, that of bringing fuel to the burning grounds. None of his other ordained tasks was inherently polluting. He maintained the village wall and guarded the gate, carried messages and tax moneys, cared for the horses of passing government officials, made public announcements for the villagers, tracked thieves, testified to true boundaries in land disputes. Mahars who inherited this post received *baluta*, gifts in kind, along with the artisans of the village, but also received a small parcel of land as hereditary due, *watan* land. They could claim fifty-two traditional rights, such as the shrouds of the dead, the hides of the carcasses, the privilege of begging for food, certain small amounts of money or grain for ritual duties at rites of passage or festival times. The number of these perquisites is traditional; not all persisted into the modern age. Degrading though they seem to be, the fifty-two rights had meaning for the pre-modern Mahar. While the origin myths deal with the reason for the untouchability, the heroic myths tell stories of the securing of these rights.

The most important Mahar legend is that of its hero, Amrutnak (the *nak* ending indicates a Mahar name). A modern poetic version begins "Great, great is the nation where the Mahar is recognized as a brave man . . . ''[8] and proceeds with considerable delicacy to tell this story: Amrutnak was soldier-courtier at the court of the Muslim king of Bidar. When the queen was missing after an attack on the royal hunting camp, he volunteered to go in search of her, but first handed the King a small box. After many brave adventures, he brought the Queen back to a grateful court. The King, however, began to worry about the days the Queen had been alone with the handsome Amrutnak! He was told to open the small box, and its contents told him that Amrutnak had made the ultimate sacrifice to insure the Queen's chastity. Amrutnak refused a *jagir* for his service; instead he asked for fifty-two rights for his people, the Mahars.

This theme of sacrifice, trustworthiness and caste loyalty is also stressed in numerous legends of Mahars offering themselves as sacrifices for the foundations of great buildings in return for privileges for their people, or for the fifty-two evidently hard-won rights.

Chokhamela the Mahar Saint

Chokhamela, a thirteenth-fourteenth century *bhakti* saint-poet, invoked
the law of karma to explain his low birth, stating in two poems, "this
impurity is the fruit of our past", (*Abhanga* 4). But he passionately
protested his birth in another: "If you had to give me this birth, why did
you give me birth at all?" (*Abhanga* 6). In one poignant poem, Chokhamela
told the story of his being turned away from the temple and beaten by the
priests for daring to wear the garland of Vithoba, the God of the bhaktas
at Pandharpur.

There is discontent in the songs of this medieval Mahar saint, there
is protest of the very idea of a polluting caste, but the overriding feeling
is one of joy in devotion to God. "Chokha is uncouth, but his devotion
is not uncouth. Why judge him by his exterior?"[9] Although he was
acknowledged as one of the saint-poets in the *bhakti* pantheon, he was
fully involved in Mahar village duties.

The Use of Myth and Legend

This is unpromising material for a modern protest movement. There is
bravery, sacrifice, loyalty, piety, but all subservient to outside divine or
human forces. The obvious duty of a caste reformer is to call for an end
to eating carrion, and this the early Mahar leaders did, loudly and clearly
through the first decades of the twentieth century. There is also a possibility for a more positive call to a self-respect in the figure of Chokhamela
The Gazetteers of the Marathi-speaking districts report many Mahars
involved in the *bhakti* sect and some of these called themselves *Chokhamelas*
rather than give their caste name, Mahar. A pre-Ambedkar reformer from
the Nagpur area, Kisan Fagoji Bansode, made great use of the fact that
the Mahars had produced a saint to try to induce self-respect. He started
Chokhamela libraries and a Chokhamela hostel, went to Pandharpur to
collect Chokhamela's poems, and presented the figure of the saint as a
hero in one of his poems:

> Why do you endure curses?
> Chokha went into the temple resolutely.
> Why do you, ashamed, stay far off?[10]

In analogous movements, Chamars of the North called themselves
Raidasis or Ravidasis after their shoemaker saint and Chamars of the

Chattisgarh area were urged toward unity and new status as Satnamis.[11]

Two theories of origin were used by early Mahar leaders to stimulate caste pride, that of the Mahar as the original inhabitant of Maharashtra, "Lords of the Earth" brought low by the Aryans, and that of the Mahar as former Kshatriya, a man of proud warrior race. Neither seems to be part of the "legendry" of the pre-modern Mahar; both were common to many Untouchable castes as they began to strive for self-respect and higher status. The Lord of the Earth theory was potentially powerful since many nineteenth century British writers had derived the name Maharashtra from "Mahar" plus "rashtra" (country) and since some Mahar duties, such as the defining of land boundaries, could be used to substantiate the idea of previous ownership. The census as late as 1931 illustrates the use of this sort of claim in its recording of "Ad-Dharm" in Punjab and United Provinces,[12] and "Adi-Dravida" in Madras[13] as a substitute name for Untouchable castes. Such a movement was begun in Maharashtra by several leaders. Kisan Fagoji Bansode not only "went from door to door in the Mahar areas of Nagpur preaching self-respect among people who felt they were being punished for previous sin"[14] but also told the Mahars they had been former rulers of the land. Gopal Baba Walangkar, a retired Mahar soldier, drew up a petition for readmission of Untouchables into the army around 1890 in the name of the Anarya Doshparikarakham at Dapoli (the Non-Aryan group for the removal of wrongs).

Walangkar's petition is the first documentary evidence of the Mahar movement,[15] and as such its consideration of the question of origin is important. The initial claim to pre-Aryan status is quickly passed over in favour of the Mahars as former Kshatriyas, brought low by the Peshwa in the eighteenth century, a claim reinforced by the Mahars' army record of long and faithful service. But even this claim is superseded by a denial of the importance of origins: the Marathas were Turks; the Chitpavan Brahmans were Barbary Jews; and the high castes of South India were mixed Australian-semitic non-Aryan African Negroes! What matters is that "God made man the highest of beings and does not make man high or low by differences in eating or outward cleanliness.... We have begun to realize our proper rights of humanity." For humanity, Walangkar uses the simple but potent Marathi word *manuski*, of mankind.

Ambedkar and the Mythic Past

B.R. Ambedkar returned to India in 1923 after nearly ten years of study in the United States and England. Thirty years after Walangkar's beginnings, twenty years after Bansode's first conference, he began his work. He was a highly educated man; his degrees, B.A., M.A., Ph.D., M.Sc., D.Sc., Barrister-at-Law are sung in a sort of incantation in one of the Mahar songs about him. He was a highly political person, practical and pragmatic. Still, for personal as well as public reasons, he had to come to terms with the Mahar myths.

The classic myth of origin, the innocent eating of beef, could be discarded as irrational and irrelevant, as it had been by earlier reformers. The earting of carrion had to be attacked, and here Ambedkar combined a simple ''don't'' with a broader view. At a large conference of the Depressed Classes at Mahad in 1927, he asked his audience to take a vow not to eat carrion, *and* to abandon the *watan* system that bound them to village rights and village duties. He also asked for two resolutions, one calling upon caste Hindus to bury their own dead animals, and another calling upon the Government to prohibit, by law, the eating of carrion.

The claiming of Kshatriya status was open to Ambedkar, and supported by the fact that his father and grandfather had been soldiers in the Bombay army. However, in Maharashtra, the clean caste of Marathas were still battling to be considered Kshatriya instead of Shudra and it would have been of little use for Mahars, even if one believed in the efficacy of a new *varna* status, to make this claim. Instead of telling the Mahars that they had once belonged to the warrior caste, Ambedkar urged them to be militant *now*. ''Goats, not lions, are sacrificed'' is one of his sayings many remember. And while he was a member of the Viceroy's executive council during the Second World War, Ambedkar aided in the creation of the Mahar regiment which allowed thousands of Mahars to enter the army in a unit which acknowledged their military worth with its very name.[16]

Identification as former ''Lords of the Land'', the pre-Aryan inhabitants of India, might have not only unified the Mahars but linked them with the important movements of Untouchables in the North and South. But in his student days at Columbia, Ambedkar had written a thesis claiming that Indian culture and the Indian people are basically homogenous,[17] and he never departed from this belief. It may be that his American experience made him wary of a separation based on racial difference. It may be that his father's devout Hinduism, which included membership in the Kabir Panth, and his own interest in the dominant Sanskritic culture urged him toward a solution more identified with India's proudest traditions.

The figure of Chokhamela was attractive, and Ambedkar did dedicate one of his books to "Nandnar, Ravidas and Chokhamela, three renowned saints who were born among the untouchables who by their piety and virtue won the esteem of all."[18] But the "Cult of Vithoba"[19] offered spiritual, not social equality.

Ambedkar did not present the Mahars with a new identity, that of former Buddhists broken in the battle with Brahmans before the fourth century A.D., until 1948. He did not leave the Mahars with a new religion correlated with that past identity until 1956, the year of his death. What he did do, in my opinion, was present the Mahars with a new Amrutnak in his own person, a hero who won rights for them, but who did not have to castrate himself to show his absolute loyalty to his sovereign. The rights were political, not tied in with traditional duty, and they were the rights of all Indians in a democratic system. Ambedkar was seen as a savior, as a giver of rights, as one who sacrificed for his people. No one referred to him as an Amrutnak, but they sang:

He was a great scholar of India,
But he had no rest.
He gave up all his comforts
To serve his people.[20]

And Ambedkar himself, in his conversion speech in 1956, urged his people to become Buddhists without fear: "I am the one who got rights in the first place, and I will be able to get them again. At least for the present, you should continue to have faith in me."[21]

Ambedkar's Image and the Mahar Stereotype

The image of Ambedkar as it is so often depicted in the homes of the Buddhists and in statues in the railway towns of Maharashra[22] is almost always as a westernized man, complete with a coat, shirt, tie, shoes, fountain pen and usually a book [representing the Constitution]. The portrait or statue shows a man serious, determined and proud. The personality which Ambedkar presented with that elitist image was arrogant, caustic, aggressive, determined. To realize the impact of this figure, one must place it alongside the stereotype of the Mahar.

An unknown poet of the ex-soldier Walangkar's period [the 1890s] wrote a bitter poem about his fellow Mahars:

> Their houses are outside the village; there are lice in their women's hair; naked children play in the rubbish; they eat carrion.
>
> The faces of the Untouchables have a humble look; there is no learning among them; they know the names of the village goddesses and the demon gods but not the name of Brahma.[23]

The Gazetteer writers of the same period were no more flattering. In Kolhapur the Mahars were "darker than Kunbis, with gaunt cheeks, irregular features, a dreamy expression and flat noses," while in Sholapur they were "tall, strong, muscular and dark, with regular features and low unintelligent foreheads."[24] The general image given of the Mahar is that which is applied to depressed groups everywhere: poor, dirty, fond of drink, and of loose morals. Added to this is a suggestion that in spite of their humble lot, the Mahar was "hated and feared", or hot-tempered. One Gazetteer notes that "maharjatica" (of the Mahar caste) is a proverbial term for a cruel man.[25]

Another Marathi proverb, *jethe gao tethe maharwada*, means "Wherever there is a village, there is a Maharwada" (living quarters outside the village proper for the Mahar), and is literally true. Mahars constitute about nine per cent of the Marathi-speaking population, and are found in every village of the Marathi-speaking area. The implication of the proverb, however, is "There's a black sheep in every flock", or "Nothing in life is perfect."

Ambedkar had no need to identify himself by dress or speech with the village Mahar. He was a Mahar and no other choice was open to him. His identity of one of the educated elite, however, could be reinforced by clothes and manner. In 1918 a Professor in the University of London recommended him for his extraordinary practical ability, adding: "his character is rather Scotch-American, though in appearance he is a fat Indian".[26] Mohandas Karamchand Gandhi met him in 1932, but "Till I went to England, I did not know that he was a Harijan. I thought he was some Brahman who took deep interest in Harijans and therefore talked intemperately".[27] Toward the end of his life, when Ambedkar did wear Indian dress, a rather romantic American writer described him as "handsome", "jet-eyed", and looking like "a serious bespectacled Roman Senator in his immaculate white Indian robes".[28]

An Untouchable whose character was seen as tough Scotch-

American, who could pass for a Brahman on close inspection, who created the image of a Roman Senator, was of more use to the Mahars as a symbol of achievement than one who could be identified with the poor and humble Mahar. While Gandhi's saint-peasant garb reinforced the identity with the Indian masses he sought, Ambedkar's western dress and his independent critical temperament underlined the new identity he sought for the Mahar. Unconsciously but very effectively, Ambedkar brought together an iconoclastic *maharjatika* image, an elite stance, and the kind of "incendiary, explosive, inspiring" protest Maharashtra had seen earlier in such Brahman nationalists as Lokamanya Tilak and Vishnu Krishna Chiplunkar.[29]

Ambedkar's Guiding Principles

In his battle to gain rights for his people, to lift the Untouchables to a status equal to the higher castes of India, Ambedkar used many techniques, many tactics. In the religious field, he at first encouraged attempts to join in religious festivals, to enter temples, to perform marriages with Vedic rites. Later he called the caste to a conference on conversion and asked them to leave the fold of Hinduism. For twenty years, following that decision in 1936, Ambedkar played with the possibilities of entering Islam, Sikhism, Christianity or any one of India's numerous sects within Hinduism. The final decision was to convert to Buddhism, which meant literally to revive a religion long dead in India.

In the political field, Ambedkar at first supported special representation for the Depressed Classes, then joint electorates with Hindus, then separate electorates, and toward the end of his life denied the workability of the reserved seats for the Scheduled Castes for which he had spent so much time and energy. Ambedkar's varying approaches in the religious and political fields, however, reflect the shifting opportunities and the changing political demands around him. There is a remarkable consistency in his total view. From his work and from his own voluminous writings. I have drawn the following list of his guiding principles:

(1) The Untouchables should revolt because they are slaves, and slavery is inherently inhuman. There is no racial difference that marks them off from caste Hindus. If Hindu religious scripture ordains the practice of untouchability, those scriptures should be rejected.

(2) Only by acknowledging their slavery, by admitting their inferior position, could Untouchables unify and press for change. Only by

Governmental acknowledgement of their deprivation as a class and the correction of that injustice by special treatment on a caste basis could equality eventually be reached.

(3) Only Untouchables could understand their own condition and needs; hence only Untouchables themselves should lead Untouchable movements.

(4) Education and politics are the chief means to equality: education, so that the Untouchable will be able to participate in society on an equal plane; political agitation and participation, so that Untouchables can secure their rights and redress their economic and social grievances by law and political policy.

(5) Untouchables are totally Indian. No foreign ideology, no foreign religion could help them achieve equality as Indians. India must be free before they are totally free, but their battle for freedom must never be subservient to other demands.

(6) Only as some Untouchables become elite can the whole group be raised. Only if ability and ambition enable some Untouchables to be at the top of the pinnacle can the mass below realize its own potential.

The Mahar in the Early Twentieth Century

The most striking difference between the Mahars and most other Untouchable castes is that their hereditary occupation did not carry over into the modern world. No one could say in 1923, as Thomas Coats did one hundred years earlier, that "although considered outcaste (the Mahars) have great weight and are of great importance as members of the community."[30] New methods of administration and communication had cut away much of the power of village officials in general, and the Mahar as "inferior village servant" was left with only the most mundane of his village tasks. The 1921 Census indicates that only thirteen per cent of the employed Mahars were in traditional occupations. The Untouchable Mang's rope and basketry work was still viable, and a third of the Mang workforce together with over half of the shoe and leather working Chambhars were still in traditional occupations.[31]

Although the majority of Mahars were probably still tied to the village as agricultural labor, it is clear that even at the time of the early Gazetteers in the 1880s a number had moved into economic independence. State public works, domestic service to Europeans, the mill industry, ammunition factories, and especially the railroad offered new opportunities to the Mahar. No Gazetteer gives statistics, but the

Khandesh writer of 1880 is explicit in reporting the nature of new occupations and their social consequences:

> Of late between landlords and village Mahars complaints and feuds have grown very common . . . . the railway has done much for the Mahars. They make excellent gangmen, and some of them, gathering capital as petty contractors and moneylenders, show much independence and manage their business without the help of any high caste clerks. Of late, too, they have begun to send their boys to school.[32]

The link between the non-traditional Mahar and the early social movement is clear. Walangkar's 1890 petition failed to reintroduce the army channel for upward mobility among the Mahars (indeed, his fellow army pensioners refused to sign it and it never was presented to the British), but there were still retired soldiers in the 1920s taking part in conferences and the temple and water *satyagrahas*. Kisan Fagoji Bansode found a receptive audience for his social concerns among the mill workers of Nagpur. His counterpart in Pune, Shivram Janba Kamble, was a butler in the Masonic Hall. A number of Ambedkar's early followers worked in the Port Trust of Bombay, and it is not a coincidence that many of the early conferences were held in small towns along the various branches of the railroad, where enclaves of Mahar railway workers formed a group ready for social change that would match their new economic status.

Economic changes, as Khandesh Gazetteer indicates, led directly into educational interests. There are records of the Mahars founding schools or hostels in Nagpur, Pune, Ahmadnagar and Amraoti (where Mahar village service had been placed on a cash basis and was no longer on the traditional *baluta* and *watan* basis). It was in response to the initiative among the Mahars that Vithal Ramji Shinde, a Maratha and the most important of the caste Hindu reformers, began his Depressed Class Mission in Pune in 1906, creating an organization that was to educate thousands of Untouchables.[33] Government schools now, in contrast to the mid-nineteenth century,[34] also admitted Untouchables, although it often involved their being placed on a veranda or in separate seating arrangements. The Mahar male literacy rate climbed from 1 in 1000 to 23 in 1000 between 1901 and 1921. The 2.3 per cent literacy rate, however, must be seen in terms of actual educated Mahars. Of the half a million on the Bombay side of the Marathi-speaking area, there were nearly five thousand male and three thousand female Mahars who were literate.[35] Of these, 288 were literate in English, and only one, B.R. Ambedkar, was a college graduate.

In economic and educational terms, then, there was at least a small group of Mahars ready for a social change that would remedy their traditional low status. An intangible factor must be added to the tangible facts -- that of a legitimization of such a social change by society. I have argued elsewhere in this context[36] that there must be approval by some elements of the elite before a mass movement gathers momentum. Criticism of the caste system and disapproval of the practice of untouchability may be found in many parts of India during this period, but in the Marathi-speaking area there seems to have been an unusual amount of radical criticism which was divorced from any program of action. Keshavsut, the first modern poet, mourned that the glory of some rested on the degradation of the Mahar.[37] R.G. Bhandarkar, Maharashtra's finest Sanskrit scholar, wrote that a great deal of intelligence was being wasted by depriving the Mahar of education.[38] Gopal Ganesh Agarkar influenced many by his totally rational approach to society's problems.[39] The most striking instance of radical thought unconnected with social action may be seen in the 1915 encounter of Gandhi with Hari Narayan Apte, the first great Marathi novelist. Gandhi attended a meeting of the Servants of India Society in Poona and heard their plans to try to arouse the Untouchables to a full realization of the injustice of their position. He told the group, ''I am afraid you will make Harijans rise in rebellion against society.'' Apte told him, ''Yes, let there be a rebellion. That is just what I want.''[40] Not many Brahmans wanted rebellion, but the creative fringe of the Brahman elite legitimized change without creating the channels which would enable the educated Untouchable to enter a new status, somewhere above his uneducated brethren. There seems to be a vacuum between thought and program waiting to be filed. For instance, it was Ambedkar himself in the late 1920s who saw to it that the second college graduate in the Mahar community secured a post as Deputy Collector,[41] the first Untouchable in India to hold such a high post in the administration.

Ambedkar's Leadership: The Southborough Testimony and its Ramifications

In 1919, during a brief period in India between segments of his overseas education, Ambedkar testified to the Southborough Committee, the group gathering information to determine the franchise for the Montagu-

Chelmsford reforms. It was his first political move, and it reveals graphically the difference between Ambedkar and other Mahar leaders as well as leaders of Untouchables in other parts of India. He spoke for no group, only as *the* college graduate among the Untouchables of Bombay province. His testimony was lengthy, sophisticated, passionate, but never beyond the bounds of a lawyer's plea. He fit his proposals into a total plan for the election procedures in the province for all groups, asking only that "the hardships and disabilities entailed by the social system should not be reproduced and perpetuated in political institutions."[42]

Attempts to influence government policies were not new to the Mahars. Shivram Janba Kamble, the Masonic Hall butler in Pune, had a talent for letter writing and petition which he often employed. His finest effort was a 1910 appeal to the government for employment opportunities for the Depressed Classes "in the lowest grades of the Public Service, in the ranks of Police Sepoys and of Soldiers in the Indian Army." One passage of the appeal reveals considerable sophistication and prophetic judgement:

> And it is most encouraging to know that the Honorable House of Commons . . . is composed, to some extent, of the representatives of the lower strata of English society, the workingmen, who, only a quarter of a century ago, were regarded as but Mahars and Paryas by the more educated and affluent classes of their nation.[43]

Kisan Fagoji Bansode, on the eastern edge of Maharashtra, also worked political interest into his messages to the Mahars. A summary of his preaching would read: do not eat carrion, do not drink, spread education, acquire citizenship, organize, press for appointments on local governing bodies, "create among caste Hindus a feeling that the downtrodden should be uplifted", do not become Christians.[44] Bansode was actually brought before Edwin Montagu during the Montagu-Chelmsford tour of 1917, together with an Amraoti Mahar, G.A. Gawai, who had studied up to matriculation, and Montagu recorded in his diary that he was struck "by their extraordinary intelligence", although "one did not speak English."[45] Kamble and Bansode were able and gifted leaders, but neither a butler nor a non-English speaker was equipped to deal with the new political opportunities of the Montagu-Chelmsford reforms.

Mahars had also been called to two conferences in the period of the Montagu-Chelmsford reform tour to express their political desires. However, both conferences were called by caste Hindus, and the resolutions of the conferences reflected the political position of those men. Shinde's Depressed Classes Mission Society held a meeting endorsing the Congress-League Scheme for self-rule and called upon the Congress to resolve that the disabilities of the Depressed Classes be removed. Congress passed such a resolution, its first statement on untouchability, in almost identical language. Another organization, led by Non-Brahman Marathas who feared devolution of British power lest it bring back Brahman rule, held a conference a few weeks later at which its Depressed Class attenders denied support to the Congress-League plan.[46] Untouchables in Madras, who were at this time perhaps even more politicized than the Mahars, followed the lead of the Non-Brahmans in that province and refused to appear before the Franchise Committee because of the objectionable statements of some of the committee's Brahman members.

Ambedkar's use of the public platform of the Governmental Commission, then, independently and confidently, fully supportive of any extension of democracy to India, was in stark contrast to that of other Untouchables. He was not bound to the Non-Brahman movement; his English was fully equal to the situation; he believed in the political process and was only anxious that the Depressed Classes share in it according to their numbers and needs.

Ambedkar asked for nine elected representatives from the Depressed Classes in a Bombay Legislative Council of 100, and for one of those to be chosen by the group to serve on the Central Legislative Council in Delhi. He claimed that the Depressed Classes were entitled to this representation because there was no "like-mindedness" and no "endosmosis" between Touchables and Untouchables and hence Touchables could not represent Untouchables. The Depressed Classes were "slaves", "dehumanized", and so "socialized as never to complain", and they must have communal representation "in such numbers as will enable them to claim redress", and under a franchise "so low as to educate into political life as many Untouchables as possible".

The final decision on franchise was to give the Depressed Classes *one nominated* member on the Bombay Legislative Council.[47] Ambedkar, undeterred, came back from his second period in London to testify, whenever possible, on matters pertaining both to the Depressed Classes and to his interests as an educated man. He spoke to the Royal Commission on Indian Currency and Finance, to the University Reforms Commission, and, of course, to the Simon Commission, at which time he served on its Provincial Committee to hear evidence as well.

This method of political action resulted in two long-term gains, although it was rarely immediately effective. One was the creation of the Starte Committee, a group designated by the Bombay Legislative Council (of which Ambedkar was now a nominated member) to hear testimony on the needs of the Depressed Classes. The Starte report, issued in 1930,[48] represents the most thorough-going inquiry into the Depressed Class condition and the most far-reaching recommendations of its time. Its recommendations on Depressed Classes scholarships and reserved places in education and in government offices, and on the creation of a special government official to look after the interests of the Depressed Classes and Tribes became, in time, official governmental policy. Its report clearly represents Ambedkar's ideas. Ambedkar's firm grasp of the British method of commission and committee methods of determining change brought the needs of the Untouchables into the purview of the Government more effectively than the Mahar could have dreamed of ten years earlier.

A second result of Ambedkar's articulate use of the parliamentary process was his selection as one of the two Depressed Class members for the Round Table Conferences in London in 1930-1932.[49] Ambedkar's sophisticated testimony to government bodies was probably not known to the village Mahar; however, his selection by the British to meet politicians and princes in London to determine the future of India was known to even the most humble Mahar in the remotest village. Other matters of a more political nature were to stem from the Round Table Conferences, and it was here that Ambedkar came into the direct conflict with Gandhi over the issue of special representaiton for the Depressed Classes. But the immediate importance of the Round Table Conferences to the Mahar movement was that Ambedkar had indeed taken their needs into the highest circle of power.

Ambedkar's Leadership: The Mahad Conferences

S. Natarajan, an astute historian of social reform, wrote that ''in 1930, by a process of repeated conferences the depressed classes were led into the camp of Dr. B.R. Ambedkar''.[50] This is something of an exaggeration, but it is certain that thousands of the Depressed Classes in the Marathi-speaking area saw and heard Ambedkar at perhaps a dozen large and innumerable small conferences from 1924 on. Mahars had been calling conferences since 1903, usually under the Mahar name, or participating in the Depressed Classes conferences associated with the Non-Brahmans or caste-Hindu reformers. Ambedkar's conferences were held in the name of all the Depressed Classes, were never associated with any other group, and at least twice formed resolutions calling for permanent organization. The Depressed Classes Institute was formed after the Barshi conference of 1924. The Scheduled Castes Federation took shape at the Nagpur conference of 1942. The conferences that were seen as the beginning of the Mahar awakening, however, were those held at Mahad, a small town in Kolaba district in, 1927.

Mahad was not only the most dramatic of the Ambedkar conferences, but also shows his pattern of organization. These factors can be seen at Mahad and also in much of Ambedkar's other work: a call by local leaders; organizational work by "new" Mahars, those freed from village dependency, and publicity in Ambedkar's newspaper; caste Hindus used as associates and legitimizers but not as decision makers or leaders; the presentation of new ideas in direct passionate speech or vivid action; mass action channeled toward some legal or political goal.

Surendranath Tipnis, the chairman of the Mahad municipal government, a follower of the reformer Gopal Krishna Agarkar and a caste-Hindu acquaintance of Ambedkar, announced the Kolaba District Depressed Classes Conference for March 1927. For weeks preceding the Conference, a former Mahar military man, Subhedar Savadkar, and other local Mahars traveled from village to village mobilizing the Untouchables. Keer reports that 10,000 people arrived from almost all the districts of Bombay,[51] and while this may be an exaggeration, Mahars from Nasik and Pune did come in large numbers to Mahad. In his Presidential address, Ambedkar reminded the Mahars of their former opportunities in the army (many recruits had come from the Kolaba and Ratnagiri districts) and of the treachery of the British in closing this door on them. He urged the Mahars to agitate against the ban on recruitment and to seek self-help, self-respect and self-knowledge.

The Subjects Committee of the Conference met that night, and decided to test a new government provision opening public places to all castes. The target was the Chowdar Tank, a large body of water in the Brahman area of Mahad. Ambedkar had not urged this, but it was he who led the procession to the Tank on the following day, stopped and first drank water. A rumor spread through Mahad that the Untouchables were going on to the Vireshwar Temple, and a group of "caste Hindu rowdies" attacked the Conference delegates. Ambedkar urged restraint on the part of the delegates and convinced the Hindus that a temple entry was not planned. Five of the attackers were sentenced to four months imprisonment and the Chowdar Tank was ceremoniously purified by

Mahad residents.

Ambedkar, back in Bombay, called for a return to Mahad on 25 and 26 December 1927: "The question whether we belong to the Hindu religion or not is to be decided by us once for all". As the date neared, some residents of Mahad filed a suit against Ambedkar and three others and secured an injunction temporarily prohibiting their use of the Tank. Nevertheless the Conference met, and Ambedkar's address this time condemned the inequality of Hinduism. At night, the *Manusmriti*, the ancient law book which sanctified differential treatment of low castes, was ceremoniously burned.[52] Rather than follow up this dramatic gesture with another satyagraha to the Tank, Ambedkar heeded the court injunction and asked the Conference to postpone its action. A procession went round the tank but did not "pollute" the water. The Conference ended with Ambedkar's address, his first, to a special group of 3000 Untouchable women, in which he asked them to dress well, educate their children, and to combat drunkenness by not feeding their husbands if they had been drinking. Ambedkar won the suit for the use of Chowdar Tank water after a three-year battle in the lower courts.

I have juxtaposed the separate elements in this narrative deliberately to stress the varied techniques Ambedkar used. What is clear is that although the Mahars were ready for militancy, Ambedkar much preferred a fight in the courts to a battle in the streets. Mass action produced unity and courage, but unless gains were legalized and protected, the masses could do little. This belief can be seen in Ambedkar's role in temple satyagrahas that followed the Mahad effort. In 1927 in Amraoti, in 1929 in Pune and 1930-35 in Nasik, there were ever larger temple entry movements. The Nasik satyagraha involved thousands of Untouchables in a five-year fruitless attempt to enter the Kala Ram temple in that pilgrimage town. Although Ambedkar was seen as the inspiration of these temple entry attempts, and his name was shouted by the marchers as they moved toward the closed temple doors, he was not the initial planner of any but the Nasik effort, nor was he the chief on-the-spot leader of any. Ambedkar's role was to give courage and a sense of protection. He saw the satyagrahas, however, as necessary efforts to unify the Untouchables and make them conscious of their lack of rights. He had no faith in the Gandhian idea of a "change of heart" among caste Hindus, and indeed neither Gandhi nor the Congress approved of these non-violent efforts to adapt the Gandhian method to their needs.

Ambedkar called off the Nasik satyagraha in 1935, choosing a railway town near Nasik for his announcement, and stating at the same time that he would leave Hinduism since it offered no sign of yielding equality either to plea or mass protest. At this juncture, the devout Kisan Fagoji Bansode of Nagpur, who had introduced Ambedkar to Nagpur Mahars in 1926 as an accomplished leader, left Ambedkar's fold. The movement, however, did not split. Mahars from the eastern side of Maharashtra had not been through the emotional mass action protests of those on the west, but they remained loyal to him. Perhaps the lack of an immediate alternative religion in place of Hinduism, perhaps the fact that Ambedkar did not seek a public show of support until a conference in 1942 in Kamti, near Nagpur, allowed a slow acceptance of a radical idea to permeate the caste.

The Satyagraha method was used only three more times on a large scale in Ambedkar's lifetime: once in 1938 to support an Anti-Khoti legislative bill; once in 1946 to back up Ambedkar's demands for separate electorates; and once in 1953 for land in the Marathwada area, a movement Ambedkar did not initiate but did help by mediating toward a satisfactory conclusion. He did, however, bequeath the satyagraha technique to his people, and in contemporary India, filled with satyagrahas for all causes, mass demonstration technique is no longer used sparingly.

Ambedkar's Leadership: Politics and Education

The success and failure of Ambedkar's political parties and his work as a national leader are well known, and there is no need to detail them here.[53] What I would like to point out, very briefly, are the nature of that success and the reasons for failure. Ambedkar's three political parties, the Independent Labour Party of 1936, the Scheduled Castes Federation of 1942 and the Republican Party of 1956, were all attempts to join Untouchables to larger groups or in a solid mass to seek political power. The very success of the Independent Labour Party in the 1937 elections, in which it won 14 of the 18 seats it contested, pointed to its limitations: fourteen legislators can do little in a political body of 100. The Scheduled Castes Federation attacked the problem in a new way: its chief aim was to secure separate electorates which would allow Untouchable representatives to enter political bodies without seeking caste Hindu support. Its election failure was nearly total, due in Bombay and Madras province, at least, to caste Hindu votes.[54] A third approach was tried with the Republican Party, which was to unite all the dispossessed, but which has remained a Scheduled Caste body. Ambedkar, obviously, never found a way to use the roughly ten per cent of the vote which he could command to secure political power. Nor did he have the organizational technique to unite groups in which the local leadership was not already committed to him or to his policy. He was a statesman, not a party boss. His success, then, was to leave large groups thoroughly politicized. Their vote and their few elected representatives have protest value, and when the dominant party is weak they have a massive committed vote to swing toward that party in return for recognition of their needs and some political favors.

Ambedkar's educational institutions have little to do with politics, save that mock elections and mock parliaments that are held in these institutions encourage the students to consider political matters. Moreover, like the political parties, they provide a way for the educated Mahar, now Buddhist, to work for his people rather than finding his own way into the elite. The educational institutions also indicate the unique quality of Ambedkar's leadership. There are now educated Untouchables all over India. Only in Maharashtra do they run a system of colleges. Beginning with the establishment of Siddharth College of Arts and Sciences in Bombay in 1945, Ambedkar's People's Education Society now supervises colleges of law and commerce in Bombay, Milind College in Aurangabad, Dr. Ambedkar College in the satyagraha town of Mahad [and twenty-eight other institutions]. Nagpur Buddhists have established their own Ambedkar College [and other institutions have sprung up all over Maharashtra]. The system is open to all, but is obviously a comfortable haven for the Scheduled Caste student. And it has pioneered in ways that reflect Ambedkar's broad vision: Siddharth College was the first to offer courses in Sociology in Bombay; Milind was the first college in the backward area of Marathwada, formerly in Hyderabad State. Ambedkar not only talked about the necessity of producing members of the elite, he enabled the production of the elite untouchable, many of them committed to the service to their people.

Another result of this stress on education, on being linked to the mass even though achieving elite status, may be seen in the vast body of Dalit (oppressed) Literature.[55] I know of no other Untouchable group which has produced literature considered seriously on the literary scene. [The neighbouring Dalits of Gujarat and Karnataka are now writing serious literature.] Beginning with Shankarrao Kharat's stories of his father as a Mahar village servant,[56] the Mahars have continually produced literature, chiefly poetry and short stories. These writers do not honor Ambedkar as "Saviour", they are far too sophisticated and much too conscious of continued humiliation. But they were clearly set free by Ambedkar's work among their fathers to declare their bitterness and their despair in eloquent literary forms [and all acknowledge their debt to Ambedkar].

Ambedkar's Leadership: The Completion of Myth

In the last ten years of his life, after decades of pragmatic political work and in the midst of national recognition of his statesmanship, Ambedkar returned to the need to create a new legend, a new history, a new identity for his people. In 1948 he published *The Untouchables* in which he argued that they had been "Broken Men", fragments of defeated tribes which were barely tolerated outside the villages of settled tribesmen, analogous to the Fuidhars of Ireland and the Alltudes of Wales in early days. The Broken Men were not absorbed in India, as they were in Europe, because they were Buddhists who clung to their religion and to their beef-eating in the face of Brahman hatred. Untouchability was born in India around A.D. 400, out of the struggle for supremacy between Buddhism and Brahmanism "which has so completely molded the history of India and the study of which is so woefully neglected by students of Indian history".[57] Here was an explanation which rationally explained untouchability, which identified the Untouchables with one of the mainstreams of Indian thought, and which even offered reasons for the separate dwelling areas and the eating of forbidden food by the Untouchable.

Ambedkar's own religious interests had leaned toward Buddhism for many years. His early heroes were the Buddha, Kabir and Mahatma Phule, all religious reformers who advocated castelessness. When he moved from a cement chaul to a home in a Brahman area of Bombay in 1934, he named the house Rajgriha, the place of the first Buddhist Council. His first college took the personal name of the Buddha, Siddhartha. But Buddhism was not a viable religion to offer his people until the emergence of an independent India which used the Buddhist wheel and Asokan pillar as its symbols and was newly conscious of its Buddhist neighbors, Ceylon and Burma.[58]

Two months before his death in December 1956, Ambedkar went to Nagpur, which he called the home of the Nagas, an ancient Buddhist people, and again, using local leadership and his own impassioned oratory and example, set the Mahars on a new path. The Nagpur newspapers called the scene of mass conversion "a new Pandharpur",[59] thus evoking images of Chokhamela and the Bhakti movement. In Bombay, ten days after Ambedkar's death, another mass conversion was held, and by the time of the 1961 Census, eighty per cent of the Mahars, locality by locality, had announced their new identity. Small enclaves of Untouchables outside Maharashtra held their own conversion ceremonies, adding half a million Buddhists to the 2,789,501 in the Maharashtra area. They were left without organization, without a *sangha* and without recognition from caste Hindus that any change in status had taken place, but with a new psychological freedom.

A recent popular article on the current problems of the Untouchables ends with this tribute to Ambedkar's image:

> The Harijans today are leaderless. What they need is an Ambedkar rather than a Gandhi because the long tale of their persecution at the hands of Caste Hindus even after Independence has shown that there is going to be no change of heart among the latter through mere gentle persuasion. It is unrealistic to talk of "solutions" for the woes of Harijans but, if there is one, it must surely lie in exploring the limitless possibilities of organized resistance to discrimination within the framework of non-violence . . . . But only an Ambedkar can galvanize the community into action. As things are, no such liberator is in sight.[60]

It is unlikely that there will be another Ambedkar. Any Untouchable leader today would compete with a dozen others who are his equal in education, in articulateness, in grasp of the political and social situation. What may happen is that those things which are in large part a legacy from Ambedkar: a sense of self-respect, opportunities for education and employment in high places, organization on the basis of local leadership for large goals, a militant claim to human rights, a tie between the new elite and the still-suffering masses, a sense of belonging completely to a rich Indian religious heritage -- all these potentially creative factors may continually produce new, smaller movements. India's depressed minority has as much dynamism as any such people's movement today, and it has more legalized governmental help. It is possible that India may solve her discrimination problem before the West finds a solution to its own.

Notes

1. Untouchable is the word used by Ambedkar himself for those castes lowest in the Hindu scale of pollution. The early governmental term was Depressed Classes; this was replaced by Scheduled Castes in 1935 when these castes were placed on a schedule as qualifying for special rights. Gandhi's name for the Untouchables, Harijan, dates from his 1933-34 campaign against untouchability, and is in general usage except among Ambedkar's followers. All those who have converted to Buddhism use the term Buddhist and reject all other nomenclature, including their original caste names. All these terms and specific names of Untouchable castes as well have been used in this paper according to time period and group usage. [Dalit--downtrodden-- has become the most acceptable term in the 1980s.]

2. Other groups of Untouchables, chiefly in urban areas, followed Ambedkar as closely as the Mahars did from the 1940s on. See Owen M. Lynch, *The Politics of Untouchability* (New York and London: Columbia University Press, 1969), and the same author's article, "Dr. B.R. Ambedkar -- Myth and Charisma", in J. Michael Mahar ed., *The Untouchable in Contemporary India* (Tucson: University of Arizona, 1972), pp. 97-112, for a study of the Jatavs of Agra.

3. Only the conference in 1936 called to determine the matter of conversion was announced as a Mahar conference. Ambedkar held that each caste must determine its religious destiny by itself.

   For a broader look at Ambedkar's total work, see Dhananjay Keer, *Dr. Ambedkar: Life and Mission* (Bombay: Popular Prakashan, 1962, rev. ed.). Recent studies, all Ph.D. dissertations and all by non-Mahars, include: Daya Ram Jatava, *Social Philosophy of B.R. Ambedkar* and *Political Philosophy of B.R. Ambedkar* (both published in Agra: Phoenix Publishing Agency, 1965); A.M. Rajasekharia, *B.R. Ambedkar: The Politics of Emancipation* (Bombay: Sindhu Publications, 1971); and W.N. Kuber, *Ambedkar: A Critical Study* (New Delhi: People's Publishing House, 1973). [See the Bibliography on Ambedkar for newer works]

4. C.M. Wagh, "Lord Beema", in *Thoughts on Ambedkar*, compiled by Hoti Lal Nim (Agra: Siddharth Educational and Cultural Society, 1969), pp. 10-11. "Beema", a shortened form of Ambedkar's first name, Bhimrao, links Ambedkar with Bhima, "the terrible", the strongest of the Pandhava brothers in the epic *Mahabharata*.

5. A Bhangi (scavenger) myth claims that Bhangis are the descendants of a Brahman sage who carried away and buried a dog that died in a Brahman assembly. See *Gazetteer of Baroda State*, Vol. 1 (Bombay, 1923), p. 222. A Chambhar myth traces their descent from a son of Shiva, who incurred his father's wrath by making a pair of shoes from his own skin to present to the God. As punishment he was damned to be a cobbler for life. *Gazetteer*

of the Bombay Presidency: Kolhapur, Vol. XXIV (Bombay, 1886), p. 109. There are many Mahar origin myths, but none refers to Mahar traditional duties.

6. A number of myths trace the Mahar fall from grace to the time of the Peshwas, chief ministers of the Maratha kingdom. The Peshwas were Chitpavan Brahmans, and are remembered as having introduced especially limiting strictures on Mahars, such as carrying pots for their spittle and brooms to erase their footsteps from the road.

7. Quoted in Alexander Robertson, *The Mahar Folk* (Calcutta: Y.M.C.A. Publishing House and Oxford University Press, 1938), p. 22.

8. C.B. Khaimode published his poetic version of the Amrutnak legend, as told him years earlier by an older Mahar, in 1961 (Pradna Publishing Company). This version has been translated by D.K. Bholay for Robert J. Miller's article, "Button, Button . . . . Great Tradition, Little Tradition, Whose Tradition?", *Anthropological Quarterly*, 39, 1, 1961, pp. 26-41. Another loyalty-castration story is told in Robertson, *The Mahar Folk*, pp. 72-3. [See "The Folklore of the Brave" in this volume.]

9. This line is from Iravati Karve's "On the Road: A Maharashtrian Pilgrimage", *Journal of Asian Studies*, XXII:1 (1962), p. 21. All other quotations were translated from *Cokhamela Abhang Gatha* (Bombay: Balkrishna Lakshman Pathak, 1950) with the help of B.S. Shinde and Mrs. Hemant Fanse.

10. *Pradip* (Nagpur: Sahrao Bansode, 1958).

11. See Lawrence A. Babb, "The Satnamis -- Political Involvement of a Religious Movement", in *The Untouchables in Contemporary India*, (*op.cit*) pp. 143-51.

12. In the Panjab, 400,000 Depressed Classes, chiefly Chamars and Churas, registered themselves as "Ad-Dharmi" (first religion) in the 1931 Census in an organized effort to claim special status. [See Mark Juergensmeyer, *Religion as Social Vision* (Berkeley: University of California Press, 1982).]

13. Rao Bahadur M.C. Rajah, an Untouchable leader from Madras, made a strong case for the Untouchable as "Adi-Dravida" (first or original Dravidian) in his book *The Oppressed Hindus* (Madras: The Huxley Press, 1925). The use of the term in the Census was at the request of the Depressed Classes.

14. Interview with S.V. Dahat of Nagpur, a knowledgeable informant on Bansode's life and the Mahar movement in the Vidarbha area.

15. A handwritten copy of Walangkar's petition in Marathi is in the Khairmode collection of Ambedkar materials at the Bombay University Library.

16. See Major General S.P.P. Thorat, *The Regimental History of the Mahar MG Regiment*. (Dehra Dun: The Army Press, 1954). The regiment was never limited to Mahars, but enlists many along with caste Hindus and still bears the Mahar name.

17. Ambedkar's seminar paper was published as "Castes in India - Their

Mechanism, Genesis and Development" in *The Indian Antiquary*, XLVI, 1917, pp. 81-95.

18. *The Untouchables* (New Delhi: Amrit Book Co., 1948).

19. See G.A. Deleury, *The Cult of Vithoba* (Pune: The Deccan College Post Graduate and Research Institute, 1960) for the fullest description in English of this important Maharashtrian sect.

20. "Song of Baba", poet unknown. This unpublished song is among the many collected by Russ Geyer, a Carleton student in Pune in 1970.

21. The Buddhist conversion speech of 15 October 1956, was published in *Prabhuddha Bharat*, 27 October 1956, in Marathi. The translation is with the help of Mrs. Rekha Damle. [The rights he refers to here are those allowed by the Government for Hindu Untouchables.]

22. Pressure from the Republican Party has resulted in a life-size statue placed at the Northwest corner of Parliament House compound. A copy of the Constitution is in one of Ambedkar's hands; the forefinger of the other points at Parliament.

23. These stanzas are from a long poem in Marathi which was attached to the handwritten Marathi petition of Gopal Baba Walangkar. The internal signature is "Pandit Kondiram", whose name I have not found in any other connection. The transaction was made with the help of Pramod Kale.

24. *Gazetteer of the Bombay Presidency: Kolhapur*, Vol. XXIV (Bombay, 1886), p. 112 and *Sholapur*, Vol. XX (Bombay, 1884).

25. The Sholapur Gazetteer reports the use of the term *maharjatica*. The protagonist of Vijay Tendulkar's new and controversial Marathi play, an amoral, hot-tempered iconoclast, describes himself as "a Mahàr although born a Brahman". See *Sakharam Binder*, translated by Shanta Shahane and Kumud Mehta (Delhi: Hind Pocket Books, 1973).

26. Government File, Education Department, No. 65-I-1918, pp. 237-38. Bombay   Archives.

27. Mahadeo Desai, *The Diary of Mahadeo Desai* (Ahmedabad: Navajivan Publishing House, 1953), p. 52.

28. Blake Clark, "The Victory of an Untouchable", *The Reader's Digest* (March 1950), p. 110.

29. The words in quotation marks were applied to Chiplunkar by Stanley A. Wolpert in *Tilak and Gokhale: Revolution and Reform in the Making of Modern India* (Berkeley: University of California Press, 1962), p. 10.

30. Thomas Coats, "Account of the Present State of the Township of Lony", *Transactions of the Literary Society of Bombay*, Vol. III, 1823, reprinted 1877, p. 210.

31. *Census of India*, 1921. Vol. VIII: *Bombay Presidency*, Part II -- Tables, (Bombay, 1922), p. 363.

32. *Gazetteer of the Bombay Presidency: Khandesh*, Vol XII (Bombay, 1880), p. 116.

33. V.R. Shinde, *The Theistic Directory* (Bombay: Depressed Classes Mission, 1912), pp. 61-2. Although Shinde's educational work was most important

in term of numbers, it was the reformist attitude of two Maratha princes, the Gaikwad of Baroda and the Maharaja of Kolhapur, which prompted them to aid Ambedkar in securing his education.

34. A Mahar boy in Dharwar had petitioned for admission to a government school in 1856 and been turned down on the basis of caste. See Syed Nurullah and J.P. Naik, *History of Education in India* (Bombay: Macmillan, 1951), pp. 421-22.

35. *Census of India*, 1921. Vol. VIII: *Bombay Presidency*, Part I, pp. 140-41, and Part II, p. 121.

36. "The Nineteenth Century Background of the Mahar and Non-Brahman Movements in Maharashtra." *The Indian Economic and Social History Review*, VII:3 (1970) pp. 397-415.

37. Keshavsut's poem, "The First Question of the Untouchable Boy", has been translated by Prabhakar Machwe in his short biography, *Keshavsut* (New Delhi: Sahitya Akademi, 1966), pp. 45-6.

38. R.G. Bhandarkar, *Collected Works*, Vol. II, edited by Narayan Bapuji Utgitkar (Pune: Bhandarkar Oriental Research Institute, 1928), p. 491.

39. See R.S. Markhandikar, "G.G. Agarkar - A Study in Radical Liberalism, 1856-1895" *Modern Review*, 118, December 1965, pp. 518-23. Many of the reformers who encouraged Bansode and worked with Ambedkar in the twentieth century were followers of Agarkar's school of thought.

40. Mahadeo Desai, *op. cit.*, pp. 52-3. [The word *Harijan* is used anachronistically here; Gandhi did not use the term until 1933.]

41. M.K. Jadhav, who had been educated in V.R. Shinde's schools, took a B.A. in Sanskrit from New Poona College in 1925, twelve years after Ambedkar secured his B.A. from Elphinstone College. Ambedkar is given credit for his appointment as Deputy Collector in Bijapur District in 1928.

42. *The Reforms Committee* (Franchise: Lord Southborough, Chairman). Evidence taken before the Reforms Committee, Vol II (Calcutta, 1919), pp. 729-39.

43. The petition is reproduced in *The Life of Shivram Janba Kamble* by H.N. Navalkar (Pune: S.J. Kamble, 1930), pp. 142-47. The petition is in English, the biography in Marathi.

44. Copies of the resolutions of early conferences of the Mahars in the Nagpur area and their resolutions are in the possession of Bansode's son, Shamrao Bansode of Nagpur. Bansode was generally Secretary of these conferences. Other early material is in the extensive collection of Vasant Moon in Nagpur.

45. Edwin S. Montagu, *An Indian Diary* (London: William Heinemann, 1930), p. 306. Montague does not record the names: these are given in N.R. Shende, *Ga, A. Gawai: Vyakti and Karya* (life and work), (Amraoti: Prabhakar Pandurang Bhatkar, 1963), pp. 32-3.

46. Ambedkar discusses both resolutions in *What Congress and Gandhi Have Done to the Untouchables* (Bombay: Thacker and Co., 1946, 2nd ed.), pp. 14-18.

47. D.D. Gholap, a Mahar from Satara and the editor of Ambedkar's first newspaper, *Muknayak*, was selected for this seat. Later two nominated representatives were allowed, and Ambedkar and P.G. Solanki, a Gujarati Untouchable and associate of Ambedkar, served from 1928 to 1930.

48. See Bombay (Presidency) Depressed Classes and Aboriginal Tribes Committee. *Report* (Bombay, 1930). O.H.B. Starte, Chairman.

49. Rao Bahadur Rettamalle Srinivasan, the leader of the Depressed Classes within the Madras Legislative Council, was the other Depressed Classes delegate to the Round Table Conference. He seems to have been a less important leader than M.C. Rajah, who was then a member of the Indian Legislative Assembly. Evidently the Madras movement was factionalized, and Rajah and Srinivasan did not work together.

50. S. Natarajan, *A Century of Social Reform in India* (Bombay: Asia Publishing House, 1962, 2nd ed.), p. 140.

51. My account of the Mahad is compounded from Dhananjay Keer, *Dr. Ambedkar: Life and Mission*, pp. 69-76; 97-105, and interviews with Surendranath Tipnis and other Mahad veterans.

52. A radical Brahman, G.N. Sahasrabuddhe, a long-time associate of Ambedkar, moved the resolution to burn the *Manusmriti*. B.S. Dhotre, a retired Mahar primary school teacher, told me that Ambedkar had read the *Manusmriti* with a pandit in the months before the Conference and had asked Dhotre to copy out those portions of it which dealt with punishment for the disobedient Shudra. [These portions were burned.]

53. See any of the volumes in footnotes 3 of my "Learning the Use of Political Means -- the Mahars of Maharashtra" in Rajni Kothari ed., *Caste in Indian Politics* (New Delhi: Orient Longmans, 1970) [And in this volume].

54. It was Ambedkar's claim that the vote count showed Scheduled Caste support, but that caste Hindu votes swung the election against the Party.

55. See the Special Issue on Dalit Literature of the *Times Weekly*, 25 November, 1973. The issue also discussed the new Dalit Panther group. [See also my articles in this volume.]

56. Three of Shankarrao Kharat's stories have been translated in Robert Miller and Pramod Kale, "The Burden on the Head is Always There", in J. Michael Mahar ed., *The Untouchables in Contemporary India*, pp. 317-59.

57. B.R. Ambedkar, *The Untouchables*, p. 155.

58. Ambedkar visited Ceylon and Burma in 1950 and 1954 respectively. He evidently hoped for continued contact with Buddhist countries.

59. *Nagpur Times*, 15 October 1957.

60. K.R. Sundar Rajan, "Harijans: The Great Betrayal -- 200 killed every year by Caste Hindus", *The Illustrated Weekly*, XCIV, 30, 30 September, 1973, p. 11.

See the Addendum at the end of Section II for new political material.

The American Experience of Dr. B.R. Ambedkar*

Very few of India's leaders have been educated in America. In the British period, England and, to a lesser extent, France and Germany were the focal points for overseas study. Even today, when Indian students flock to America, their education is generally in the field of technology or science, and they do not enter politics. As far as I have been able to find out, only three men well known in public life have been thoroughly exposed to an American experience: Jaya Prakash Narayan; the late Chief Minister of the Punjab, S. Pratap Singh Kairon; and Dr. B.R. Ambedkar. As an American, one inevitably wonders what effect this country has had on the lives and thinking of these men.

It is clear that J.P. Narayan's direct contact with American poverty during the Depression era and with American radical thinkers somewhat influenced the development of his socialist attitudes. It is possible that Kairon learned some of his expertise with mass politics during his stay in America. In the case of Dr. Ambedkar, the influence seems to be chiefly in developing his commitment to a pragmatic, flexible democratic system. Ambedkar spent three years from 1913 to 1916 at Columbia University in New York City. There is little material on his political thought from the pre-1913 period with which to compare his post-1916 writings, but even so I would like to suggest that the American experience did influence the thought and action of this unusually gifted and innovative son of Bharat.

B.R. Ambedkar entered the Graduate School in Columbia University in 1913 after graduating from Elphinstone College in Bombay. His patron was Sayajirao Gaikwad, Maharaja of Baroda, who was distinguished for his financial support of reform measures, and had already assisted Ambedkar in securing his college education. Gaikwad sanctioned a stipend for Ambedkar's study in America through the Baroda

*Written for R.D. Suman ed., *Dr. Ambedkar: Pioneer of Human Rights* (New Delhi: Bodhisattva Publications, Ambedkar Institute of Buddhist Studies, 1977). Another version of this theme appeared in *Vision* (New York: 21 April 1979).

State Education Department, though it is not known who suggested that Ambedkar should go to America for higher studies. However, Ambedkar was 23 at the time and he seems to have been intellectually mature, with his interests already established. From the time of Jotiba Phule, there has been a sense of appreciation among the leaders of Non-Brahman Movement for America's effort to create an egalitarian democracy. Ambedkar was aware of this, and it is quite possible that he himself decided to go to America.

As a student at Columbia, Ambedkar explored as widely as possible the economic and social aspects of American development. He took an enormous number of courses ranging from the economics of American railways to American history, auditing what he could not take for credit. He seems to have exposed himself to as many of the top-ranking professors at Columbia as he could, whatever their field. Columbia at this time was in its Golden Age, and the list of men with whom Ambedkar studied represents a catalog of important early twentieth century American thinkers. John Dewey, James Shotwell, Edwin Seligman, James Harvey Robinson, Franklin Giddings, and Alexander Goldenweiser were all men of great importance in the development of American thought, and probably nowhere else could Ambedkar have received such a broad and deep exposure to an optimistic, expansive, pragmatic body of knowledge.

Interestingly enough, Ambedkar's own original research at Columbia was concerned with Indian themes. In his primary field of economics, under the guidance of Edwin Seligman, he wrote a dissertation for his Ph.D. on 'The Evolution of Provincial Finance in British India' (published in 1925 by P.S. King and Company, London). His thesis was critical of the imperial British system and its harmful effect on Indian development. The other major publication coming out of the Columbia experience was a paper on "Castes in India, Their Mechanism, Genesis and Development", which was first presented at a seminar in Anthropology with Alexander Goldenweiser and published in May 1917 in *The Indian Antiquary*. Both studies make it clear that although Ambedkar was gaining all he could from his educational opportunity in America, his attention was centered on using that knowledge to analyze the Indian situation.

Ambedkar's paper on caste was not a diatribe against the iniquities of the caste system but rather an effort to present a theory of the development of the system. His two main points are significant. First, there *was* a basic, unified Indian culture. He wrote, "Ethnically all peoples are heterogeneous. It is the unity of culture that is the basis of homogeneity. Taking this for granted, I venture to say that there is no country that can rival the Indian peninsula with respect to the unity of its culture''. Second, he denied that caste stratification arose through racial, color or occupational factors. He stated that the caste system grew through a process by which other groups imitated the endogamy of the Brahman priest caste. There is no development of a theory of untouchability in the paper; that was to come late in Ambedkar's life. These two premises, however, remained constant in his thought. His later theory of the development of untouchability and his work for the eradication of untouchability were based on these theories, namely, that Indian culture was basically unified and basically valuable, and that caste inequalities were a social development without a racial origin.

It is difficult to say what influence the study of anthropology and sociology under Goldenweiser and others at Columbia had on Ambedkar. Certainly he felt such systematic study of society was valuable, for he instituted a Department of Sociology at Siddharth College in Bombay at a time when sociology was not usually offered in Indian colleges. Also, the sociological vocabulary lingered, and perhaps some of the concepts behind the American jargon. Shortly after returning to India, Ambedkar testified to the Southborough Committee on Franchise, the group which was preparing the election procedure for the Montagu-Chelmsford Reforms instituted in 1921. Ambedkar's lengthy testimony before this body stressed the lack of "endosmosis" or "like-mindedness" between Touchable and Untouchable—phrases evidently borrowed from American social analysis. Ambedkar's solution was to educate and politicize the disadvantaged group into full use of popular assemblies so that the new political institutions would not continue the "hardships and disabilities entailed by the social system". Ambedkar may have observed the ethnic groups in New York, the Irish, Italians and Jews, gaining political power through unified political pressure. The early twentieth century American dream of social and political equality in the great melting pot was apparent in both academic circles and New York life during Ambedkar's stay at Columbia University. Both Ambedkar's study and experience would have encouraged him to look beneath cultural dfferences for a basic national cultural unity and to look to the political process as the way in which different groups attained their proper place on the national scene.

A direct comparison between the Negroes of America and the Untouchables of India does not appear in Ambedkar's writings. This is natural, since Ambedkar denied that there was a racial basis for untouchability. In contrast to the leaders of almost all other Untouchable movements, he refused to claim that Untouchables were "Adi-Dravida", (the first Dravidians), or "Ad-Dharm", (the first religion, i.e. pre-Aryan), but stressed that they were of the same racial background as other Indians. His observation of the obvious racial differences between Negro and white Americans, and the segregation based on race in America may have heightened his belief that the Untouchables' way to equality lay in asking for political and educational privilege because of social discrimination, not because of a separate racial background.

Ambedkar's understanding of the American situation was quite sophisticated. Jotiba Phule, as early as 1873, had dedicated his book *Gulamgiri* (slavery) to "the good people of the United States ... for their sublime, disinterested and self-sacrificing devotion in the cause of Negro Slavery." But Ambedkar noted the political expediency of Lincoln's action in freeing the slaves. In his criticism of Mahatma Gandhi in *What Congress and Gandhi have Done to the Untouchables* (2nd edition published by Thacker and Company in 1942), he compared Gandhi and Abrahām Lincoln, stating that both were concerned with freeing the depressed groups in their countries for the political compulsion of preserving national unity. This view of Lincoln's Emancipation Proclamation now has currency among American Blacks, who no longer view the freeing of the slaves as "disinterested and self-sacrificing". Although Ambedkar did not identify with the American Negro in words, he understood their position well enough to anticipate their criticism of Lincoln. Ambedkar's understanding of the reformer as politician was based on bitter experience, but it also reflects his grasp of comparative history. He did not borrow wholesale from the American experience, but he used his knowledge of American culture to analyze his own country's social situation.

Although the study of economics was Ambedkar's major interest in both the United States and in London, there was little scope for him to take action in this field in his public life in India. His stance was basically socialist, but he did not align himself with any socialist party except for specific election alliances. He admired a number of economic measures taken by the Soviet Union to reform their economy, and at one time advocated state control of the land. But, at the same time, he criticized the political system of the Soviet Union, and he was not a Marxist. The theory that history was the result of economic forces held little meaning for him.

If Ambedkar had succeeded in becoming head of the Planning Commission (and it is probable that this was his wish), he might have developed some of his socialist ideas within the context of democracy. His chief economic measures, however, were limited to those taken while he was Member for Labour in the Viceroy's Executive Council in the years before Independence. While holding the Labour portfolio, he instituted a Tripartite Labour Conference to consider such matters as a Joint Labour Management Committee and an Employment Exchange, and he attempted to institute social security measures for industrial workers. In these matters, both American and British policies offered some guidelines.

It is in the *basis* of Ambedkar's politics that American influence seems strongest. Behind all of Ambedkar's seeming separatism -- separate political parties for the backward classes, special reservation of seats in political assemblies and in government jobs -- there was a strong, unwavering belief in the power of democratic institutions to bring about social equality. India's case might demand special techniques not found in the West, but Ambedkar's basic faith was in representative political bodies. It may be too much to say that Ambedkar's American experience created this belief, but it is clear that it strengthened it. John Dewey's philosophy especially was meaningful to Ambedkar, for it offered encouragement that educated and politically aware peoples could work out their own political destiny in a pragmatic way, pruning the useless and preserving the useful in their societies. In his *Annihilation of Caste*, Ambedkar quotes John Dewey, "who was my teacher, and to whom I owe so much". "Every society gets encumbered with what is trivial, with dead wood from the past, and with what is positively perverse. As a society becomes more enlightened, it realizes that it is responsible *not* to conserve and transmit the whole of its existing achievements, but only such as make for a better future society".

Ambedkar's methods were directly related to Indian conditions. The ideology behind those methods was closely associated with optimistic, pragmatic American democracy, which preached (although it did not always practice) equality, no barriers to upward mobility, the use of machinery to produce leisure, and an attitude of respect for every individual.

Ambedkar's first political party, the Independent Labour Party founded in 1936, took its name from British politics. Two things, however, prevented Ambedkar's identification with British parties: the colonial presence of the British in India, and the preference of British liberals for Gandhi and his non-violent direct action campaigns for independence over Ambedkar and the slow parliamentary path. It also seems likely that American optimism, and the lack of an obvious class system in America, met a natural response in Ambedkar.

Ambedkar's American contacts did not end when he left Columbia University in June 1916, although one must admit they became minimal. He continued to correspond with Edwin Seligman, his teacher in Economics at Columbia, and occasionally recommended Indian students to Seligman. In 1930, Ambedkar wrote an article for the Columbia alumni magazine which reveals quite a sentimental attachment: "The best friends I have had in my life were some of my classmates at Columbia and my great professors, John Dewey, James Shotwell, Edwin Seligman and James Harvey Robinson." In 1952, Ambedkar went back to Columbia to receive an honorary degree of Doctor of Laws and it is clear that this recognition of his work meant much to him. It was in this period of the early 1950s that Ambedkar was publicly critical of India's foreign policy of non-alignment, which seemed to him to cut India off from American contacts.

I shall end with two stories, since this is not so much a scholarly tract as an essay which attempts to explore an American-Indian cultural interaction in a personal way. Mrs. Savita Ambedkar tells a touching story of Ambedkar happily imitating John Dewey's distinctive classroom mannerisms -- thirty years after Ambedar sat in Dewey's classes. It is impossible to find in Ambedkar's life story any hint of a living guru or a personality which dominated him, but here at least is a suggestion that he was fond of both Dewey the philosopher and Dewey the man.

The other story concerns a letter of recommendation written about Ambedkar by Edward Cannon, Professor of Political Economy in the University of London, to the head of Sydenham College, where Ambedkar applied for a teaching position in 1918. Professor Cannon wrote: "I don't know anything about Ambedkar except that he came to do a thesis and attacked it and me in a way which showed he had quite extraordinary practical ability. . . I rather wonder if he is a pure Indian; his character is rather Scotch-American". There is absolutely no doubt that Ambedkar was pure Indian, and no one who knew his background and the history of his caste would assign any other nationality to him. But this depiction of his character as "Scotch-American" rather delights me. Ambedkar's pragmatism, his wide-ranging intellectual interests, his realistic approach to social matters, his uncompromising attitude toward those he felt were his opponents -- all these factors make his character and work very understandable to an American. Even his bitterness can be understood by an American who has seen social injustice at work in the midst of American democracy. I am tempted to end this essay with the thought that American influence on Ambedkar really counted for very little. It is more likely that in those early years in America his own natural proclivities and interests found a healthy soil for growth, and the experience served chiefly to strengthen him in his lifelong battle for dignity and equality for his people.

Learning the Use of Political Means: The Mahars of Maharashtra*

I

Among all the Scheduled Castes in India, the Mahars of Maharashtra have used political means most consistently and unitedly in their attempt to better their condition. The term ''political means'' covers both early efforts of scattered groups to secure governmental benefits and representation on legislative and political bodies, and later more direct efforts in the form of political parties that secured representation of their special interest, agitated for constitutional guarantees, and created for themselves a firm electoral base. My attempt in this paper is to describe the process by which the Mahars, operating under conditions of social degradation, perceive the potency of politics as a means of ameliorating their social condition.[1] Our concern, however, is not so much to evaluate the extent to which they achieved these ends but rather to identify and describe the manner in which a community like this participates in the political process for the improvement of their social conditions, in turn acquires political skills and capabilities and develops behaviors and responses favorable to their assimilation in the broader political culture of the nation.

Mahars and Buddhists account for about nine per cent of the present-day population of Maharashtra. The two next largest Scheduled Castes in Maharashtra are smaller in comparison: Mangs, 1.8 per cent and Chambhars, 1.3 per cent. The total Scheduled Caste population including those who converted to Buddhism constitutes 12.68 per cent of the State population of Maharashtra, somewhat lower than the nearly 15 per cent average for India as a whole.[2]

---

*First published in Ranjit Kothari ed., *Caste in Indian Politics* (New Delhi: Orient Longmans, 1970, reprinted in 1986). Minor corrections and deletions have been made. The use of the word Mahar in this essay is by no means an indication that Dr. Ambedkar's influence was limited to one caste, but an attempt to analyze how he was able to influence one group. For another caste, see Owen Lynch.

Mahars are found in almost every village of Maharashtra, and are always in a minority. Their quarters, called the *maharwada*, are set apart, usually east of the village proper. A Marathi proverb, *jethe gao tethe maharwada* (wherever there is a village, there is a *maharwada*), under-lines their prevalence and also their low status, since it is used idiomati-cally to mean the same as the English proverb, "There's a black sheep in every flock".[3] A contemporary anthropologist, Irawati Karve, found the Mahars, and not the dominant agricultural caste of Marathas, the most thoroughly widespread caste of Maharashtra and ended an essay on "Mahars and Maharashtra" with the statement of a Mahar minor village official on the border between Marathi and Hindi-speaking peoples, *jethaparayant mahar pochle tithaparayant maharashtra* (as far as the Mahars have gone, there is Maharashtra).[4]

A theory held by some scholars and writers is that the Mahars are the original inhabitants of Maharashtra. One of the old names used for them, *dharniche put* (sons of the soil) as well as some of their traditional village duties -- the arbitration of boundary disputes and the care of the village goddess Mariai -- suggest that they may at one time have owned the land. At least one early Mahar leader, Kisan Fagoji Bansode of Nagpur, spoke of pre-Aryan land ownership to try to build the pride and spirit of the Mahars, but the most important Mahar leader in this country, Dr. B.R. Ambedkar, did not exploit this belief.[5]

The traditional place of the Mahar in the village community was as a *balutedar* or *watandar*, a village servant whose duty was to the village and whose recompense (*baluta* or gifts in kind, and *watan* or land) came from the village. The Mahar's hereditary duty may, in former times, have involved membership of the village governing body when the village servants, including the *patil* (headman, usually a Maratha) and the *kulkarni* (accountant, usually a Brahman), sat as a panchayat.[6] The Mahar *balutedar's* duties included arbitrating in boundary disputes, acting as the village watchman, mending the village wall, serving as guide and messenger to government servants, calling landowners to pay land revenue at the village *chaudi* (village hall), sweeping the village roads, escorting the government treasury, tracking thieves, carrying death notice and messages to other villages, bringing fuel to the crema-tion ground, and removing the carcasses of dead cattle from the village. The Mahar also had fixed duties in religious matters, including the kindling of the first *Holi* festival fire from which other fires were lit and guarding the shrine of goddess Mariai which was in the *maharwada*. Recompense given by the village for these duties included not only grain and the skins of the dead cattle, but a small amount of land known as *watan* and a host of other perquisites legendarily numbering fifty-two. The Mahars not required for *balutedar* work (in recent decades at least, they have worked in turn) did agricultural labor, their own *watan* lands being insufficient to support them. This set of duties holds for the Konkan (coastal) and Desh (plains) areas of Maharashtra; in the Vidarbha region to the east, where a looser social structure prevailed, some Mahars were also weavers, tradesmen, and *malguzars* (village revenue collectors).

The Mahar's duties were performed in the context of his untouchability; his touch was polluting and he did not come into direct contact with a caste Hindu or enter a caste Hindu home. The temple, the school, the village well were closed to him. Some restrictions in clothing, ornaments, metal household wares and the observance of ceremonies seem to have been enforced. The Mahar role in the village festivals was clearly specified and generally, though not always, indicative of his inferior status. The Mahar practice of eating the carrion beef, an early target of the Mahar reformers, was the justification, in the mind of the caste Hindu, for his untouchability.

The Mahar *balutedar* duties gave him a widely held reputation for cleverness and curiosity and fairly close association with caste Hindus and government officials in spite of the polluting consequences of his touch and, in some areas, even his shadow. Many of his duties are those of Untouchable castes in other areas, but some appear to be unique to the Mahar. The curious position of the village Mahar, inferior and yet responsible in a way beyond that of servants, is seen in the 1845 description of R.N. Gooddine: "[The Mahar is] the watchman and guardian of the village and the living chronicler of its concerns", to which R.D. Choksey adds, "He, it appears, was acquainted with everybody's affairs, and his evidence was required in every dispute."[7] C.B. Agarwal, in *The Harijans in Rebellion*, writes, "In cases of [land] dispute, his decision was willingly accepted by both the parties. The Mahar, therefore, played the part of a witness and judge simultaneously".[8] But, interesting as it is, there are few factors in the Mahar village position which are indicative of castewise unity. The inter-village contact of Mahars in *tamasha* and *jalsa* (traveling village entertainment and singing groups) may have created channels for the communication of new ideas, but the ideas and the impulse for organization came from non-village factors.

With the advent of British rule, other opportunities for work were opened to the Mahar, his traditinal role being such that he was both free and pressed to take whatever new vocation presented itself. While the other Untouchable castes in Maharashtra had tasks which carried over into modern life, the Chambhar leather and shoe work quite successfully and the Mang basket and rope-making with less financial success, the Mahar position as an 'inferior village servant' (a British term) lost significance with new methods of communication, justice and government. The post office, the courts, and the police replaced the Mahar as messenger, arbitrator of land disputes, and watchman. The system of *balutedar* work itself could not expand to care for increasing numbers of Mahars. Work on the docks, the railways and the roads, in textile mills, and in government industries such as ammunition factories[9] became the outlets for Mahar labor, from the 1860s on.[10] Although Mahars evidently did not flock to the cities in as great numbers as did other castes (even now the percentage of urban Mahars including Buddhists is lower than the urban percentage for Maharashtra as a whole[11]), the railway centres and the mill towns, as well as Bombay, Pune and Nagpur, became the loci for a new Mahar push for education and improved social status. Major consequences followed such exposure. Stimulated through contact with city relatives or to the traveling Mahar propagandists and entertainers, the Mahars remaining in the village began to discard both duties and caste practices that were associated with their low status: the dragging out of carcasses and the subsequent eating of carrion, begging for food, wearing the clothes of the dead. Eventually, under Dr. Ambedkar's leadership, the *watan balutedar* system itself was attacked.[12]

II

While the new economic opportunities presented to the Mahars undoubtedly encouraged a movement up from their inferior position, another factor that contributed both to their economic and social progress and to their caste spirit derived from the Mahar military service. Even before the arrival of the British, the Mahars had an outlet from traditional work in the time of Shivaji as guards in the hill forts and soldiers in the artillery. It is fairly clear that they had their own units in the later armies of the Peshwas. But it is from the records of their service in the armies of the British that the Mahars draw the contention that they are a martial race. A military monument at Koregaon near Pune serves as a focal point in the legend of Mahar heroism, and a number of Mahar gatherings have been held at its foot. The Koregaon pillar commemorates the soldiers of the British Army who fell during an 1818 battle with the Peshwa's forces. Of the 49 names of the 2nd/1st regiment recorded there, twenty-two are

Mahar, or *Parwari*, as army Mahars were known then (identifiable by the *nak* ending of the names, a designation used for Mahars into the early years of this century), sixteen are Maratha, eight Rajput and other Hindu, two Muslim and one probably Indian Jewish.[13]

Though their record of military service dates back to the pre-British period and may lend some plausibility to their claim to the status of a martial group, it was their entry into the British army which proved significant for the subsequent history of the Mahar movement. It is important to gauge this significance. It consists not in any automatic elevation in the social hierarchy through military service, which indeed is ruled out in a hierarchical system governed by considerations of ascriptive status and ritual purity. It rather consists in the fact that military service at such an early date exposed them to British institutions much before the dissemination of western culture took place on a large scale. Such an exposure socialized them sufficiently early to the new political order so that when new opportunities and alternatives became available, they were found prepared to use them more effectively than those groups which did not have this experience.

Dr. Ambedkar, probably basing his belief on the army experience of his ancestors on both sides for several generations, attributed the beginning of the Untouchables' movement almost solely to their contact with the British Army:

> Until the advent of British, the Untouchables were content to remain Untouchables. It was destiny preordained by the Hindu God and enforced by the Hindu State . . . . Fortunately or unfortunately, the East India Company needed soldiers for their army in India and it could find none but the Untouchables . . . . In the army of the East India Company there prevailed the system of compulsory education for Indian soldiers and their children, both male and female. The education received by the Untouchables in the army . . . gave them a new vision and a new value. They became conscious that the low esteem in which they had been held was not an inescapable destiny but was a stigma imposed on their personality by the cunning contrivances of the priest. They felt the shame of it as they never did before and were determined to get rid of it.[14]

With the abolition of the old Presidency armies in 1893 and the establishment of units on a class basis, together with the increased recruitment from the northern martial races, the Mahars were denied further recruitment in the army. Ambedkar's father was of the last generation to be able to use this channel of financial security and social prestige. Two documents, one from the late nineteenth century and the other from the early twentieth, illustrate the importance of army service to the Mahars. These were clearly the beginnings of their efforts to induce government to intervene on their behalf, and their questioning of their traditional inferior status.

In 1894, Gopal Baba Walangkar, a Konkani military man, drew up a petition in Marathi requesting re-acceptance of Untouchables into army ranks, but secured little support from his less audacious caste fellows.[15] The petition was never translated into English or presented to the British, but it serves as a document for Mahar attitudes of the time. Sent from the *Anarya Doshpariharakham* at Dapoli (Non-Aryan Group for the Removal of Wrongs at Dapoli, an army pensioners' center in Ratnagiri), the petition speaks for Parwari (Mahar), Mochi (Chambhar) and Mang peoples who have served loyally in the past in both the army and domestic service. It makes the claim that the Untouchables were former Kshatriyas, demoted by the Peshwa at the time of the Mahadurgadevi famine in 1676 for eating whatever they could find to save their lives. Because of education in the army, they have begun to read the religious books of the Hindus and to question the behavior, thoughts and the ancestry of the caste Hindus. A challenge was issued by the author of the petition several years earlier, asking what religious scriptures proved that these people were low and what remedies there were in Hinduism that would remove this lowness. The writer claimed that "none of the caste-proud or their priests" have proved the Untouchables' lowness. Examples of the bravery of both Untouchable soldiers and domestics are given, and a plea made that Untouchables should be recruited in the army, police and civil administration in accordance with the promise made by Queen Victoria after the Mutiny.[16]

The Mahars of Pune, a large army camp centre, found themselves better organized and with a spokesman, Shivram Janba Kamble, who was eloquent in English. Ten years after Walangkar's effort, a memorandum was sent to the Governor of Bombay on behalf of fifteen hundred Mahars in the Deccan (the Desh area) and Konkan. The reply from the Poona Collector's office indicated that he could do nothing about their requests: admission to the lower grades of public service, removal of restrictions in public schools, permission to join the police and the Indian Army. A longer and more sophisticated document was sent in 1910 by the Conference of Deccan Mahars, with Subhedar (Captain) Bahadur

Gangaram Krishnajee as president and the same Shivram Janba Kamble as secretary to the Earl of Crewe, Secretary of State for India, asking for employment in the lowest grades of the public service, in the ranks of police sepoys and of soldiers in the Indian Army.[17] The petition appealed for consideration for Mahars on the grounds of former service, English justice and human worth. The authors claim, "Our people [have] been employed in the Indian Army from the very commencement of the British Raj in our country, and they have risen to the highest positions by their valour and good conduct," and list the names of 107 Mahar officers (Jamadars, Subhedars and Subhedar Majors) in the infantry, rifles and marines as proof. Several strong pleas on the grounds of British morality were made including this one:

> And it is most encouraging to know that the Honourable House of Commons, as constituted in these times, is composed, to some extent, of the workingmen, who, only a quarter of a century ago, were regarded as but Mahars and Paryas by the more educated and affluent classes of their nation. If the Brahmanical castes and the Muhammadans have been given the full rights of British citizenship, we must be given the same.

The petition held up to the British "the noble part which Japan played in the elevation of its outcastes".

There seems to be no record of an answer to the 1910 Petition. Mahars enlisted in labor units of the army in World War I and toward the end of the War, the 11th Mahars was raised but shortly disbanded. During World War II the need for troops plus the presence of Dr. Ambedkar in the Viceroy's cabinet resulted in the raising of a Mahar regiment, now known as the Mahar Machine Gun Regiment.[18] In spite of the lack of immediate response to the Petition, it was important in setting a pattern for future Mahar petitions and protests to the government. The appeal is in terms of the rights of citizens; there is no attempt to invoke Kshatriya status as proof of worth as there was in the 1894 petition, nor does any other major twentieth century Mahar document attempt to manipulate the varna system in order to claim a higher status.[19]

The 1910 petition made little mention of religion. The British were reminded that Mahars as Christian converts had attained a high status in the professions and that "the kindly touch of the Christian religion elevates the Mahar at once and forever socially as well as politically". But aside from expressing the view that "the abomination of caste, which

sins both against God and Man, has no authority in the Vedas," reinforced by a quotation from Max Muller, the petitioners dealt with the
matter of their condition in political and social not religious terms.

III

There is also considerable evidence that Mahars freed from traditional
village services saw a need to try to adopt a Hinduism more sophisticated
than that offered by village gods. A poem, probably by a Mahar, attached
to the handwritten copy of the 1894 petition depicts the hardships and the
bad habits of Untouchables in rough and direct language, and includes
the complaint:

> Our religious names are Satvi, Jarvai, Mesai, Vetal, Mhasa, Bahiri,
> Bhadvi, Mariai. We do not know Brahman, Vishnu, Mahesh, Krish-
> narai, Rukhamai, Ram, Sita, Lakshman.

Many of the military Mahars joined the Kabir and Ramanandi
panths, the sects which stressed equality. The fact that many Mahars of
the Bawani sub-sect in Vidarbha joined the Mahanubhav *panth* may be
related to their high status in the Mahar caste itself and to the greater
economic freedom in their area, which permitted Mahars to be weavers,
traders and shopkeepers.

Were the Mahars to have continued an effort to relate to Hinduism
on a higher level than village status allowed, they had a natural channel
in the person of their own saint, Chokhamela, a fourteenth century poet-
saint. Chokhamela's *abhangas* (songs) are still sung by pilgrims of the
warkari cult on pilgrimage to Vithoba's temple at Pandharpur.[20] There
seems to have been a beginning toward using the name Chokhamela as
a caste name, building temples in his honor, naming groups and institutions after him, much in the same way that the Chamars of Uttar Pradesh
have used the name of their saint, Ravidas, in an attempt to gain status.[21]
The resolutions of the Chokhamela Reform Society meeting at Ramtek,
a pilgrimage center near Nagpur, in 1923, illustrate the methods of this
approach: (1) a temple should be built where Untouchables as orthodox
Hindus can have equal rights in weddings and thread ceremonies along
with Brahmans, Kshatriyas and Vaishyas; (2) there should be religious
education to bring about the unity of the Hindu people; (3) upper class
people should help educate the so-called Untouchables, and government
should give concessions to the upper-classes to encourage them.[22] But

even such a document dealing primarily with religion includes a recognition of the importance of education and a hint at the necessity of governmental help if change is actually to come.

There were numerous scattered efforts to create specific Mahar institutions within Hinduism, to join a reforming caste Hindu organization or to adopt higher caste ritual practices (*Sanskritization*, in M.N. Srinivas' useful term) throughout the first third of the twentieth century. As examples: Gopal Baba Walangkar, author of the 1894 army petition, encouraged the replacement of Brahman *joshis* who cast wedding horoscopes, one of the few duties performed by Brahman priests for Mahars, with Mahar *joshis*. Kisan Fagoji Bansode of the Nagpur area and G.A. Gawai of Amravati, both important Mahar social reformers and spokesmen for increased participation in a higher form of Hinduism, joined the Prarthana Samaj in 1910. Vithoba Raoji Sant Pande built a separate bathing place for Mahars at Ramtek near Nagpur around 1914 and "placed the whole community under a deep obligation".[23] In the late 1920s, Mahars in the Bombay area attempted to participate in the public worship of Ganpati at Dadar, started performing weddings in accordance with "vedic rites", and at least on one occasion donned the symbol of the high caste Hindu, the sacred thread.

The most vigorous efforts by Mahars and other Untouchables to claim religious rights as the equal of the caste Hindus were three temple entry attempts: an abortive temple-entry satyagraha at Amravati in 1927; a lengthy, somewhat violent (several Untouchables ended up in the hospital) attempt of Untouchables together with several caste Hindu reformers in 1929-30 to climb Pune's holy hill, Parvati; and a five-year long satyagraha at Kala Ram Temple in Nasik, ending in 1935, which served to unify and organize the Mahars and won them sympathy in England during the negotiations of the Round Table Conference in 1930-32, but did not open the doors of the temple to Untouchables.

In 1935 Dr. Ambedkar, by then the recognized leader of the Mahars, announced his decision to leave Hinduism. A conference of Mahars, called in Bombay the following year, took a similar decision for the caste as a whole. From that date onward, there is no record of any organized attempt by Mahars to participate in Hindu ritual activities. The energy and sense of unity stimulated by the temple entry attempts could be turned to political and educational matters without losing momentum.

The nineteenth century claim that the Mahar was of Kshatriya status was dropped in the twentieth century, replaced by the claim that the Mahar was of worth simply as a human being. The fact that the Maratha was also involved in a battle for Kshatriya status at this time rather pre-empted this action. But more important than this is the fact that their goal -- re-entry into the army, places in the police force and civil services -- required dealing with the British on western terms. The Mahar military past was now no longer employed as a ground for higher varna claims, but as a source of discontent with their economic and social status, and of a mystique of militancy used by the Mahar reformers to break down the apathy and sense of inferiority of the traditional Mahar.

The claim to religious rights lost ground as the consciousness of the importance of education and political power, articulated by the western-educated Ambedkar, increased. Further, the experience of failure of religion-centred activity prepared Mahars to reject Hinduism altogether. The figure of Chokhamela remained as a source of caste pride rather than a stimulant to claiming a place of worth in the Hindu hierarchy. They now increasingly came to rely on the opening of new avenues for rising in status in a new stratificatory system that was beginning to be established with the advent of formal education and change in traditional occupa-tional system.

Ambedkar's letter to the leader of the Nasik satyagraha in 1934 proposes the new way upward for the Mahar. He suggests that the satyagraha should be stopped:

> I would advise the Depressed Classes to insist upon a complete overhauling of Hindu Society and Hindu theology before they consent to become an integral part of Hindu Society. I started temple entry satyagraha only because I felt that that was the best way of energizing the Depressed Classes and making them conscious of their position. As I believe I have achieved that, therefore I have no more use for temple entry. I want the Depressed Classes to concen-trate their energy and resources on politics and education.[24]

As against this Kisan Fagoji Bansode, 1879-1946, a labor leader, newspaper editor, social worker and a poet of the Nagpur area, persisted with the approach of the Mahar claim to religious worth. Bansode went almost all the way with Ambedkar in social and political matters, but retained the belief that progress could be made within Hinduism. A poem illustrates his attitude, as militant as Ambedkar's, but couched in religious terms:

Why do you endure curses?
Choka went into the temple resolutely,
Why do you, ashamed, stay far off?
You are the descendants of Choka,
Why do you fear to enter the temple?
Brace yourself like a wrestler, come,
together let us conquer pollution.[25]

Respected as Kisan Fagoji Bansode was in the Vidarbha area, the
Mahars there followed Ambedkar perhaps even more enthusiastically
than their caste fellows elsewhere.

The factors that led to the Mahar social awakening --military service
and other contacts with British; employment opportunities outside the
village patterns; the beginnings of education, provided at first by caste
Hindu reformers and Christian missions and from the 1920s onward at
least, in part, by their own efforts; a latent caste spirit stimulated by
reminders of their military past and the religious worth of Chokhamela;
and a highly educated leader, Dr. Ambedkar, capable of forming them
into a political force -- equipped them for the use of political means
toward a modern goal of social equality.

IV

The petitions to Government for reinstatement in the army represent the
first Mahar attempt to use what I have broadly defined as political means
to gain their goals--at that time a modest goal of economic opportunity.
The increased democratization of British rule in India after World War
I offered a chance to engage in political activity on a larger scale. Two
Mahars, G.A. Gawai of Amravati, and B.R. Ambedkar, offered testimony to the Franchise Committee (Southborough) which was gathering
material for the implementation of the Montagu-Chelmsford Reforms.
Gawai spoke on behalf of the Depressed India Association, requesting
separate electorate for an enlarged and more responsible provincial
assembly.[26] Ambedkar's testimony, making the same basic point, filled
ten closely printed pages and initiated what can only be called the
Ambedkar Era among the Mahars.

B.R. Ambedkar, a Mahar from a Ratnagiri army family, appeared on
the political scene for the first time in 1919, when he was called to testify
to the Southborough Committee. The Mahar community had exhibited
an early interest in political means, exemplified by the petitions and the

Depressed India Association begun in 1916, which G.A. Gawai represented. Ambedkar, highly educated and with a dedication to western parliamentary democracy, was able to guide this political awareness into far more effective channels. His education both enabled him to speak in modern political terms and won him the respect and admiration of his caste. By the time the Southborough Committee hearings took place, Ambedkar was a graduate of Elphinstone College, had spent three years at Columbia University and one year at the London School of Economics. His higher education was made possible by the financial support of the Gaikwad of Baroda.[27] He returned to India in 1917 and was a professor at Sydenham College at the time of the Southborough Committee meetings. Later he resumed his London studies with the help of the Maharaja of Kolhapur[28] as well as his own savings, secured a D.Sc. from London University and was called to the Bar in 1923. His degrees indicated an accomplishment rare for an Indian, almost incredible for an Untouchable. The Mahar reaction is shown by a song about Ambedkar, part of an enormous Mahar-Buddhist-Ambedkar song literature, that begins by listing his degrees: B.A., M.A., Ph.D., D.Sc., Bar-at-Law, in a sort of incantation.

In response to a question, Ambedkar told the Southborough Committee that there was, among the Depressed Classes of Bombay State, one B.A.(himself), six or seven matriculates, and about twenty-five men who had passed the sixth or seventh standard and who consequently would be literate in English. Gawai's testimony to the Committee in the Central Provinces added three or four matriculates to this number among the Untouchables in his area. Ambedkar did not see the lack of education among his people as a bar to political participation, but pleaded that the franchise for the Depressed Classes should be "so low as to educate into political life as many Untouchables as possible".

Ambedkar's testimony informed the Committee, in words that reflected his Columbia courses with John Dewey and Franklin Giddings, that India's social divisions on the basis of "lack of like-mindedness and endosmosis", were not Hindu, Mohammadan, Christian, Parsi, Jew, etc. but Touchable Hindu, Untouchable Hindu, Mohammadan, Christian, Parsi, Jew, etc. In a statement that ranged far beyond demands for the Depressed Classes, he urged joint electorates with reserved seats for Mohammadans, lest communal representation sharpen the angularity of the division between Hindus and Muslims, and low-pitched franchise for the Marathas, which would serve that large community better than reserved seats or separate electorates in allowing them a voice free from

Brahman domination. But he argued that Untouchables, whom he characterized as "slaves", "dehumanized", and "socialized as never to complain", must have communal representation since "untouchability constitutes a definite set of interests which the Untouchable alone can speak for", and representation "in such numbers as will enable them to claim redress".

Of the Legislative Council of Bombay Presidency's proposed 100 members, he suggested that the Untouchables be allowed nine representatives, eight for their percentage of the population and one from among the nine to be elected by them to the Imperial Legislative Council. He stigmatized the Congress followers as "political radicals and social Tories", and summarized his position in these words: "British rule in India was meant to provide equal opportunity for all, and . . . in transferring a large share of the power to popular assemblies, arrangements should be made whereby the hardships and disabilities entailed by the social system should not be reproduced and perpetuated in political institutions."[29]

Ambedkar's first public political plea in 1919 resulted in failure. The Southborough Committee, ignoring Ambedkar, Gawai and a number of caste Hindus from Bombay, including Vithal Ramji Shinde, V.J. Patel, R.P. Paranjpye and M.M. Joshi, who urged direct representation of the Depressed Classes, gave them one *nominated* representative in the Bombay Legislative Assembly. The first man selected for representation was D.D. Gholap, a Mahar from Satara who had been in charge of Ambedkar's paper, *Muknayak*. Following the Muddiman Committee report on the working of the Montagu-Chelmsford Reforms in 1925, which among many other matters contained an admonition on the need to correct the Depressed Class status, another nominated Untouchable representative was added to the Bombay Legislative Council, and Ambedkar was named to this seat in 1926.

The presence of two Untouchables on the Bombay Legislative Council probably had little effect on the nature of its laws. A resolution was passed in 1923 urging that all public places and institutions maintained by public funds be open to Untouchables, and an attempt to put teeth in the resolution was made in 1926 by advising the Government not to grant money to municipalities which did not observe the rule. But these resolutions were the work of S.K. Bole, a caste Hindu reformer from the Bhandari community. Early bills presented by the Depressed Class representatives, but not passed, pertained to education for Untouchables, and that the Mahar *watan* land be made *ryotwari*, and hence eligible for sale, a strike at the bonds of the *balutedar* system.

In the decade between the sessions of the Southborough Committee and those of the Simon Commission in 1928, which provided the next opportunity for Untouchables to plead for direct representation, a great deal of organizational and educational work went on in the Mahar community. In the pre-Ambedkar era, Shivram Janba Kamble had organized conferences as early as 1903; the Depressed India Association was formed in Nagpur (and continued to function in the 1920s, but without Ambedkar's cooperation); and four conferences were held in Bombay in 1917-18, some under caste Hindu leadership, all concerned with the Untouchables and their increased political importance in the coming Reforms.[30] Ambedkar's first full-scale conference seems to have been in March 1920, at Mangaon in Kolhapur, a princely state whose ruler, Shahu Maharaj, had been active in the non-Brahman movement of the Marathas and in education for backward classes, including Untouchables. Ambedkar also spoke at the first all-India conference convened by Untouchables at Nagpur later in 1920, before his return to England. At Nagpur, he persuaded all Mahar sub-castes, at that time endogamous groups, to eat together, although not all Untouchable castes were prepared to interdine.[31] Ambedkar also propounded a theory at Nagpur, which has held for the subsequent Mahar political movement, that the caste Hindu could not know the mind of the Untouchable, and hence could not lead him. He criticized Vithal Ramji Shinde, the most active of the caste Hindu workers among Untouchables, for suggesting that Untouchable representatives should be selected by members of the Legislative Council rather than by the Government or institutions of the Untouchables themselves.[32] Direct representation was their goal; if that was not possible, then a neutral British government or their own organized groups should select members, not a largely caste-Hindu body.

Ambedkar presided over or spoke at a number of conferences in the Maharashtra area after his return from England in 1923, but the Mahars themselves date their political awakening from a conference held in 1927 at Mahad, a town in Kolaba district south of Bombay. As is true of most conferences and organizations of the Untouchables in the 1920s and 1930s, caste Hindus played a part in this event. A C.K.P. (Chandraseniya Kayastha Prabhu),[33] supporter of Ambedkar, S.G. Tipnis, the then head of the city council of Mahad, invited Ambedkar to hold a conference of the Depressed Classes there. The venue of the conference was a field belonging to a Muslim outside the town. At the meeting, evidently without previous planning, a decision was reached to test the 1923 resolution of the Bombay Legislative Council, which had been confirmed by the Mahad city council, that all public places should be open to Untouchables. The conference attenders marched to Chowdar tank, a large pond on the outskirts of the town in a caste Hindu area. Leaders of the procession then stopped and drank water, attempting a symbolic fulfillment of the law, but a rumour had spread through Mahad that the Untouchables were going on to the Vireshwar Temple to attempt entry, and the procession and conference ended in an attack.

The caste Hindus purified the tank and the Untouchables planned another demonstration. At the second conference, held later in the year, a copy of *Manusmriti*, the ancient law book which symbolized Hindu injustice to the Untouchables, was ceremoniously burned, but a second satyagraha for water did not take place. The district magistrate appeared with an injunction, based on a suit initiated by caste Hindus on the ground that the tank was private property. Ambedkar evidently preferred to fight in the courts rather than on the streets, and persuaded the conference members to disperse. The legal struggle ended ten years later, with the judgement in favour of Ambedkar.

The Mahad satyagraha failed to achieve its specific purpose at the time, but was successful as a rallying point for the internal reform of the Depressed Classes, the public expression of their grievances, and the stimulation of a sense of unity. The resolutions of Mahad conferences express the mood of the 1920s. The first conference "appealed to the caste Hindus to help the Untouchables secure their civic rights, to employ them in services, offer food to Untouchable students, and bury their dead animals themselves". The government was requested to pass laws prohibiting Untouchables from eating carrion, enforcing prohibition, providing free and compulsory education, and making the Bole Resolution of 1923 effective. Ambedkar addressed a meeting of the Depressed Class women urging them to dress well, not to observe caste restrictions in dress or ornaments, to be clean, not to feed husbands or sons if they were drunkards, and to send their children to school.[34]

The large numbers of Untouchables at the Mahad conferences, the unsuccessful but dramatic satyagraha at Chowdar Tank, and the burning of *Manusmriti*, which is remembered even today by Mahar and caste Hindu alike, made the Mahad conferences a legend in Mahar history. Its anniversary was celebrated as "Independence Day" thirteen years later.[35]

As the Mahar political movement gathered momentum, the non-Brahman movement, with which it was partially identified, died away, or rather took a new form as its leaders were slowly absorbed into the

Congress. The two movements had some things in common: both groups had grievances against the Brahmans; both looked back on the nineteenth century figure of Jotirao Phule as a prophet;[36] such non-Brahman leaders as Shahu Maharaj and Keshavrao Jedhe knew Ambedkar and attended Untouchable conferences. But the caste difference between the two groups and their social situations -- the Marathas were a land-owning dominant caste, the Mahars a nearly landless minority -- worked against any real cooperative effort between them. Although the Mahar griev-ances were voiced chiefly against the Brahman, the Mahar village protests in the form of quitting *balutedar* duties or claiming some form of social equality increased, and the village boycott directed by the non-Brahman castes proved an effective weapon against the Untouchables. The inability of a leader like Ambedkar to accept a subordinate role in a caste Hindu organization also mitigated against cooperation. Just as the Justice Party in Madras failed to include significant numbers of Untouch-ables, the non-Brahman movement in Maharashtra could not make common cause with the Untouchables.

V

The reaction of the Depressed Classes to the Simon Commission's tour of India was far different from that of the Congress or the moderates. Eighteen Depressed Classes associations testified willingly to the Commission, sixteen of them asking for separate electorates for Un-touchables. While his students walked out of his class at Government Law College in protest, Ambedkar told the Commission that the Un-touchables were relieved of anxiety because the Simon Commission did *not* include an Indian, since such a nominee could not be truly represen-tative of all groups. However, he did not renew his 1919 request for separate electorates. Adult franchise and reserved seats, up to 22 in all in a Bombay Assembly of 140 (15 according to their numbers plus seven as weightage to insure their rights), would satisfy him and the organization he spoke for, the Bahishkrit Hitakarini Sabha (Depressed Class Association).[37] He also requested guarantees for the Depressed Classes, as did an appeal from the Central provinces Depressed Class Association, signed by five Mahars (including Kisan Fagoji Bansode), two Chamars, one Mang and one Bhangi, which expressed a similar view of rights and privileges in even stronger and more distrustful language. This group requested: (1) an increase in the government power of veto for protection of the minority, (2) separate representation not only in legislatures, but all public bodies including universities in proportion to their numerical strength, (3) posts in government service for Depressed Class members, with minimum qualifications required, (4) representation in the cabinet dependent only upon Depressed Class votes, (5) special grants for education, (6) no application of a bill affecting the Depressed Classes if three-fourths of the community opposed it.[38] Both the Vidarbha and the Bombay demands reflect the feeling of the need for education (2.9 per cent of the Mahars were literate, according to the 1931 Census), the need for government jobs (Ambedkar pointed out that there was not one Depressed Class clerk in government service), and a desire for the Depressed Classes not only to participate in all public bodies but to be able to control any legislation affecting them.

Ambedkar's nomination to the 1930 Round Table Conference called to discuss India's future constitution was an acknowledgment of the leadership he had gained, and the very fact of this participation extended his fame to every corner of Maharashtra and beyond. For Ambedkar, his and Dewan Bahadur R. Srinivasan's nomination meant ''that the Untouchables were regarded not merely as a separate element from the Hindus but also of such importance as to have the right to be consulted in the framing of a constitution for India''.[39] Subhas Chandra Bose voiced another interpretation of Ambedkar's political rise: ''In 1930 and after, Dr. Ambedkar has had leadership thrust upon him by a benign British Government, because his services were necessary to embarrass the nationalist leaders''.[40] However, Ambedkar, on his own terms, identified himself with nationalism, if not with the nationalists. Before the first Round Table Conference held in August 1930, Ambedkar said at Nagpur:

> I agree with the Congressmen that no country is good enough to rule over another. But I must also take the liberty to tell them point-blank that the proposition does not end there and that it is equally true that no class is good enough to rule over another class.

He added, ''It is only in a Swaraj constitution that you stand any chance of getting the political power into your own hands without which you cannot bring salvation to your people'',[41] but he found it necessary to continue to press for political safeguards for the Depressed Classes while the British continued to rule India, not trusting that those who put independence above social reform would allow the Untouchables equality.

At this Nagpur conference, shortly before he left for London, Ambedkar stated that he would be satisfied with joint electorates provided that there was adult franchise and reserved seats. Earlier, in 1919, he had asked for separate electorates, as did Jains, Marathas, Lingayats, Marwaris and a number of other groups in a sort of separate electorate fever, but in 1928, before the Simon Commission, he reversed his position. There he used the argument against separate electorates which Gandhi was later to use against him -- that this would result in increased disunity. This ambivalence seems to show that Ambedkar's goal was direct, effective representation; the method of achieving that goal varied with the circumstances. At the Round Table Conference, however, he reversed himself on the matter of electorates again. Perhaps under a sense of representing all Depressed Classes, most of whom wanted separate electorates, perhaps because communal electorates for Muslims seemed to be guaranteed, perhaps because Gandhi would not even concede that reserved seats for Untouchables were necessary, Ambedkar came out strongly for separate electorates for the Depressed Classes and held his position through the three Round Table sessions. From this time on, "separate electorates" was the battle-cry of the Untouchables under Ambedkar's leadership until Independence.

At the second Round Table Conference, the only one Mahatma Gandhi attended, Ambedkar's attitude toward Gandhi hardened. At the time of the temple road satyagraha at Vaikam in Travancore, in 1924-25, Ambedkar had referred to Gandhi critically but not without respect. He felt that Gandhi did not give as much importance to the removal of Untouchability as he did to the propagation of Khadi and Hindu-Muslim unity. "If he did, he would insist on the removal of untouchability as a precondition for voting in Congress". But he concluded, "When no one else comes near us, even Mahatma Gandhi's sympathy is of no little importance".[42] Later, at the 1930 Nagpur conference, Ambedkar referred to Gandhi's moral influence in the struggle for Untouchables' rights. However, an unproductive meeting between the two and the confrontation in London in 1931, where Gandhi denied the recognition of the Depressed Classes as a minority and hence eligible for political safeguards, made Ambedkar bitterly critical.

After the third Round Table Conference, the General Secretary of the Depressed Classes Institute, S.N. Shivatarkar, a Chambhar, wrote in Ambedkar's paper, *Janata*, a criticism of the Congress and Gandhi that reflects the feeling on Ambedkar's side:

In spite of the fact that the removal of the untouchability has been included in the constructive programme of the Congress, practically nothing has been done so far by the body to achieve that object, and in our fights against untouchability at Mahad and Nasik most of the local Congress leaders have been our bitter opponents.

Gandhiji was prepared to concede [at the Round Table Conference] on behalf of the Congress special claims of the Mohammedans and the Sikhs including their demand for separate representation on "historic grounds", but he was not willing even to concede reserved seats in general electorates to the depressed classes, although he knew, at least he ought to have known what sort of treatment they would get, should they be thrown at the mercies of the caste Hindus.

The greatest presumption on Gandhi's part at the Round Table Conference was that he claimed that he represented the depressed classes and not Dr. Ambedkar .... Leadership cannot be imposed, it must be accepted by those on whose behalf it is claimed. Congress is now dissecting the community of untouchables by playing one section of that community against the other.[43]

The *Free Press Journal* reported in 1931 that "a large section which embraces the vast majority of the Depressed Classes community", under the leadership of "P. Balu, B.J. Deorukhakar and Mr. Patel", repudiated Ambedkar's position on separate electorates and special representation and declared their faith in the Congress and Mahatma Gandhi.[44] There are indications, however, that Ambedkar's active supporters were more numerous. When Ambedkar returned from the second Round Table Conference, 114 Depressed Classes associations of Bombay city and the Presidency presented addresses of welcome. The Muslim leader, Shaukat Ali, and Ambedkar came back on the same boat and addressed crowds of Muslims and Depressed Class members from the same platform. When Gandhi had returned a month earlier, Shivatarkar had organized a black flag demonstration. A free-for-all ensued between Congress supporters and some 8,000 Depressed Class Demonstrators.[45]

Gandhi's fast against separate electorates, which had been granted to the Depressed Classes by the Communal Award of 1932, brought Ambedkar and a number of caste Hindus to Pune, where Gandhi was imprisoned in Yervada jail, to negotiate an agreement that would somehow satisfy the Depressed Classes and yet allow Gandhi to end the fast. The Poona Pact of 1932 which resulted gave the Depressed Classes a greater number of representatives in provincial legislatures, 148 seats in place of the 71 allowed by the Communal Award. But a system of primary elections in which only the Depressed Classes were to vote, to be followed by the general election in which caste Hindus and Untouchables would vote together, took the place of the double vote, one in a separate electorate and one in the joint constituency, which the Communal Award had already provided. Both sides were later unhappy with the Poona Pact, the caste Hindus because they felt their own representation lessened, and the Depressed Classes because the double elections for their candidates seemed expensive and cumbersome, and not a proper substitute for a separate electorate. Nor did the long and arduous campaign against untouchability which Gandhi undertook after his release from prison or the establishment of the Harijan Sevak Sangh win over Ambedkar. Ambedkar was named to the Board of the Harijan Sevak Sangh, but resigned when he felt his views were not being considered.[46] One way of explaining the conflict between Ambedkar and Gandhi, perhaps an oversimplification, is to say that Ambedkar saw advancement for the Untouchables in terms of using political means to achieve social and economic equality with the highest classes in a modern society, while Gandhi held to a more traditional concept of varna system, cleansed of untouchability, in which Untouchables would be Shudras and their unclean work made honorable.

One outcome of the Poona Pact, however, was to bring Ambedkar to the limelight again, adding to his fame and giving his leadership more of an all-India stature. An Englishman said of him in 1932: "I think we may accept Dr. Ambedkar as the most important leader and accredited spokesman of the depressed classes. None of the local leaders have either his education, forensic ability, or pugnacity, and his recent conduct during Mr. Gandhi's fast, the extraordinarily favourable agreement which he exacted from Hindu negotiators, reveal him as a political tactician of quality".[47] Ambedkar's chief rival for the Depressed Class leadership, Rao Bahadur M.C. Rajah of Madras, was also involved in political action. Rajah, the first nominated member from the Depressed Classes on the Central Legislative Assembly, also instituted Depressed Class conferences, testified to the Simon Commission, and had some following among the Mahars of Vidarbha as well as in South India. He and Dr. B.S. Moonje of the Hindu Mahasabha brought forward a compromise plan allowing reserved seats in a general constituency for the Depressed Classes in 1932 before the Poona Pact was signed, but although M.C. Rajah was present at the Poona Pact negotiations, he was eclipsed in importance by Ambedkar.[48]

VI

As the 1937 elections for provincial legislatures under the new Constitution approached, Ambedkar gave the political movement a specific focus by establishing the Independent Labour Party. According to a news release issued in August 1936,[49] he had been persuaded by friends to form a party with a broader base than the Depressed Classes alone, and a party modelled on the English Labour Party came into being. The program of the new party was "mainly to advance the welfare of the labouring classes", and contained little direct mention of what were, by then, called the Scheduled Castes. Socialist in flavor, the party accepted "the principle of State management and State ownership of industry whenever it may become necessary in the interests of the people". Aid to agriculturists through land mortage banks, cooperatives and marketing societies; technical education and the promotion of new industries; reform of the *khot*, *talukdari* and *watan* tenant systems; free and compulsory primary education; and a pledge to bring about a fair mixture of castes in the administration were planks in the platform. The executive committee of the party included many of the caste Hindus who had worked with Ambedkar in social affairs for the previous ten years. In the elections of 1937, the party won ten of the fifteen reserved seats for the Scheduled Castes and three general seats in the Bombay Legislative Assembly, and three of Central Provinces and Berar's reserved seats.

The list of candidates reveals something of the nature of the Mahar political movement in the 1930s. The majority of tickets were given to Mahars, although there were at least two candidates from other Untouchable castes, a Mang and a Gujarati Scheduled Caste man. Two of the caste Hindus elected were C.K.P.; one was a Brahman. Candidates such as R.R. Bhole (Pune) and D.G. Jadhav (Khandesh) represented the new college-trained generation of Mahars; others such as B.K. Gaikwad (Nasik), had less formal education but a history of work in the various Mahar satyagrahas and conferences.

The absence of Chambhars, the wealthiest, ritually highest group among the Scheduled Castes in Maharashtra, is striking. The secretary of Ambedkar's Depressed Classes Association had been a Chambhar and the secretary of the coming Scheduled Castes Federation was to be a Chambhar, P.N. Rajbhoj, yet the caste as a whole did not follow Ambedkar. Chambhars had already achieved some degree of economic advancement with their leather work, while the Mangs were the most educationally and economically backward of the three groups, but

neither Chambhars nor Mangs could see a Mahar leader as their salvation. Ambedkar seems to have attempted to win these castes over,
frequently appearing at Chambhar or Mang meetings. He gave a detailed
reply to criticism raised at a Chambhar conference in 1939[50] and devoted
space in *Janata* in 1941 to a long letter from a Mang accusing him of
being only a Mahar leader,[51] but by this time the Mahar conversion
announcement had further alienated other castes. Neither group was
active to a large degree in the Independent Labour Party or its successor,
the Scheduled Castes Federation. Nor was the attempt to make the
Independent Labour Party a working class party successful. Caste Hindu
labor was not ready for Untouchable leadership, nor could the identification of the Congress with Independence be overcome.

During its short lifetime, from 1937 until 1939, when the Congress
ministries resigned, the Independent Labour Party functioned with vigor
but without much effect in the Congress-dominated Bombay legislature.
Ambedkar protested at the minimum salary proposed for ministers,
which he felt was impractical idealism. The I.L.P. members also protested
against the use of the word *Harijan*, which the Untouchables felt was
patronizing, in a proposed Local Boards Act, the Wardha Scheme of
Education, and against increased powers of the city police in matters other
than riots. The education of Scheduled Caste students, the problems of
Scheduled Caste teachers, the lack of adequate water supplies for
Untouchables, and the need to abolish the *watan* system were raised at
various times. The Harijan Temple Entry Bill passed evidently without
comment by the I.L.P. members, although orthodox Hindus protested
outside the Council House.

In two matters the I.L.P. participated in extra-parliamentary ways to
add strength to their parliamentary voice. There was a march of peasants
in Bombay in 1938 to protest againt *khoti*, a land tenure system in
Ratnagiri against which Ambedkar had introduced a bill. Also in 1938,
the I.L.P. joined the Communists in calling a one-day strike to protest
aginst the Industrial Disputes Act, which Ambedkar declared ought to be
called "The Workers Civil Liberties Suspension Act".[52] The Khoti
Abolition Bill was not passed; the Industrial Act was.

With the conversion announcement in 1935, the establishment of a
political party in 1936, and considerable success in the 1937 elections,
the shift from attempting to gain status in matters of religion to organizing for political activity was nearly complete. Ambedkar considered but
rejected various possibilities of converting to a religion that offered
political as well as social advantages -- Sikhism or Islam. The announce-

ment of intent to convert was followed by a twenty-year hiatus, culminat-
ing in conversion to Buddhism, a religion that offered release from Hindu
concepts of caste and a high moral standard but had no political
overtones. Lloyd and Susanne Rudolph's general statement that, as the
processes of democratic politics began to reach the mass electorate, the
aims of caste associations changed, and "instead of demanding temple
entry and prestigious caste names and histories in the census, the
association began to press for places in the new administrative and
educational institutions and for political representation",[53] can be applied
to the Mahars. Their political movement overrode efforts to claim
religious rights, failed in its attempts to represent class or all labor, and took
on much of the nature of a caste association functioning in the political
arena. [However, other castes were always included.]

A note by a Harijan Sevak Sangh research worker indicates the depth
of the political awakening and some of its consequences on the local
level:

> Harijan leaders, especially those belonging to Dr. Ambedkar's
> party, have become fully conscious of their civic rights and encour-
> age their followers to assert them. But as this is done in a somewhat
> defiant manner and no attempt is made for persuading the caste-
> Hindus or to secure the cooperation of the Harijan Sevak Sangh,
> often they arise as a result severe conflicts, boycotts, and even
> belabouring of Harijans by Hindu villagers.[54]

The next step of the Scheduled Castes associated with Ambedkar
was a move further in the direction of separation from caste Hindu
society. In July 1942, the All India Depressed Classes Conference was
held at Nagpur. The meetings were attended, according to Dhananjay
Keer, by 70,000 people,[55] with representatives from Bengal, Bombay,
Punjab, the Central Provinces and Berar, the United Provinces and with
N. Shivraj from Madras as the President, but Mahars undoubtedly pre-
dominated. The first resolution of this Conference condemned the
proposals of His Majesty's government regarding the constitutional
changes brought to India by Sir Stafford Cripps as a betrayal of the
interests of the Scheduled Castes and a breach of the assurances given to
them that a constitution would not be imposed upon them without their
consent. Further resolutions restated the demands that had been part of
Scheduled Caste political activity in some form since the earliest days of
the movement, funds for primary and advanced education for the

Scheduled Castes, representation in the public services and all legislative bodies, and separate electorates. The two final resolutions were of a new kind. "After long and mature deliberation", the conference came "to the conclusion that a radical change must be made in the village system, now prevalent in India and which is the parent of all the ills from which the Scheduled Castes are suffering for many centuries at the hands of the Hindus". The resolution continued to ask for a constitutional provision for transfer of the Scheduled Castes to separate Scheduled Caste villages, "away from and independent of Hindu villages". The last resolution established a political party for the purpose of carrying on the political movement of the Scheduled Castes, to be called Scheduled Castes Federation.[56]

It is difficult to say how much the separate village resolution reflected the mind of the village Mahar, and how much it indicated an attempt by Ambedkar[57] to establish the desperate seriousness of Scheduled Caste demands. It was made at a time when the Muslim League's demand for Pakistan was of great concern to both the Congress and the British, and when the early Cripps proposals seemed to overlook the problems of the Scheduled Castes in their anxiety to heal the Hindu-Muslim rift and carry on the war. The demand for separate villages was ignored by the British as was the demand for separate electorates, although at least in the case of the latter there was a longstanding and widespread opinion among the Scheduled Castes that separate electorates were necessary for them to be truly represented in the legislatures.

The 1945 elections for the Provincial Legislatures saw the newly established Scheduled Castes Federation utterly defeated. Ambedkar's official position as Labour Member in the Viceroy's Executive Council prevented him from taking an active part in the party organization, which may have been a factor in the defeat. He himself produced official election figures for the Cabinet Mission which showed that in the primary elections, in which the Scheduled Castes alone voted, the Scheduled Castes Federation had received a larger percentage of votes than the Congress had done in Madras, Bombay and the Central Provinces.[58] He also offered proof that, in each province, the majority of Scheduled Caste votes had gone to non-Congress candidates.[59] There had been some violence in Nagpur and Bombay at the time of the elections, and Ambedkar charged terrorism and intimidation as well as open hostility on the part of returning and polling officials as reasons for the election defeat.[60] But Sir Stafford Cripps felt that it was not possible, "even had we decided to do so, to arrange for Dr. Ambedkar's organization to have any special right of election of the Constituent Assembly. It had failed in the elections and we could not artificially restore its position".[61]

Ambedkar resorted to extra-parliamentary action to press the demand for recognition, and the Scheduled Castes conducted large-scale satyagrahas for separate electorates before state legislatures at Pune, Nagpur, Lucknow and Kanpur in 1946. The satyagraha and demonstration methods of political activity had been sparingly used in the Mahar movement. The Mahar satyagraha for water; the full-scale temple satyagrahas, one at Pavarti in Pune without Ambedkar's aid and one at Nasik with his early approval and later disinterest; the peasant march against Khoti and the one-day strike protesting against the Industrial Disputes Bill are the chief examples, and the Scheduled Castes together with caste Hindus participated in all of them. Petitions, attempts to secure favorable legislation and occasionally battles in the courts were preferred to satyagraha when the issue concerned British law and administration. The comparatively small numbers of the Scheduled Castes and their dependent position in the village made demonstrations vis-a-vis caste Hindus a dangerous and not very effective weapon. On the eve of Independence and even thereafter, the method of extra parliamentary demonstration became more widely used, probably both because of the increasing political awareness of the Mahars and the change in the nature of the governmental adversary.

The 1946 satyagrahas were conducted solely by the Scheduled Castes demonstrating for separate electorates and recognition of their demands by those planning for Indian Independence. The failure of all other methods, including numerous memoranda to the concerned bodies for Scheduled Caste demands; Ambedkar's book entitled *What Congress and Gandhi have Done to the Untouchables*, which stressed the necessity for considering the Scheduled Castes as a separate element in Hindu society, and a fruitless trip to London by Ambedkar, evidently prompted the use of the demonstration method.

The phenomenon of "separatism" which marked the political movement under Ambedkar from 1939 until Independence was strong enough even before the formation of the Scheduled Castes Federation for M.R. Jayakar, a Bombay political figure and judge, to write to his fellow-moderate, Tej Bahadur Sapru, in April 1941: "The depressed classes, under Ambedkar's guidance, are becoming more conscious of their separateness and not of their unity with Hinduism and perhaps in a short time a cry will go up for Mahar-stan".[62] Undoubtedly separatism was stimulated by the demands of the Muslims for Pakistan. It may also have been a macrocosm of what has been noticed on the village scale when the Scheduled Castes' attempts to gain status are defeated. F.G. Bailey writes of the Boad Outcastes of a village in Orissa, "They are moving out of the social structure of the village . . . . They cannot rise within the existing ritual and political structure of the village . . . they are showing the first signs of becoming a separate village community".[63] But both on the village and national level, separatism requires an outside force to relate to, if any gains are to be made. For the Boad Outcastes, it was the Congress government; for the Mahars, it was the British. With the advent of Independence, separatism as a political device lost its value.

VII

The situation changed for the Scheduled Castes with the coming of Independence. Replacing the British Raj was the Congress Government, committed by its long association with Gandhi to the removal of untouchability. The triple prongs of a British government willing to engage in social reform when it did not endanger its position, an Indian elite which accepted the necessity of correcting ancient injustice, and a Scheduled Caste political movement which articulated specific needs had resulted in considerable legislation. The Congress Government continued to add legal prohibitions of untouchability, ameliorative economic and educational benefits, and reservations in public bodies and governmental posts. Lelah Dushkin wrote in 1957, "Probably nowhere in the world is so large a lower-class minority granted so much favourable special treatment by the government as are the Depressed Classes of India today".[64] The actual function of the political party under Ambedkar's leadership from Independence until 1956 was to see that the special treatment provisions were properly used, that the discrimination and injustice still practised was brought to public attention, and that the seats reserved for the Scheduled Castes in legislatures were filled by men under obligation to speak for Scheduled Caste interests, although its platform was far broader than this.

The early years of Independence found Ambedkar in a position from which he was able to operate constructively and cooperatively. He had won a seat in the Constituent Assembly from Bengal in 1946, and later, after Partition, from Bombay. He was named Chairman of the drafting committee for the Constitution, which meant he was responsible for guiding it through the Assembly, and was included by Nehru as Law Minister in the first cabinet, one that "contained a strikingly careful

selection of representatives of communities and regions -- far more so
than any later governments".[65] And Ambedkar responded with words
which indicated separatism was a thing of the past. In a public meeting
at which he was presented a golden replica of the draft copy of the Indian
Constitution by the Scheduled Castes Federation in Bombay, he told his
audience to place the country above their community to avoid "our independence being put into jeopardy". The Scheduled Castes, he said,
should forget the narrow outlook of the past and think of the wider
interest as a whole; they should forget past differences with the Congress
and other political parties. Cooperation, although not federation with any
other organization, should be the goal.[66]

The era of cooperation ended in the fall of 1951, just before India's
first general elections. Ambedkar resigned from the cabinet primarily
because of lack of Congress support for the Hindu Code Bill, for which
he as Law Minister was responsible, but also because he felt he had little
voice in the cabinet, and because, he charged, the old oppression of the
Scheduled Castes still existed. Nehru's foreign policy had cost India its
friends, and the official position on Kashmir caused an unnecessary
impasse, he stated. Ambedkar participated in the 1952 elections not as a
friend of the administration, but as a bitter opponent.

The Scheduled Castes Federation entered the elections as one of a
few parties with previous election experience. In its platform, the
Federation pledged that it would insist on reservations subject to minimum qualifications, so long as the Backward Classes, Scheduled Castes
and Scheduled Tribes "are not able to find their place in the Civil and
Military services of the country". Otherwise, the party's statements dealt
with larger issues. Expansion of production, birth control, cooperative or
collective farming, the need to partition Kashmir, the abandonment of
neutralist foreign policies in favour of cooperation with the parliamentary democracies, the abolition of prohibition, the nationalization of
insurance, the formation of linguistic provinces -- all were approved by
the party.[67]

In the elections of 1951-52, the Scheduled Castes Federation lost
badly. In Bombay state, four candidates contested seats for the Lok
Sabha; only one, P.N. Rajbhoj, standing from Sholapur, was successful.
Ambedkar was defeated by his long-time Chambhar opponent, N.S.
Kajrolkar, in the Bombay (North) constituency.[68] The Federation had put
up thirty-eight candidates for the Bombay legislative Assembly, its
ambition going beyond the twenty-seven seats reserved for the Scheduled Castes. With the exception of B.C. Kamble, standing from the

Chinchpokli-Lower Parel-Love Grove constituency in Bombay, all lost. Before the election, "at one stage there was an attempt to invite Dr. Ambedkar to stand on a Congress ticket. According to S.K. Patil, the Congress had kept a seat vacant for Dr. Ambedkar until the last moment, till it came to be known that his party entered into an electoral alliance with the Socialist Party".[69] The Congress had not read Ambedkar rightly. Even in the halcyon days of the Constituent Assembly and the first cabinet, Ambedkar had advised the Scheduled Caste Federation to preserve its independence, and his resignation from the cabinet was not likely to change that position.

The alliance with the Socialist Party, which was the logical group for the Scheduled Castes Federation with its socialistic platform to cooperate with, was not a happy experience for either group. In a study of the elections, Venkatarangaiya reports that some Socialists felt the alliance with the Scheduled Castes Federation had been injurious. Middle class resentment was increased because of the alliance of the federation with the Peasants and Workers Party in some parts of the state and also because of alleged attacks by the Federation leaders on Gandhi.[70] In another report, Venkatarangaiya adds that Ambedkar's proposal to include Bombay in Maharashtra cost him and the Socialists the Gujrati vote.[71] Ambedkar himself said he was "at a loss to understand the defeat".[72] The facts that the proportion of votes per candidate was higher for the Federation than for any other party but the Congress; that the Scheduled Castes Federation had tripled its 1946 vote, which the Congress did not quite do; and broadened its area of influence, winning twelve seats in the Legislative Assemblies of six states (Hyderabad, Madras, Pepsu, Bombay, Himachal Pradesh), did not relieve the general gloom. Hugh Tinker writes, "The most disappointed candidates were those of the Scheduled Castes Federation.... The great majority of these "reserved" seats went to the nominees of Congress: non-entities for the most part, but returned by the magic name of Nehru".[73]

In 1954, Ambedkar and his 1952 running partner, Ashok Mehta, contested the bye-election in Bhandara, a district near Nagpur. Mehta, running on the Socialist Party ticket for the general seat, won; Ambedkar, as a Scheduled Castes Federation candidate for the reserved seat, lost. The factors in the loss of the Bhandara by-election seem to be the failure of those voting for Mehta to also support Ambedkar; the alienation of caste Hindus by Ambedkar's bitter denunciation of Nehru, the Congress, and Gandhian policies; the thorough coverage of the area by a high powered group of Congress leaders; and possibly the defection of G.M.

Thaware, a Mahar leader who had broken with Ambedkar and joined
Congress before his death in 1952.

The chief reason, however, for the Scheduled Castes Federation
defeat was that they had nowhere to go with their political power. The
Federation constituency was limited to a minority by the factor of caste.
In the 1937 election, the reserved seats in Bombay had evidently been left
to the Scheduled Castes at the time of voting; votes recorded for these
seats were in most cases considerably fewer than votes recorded for
general seats. In the following elections, this factor does not seem to have
held. With the coming of Independence and the Partition, separate
electorates became a psychological impossibility both for the Muslims
and Scheduled Castes, and the occupant of the reserved seat was to be
determined by the general vote. Ambedkar evidently realized the necessity of both winning the reserved seats and using the votes from that limited
number of seats in a larger alliance. In 1948 he told an Uttar Pradesh
Scheduled Castes Conference, according to a newspaper report, that
political power was the key to all social progress and that the Scheduled
Castes could achieve salvation only if they captured political power
by organizing themselves into a third party and holding the balance of
power between the Congress and the Socialists.[74] The 1952 election
alliance with the Socialist Party was evidently an attempt to use this
strategy, but the overwhelming victory of the Congress made it clear
that they were not equal political groupings and hence a balance of
power could not be held this way.

VIII

In 1956 Ambedkar made an attempt to transform the Scheduled Castes
Federation into a party which would speak for all the "dispossessed", the
Scheduled Castes, Scheduled Tribes and Backward Classes. The move to
create the Republican Party came about the same time as the conversion
to Buddhism in Nagpur on 14-15 October 1956. Both were efforts to take
the Scheduled Castes out of untouchability and into a larger group, one
religious and the other political.[75] Both trace back in origin to decisions
made twenty years earlier when the Mahar conference in 1936 in
Bombay opted out of Hinduism and the Independent Labour Party was
founded. And in spite of Dr. Ambedkar's intentions, both movements
have been largely confined to the Mahars and other groups which had
been involved in political activities under his leadership. Dr. Ambedkar
died on 6 December 1956, two months after setting the conversion

movement and the idea of a new poltical party in action and without making plans for the development of either.

The Republican Party was not formally organized until October 1957, and the elections earlier in the year were fought by the Scheduled Castes Federation under its old name and with its old personnel. The factor which entered into the election was not the Buddhist conversion, but the battle-cry for a linguistic state of Maharashtra. The Scheduled Castes Federation campaigned in the elections under the banner of the Samyukta Maharashtra Samiti (United Maharashtra Committee).[76] In the spirit of unity engendered by linguistic state feeling, plus the careful allotment of tickets, the Federation won nineteen places in the state Legislative Assembly (counting those won in later by-elections), and six in the Lok Sabha. The lesson learned by the Party in the election was that no harm seemed to come from cooperating with other parties, even the Communists hitherto avoided because they did not come in Ambedkar's category of groups committed to parliamentary democracy, and that a statewide issue helped the constituents to forget caste.

The next elections reinforced the need of the Party both for issues that identified them with the larger electorate and for control of the number of candidates in each constituency. Without either, the Party lost the 1962 elections to the Congress, winning only three seats in the Maharashtra Legislative Assembly and none in the Lok Sabha from that state.[77]

The figures on winning candidates from the Republican Party in the 1962 elections conceal the Party's strength in Maharashtra. In actual number of votes, the Party is second to the Congress with 11.66 per cent of the total, twice as much as the nearest opposition party.[78] At the local level, the Republican Party has a strong voice in a number of Maharashtrian urban centres, particularly in Vidarbha and in the railroad towns. In Zilla Parishad elections the Party gained at least one seat in twelve of twenty-five districts, a better record than the Communist Party's, or the Jan Singh's. In Amravati district, the Republican Party ran a number of caste Hindu candidates and won, defeating the Congress by twenty-three to twenty-one seats.[79] But even the victories make it clear that only when the solid Mahar strength behind the Republican Party can be combined with a larger issue or with other groups in election alliances can the Party show that strength in the polling results.

In addition to the problem of alliances, the Republican Party faced the difficulty of splits in the Party leadership. A group led by B.C. Kamble, a Bombay lawyer, and some other generally young and well-educated men pulled away from the party dominated by B.K. Gaikwad, Ambedkar's long-time associate, in 1959 and contested the 1961-62 elections separately, adding to the disastrous results for the Party as a whole. In Bombay city itself, the Kamble group put up 21 candidates for the municipal elections, the R. D. Bhandare group ran twenty candidates. A chart showing seats contested and won by the Scheduled Castes Federation over a period of four municipal elections suggests the effect of the split:[80]

Year	Seats contested	Seats won
1948	9	7
1952	11	5
1957	14	12
1961	41	6

While the Kamble split now seems confined to Bombay city, a new rift has come with Bhandare's expulsion from the Party. The factionalism that was kept more or less in order during Ambedkar's lifetime has now come to visible ruptures, and the ensuing competition for leadership may cut into the Mahar political unity severely. Still another problem affecting the political leadership is that most educated Mahars and Buddhists enter government service, one of the few ways up economically that are open to the Scheduled Castes, which effectively places them beyond political activity.

Faced with the inconsequential representation in the legislatures, the Party seems to be turning more to extra-parliamentary methods, as perhaps are other opposition parties also, to press its demands. Two massive land satyagrahas have been held, one in 1954 in the Marathwada area of Maharashtra, the second in 1959 around Nasik, Jalgaon, Dhulia and Ahmednagar, evidently with some result in the distribution of wasteland to the landless. Silent marches in a number of cities in 1964 called attention to the harassment of Buddhists in a Maharashtrian village, where a personal quarrel had erupted on a caste basis, ending in public insult of Buddhist women. A large but scarcely publicized satyagraha was held in Uttar Pradesh and Maharashtra and a few areas in other states in December 1965 and January 1966 in which the party claims 300,000 satyagrahis participated. A conference between B.K. Gaikwad, Barrister B.D. Khobragade and B.P. Maurya, leaders of the Republican Party, and Congress leaders, including the Prime Minister, ended the satyagraha, which had filled the Maharashtrian jails. The Charter of Demands for which the demonstration took place details the present aims of the Republican Party: (1) a portrait of Dr. Ambedkar as "Father of the Indian Constitution" in the central hall of Parliament,[81] (2) the nation's land given to the tiller, (3) idle and wasteland given to landless labor, (4) adequate distribution of grain and control over rising prices, (5) improvement of the situation of slum dwellers, (6) full implementation of the Minimum Wages Act of 1948, (7) extension of Scheduled Caste privileges to the Scheduled Caste members who have embraced Buddhism,[82] (8) the ceasing of harassment of the Depressed Classes, (9) full justice under the Untouchability Offences Act, and (10) reservation in services for the Scheduled Castes and Scheduled Tribes completed by 1970.[83]

Since that large satyagraha, two smaller demonstrations have been organized. A *morcha* (protest procession) of 5,000 men and women marched to the Council House in Bombay on 13 July 1965 "to protest against the single member constituency on behalf of the Republican Party".[84] Also in July, Republican Party members joined other opposition parties in "anti-starvation" protest, chiefly in Satara and Kolhapur,[85] calling off the agitation only when the Kashmir trouble erupted.

In the 1967 elections, the Republican Party again faced the problem of alliances. The Buddhist conversion lessened the number of reserved seats in Maharashtra. The Republican Party repudiated the concept of reserved seats, however, as had the Scheduled Castes Federation in 1955, a pragmatic decision based on the inability of a minority group to determine the outcome of the vote. A way out of the dilemma is an agreement on the distribution of tickets at the top level. This fact, plus the liberal record of the Congress under the leadership of Yeshwantrao Chavan in Maharashtra, seem to have led to an attempt at an entente with Congress in that state. A press interview with the Republican Party President, B.K. Gaikwad, in the summer of 1966 indicated that the Republican Party might cooperate with the Congress in Maharashtra, trading its support for a suggested fifty Assembly and fifteen Lok Sabha seats, a number far above those previously reserved for the Scheduled Castes. The alliance would be minimal, and the Republican Party candidates would contest seats under their own banner: "The Republican Party would prefer annihilation to contesting the elections on the Congress ticket".[86] Whether the Congress will agree to an alliance so favourable to the Republicans; whether Mahars and Buddhists will vote according to plan, forgetting the twenty years of belief that the Congress is the arch enemy; whether Republicans yoked to the Congress can retain independence in the legislatures -- these are questions to be answered in time.

Notes

1. The political movement which the Mahars have dominated has never been confined exclusively to their caste and from 1936 has included non-Marathi speaking groups. Since 1956, a majority of the Mahars have converted to Buddhism and no longer use the caste name. Nevertheless, in the interests of a workable title, and to bring into relief the substance of the movement we are about to consider, I have used the present title.

2. Scheduled Caste Census figures are from *Census of India*, 1961, Volume X, Maharashtra, Part V-A, by B.A. Kulkarni (Delhi: Government of India, 1964), p. 29. Buddhist figures are from the same volume, p. 31.

   The term, Scheduled Caste, came into use with the Government of India Act of 1935. Previously the terms Untouchable and Depressed Class were generally used. Mahatma Gandhi's term Harijan which gained currency around 1933 is unacceptable to the Mahars.

3. Alexander Robertson, *The Mahar Folk* (Calcutta: Y.M.C.A. Publishing House and Oxford University Press, 1938), p. 1.

4. Irawati Karve, *Paripurti* (Fulfillment) (Pune: R.J. Deshmukh, 1951), p. 81; in Marathi. This and other translations have been made with the help, at various times, of Rekha Damle, M.D. Panchbhai, Lalita Khambadkone, D.R. Maheshkar, S.D. Gaikwad, and Pramod Kale, but I am to be charged for any inaccuracies in the final version.

5. Dr. Ambedkar, asked if he were a pre-Aryan during the question period after his report to the Simon Commission, said, "Well, I do not know. That is a view." *Indian Statutory Commission*, Vol. XVI (London: H.M.S.O., 1930), p. 54.

   In his book, *Who Were the Shudras?* (Bombay: Thacker & Co., 1946), Ambedkar claimed the Shudras of Indo-Aryan society were Kshatriyas, but that the Shudras of today are unrelated to the ancient Shudras. In *The Untouchables* (New Delhi: Amrit Book Co, 1948), he denied a racial origin for untouchability and proposed the theory that the Untouchables were "Broken Men" who, in contrast to "Settled Tribesmen", did not give up Buddhism when Brahmanism triumphed in India.

6. A.S. Alteker, *History of Village Communities in Western India* (Madras: Oxford University Press, 1927), p. 43.

7. R.D. Choksey, *Economic History of Bombay, Deccan and Karnatak --* 1818-68 (Pune: R.D. Choksey, 1945), pp. 66-7.

8. C.B. Agarwal, *The Harijans in Rebellion* (Bombay: Taraporevala and Sons, 1934),   p. 7.

9. The British seem to have employed large number of Mahars in their ammunition factories, and the towns in which these factories are situated today seem to have a disproportionately large number of Mahar residents. Harold Mann's *Land and Labour in a Deccan Village* (Bombay: Oxford University Press, 1917) offers some witnesses to this and also suggests that village Mahars within cycling distance of some plant were factory employees. In the villlage he studied were ten Mahar *watandar* families, too many for the necessary watan duties. Of the 30 Mahar men in the village, 24 were employed at the Kirkee ammunition factory.

10. One of the few available dates for the beginning of Mahar urbanization is found in Morris David Morris, *The Emergence of an Industrial Labour Force in India* (Berkeley and Los Angeles: University of California Press, 1965), p. 73n: "One would probably be safe to suggest as a first approximation from the census data that before 1864 untouchables were much less likely to move to Bombay than other groups and that afterwards they tended to move in at a slightly more rapid rate than all other groups combined, at least until 1921".

11. The 1961 Census indicates that 13.81 per cent of Mahars and 20.8 per cent of Buddhists in contrast to 28.22 per cent of Maharashtra's general population is urban. Mahar and general percentages form *Census of India* 1961, Vol. X, Maharashtra, Part V-A: 32-3. Buddhist percentage taken from figures in *Census of India,* Paper No. 1 of 1963, 1961 Census -- Religion (Delhi: Government of India, 1963, p. 24.

12. In a paper entitled "Social Condition of the Mahar in Poona and Vicinity", read at the Association for Asian Studies, New York, April 1966, Robert J. Miller said, "I . . . emphasize the readiness of the Mahar ultimately to follow leaders who attacked the system *as a whole* . . . . The most renowned leader of them, B.R. Ambedkar, proposed a breaking of the link with the system at its only point of strong connection with the village Mahars - abolition of the status of hereditary servant".

13. Sir Patrick Cadell, *History of the Bombay Army* (London: Longmans, Green and Co., 1938), pp. 154-55.

14. B.R. Ambedkar, *What Congress and Gandhi have Done to the Untouchables*, 2nd ed. (Bombay: Thacker and Co. Ltd., 1946), p. 189.

15. Vithal Ramji Shinde, *Majhya Athvani va Anubhav* (My Memories and Experiences) (Poona: R.B. Andre, Shri Lekhan Wacan Bhandar, 1958), p. 214; in Marathi.

16. A handwritten copy of the petition is in the C.B. Khairmoday collection of materials on Ambedkar and the Mahars now in the University of Bombay Library.

17. The memoranda and the 1904 reply are reproduced in English in the Marathi biography of *Shivram Janba Kamble* by H.N. Navalkar (Pune: S.J. Kamble, 1930), pp. 157-64, 166-68.

18. A military history of the Mahars may be found in *The Regimental History of the Mahar MG (Machine Gun) Regiment* by Major General S.P.O. Thorat (Dehra Dun: The Army Press, 1954). Photographs show a replica of the Koregaon pillar and the word "Koregaon" on the cap badge of the Mahar Regiment from 1942 until Independence.

19. The Somwanshi sub-caste of Mahars may have made some effort to identify themselves with the Rajputs, and G.M. Thaware, a Nagpur Mahar leader, made the claim, "The Scheduled Castes formerly belonged to a class of Warriors and from the Indian History these classes and specially the Mahar community rose to a high position in Shivaji's Raj" in a letter to Gandhi. *Gandhiji's Letters Re: Untouchables* by G.M. Thaware (Nagpur: L.P. Meshram and M.G. Dongre, c 1941), p. 52. Nevertheless, the emphasis on Kshatriya status has been a minor part of the Mahar movement. For contrast, see the history of the Jatava caste of of Chamars in Agra in Owen M. Lynch's "The Politics of Untouchability", a paper read at the Conference on Social Structure and Social Change in India, 3-5 June 1965. [Now a book: Owen M. Lynch, *The Politics of Untouchability* (Now York and London: Columbia University Press, 1969.)]

20. For a historical and contemporary account of the Bhakti religion centered at Pandharpur, see G.A. Deleurey, S.J., *The Cult of Vithoba* (Pune: Deccan College, 1960).

21. See Bernard S. Cohn, "The Changing Status of a Depressed Caste", in McKim Marriot ed., *Village India*, 4th impression (Chicago: University of Chicago Press, 1960), pp. 53-77. Ravidas is also honoured by the Chambhars of Maharashtra.

22. A copy of the resolutions of the Chokhamela Sudharak Mandal in Marathi is in the possession of Vasant Moon of Nagpur [who maintains an extensive library of research materials on Dalit movements.]

23. From the minutes of the Loyal Mahar Sabha, in English, in the possession of Vasant Moon of Nagpur. A separate ghat was also built for Mahars at Nasik on the Godavari river, but I have no information on its date.

24. Letter to B.K. Gaikwad, 3 March 1934.

25. Kisan Fagoji Bansode, *Pradip*, edited by Shamrao Bansode (Nagpur: Jagruit Prakashan, ca. 1958), p. 48, in Marathi. Choka is an abbreviation of the name of the Mahar poet-saint Chokhamela.

26. (Franchise) Evidence Taken Before the Reforms Committee, Vol. I (Calcutta: Government of India, 1919), pp. 723-25.

27. The support of Ambedkar's education was one of the many gestures toward reform made by Maharaja Sayajirao Gaekwad of Baroda, who had encouraged the education of Untouchables in his own state. In return for the financial aid, Ambedkar was to give ten years service in Baroda State. He

actually gave only a few months service at two different times, claiming that the treatment he received in the Baroda offices and the lack of suitable housing available for an Untouchable made it impossible to stay.

28. Shahu Maharaj of Kolhapur was an important figure in the Non-Brahman movement. He established a hostel for Untouchables in Kolhapur around 1908 and was in close contact with Ambedkar until his death in 1922.

29. *The Reform Committee*, Vol. II, pp. 729-39.

30. One conference was held under caste Hindu leadership to rally Untouchable support for the Congress-League scheme; the conference in turn asked for a Congress resolution for the removal of the disabilities of the Depressed Classes. The second conference was held later in 1917 under Non-Brahman Party leadership to counteract the pledged support of the first conference to the Congress-League scheme. A third conference was held in 1918 under the leadership of Subhedar Ganpatrao Govind Rokde, probably a Mahar, demanding separate electorates. A fourth conference was held by V.R. Shinde's Depressed Classes Mission and produced an All-India Anti-Untouchability Manifesto.

31. Dhananjay Keer, *Dr. Ambedkar, Life and Mission* (Bombay: Popular Prakashan, 2nd edition 1962), p. 43.

32. C.B. Khairmode, *Dr. Bhimrao Ramji Ambedkar*, Vol. I (Bombay: Y.B. Ambedkar, 1952); p. 267; in Marathi.

33. The C.K.Ps. are among the "advanced castes" of Maharashtra. In Ambedkar's circle of caste Hindu supporters and friends, the majority were from this community. A possible reason is that they were, in certain situations, in competition with the Brahmans.

34. Dhananjay Keer, *op.cit.*, pp. 70-1, 104-05.

35. *Times of India*, Bombay: 21 March 1940 [a picture book on the Mahad satyagraha, with Marathi text, has recently appeared].

36. Jotiba Phule, 1827-90, began the Satya Shodhak Samaj (Truth-seeking society) in 1873. Its objects were "to redeem the Shudras and Atishudras (Untouchables) from the influence of Brahmanical scriptures. . . to teach them their human rights, and to liberate them from mental religious slavery". Dhananjay Keer, *Mahatma Jotirao Phooley—Father of Our Social Revolution* (Bombay: Popular Prakashan, 1964), p. 126. Phule belonged to the Mali caste, an agricultural community ranked with the Marathas. He was the first Hindu to conduct schools for the Untouchables. Ambedkar considered him one of his three *gurus*, along with the Buddha and Kabir, and Phule's picture is often found in Mahar institutions.

37. *Indian Statutory Commission*, Vol. XVI, pp. 27-37. Dr. Ambedkar was also a member of the Provincial Committee in Bombay. His report in that capacity appears in Vol. III of the Indian Statutory Commission. The Bahishkrit Hitakarini Sabha was an organization founded by Ambedkar in 1924 to work for the social and economic betterment of the Depressed Classes.

38. Petition to the Indian Statutory Commission from the Central Provinces

Depressed Classes Association, Nagpur, 24 February 1929; privately printed.

39. B.R. Ambedkar, *What Congress and Gandhi...*, pp. 40-1. Srinivasan was a member of the Depressed Classes from Madras who seems to have faded out of the political picture after the Round Table Conferences.

40. Subhas Chandra Bose, *The Indian Struggle*, Part II -- *Netaji's Life and Writings*, 1920-34 (Calcutta, Thacker, Spink and Co., 1948), p. 40.

41. "All India Depressed Classes Conference", Nripendra Nath Mitra ed., *The Indian Annual Register*, Vol. II (Calcutta: Annual Register Office, 1930), pp. 367-74.

42. C.B. Khairmode, *Dr. Bhimrao Ramji Ambedkar*, Vol. II, pp. 117-18; in Marathi.

43. *Janata*, 9 January 1932, Bombay; in Marathi.

44. *Free Press Journal*, 11 October, 1931, Bombay.

45. Dhananjay Keer, *Dr. Ambedkar...*, pp. 191-93.

46. B.R. Ambedkar, *What Congress and Gandhi...*, pp. 134-40.

47. John Coatman, in a speech before the East India Association, published in *Asiatic Review*, Vol. XXIX, No. 97C (London: January 1933), pp. 46-7.

48. M.C. Rajah and Dr. Ambedkar joined forces only in 1942, when they protested together against the lack of provision for separate electorates for the Scheduled Castes in the Cripps Proposals. *Times of India*, 1 April 1942, Bombay.

49. *Times of India*, 15 August 1936, Bombay.

50. *Bombay Chronicle*, 4 July 1939. The Chambhar criticism is not available. Ambedkar replied that "he had no ambition for the Mahars, in fact would do everything in his power to liquidate it as a community though he would want them to progress as human beings". He accused the Congress of playing a political game, giving as an example: "Although it was the Mahars who fought for right of entrance in the Police Training School at Nasik it was all non-Mahars who were admitted".

51. *Janata*, 14 June 1941, Bombay; in Marathi. The letter from "the first educated Mang in the Nizam's state", D.N. Kamble, makes the following requests: (1) Mahars must consider Mangs as equals, (2) promising Mang young men should have a chance to go forward, (3) Mahars must not obstruct Mang processions, (4) Mahars must not take *watandari* rights from Mangs, (5) Ambedkar must give as much concern to the improvement of Mangs as to Mahars. Ambedkar replied that he had successfully encouraged inter-caste dining, that the Mahar hostels were open to all, and that the Independent Labour Party considered quality, not caste, and warned the Mangs against taking the way of Congress.

52. Ambedkar's lengthy testimony is in the *Bombay Legislative Assembly Debates*, Vol. IV, Part I, pp. 1330-59.

53. Lloyd and Susanne H. Rudolph, "The Political Role of India's Caste Associations", *Pacific Affairs*, Vol. XXXIII, No. I, March 1960, p. 7.

54. Vamanrao A. Bhatt, *The Harijans of Maharashtra* (Delhi: All India Harijan Sevak Sangh, 1941), pp. 16-17.
55. Dhananjay Keer, *Dr. Ambedkar...*, p. 348.
56. *Report of the Depressed Class Conference* (Nagpur: G.T. Meshram, 1942).
57. As early as 1926, Ambedkar had suggested at a meeting in Jejuri that Untouchables seek land for colonization: Keer, p. 63. In 1929 at a conference in Ratnagiri District at Chiplun, Ambedkar said he would try to secure land for cultivation in Sind and in Indore State for Untouchables: Keer, p. 127. A recommendation of the Starte Committee, of which Ambedkar was a member, stated: "we also consider it possible that some of the Depressed Classes would take up land in Sind if a suitable scheme could be worked out by the Barrage Revenue authorities in consultation with the Backward Classes officer". *Report of the Depressed Classes and Aboriginal Tribes Committee*, Bombay Presidency (Bombay: Governmental Central Press, 1930), p. 42.
58. A copy of his chart is in C.B. Khairmoday's collection of Ambedkar materials in the Bombay University Library.
59. B.R. Ambedkar, *What Congress and Gandhi...*, pp. 378-86. The charts are not entirely convincing.
60. B.R. Ambedkar, *The Cabinet Mission and the Untouchables* (Bombay: privately printed, no date).
61. Anil Chandra Banerjee and Dakshina Rajan Bose, *The Cabinet Mission in India* (Calcutta: A. Mukherjee, 1946), p. 108.
62. Jayakar to Sapru, 7 April 1941, Letter J 65 in the Sapru Collection, National Library, Calcutta.
63. F.G. Bailey, *Caste and the Economic Frontier* (Manchester: Manchester University Press, 1957), pp. 224-26.
64. Lelah Dushkin, "The Policy of the Indian National Congress Toward the Depressed Classes -- An Historical Study", Unpublished M.A. thesis, University of Pennsylvania, 1957. Dushkin has also discussed Scheduled Caste policy in a series of three articles in *The Economic Weekly*, 28 October, 4 and 18 November 1961, Bombay. See also Dushkin's "Scheduled Caste Politics" in J. Michael Mahar ed., *The Untouchables in Contemporary India* (Tucson: University of Arizona Press, 1972).
65. W.H. Morris-Jones, *The Government and Politics of India* (London: Hutchinson University Library, 1964), p. 87.
66. *Times of India*, 12 January 1950, Bombay.
67. *Asian Guide to the First Elections* (Bombay: Asia Publishing House, 1951), pp. 191-93.
68. It is probable that Ambedkar was defeated by caste Hindu votes. The Scheduled Castes Federation with 16.92 per cent of the electorate in the Bombay North constituency got 17.27 per cent of the valid votes. M. Venkatarangaiya, *The General Election in the City of Bombay* (Bombay: Vora and Co., 1953), p. 40.

69. *Ibid.*, p. 40.
70. M. Venkatarangaiya, "Bombay City", In *Reports on the Indian General Elections, 1951-52*, by S.K. Kogekar and Richard L. Park (Bombay: Popular Book Depot, 1956), pp. 66-7.
71. M. Venkatarangaiya, *The General Election...*, p. 146.
72. M. Venkatarangaiya, in Kogekar and Park, *op.cit.*, p. 65.
73. Hugh Tinker, *India and Pakistan -- A Political Analysis* (New York: Frederick A. Praeger, 1962), p. 55.
74. A.P.I. news release, 27 April 1948.
75. For a fuller discussion, see "Buddhism and Politics in Maharashtra" by Eleanor Zelliot, in Donald Eugene Smith ed., *Religion and Politics in South Asia* (Princeton: Princeton University Press, 1966); [and in this volume].
76. Ambedkar had reluctantly given the party permission to align with the Samyukta Maharashtra Samiti in the fall of 1956. He had been an early supporter of the idea, publishing a defense of *Maharashtra as a Linguistic Province* (Bombay: Thacker and Co.), in 1948. Later he feared the possible "nationalism" of large linguistic states, and the rule of the numerically dominant caste (in Maharashtra, Marathas, not Brahmans), and recommended that Maharashtra be divided into four states. *Thoughts on Linguistic States*, privately printed in 1955.
77. The number was later reduced to two. D.P. Meshram was declared unqualified, as a Buddhist, to hold a reserved seat after a legal battle that reached the Supreme Court. The Republican Party in Uttar Pradesh, allied with the Muslims in some areas in 1962, had more success, winning three Lok Sabha and nine Legislative Assembly seats in that election.
78. *Report on the 3rd General Elections in India*, Vol. II, Statistical (New Delhi: Indian Election Commission, n.d.), pp. 12-13.
79. A discussion of the Zilla Parishad elections in Maharashtra is available in Barbara J. Ravenell's "The Scheduled Castes and Panchayati Raj", unpublished M.A. thesis, University of Chicago, 1965, pp. 102-04. The Amravati figures are from the *Times of India*, 6 June 1962, Bombay.
80. B.A.V. Sharma and R.T. Jangam, *The Bombay Municipal Corportaion -- An Election Study* (Bombay: Popular Book Depot, 1963), p. 54.
81. This demand indicates the need of Untouchables for recognition of their place in Indian history, represented by the contributions of Dr. Ambedkar. Allied to it are attempts to enhance the prestige of Buddhism, such as the proposal of Maharashtrian Republicans that the Buddha's birth-date be a public holiday. *Maharashtra Legislative Assembly Debates*, Vol. I, No. 30, 18 August 1960.
82. In Maharashtra, "The State Government has from 1st May 1960 extended all concessions and facilities available to Scheduled Castes also to the Scheduled Caste converts to Buddhism except the statutory concessions under the Constitution and certain special schemes for the removal of un-

touchability, etc. which cannot by their very nature apply to non-Hindus''. Government Resolution Education and Social Welfare Department, SCW 2260, 6 July 1960. *Census of India* 1961, Vol. X, Part IV-A, p. 31. In other states and in matters pertaining to the Central Government, converts to Buddhism lose their privileges [in 1990, Buddhists were included in Central Government reservations.]

83. *The Charter of Demands* (New Delhi, Dada Sahib B.K. Gaikwad, B.P. Maurya and B.D. Khobragade for the Republican Party of India, 1964).

84. *Danik Maratha*, 13 July 1965, Bombay; in Marathi.

85. *Maharashtra Times*, 21 and 22 August 1965, Bombay; in Marathi.

86. *Maharashtra Times*, 28 May 1966, Bombay; in Marathi.

Buddhism and Politics in Maharashtra*

In the period between the 1951 and the 1961 Census, the number of Buddhists in India jumped 1,670.71 per cent. There are now 3,250,227 Indian Buddhists, a census figure which is probably minimal.[1] Of this number, 2,789,501 are in Maharashtra, where only 2,487 Buddhists were counted in 1951. The Buddhist community in that state now is five times as large as the Christian community, almost as large as the Muslim, and accounts for 7.05 per cent of the total population. This rather staggering conversion figure is the work of one man, Dr. B.R. Ambedkar, and has taken place largely within his caste, the Mahars, a Maharashtrian Scheduled Caste.[2]

The initial conversion ceremony was held on 14 October 1956, in Nagpur. Dr. Ambedkar took *diksha* at the hands of the oldest Buddhist monk in India and then administered simple conversion rites to a crowd estimated at between 300,000 to 600,000 people. Conversion spread rapidly at first, more slowly later, chiefly in the area that is now Maharashtra, but also in Madhya Pradesh (113,365 Buddhists in 1961 in contrast to 2,991 ten years earlier), Punjab (14,857 in contrast to 1,550), Uttar Pradesh (12,893 in contrast to 3,221). The areas in which there were mass conversions correspond, with the exception of Madras,[3] to those areas in which Dr. Ambedkar and his political party, the Scheduled Castes Federation, had some direct influence.

Conversion to another religion as a way to escape the disabilities of untouchability in Hinduism is not a new idea in Indian history. Islam and Christianity grew in large part by the conversion of lower caste peoples. The differences between the 1956 conversion to Buddhism and the earlier movements are that (1) the Buddhist conversion involves the greater part of one entire caste; (2) the Untouchables have not joined an established larger body, as in the case of Islam or Christianity, but are themselves building a new religious organization, retaining much of

---

*First published in Donald E. Smith ed., *South Asian Politics and Religion* (Princeton: Princeton University Press, 1966, 1969). Minor corrections have been made.

their social structure, caste loyalty and old leadership; (3) the conversion has taken place among a people who were already involved in an independent party, in opposition to the Congress.[4]

Now, not many years after the initial mass conversion, it is too soon to judge whether or not the acceptance of a new religion by Untouchables can secure a higher status for them. What can bé recorded is the relationship of that conversion to the previous struggle for equality with higher castes, and the relationship of the conversion to their political life. This paper will deal with these questions largely from the standpoint of the involvement of the Mahars.

The Buddhist conversion has touched, according to the census figures, less than 1 per cent of India's population, about 5 per cent of the Scheduled Castes. About 75 per cent of the Mahars, a number of Jatavas (a Chamar caste in Uttar Pradesh who came strongly under Ambedkar's influence) and pockets of the Scheduled Castes in Gujarat, Punjab, Rajasthan, Mysore and Madhya Pradesh have declared themselves Buddhists. Generally speaking, Buddhist conversion has occurred among castes which have some history of a struggle for rights independent of the Congress and caste Hindu organizations. Most Scheduled Caste communities, including Maharashtrian Scheduled Castes other than the Mahars, remain acknowledged Hindus and generally support the Congress Party.

At the moment, only Buddhists in Maharashtra, placed in the Backward Classes category in 1961, retain the rights given to the Scheduled Castes previously in matters of education and economic benefits. Elsewhere, and in all matters relating to the Central Government, a Scheduled Caste convert to Buddhism loses privileges. How many Scheduled Caste individuals think of themselves as Buddhists but retain their Scheduled Caste status out of economic necessity is impossible to judge.[5] A satyagraha held in December 1964-January 1965 organized by the Republican Party and involving, it is claimed, 300,000 volunteers, mostly in Maharashtra, Uttar Pradesh and Punjab, stressed as one of its demands the retention of the Scheduled Caste privileges in education and government positions by converts to Buddhism. Assurances by the then Prime Minister Lal Bahadur Shastri that the demands would be considered brought the satyagraha to an end. Whether the valued rights of educational scholarships and a percentage of reserved places in all government offices will actually be given to Buddhists, and what difference this will make in the numbers who declare themselves converted, remains to be seen.

Ambedkar the Rebel

The key figure in the Buddhist conversion movement and in the political history of the Mahars is Dr. Bhimrao Ramji Ambedkar, a Mahar who was born in 1891 and who died on 6 December 1956, two months after the initial conversion ceremony. A catalyst of aggressive forces within the Mahar community already pushing upward, an innovator of new tech- niques for rising, and a symbol of achievement for many untouchables outside the Mahar caste as well as within, Dr. Ambedkar still dominates both the conversion movement and the political activities of the Repub- lican Party. The history of the movement and of the Party can be written only in terms of his life.

Prior to Ambedkar's first public statement on the political rights of the Depressed Classes in 1919, the Mahars' attempts to raise their social and economic status were made through claims to recognition of worth within the Hindu religion, and use of British-created economic opportunities. Four of the best-known Mahar leaders in the pre-Ambedkar era illustrate the use of both paths. Gopal Swami Yagavkar, a saint whose *samadhi* (memorial) is still venerated by both Mahars and caste Hindus, was a paymaster in the British Army. Gopal Baba Walangkar, also a soldier in the British Army, wrote an essay showing that the Vedas did not support untouchability.[6] Kisan Fagoji Bansode, from the Vidharba region, collected the songs of Chokhamela, the Mahar saint in the Pandharpur pantheon, wrote Chokhamela's biography, and joined the Prarthana Samaj.[7] Shivram Janba Kamble, a butler in a British club in Pune, directed an unsuccessful satyagraha at Parvati, Pune's holy hill.

Shivram Janba Kamble was the chief author of a petition written in 1910 which pleaded for the re-establishment of Mahar enlistment in the army. The document, which seems to have been ignored by the British government, illustrates both the consciousness of low position and the aspirations of the Mahar of that time:

> We, the Mahar inhabitants of India, residing in the Bombay Presi-
> dency, have experienced the vitalizing influence of the general
> awakening of our Indian People, and long to participate in the new
> privileges which have been granted by our illustrious Emperor. . . .
> We do not aspire to high political privileges and positions, since we
> are not educationally qualified for them, but humbly seek employ-
> ment in the lowest grades of the public service, in the ranks of police
> sepoys and soldiers in the Indian army . . . . We have been excluded

from the military service entirely, for reasons unknown to us . . . . If the other castes of the Hindus should object to our enlistment in the same regiments with them...we would request that separate regiments of our people might be created, or separate companies of our people might be attached to Muhammadan regiments . . . . The kindly touch of the Christian religion elevates the Mahar at once and forever socially as well as politically, and shall not the magic power of British law and British justice produce the same effect upon us, even as followers of our own ancestral faith?[8]

Eight years later, more "new privileges" were to come to the Indian people as the British raj attempted to broaden the representative base of its power. The opportunity to testify to the Southborough (Franchise) Committee, which prepared a report to be used in the Montagu -Chelmsford reforms, coincided with the arrival on the scene of a Mahar who was well educated enough to "aspire to high political privileges". Dr. Ambedkar, himself from a Mahar army family and the second high school graduate among the Mahars, had returned in 1917 from three years of education in America (MA, PhD, Columbia University), and one year in England, made possible by the liberal Gaikwad of Baroda as part of his program of educating the lower castes. One of the two Untouchable witnesses, the other also a Mahar,[9] Dr. Ambedkar used the opportunity to outline a complete franchise system for Bombay Presidency. But his main plea was for direct representation of the Depressed Classes in the Bombay legislative council in proportion to their population, through their own electorate separate from that of the caste Hindus. His testimony gave a gloomy picture of the state of the Untouchable in 1919:

Socio-religious disabilities have dehumanized the untouchable . . . The untouchables are so socialized as never to complain of their low estate . . . . The exact description of the treatment cannot be attempted. The word untouchable is an epitome of their ills and sufferings. Not only has untouchability arrested the growth of their personality but it comes in the way of their material well-being. It has also deprived them of certain civil rights.... The principal modes of acquiring wealth are trade, industry or service. The untouchables can engage in none of these because of their untouchability.... In the whole Bombay Presidency there [are] one B.A. [himself] and six or seven matriculates among the depressed classes.[10]

In Ambedkar's testimony were various elements which were to recur again and again throughout his career; some of these bear a relationship to the final conversion to Buddhism. He emphasized the need of the Untouchable for self-respect; the reality of the division between caste Hindu and Depressed Class, which had to be acknowledged if any justice was to be done; the belief that the Brahman's "deep ingrained ethnocentrism has prevented a reconstruction of Hindu society and stood in the way of a revision of vested rights for the common good"; distrust of Congress as a group composed of social conservatives; the representation of Untouchables by Untouchables, because caste Hindus, however sympathetic, could not properly represent their wants and grievances; and the need for political power and political education for the Depressed Classes. Ambedkar appeared before the Southborough Committee in the hope that the coming transfer of some power to popular assemblies would include direct representation of the Depressed Classes so that "the hardships and disabilities entailed by the social system should not be reproduced and perpetuated in political institutions". His plea was ignored by the Southborough Committee, which in its final report gave one nominated seat (Ambedkar had asked for nine elected seats) to the Depressed Classes in the Bombay Presidency. But Ambedkar was to continue to use every opportunity which presented itself to attempt to secure political power for the Depressed Classes.

Another trip to England, financed by the Gaikwad of Baroda and also the Maharaja of Kolhapur, an active figure in the Non-Brahman movement, gave Ambedkar the additional qualifications of barrister-at-law and M.Sc. and D.Sc. (Economics) from the London School of Economics and Political Science. After his return, he gave some attention to the process of improving the Untouchables' status by the traditional means of emulating the religious practices of the higher castes, but there was ambivalence in his attitude toward Hinduism. In an early editorial in *Muknayak* (The Voice of the Dumb), his first newspaper started in 1920, he wrote: "We are not yet ready to give an answer to the question of whether the Untouchables should have a temple of their own or attempt to enter the Hindu temple".[11] On a few occasions, Ambedkar made some attempt to enter, physically or symbolically, a Hindu temple. The right to participate in the public Ganpati festival was secured; on at least one occasion, Ambedkar and his followers donned the sacred thread symbolizing rebirth worn by the three higher castes; an abortive attempt to enter the temple at Amravati was followed in 1930 by a large-scale satyagraha at the Kala Ram temple in Nasik.

Even the Nasik satyagraha may have been more of a social device than a battle for religious rights, for in 1934 Ambedkar himself wrote to the Nasik leader, Bhaurao Gaikwad, that the proposed renewal of the attempt (still unsuccessful) to gain entrance to the temple should be stopped altogether:

I did not launch the temple entry movement because I wanted the Depressed Classes to become worshippers of idols which they were prevented from worshipping or because I believed that temple entry would make them equal members in and an integral part of Hindu society. So far as this aspect of the case is concerned, I would advise the depressed classes to insist upon a complete overhauling of Hindu society and Hindu theology before they consent to become an integral part of Hindu society. I started temple entry satyagraha only because I felt that that was the best way of energizing the Depressed Classes and making them conscious of their position. As I believe I have achieved that, therefore I have no more use for temple entry. I want the Depressed Classes to concentrate their energy and resources on politics and education''.[12]

But if he did not stress the need for the Untouchables to become "an integral part of Hinduism", Ambedkar did insist that Untouchables should look and act like the highest of caste Hindus. In his newspapers and at innumerable conferences he enjoined: stop the traditional Mahar work of dragging the dead cattle out of the villages and the practice of eating carrion; dress well; don't drink; don't beg; get educated and send your children to school; be self-respecting. In 1942 when recalling the progress made during twenty years of work, Ambedkar's references were not only to political gains but also to the process of self-purification of those practices which "justified" the untouchability of the Untouchable. The Scheduled Caste man, he declared, has stopped eating dead animals and observing meaningless Hindu customs, and now had the privilege of sending representatives to the legislature.[13] On another occasion in the same year he congratulated his audience on its political awareness (75,000 people had attended the public meeting), good progress in education, and entry into the police and the army. However, "the greatest progress that we have made is to be found among our women folk. Here you see in this conference these 20 to 25 thousand women present. See their dress, observe their manners, mark their speech. Can any one say that they are Untouchable women"?[14]

While the process of purifying and modernizing was going on within the caste, Ambedkar had further opportunities to bring Untouchables' grievances and demands before the British government. The emphasis on the Depressed Classes as a separate element in Indian society was intensified, and Ambedkar increasingly urged constitutional arrangements which would accentuate this separateness. The demand for joint electorates with adult franchise before the Simon Commission in 1928 gave way to insistence on separate electorates at the Round Table Conference in 1930, probably in the light of the Muslim minority's demands. Ambedkar argued that the Depressed Classes "must be regarded as a distinct and independent minority . . . . We cannot be deemed part of the Hindu community".[15] This was later softened, however, to a plea for the Depressed Classes to be called "Protestant Hindus" or "non-caste Hindus".[16]

For Dr. Ambedkar, the selection of two Depressed Class members (Rao Bahadur R. Srinivasan from Madras and himself) as delegates to the first Round Table Conference in 1930 was in itself recognition of the right of the Depressed Classes to be considered a separate element on the Indian political scene, and he felt the Conference acknowledged that as a fact. At the second Round Table Conference in 1931, however, Mahatma Gandhi was also present, representing the Congress and speaking strongly against the idea of the Untouchables as a separate entity in Indian society. In Gandhi's mind, separate electorates might allow Dr. Ambedkar himself to "mount to power and position but nothing good will accrue to the 'Untouchables'."[17]

The conflict at the Round Table Conference over who represented the Untouchables and whether they were or were not a separate group was heightened a year later when the Communal Award was announced. In an attempt to meet both the demands of Ambedkar and Gandhi, the British government announced that Depressed Class members were to have a double vote: one in the general electorate, the other in a special electorate only for Depressed Class voters. Gandhi, confined in the Yervada Jail in Pune, went on a fast[18] to protest this decision on the ground that it would be harmful for the Depressed Classes and would vivisect and disrupt Hinduism, would serve neither as penance for caste Hindus nor as a remedy for the degradation the Depressed Classes had groaned under for centuries.[19] Gandhi claimed the Depressed Classes question was predominantly a religious matter. Ambedkar regarded political power as vital for the Untouchables' progress; direct election of Depressed Class members to legislatures, without the possibility of caste

Hindu votes determining the outcome, was essential. He had by that time no interest and little faith in the Depressed Classes' full assimilation into Hinduism.

Gandhi's fast unto death against separate electorates placed his life in Ambedkar's hands. Ambedkar agreed to the Poona Pact, capitulating on the matter of separate electorates at the price of an increased number of reserved seats for Untouchables in legislative bodies, and Gandhi gave up his fast.

The conflict with Gandhi had been foreshadowed in a speech given by Ambedkar in Nagpur in 1920 in which he criticized V.R. Shinde, organizer of the pioneering Depressed Class Mission and a Maratha by caste, for suggesting that the representatives of the Untouchables should be selected by the members of the legislative council, not by government or by Untouchable institutions. Dr. Ambedkar's objection was that since the caste Hindu could not know the mind of the Untouchable therefore caste Hindu organizations for the uplift of the Depressed Classes should be opposed.[20]

Ambedkar considered Gandhi an enemy of the Untouchables from the time of the Round Table Conference until Gandhi's death in 1948. The conflict between the two men can be defined in several ways: Ambedkar's insistence on the *rights* of the Depressed Classes versus Gandhi's stress upon the *duty* of the caste Hindus to do penance; Ambedkar's complete rejection of caste versus Gandhi's defense of *chaturvarna* (the idealized four-caste system with no untouchability) as necessary to Hinduism; Ambedkar's rational democratic liberalism versus Gandhi's appeals to traditional modes of thought; and the inevitable clash between the aggressive demands of a minority group leader and the slower, broader-based and somewhat paternalistic extension of rights by the majority group reformer.

Ambedkar was critical of the British government in India, but he was of the school which demanded social reforms before political reforms, and he preferred British raj to a "Hindu raj" in which the Untouchables would not have established rights. A few years after the Poona Pact he took two steps, one religious and one political, which underlined his position as the leader of a group independent of Hinduism and Independent of the Congress. Criticism of Hinduism became a flat rejection in 1935 at a conference at Yeola (near Nasik), when Ambedkar stated: "I was born in the Hindu religion; but I will not die in the Hindu religion".[21]

A conference of Mahars which met next year in Bombay resolved to leave Hinduism, to stop participating in worship and festivals. The reaction to this announcement among the Mahars beyond the reach of the conference is hard to judge; certainly any attempt to stress religious practices as a way toward a higher social status was abandoned. But it is doubtful that disbelief in the efficacy of prayers and vows to the Hindu gods suddenly descended, and such Hindu rituals as were used for weddings and other ceremonies undoubtedly continued. The reaction to the announcement among caste Hindus was vigorous and almost totally critical. The reaction of other religions was to offer hospitality to Dr. Ambedkar and the Depressed Classes without question. Muslims, Sikhs and Buddhists sought him out. Christians, not convinced of the appropriateness of mass conversion, expressed great interest but maintained a little distance.

The conversion announcement was made without reference to any religion. Dr. Ambedkar seemed to be inclined toward Sikhism, explaining later that "conversion to Islam or Christianity would denationalize the Depressed Classes".[22] But after several interactions with the Sikhs, including the building of a college in Bombay by Sikhs as expression of goodwill towards the Scheduled Castes, Dr. Ambedkar let the issue of conversion lapse, probably because he felt that the reserved seats won for the Depressed Classes might have to be sacrificed by conversion to Sikhism. In 1946, when Dr. Ambedkar was asked by a Christian minister why his first choice had been Islam rather than Christianity, which was the strongest rumor of that time, he said that it was not easy to uproot humanity. The Untouchables were willing to stay where they were provided they had political safeguards, and there was no agreement among them as to where to go.[23]

In 1936, the same year the Mahar conference resolved to abandon Hinduism, Dr. Ambedkar founded the Independent Labour Party to fight the Congress in the elections to be held in 1937. The Independent Labour Party issued a platform quite broad in scope, mildly socialistic, with only incidental mention of the Depressed Classes. One section urged legislation to prevent social reformers from being outcasted by the orthodox and to penalize terrorism or boycotts used to prevent individuals or classes from exercising their rights. Another plank was the demand for facilities for higher education and foreign education for communities which were educationally backward. A third asked for modernization of *watan*, the village system that gave land rights for traditional services from its village servants, which Ambedkar considered detrimental to the progress of the Mahars. A few caste Hindus were influential in the party, and its general program was to rectify the injustices suffered by any underprivileged group. In the 1937 elections, the Independent Labour Party scored considerable success, winning 16 of the 18 seats contested, including 3 general and 10 reserved seats out of 15 in the Bombay state legislature, and 3 reserved seats in the Central Provinces and Berar.

In 1942, along with increasing pressure for separate electorates, Ambedkar turned the Independent Labour Party into the Scheduled Castes Federation, making a direct appeal to the Scheduled Castes to win power through unity. A large meeting at Nagpur brought together delegates from Bombay, the Central Provinces and Berar (who were for the most part Mahars), and also from Madras, Bengal, Punjab and the United Provinces. The first article of the new party's constitution read: ''The object of the All-India Scheduled Castes Federation is the attainment by the Scheduled Castes of a status as a distinct and separate element in the national life of India and to obtain for them their political, economic and social rights to which they are entitled by reason of their needs, their numbers and their importance.''[24]

This would have been the strategic time, with many Congressmen in jail, for the development of a strong all-India organization that might have welded the Scheduled Castes into the force Ambedkar dreamt of. But Ambedkar was the Labour Member of the Viceroy's Executive Council and was hampered by that official post from large-scale political activity. His own temperament also prevented him from using the war years to build his organization, as M.A. Jinnah did with the Muslim League. Dhananjay Keer has written in what seems an accurate judgement:

Ambedkar did not try to organize his political party on modern lines. He had no taste for individual organization. There were no regular annual conferences or general meetings of the organizations with which he was connected. Where and when he sat was the venue of conference and the time of decision .... When he wanted his people to assemble under his banner, he simply gave them a clarion call and the organization sprang up like the crop in the rainy season. In the summer there would be nothing in the field, the banner resting in his study corner and the people at home.[25]

Resolutions, petitions, memoranda, large-scale satyagrahas at provincial legislatures in Pune, Nagpur, Kanpur and Lucknow, and a flying visit to England in 1946, all failed to bring British recognition of what Ambedkar felt were the rights of the Scheduled Castes to a separate electorate. Independence in 1947 brought partition and with it the end of the question of separate electorates for the Muslims, and for the Scheduled Castes too. And with Independence came the surprising and gracious gesture, in view of his outspoken criticism of the Congress, Gandhi and Nehru, of Ambedkar's appointment to the Constitution drafting committee, then to the committee chairmanship and to Nehru's first cabinet as law minister.

The proposed "Constitution of the United States of India" which Ambedkar published in *States and Minorities* in March 1947, before his appointment, is quite different from the actual draft Constitution he defended before the Constituent Assembly in November 1948. Gone is the provision for agriculture as a state industry, which Ambedkar regarded as the only solution to the problems of the Scheduled Castes, the great majority of whom were agricultural laborers.[26] Gone also were the provisions for separate electorates and separate villages for the Scheduled Castes. Similar in both documents are anti-untouchability clauses, an officer to look after "minority affairs", representation of the Scheduled Castes in Legislature and the services, and special governmental responsibility for the education of the Scheduled Castes. The Constitution, of course, is the reflection of the thinking of Congress leaders of the time, not only a product of Ambedkar's mind. Actually, his main contributions to the Constitution may have been in the general fields of stressing centralized government and a unitary judiciary, plus his skill in guiding the draft Constitution through the Constituent Assembly.

Ambedkar became known as the draftsman or author of the Constitution, but his efforts to get the Hindu Code Bill as a whole through Parliament, an achievement he desired even more, failed. He resigned in 1951, chiefly over the failure of the cabinet to support the Bill. Out of the cabinet, Ambedkar faced two election defeats and increased illness in the final years of his life. But the last two public acts of his life, the Buddhist conversion and the founding of the Republican Party, are not symptoms of failures or renewed expressions of separatism.

Refuge in Buddha

The conversion to Buddhism in October 1956, which came just before Dr. Ambedkar's death, was the result of personal conviction as well as a conscious effort to lay down a way his people could follow after his death. Dr. Ambedkar's own path to Buddhism cannot be entirely correlated with his political life. His interest began when a Bombay teacher,

K.A. Keluskar, gave him a copy of the life of Buddha in 1908, on the occasion of his passing his matriculation examination, an incident which is part of the religious lore of the Buddhists today. Sometime in the 1920s he corresponded with Maharshi Shinde, the Maratha reformer of whom he was very critical on other points, about Shinde's interest in Buddhism.[27]

In 1934 the house he had built in the predominantly Brahman Hindu colony in Dadar, Bombay, was named Rajgriha, after the ancient city of the Buddhist kings. The first of the colleges established by his People's Education Society, which began in 1946 in hutments in Bombay, was called Siddharth, Buddha's personal name. In 1948 he republished *The Essence of Buddhism*, first published in 1908, and noted in the introduction that the author, Lakshman Narasu, had battled not only against caste but also against British high-handedness. And in the same year he published his own book, *The Untouchables*, with its thesis that the Untouchables had been Buddhists, degraded and banished from the villages because they had held fast to their Buddhism when others returned to Brahmanism. As early as 1951 he urged his followers to convert to Buddhism, and that year he began writing the "Bible", *The Buddha and His Dhamma*, a secular, rational, social interpretation of Buddhism, which he felt was needed to bring Buddhism to the masses.

The conversion actually came twenty-one years after the initial announcement that the Scheduled Castes should leave Hinduism. It has been called a "political stunt" by many, but it makes little political sense except as a unifying force for the Mahars, who probably would have remained cohesive in any case, or as a corollary to the Republican Party then being formed, an effort to weld the Scheduled Castes, Scheduled Tribes and Backward Classes into a powerful political group. It is fairly certain that most of Dr. Ambedkar's political lieutenants were against conversion, thinking that it might result in the loss of hard-won rights to reserved seats and reserved government jobs and serve no positive political purpose. But Dr. Ambedkar's leadership of the Scheduled Castes Federation and of the Mahars was unchallengeable, and the day of conversion found the political leaders as well as the masses, mostly Mahars, dressed in white and assembled in Nagpur, ready to become Buddhists.

There seem to have been two main purposes for the conversion in the mind of Dr. Ambedkar: (1) the rejection of Hinduism and in consequence the status of untouchability; (2) the establishment of a religion which would serve as a bulwark against communism and to which all Indians could eventually turn. The first purpose is illustrated by the stories of his ill-treatment as an Untouchable which Dr. Ambedkar related during the *diksha* speech, and by the references to Hindu practices in six of the twenty-two oaths used during the ceremony. The oaths, in Marathi, are used at each conversion ceremony. They proclaim belief in the Buddhist way of life, but also such statements as: "I will not regard Brahma, Vishnu and Mahesh as Gods nor will I worship them"; and "I embrace today the Buddha Dhamma discarding the Hindu religion which is detrimental to the emancipation of human beings and which believes in inequality and regards human beings other than the Brahmans as low-born".[28]

The second purpose is illustrated by an address on "Buddha and Karl Marx" delivered by Ambedkar at the World Fellowship of Buddhists meetings at Kathmandu shortly after his conversion. In this address he regarded Buddhism as a substitute for communism: "If we can become one-tenth as enlightened as the Buddha was, we can bring about the same result by the methods of love, of justice and good will".[29] As early as 1950, Dr. Ambedkar wrote in the *Maha Bodhi Journal*: "Some of those who believe that only the acceptance of the gospel of Buddha can save the Hindus are filled with sorrow because they do not see much prospect of the return or revival of Buddhism. I do not share this pessimism".[30] He felt that not only all the suppressed and the downtrodden but also all those who felt there was something wrong with Hinduism would turn to Buddhism, much as the masses in the Roman Empire had turned to Christianity for "mental and moral relief". At the time of conversion, he told his people that they must be honorable, respectable, responsible Buddhists, and if they could accomplish this, "We will save our country".[31]

The first of these purposes seems, from the standpoint of those who converted, well served. The conversion was accompanied by the throwing out of the Hindu gods from the *maharwada*, the Mahar quarter of the village, sometimes quite unceremoniously and with obvious intent to defy the caste Hindus, in other places immersed in rivers or tanks or buried more courteously. The palanquin of the village goddess, usually kept by the Mahars, was given over to the keeping of the caste Hindus. Along with the break with Hindu religion went an intensification of the process of abandoning ritual duties or work traditionally given to the Mahar as part of his service to the village. The conversion encouraged the Mahars to make the last break with any village duty that defined their low position and this action, more than the actual conversion, brought some reprisals from caste Hindus. Even now, newspaper reports tell almost monthly of violence in some villages where Mahars (or Buddhists) refuse to do village sanitation work, refuse to carry petromax lamps on their heads for weddings, or refuse to do road work without cash payment in advance.

The conversion seems also to have been successful in removing from the Mahar himself any vestige of a feeling of inferiority. Buddhists often say that they experienced a sudden sense of release, a psychological freedom. A Brahman teacher who was at Siddharth College in 1956 reported that his Buddhist (formerly Mahar) students not only threw out their gods and goddesses but also were noticeably filled with a new spirit of self-confidence. A sociologist who spent several months in 1962 surveying the situation of Untouchables in villages stated: "The Buddhists are still in a gallant mood. They haven't cooled down yet".[32]

The conversion continues the "purifying process" that has been part of the movement all along, a "Pali-ization" rather than a "Sanskritization" of practices, to use the Buddhist equivalent for M.N. Srinivas's useful word for the emulation of high caste practices.[33] A part of the conversion ceremony, and of any Buddhist occasion, is the taking of the Panch Sila in Pali -- five moral affirmations which announce the intent to avoid doing harm to any living being, to refrain from taking what is not given, to refrain from sexual misconduct, to refrain from wrong speech, and to refrain from intoxicating liquor and drugs. The vow to refrain from alcohol is particularly important in the Indian context. The Buddhists themselves and some observers (not all) say that there has been a decrease in drinking among the converts. Community pressure is not infrequently used to bring an indulging Buddhist into line. Since the conversion there have also been increased efforts to secure education, particularly in the villages, this again an intensification of a process of awakening that can be traced back to 1890 in some areas.[34]

The social significance of Buddhism is that it has become the culmination of the process begun years before, denying the doctrine of untouchability, attempting to remove any low caste characteristics that separated the Untouchables from caste Hindus, and cutting any ritual or economic ties that reinforced the low position of the Untouchable. The adoption of the name "Buddhist" is not an escape for the Untouchable; it is now a synonym for Mahar or Untouchable. But it gives the Mahar a sense of freedom, of progress, of change from Hinduism without a lessening of his Indian-ness. While the Buddhist today claims Buddhist tradition and Buddhist history as his heritage, he rejects any implication that Buddhism is part of Hinduism.

The Buddhist is also caught in a situation in which he rejects the idea of his untouchability and yet does not reject the benefits conferred upon Untouchables by government, which he feels Dr. Ambedkar won for him and which are recompense for the ill-treatment of the past. Some Buddhists would prefer to cut all links, helpful and unhelpful, with their former status; most do not see why they should lose benefits which attempt to correct former injustice, economic and educational, because they themselves reject social injustice by conversion. Many have hopes that the problem will be resolved for their children, who will be "true Buddhists" without caste.

The Republican Party

Plans for the Republican Party, and the name indicates Ambedkar's hope for a broader base than the Scheduled Castes, were not completely formulated before his death. Correspondence with Rammanohar Lohia of the Socialist Party, and letters written to P.K. Atre and S.M. Joshi, leaders of the Maharashtra opposition to the Congress, just before his death (but not mailed), are evidence of a hope for some new sort of alliance. Although he gave permission in the autumn of 1956 for the Scheduled Castes Federation to join the Samyukta Maharashtra Samiti, a group of all opposition parties which successfully pressed for a Marathi-speaking Maharashtra as a separate state, he made no long-range plans for the operation of a new allied party. When the manifesto of the Republican Party appeared, after his death, it expressed interest in cooperating with the organizations of the Backward Classes and the Scheduled Tribes, which it considered lacking in political consciousness. It also expressed hope for the emergence of all-India party in opposition to the Congress, of which it could be a unit, but no more specific foundation for a new force was laid.

In Maharashtra, the Republican Party members are Buddhists;[35] Buddhists are republicans. The number of Congress Buddhists can be counted on the fingers of one hand. Ostensibly, the leaders of the Republican Party are the leaders of the Buddhist movement. But there is another group of religious leaders who are apart from politics. The writers of the dozens of pamphlets on Buddhist ceremonies and doctrine, the pilgrims to Bodh Gaya and Sarnath, the young men who learn enough Pali to lead *wandana* (prayer) and conduct wedding, naming and funeral ceremonies, the thinkers, the warriers, are usually apolitical. There is an effort to create a new religious culture that is unrelated to the political field.

Dr. Ambedkar's hope that the Republican Party would be a more broadly based political group than the Scheduled Castes Federation has not been fulfilled. In the 1962 election, the Republican Party captured 3 seats in Maharashtra legislative assembly (in contrast to19 during the Samyukta Maharashtra Samiti period), 8 seats in the Uttar Pradesh assembly (due to a Republican-Muslim alliance that was temporary), and 3 seats in the Lok Sabha from Uttar Pradesh. It lost the 5 state assembly seats it had won in 1957 in Punjab, and the Lok Sabha seats it had formerly held from Madras, Mysore, Gujarat and Maharashtra.

In Maharashtra, the same factor that accounts for the strength of the Party (it claims to be second in strength, after the Congress) imposes corresponding limitations. The solid bedrock support of the Mahars or Buddhists provides a powerful base, and in certain favorable situations (railroad towns, mill towns, areas where the Buddhists are 15 per cent of the population or more) a significant number of elected places in local governing bodies have gone to the Party. But the support is limited by the number of Buddhists, since the identification of the Party with the Buddhists defines its constituency. Historically, the Republican Party and its predecessor, the Scheduled Castes Federation, have been related in one way or another with almost every other political group on either the national or local scene -- an inevitable consequence of being too small to stand alone and too united to be of no consequence. What direction the Party will go now to gain electoral strength is unrelated to the fact of the Buddhist conversion.

Because of its program, the natural alliance for the Republicans would be a socialist party. But the Socialist Party-Scheduled Castes Federation alliance of the first general elections in 1952 was not an entirely happy experience. The Federation felt it had not received promised support. In the Bhandara by-election in 1954 the Socialist leader, Ashok Mehta, was elected to the general seat; his running mate, Dr. Ambedkar, lost the reserved seat. For their part, the Socialists felt that the Mahars could be counted on to vote for the Mahars, but not necessarily other party-endorsed candidates. Some Socialists were unhappy about the party's outspoken criticism of Gandhi and Nehru; some felt uncomfortable with the social status of the Federation's members. A recent invitation from the Samyukta Socialist Party to the Republican Party to join its alliance was turned down on the grounds that the Socialists were concerned only with economic matters and the problems of the Scheduled Castes and Buddhists demanded action on more than one front.

The Scheduled Castes Federation joined forces with the communists only once, in the Samyukta Maharashtra Samiti,[36] along with every other opposition party in Maharashtra. There is an assumption among some Buddhists and some political observers that the natural political direction of the Untouchables is toward communism. Windmiller and Overstreet note the small number of Untouchables (three) among the 139 delegates to the Communist Party of India Congress in 1943, and add: "It is interesting to note the number of Untouchables was so small, for this oppressed class would seem to be a rich source of recruits for this party".[37] Some Buddhists themselves say that except for Dr. Ambedkar, who was always critical of the Communist Party, and for the Buddhist conversion, the Mahars would be communists.

The theory that the Untouchable would inevitably be drawn to communism is not substantiated by the American counterpart of the Indian situation; few Negroes have found the Communist Party an acceptable home. In India, support for the Communists comes from Untouchable castes only in Andhra and Kerala. In other states they are by and large Congressite or Republican. The attraction of communism for the middle-class unemployed youth is not found to any significant degree among the Mahars or Buddhists. The educated Buddhist at the moment finds unemployment no problem because his numbers are not yet great enough to fill the reserved government jobs available to him, and hence he is not as subject to the frustration of unemployment or as open to radical theories. Added to this is the fact that all Ambedkar's influence was on the side of parliamentary democracy. He was never attracted to communism, either in his years abroad or in India. The Communist Party in Bombay was for him "a bunch of Brahman boys".[38]

For Ambedkar, and for many Republican leaders, theoretical communism is synonymous with economic justice. In his last speech on Buddhism, given in 1956, at Kathmandu, Dr. Ambedkar said that Buddhism contained all of communism's economic and egalitarian benefits without violent methods. If the push for education produces Buddhists ready for white-collar jobs in such numbers that reservations no longer provide them, or if the communists find a way to organize the vast depressed army of agricultural laborers, the Buddhists may become more interested, or the Republican Party itself may find reason for common cause.

The most effective political alliance of the Buddhists today [1966] is with the Muslims in Uttar Pradesh. Three of the eight Republican Party MLAs and one of the three MPs are Muslims. Although that grouping has brought election results, it is limited to U.P. There is some cooperation and undertaking between Buddhists and Muslims in daily life. The Buddhists do not feel in economic or social competition with the Muslims, do not feel that the Muslims regard them as Untouchables. In cities and small towns, the Muslim localities often neighbor those of the Buddhists. Buddhist functions may be held in Muslim institutions more easily than in caste Hindu buildings. Dr. Ambedkar understood the mind of the Muslim minority well enough to produce the prophetic *Thoughts on Pakistan* in 1940, a book which delineated all the reasons why the Muslims were part of India and should not want a separate state but declared that the mental attitude of nationhood was stronger than race, language or habits, and that therefore Pakistan was inevitable. However, many Buddhists today do not differ from the normal caste Hindu feeling about Pakistan or Kashmir, and many hold the same stereotype of the Muslim as a militant person whose first loyalty is outside India. It does not seem likely that localized political cooperation in some parts of U.P. and in a few Maharashtrian cities will spread.

Temporary alliances with conservative parties such as the Jana Sangh in local elections are not unknown, but the primarily high caste constituency and conservative economic platform of the Jana Sangh, plus Dr. Ambedkar's warning against right-wing parties, make extensive cooperation unlikely. Thirty years of anti-Congress teaching would make it difficult for the Republican Party to cooperate closely with the Congress, although there have been a few arrangements made at high levels for voting support. Rumors persist that this, or that, leader, or indeed the whole party, will go over to the Congress. But at this time, any leader transferring his allegiance from the Republican Party to the Congress loses the support of his own people in gaining a reserved seat or a cabinet post.

In addition to the problem of limited constituency and unsatisfactory alliances, the Republican Party is troubled by a split which occurred in 1959 ostensibly over the issue of communism (continued alliance with the Samiti, in which the Communist Party was very active), but more probably over the question of leadership. Republicans in Maharashtra are still divided into two hostile groups, although the power of the new faction is waning. A recent split in Bombay adds a third faction in that area. There is in spite of the general unit and cohesion of the Buddhists, much quarreling over leadership and much local factionalism. Both the split and the leadership rivalry reflect the fact that the party has had no one clear leader since the death of Dr. Ambedkar; his long-time associate, B.K. (Dadasaheb) Gaikwad of Nasik, comes the nearest and commands general respect, but not total obedience. A number of Buddhists remark on the political situation with considerable bitterness: "Each man is a little Ambedkar". "It is like brothers quarreling over their inheritance".

Two other factors affect the leadership of the party. One is the almost irresistible temptation to a man from a low economic status to make secure his new-found position at the expense of a larger ideal, an affliction that hampered the effectiveness of the Justice Party at an earlier date in South India. The other is in the fact that the way up for a Buddhist or a Scheduled Caste man is through government service. Position in private industry, teaching posts in secondary school or college, or a small business of his own, are either very difficult for the Buddhist to secure or of less economic advantage than a government job. This governmental path upward effectively removes most of the educated, concerned Buddhists from direct political activity.

One effect of both the Buddhist conversion and the work of the Republican Party has been to link those who have progressed economically and socially with those still backward, thus limiting the tendency of those in the upper strata to cut themselves off from their past and to form a new urban caste, neither high nor Untouchable.[39] Although many Mahars do "pass", the sense of identity and pride in the community is still strong, giving the whole caste a feeling of moving upward as individuals within the group improve their position or gain recognition for worth.

Leader, Religion, Political Party

The figure of Dr. Ambedkar, dominating both Buddhism and the Republican Party, is the key to the direction of both movements. The respect accorded him borders on devotion, both for village Buddhists and for the educated. Not only is there a photograph or painting of Dr. Ambedkar in almost every home and at every meeting, both religious and political, but his very name has become a symbol. The Indian nationalist cry, *Jai Hind*, has been transformed into *Jai Bhim* (for *Bhimrao* Ramji Ambedkar), with *Jai Buddh* added at religious occasions. On Buddhist invitations the traditional Hindu salutation *Saprem Namaskar* becomes *Saprem Jai Bhim*. Occasionally in political meetings the term *Bhim Raj* will be used to replace the Hindu term for the ideal government, *Ram Raj*. A great body of songs has grown up with Ambedkar's life and teachings as their theme, and singing parties in many areas celebrate the lives of Ambedkar and Lord Buddha.

The devotion to Dr. Ambedkar would seem to assume the nature of a cult, except that its entire direction is to lead the Buddhist into the westernized, educated, secular world. The photographs of Dr. Ambedkar more often than not show him in a blue pinstripe business suit surrounded by books, and even those pictures which portray him as a Boddhisatva in a yellow robe look somehow very western. Often pictures showing him with the late President Rajendra Prasad or the late Prime Minister Jawaharlal Nehru are prized, as if to say: "We too share in the leadership of our country". The recent Republican Party satyagraha included, along with demands for land, slum clearance, justice to the Untouchable and implementation of the Minimum Wages Act, a demand that a portrait of Dr. B.R. Ambedkar, "The Father of the Indian Constitution", be placed in the central hall of Parliament. [In 1989, Ambedkar's portrait was unveiled in the central hall of Parliament House.] In his delineation of the values established by the advanced castes and adopted by low castes in the hope of raising their status, Richard Lambert adds a new idea to the usual list of cleanliness, literacy, economic or political power -- the value or sharing in and contributing to the mainstream of cultural accomplishment.[40] It is largely through Dr. Ambedkar as a national figure that the Buddhists claim this achievement.

The figure of Dr. Ambedkar and what he stands for identifies the nature of both the Buddhist movement and the Republican Party: A push upward, independent of caste Hindu groups, towards modern, democratic and often material values, a movement that rejects traditional Hinduism but clings tightly to its Indian-ness. Those groups which have joined the movement have a sense of self-respect, a feeling of unity, an ambition for higher social and economic status, and a political awareness which may yet aid significantly in the solution of India's age-old problem of untouchability.

Notes

1. Census of India, Paper No. 1 of 1963, 1963 Census -- Religion (New Delhi, 1963). The figures are minimal because some Scheduled Caste members who have participated in a conversion ceremony still list themselves as Hindus in order to claim government benefits reserved for Scheduled Castes. The Buddhists themselves claim that the census figures are not

accurate because census takers prefer to minimize the extent of the conversion. The figures in the first and second paragraphs are all from this census paper.

2. A note on nomenclature: four terms are used to describe the same group: Untouchable, Depressed Class, Scheduled Caste, Harijan. The word Untouchable is used freely among the Untouchables themselves. Those Untouchables who are influenced by Gandhi's organization, the Harijan Seva Sangh, and most caste Hindus use the term Harijan (people of God). Its use by an Untouchable indicates that he is of the Congress, not one of Dr. Ambedkar's followers. Depressed Class was the term used widely until Scheduled Castes came into currency in 1935, according to the schedule prepared under the Government of India Act. The term neo-Buddhists, generally used for the converts, is unacceptable to them. They call themselves, simply, Buddhists.

3. Madras has some history of lingering Buddhist influence. N. Shivraj, president of the Scheduled Castes Federation and later the Republican Party, called himself a Buddhist, as did his father. Nevertheless, there has been no major conversion movement to Buddhism in the Madras area.

4. The Independent Labour Party, founded by Dr. Ambedkar in 1936, became the Scheduled Castes Federation in 1942, and that group in turn took the name, the Republican Party, in 1957. The leadership and the program, allowing for time change and loss of caste Hindu supporters of Dr. Ambedkar in Bombay when the party took on a direct Scheduled Caste relationship in 1942, has remained much the same.

5. Scheduled Caste privileges include some economic aid in housing and small industry, scholarships at both state and central government level at all stages of education, reservation of 12½ per cent of all posts in government service. For a discussion of the effect of conversion on Scheduled Caste privileges see Donald E. Smith, *India as a Secular State* (Princeton: Princeton University Press, 1963), pp. 322-26.

6. Gopal Baba Walangkar also made some effort to deny Brahman superiority. He formed a group of Mahar *joshis* to perform the astrological services that normally were the prerogative of the Brahman *joshi*. The fixing of the proper astrological time for ceremonies was the only service generally performed for the Mahar by the Brahman priest. It is said that Dr. Ambedkar greatly admired Walangkar for his independent spirit.

7. Kisan Fagoji Bansode is the only one of the group without a British connection. Although attracted to Ambedkar, he remained attached to Hinduism and was critical of the announcement of conversion in 1935.

8. The full document is quoted in H.N. Navalkar, *The Life of Shivram Janba Kamble and Brief History of the Poona Parvati Satyagraha* (Pune: S.J. Kamble, 1930), pp. 142-57.

9. G.A. Gawai of Amravati, who reported to the committee from the Central Provinces and Berar.

10. *Evidence taken before the Reforms Committee (Franchise)*, Vol. 2 (Calcutta: Government of India, 1919), pp. 729-39.

11. Cangdeo Bhavanrao Khairmode, *Dr. Bhimrao Ramji Ambedkar*, Vol. 1 (Bombay: Yeshwantrao Ambedkar, 1952). p. 266 (in Marathi). This sentence, and other translations from the Marathi, were made with the help of D.R. Maheshkar and Mrs. Y.B. Damle.

12. A typed copy of the letter dated 3 March 1934, in English, is in the Khairmode files at the University of Bombay Library.

13. *Times of India*, 27 April 1942, reporting Dr. Ambedkar's speech on the occasion of his fiftieth birthday.

14. *Report of Depressed Class Conferences, Nagpur Sessions* (Nagpur: G.T. Meshram, 1942), pp. 28-9.

15. *Indian Statutory Commission*, Vol. 16, "Selections from Memoranda and Oral Evidence by Non-officials (Part I) (London, 1930), p. 54.

16. "Supplementary Memorandum on the Claims of the Depressed Classes for Special Representation, submitted to the Round Table Conference by Dr. Bhimrao R.   Ambedkar and Rao Bahadur R. Srinivasan," 4 November 1931. Quoted in B.R. Ambedkar, *What Congress and Gandhi have Done to the Untouchables* (Bombay: Thacker & Co., Ltd., 1946), pp. 315-17.

17. Quoted in *ibid.*, p. 71.

18. *The Epic Fast* is the title of Pyarelal's book (Ahmedabad: Navjivan, 1932) describing Gandhi's 1932 fast in Yeravda Jail against the principle of separate electorates.

19. Gandhi's letter to Sir S. Hoare, 11 March 1932, quoted in *ibid.*, pp. 99-103.

20. Dhananjay Keer, *Dr. Ambedkar, Life and Mission* (Bombay: Popular Prakashan, second ed., 1962), pp. 42-3.

21. Shankarro Kharat, *Asprishyanca Muktisangram* (The Battle of the Untouchables for Freedom) (Pune: Shri Joshi and M.D. Lokhande, n.d.), in Marathi, p. 204.

22. *Times of India*, 24 July 1936, quoted in Keer, *op.cit.*: 278.

23. *Jai Bheem*, 25 December 1946, Madras. Typed copy in the files of Nanak Chand Rattu, New Delhi. The interview, originally in the *Globe*, was with the Rev. Gordon Livingston.

24. *Constitution of the All-India Scheduled Castes Federation*, printed in *Report of Depressed Class Conferences* (Nagpur: G.T. Meshram, 1942).

25. Keer, *op.cit.*, 477.

26. Dr. Ambedkar did make such a proposal to the drafting committee, but dropped it when it received little support. G.A. Austin, "Tryst With Destiny: The Indian Constituent Assembly and the Framing of the Indian Constitution", D.Phil. thesis, Oxford University. I am grateful to Mr. Austin for some of my ideas about Dr. Ambedkar and the Constitution, although he is not responsible for my interpretation. [See Granville Austin, *The Indian Constitution: Cornerstone of a Nation* (Bombay: Oxford University Press, 1972).]

27. Principal M.P. Mangudkar of Shri Shahu Mandir Mahavidyalaya, Pune, reports seeing these letters among the Shinde papers. Principal Mangudkar's discussion of Dr. Ambedkar's pragmatic philosophy has been of great help to me.

28. The Twenty-two Oaths are printed in English in a leaflet entitled *Dhamma Deeksha*, published by the Buddhist Society of India, Ambedkar Bhavan, New Delhi.

29. The speech, given on 20 November, 1956, at the fourth conference of the World Fellowship of Buddhists at Kathmandu, has been published in a pamphlet, *Buddha and Karl Marx* (Nagpur: M.D. Panchbhai).

30. *The Maha Bodhi*, Vol. 58, April-May 1950.

31. From the Marathi speech of Dr. Ambedkar on October 1956 in Nagpur, as published in *Prabuddh Bharat*, 27 October 1956.

32. Dr. M.G. Kulkarni of the Gokhale Institute of Politics and Economics, Pune, has made available to me his reports on surveys of villages in Buldana and Nasik districts in 1962. I have quoted only his personal remark, but his detailed knowledge of the village situation has added to my understanding of present conditions.

33. The term was first used by Dr. Srinivas in *Religion and Society Among the Coorgs of South India* (Oxford: Oxford University Press, 1952), p. 30, and is detailed in "A Note of Sanskritization and Westernization", first published in the *Journal of Asian Studies* and now reprinted in *Caste in Modern India* (Bombay: Asia Publishing House, 1962).

34. Since the Buddhists are no longer counted as Scheduled Castes, no figures on their literacy are available. *The Census of India*, 1961, Vol. 10, Maharashtra, Part V-A, "Scheduled Castes and Scheduled Tribes in Maharashtra -- Tables", (Delhi: 1964), does give figures on literacy and education for those who registered themselves Mahars. The Mahar literacy rate in 1961 was 15.69 per cent, compared to 29.82 per cent as a general figure for Maharashtra, and was considerably lower than that for the Chambhars, another Scheduled Caste group primarily found in cities. However, among those Scheduled Caste individuals who have matriculated or gone on for higher education, the Mahars predominate. It is a general belief in Maharashtra that the Mahars' (and Buddhists') eagerness for education surpasses that of all but the highest castes.

35. The Buddhist who wishes to contest a reserved seat must register himself as a Mahar. A recent Supreme Court decision deprived D.P. Meshram of Nagpur of his seat in the Maharashtra legislative assembly on the grounds that his activities in the Buddhist religion proved him a Buddhist, and as such not eligible for the reserved seat. The decision was generally approved by Buddhists, since it underwrote their conviction that they are no longer Hindus. The Republican Party's inability to win a majority of the reserved seats from Congress candidates, in any case, has caused them to ask for non-renewal of reservations on the state and national level in legislative bodies.

36. The Communists' hope that perhaps the Samiti had "laid the basis of healing the great split between the democratic movement and the Untouchable masses, led by the late Dr. Ambedkar", has remained unfulfilled. Quoted from B.T. Ranadive, "Maharashtra Election Review", *New Age*, July 1957, p. 15, in Selig Harrison, *India, The Most Dangerous Decades* (Madras: Oxford University Press), pp. 192-93.

37. Gene D. Overstreet and Marshall Windmiller, *Communism in India* (Barkeley: University of California Press, 1959), p. 358. The recent dismal record of the Communists in Maharashtra is perhaps the major factor behind Untouchable disinterest.

38. From an interview with Dr. Ambedkar quoted in Harrison, *op.cit.*, p. 191.

39. Harold R. Issacs has described this situation in terms of the educated ex-Untouchables who "do not quite get *nowwhere*, but neither do they get *somewhere*". See India's *Ex-Untouchables* (New York: John Day Co., 1965).

40. R.D. Lambert, "Untouchability as a Social Problem: Theory and Research", *Sociological Bulletin*, Vol. 7, No. 1, March 1958, Bombay.

See the Addendum at the end of Section II for recent material.

Gandhi and Ambedkar:
A Study in Leadership*

The Constituent Assembly of independent India passed a provision legally abolishing untouchability on 29 November 1948, nine months after the death of Mahatma Gandhi. As the measure was approved, the house resounded with cries of *Mahatma Gandhi Ki Jai*—victory to Mahatma Gandhi—a tribute to Gandhi's thirty-year effort to remove the practice of untouchability from Indian society. Present at that session of the Constituent Assembly as chairman of the drafting committee for the constitution was Dr. B.R. Ambedkar, an Untouchable. Three years before, he had ended his book *What Congress and Gandhi Have Done to the Untouchables* with the bitter words, "The Untouchables . . . have ground to say: 'Good God! Is this man Gandhi our Saviour?'"

The irony of the moment was lost on those present—a legalistic measure was taken in the name of Gandhi who had no use for legal means, coupled with the lack of recognition for Ambedkar, the Untouchable who had drafted the measure and who had bitterly fought Gandhi to secure legalistic solutions to the problem of untouchability. The amalgamation of the two approaches to the problem in that moment, however, does symbolize India's continuing attempt to synthesize the ways of Gandhi and Ambedkar in efforts to remove the stigma of untouchability from democratic national life.

Both Mohandas K. Gandhi and Bhimrao Ramji Ambedkar are known, to different groups, as the "saviour of the Untouchables". Gandhi was a caste Hindu, the "Father of Independence" who is said to have spoken and written more on untouchability than on any other subject. Gandhi publicly put the abolition of untouchability, along with Hindu-Muslim unity, as the essential prerequisite for India's true independence. He also made popular the term "Harijan" (children of God) for the Untouchables. Ambedkar was the most highly educated Untouchable in India, recognized by many as the Untouchables' chief spokesman,

*First published in J. Michael Mahar ed., *The Untouchables in Contemporary India* (Tucson: University of Arizon Press, 1972), reprinted by Triratna Grantha Mala, Pune, 1983.

the founder of a political party for Untouchables, and the moving spirit behind organizations, schools, and colleges established for their uplift. One of Ambedkar's final acts was the initiation of a Buddhist conversion movement that ultimately attracted more than 3 million Untouchable adherents. On the day after Ambedkar's death, Nehru described him as "a symbol of the revolt against all the oppressive features of Hindu society" (*New York Times*, 6 December 1956).

Despite their common concern, Ambedkar and Gandhi were often at odds in their programs for the abolition of untouchability. In 1932 Gandhi thwarted Ambedkar's attempt to gain political concessions from the British, concessions that Ambedkar believed to be essential for the Untouchables' progress. Ambedkar retaliated by criticizing Gandhi more harshly than he did the orthodox Hindus who upheld untouchability as a religious essential. The conflict between these leaders is examined below in terms of their ideological differences and the different solutions which they advocated for the resolution of one of India's major social problems.

Gandhi may be described as a dominant group leader working for a national goal who was concerned, both from a moral standpoint and from a realization of the need for unity, about injustices to a low status group within the nation. Ambedkar's correlative role was that of the militant leader of a politically conscious segment of the same depressed group. Seen in this light, the conflict between these two men has some parallels with certain aspects of the Black Power movement versus "White Liberals" in America of the 1960s.

The Indian situation, however, included several unique elements in that the leadership of the majority and minority groups represented, in simplistic terms, idealistic Hindu traditionalism and Western-influenced modernism. The Indian scene was also marked by a society-wide hierarchical system of social groups justified by religion; by the presence of other vocal minorities, especially that of the Muslims; and by the administrative power of still another group, the British government in India.

This study is concerned with the interaction of Gandhiji and Ambedkar in the Indian Milieu, more specifically with Ambedkar's standpoint on Gandhi's policies and actions. Although a view from Ambedkar's standpoint of Gandhi's efforts to eradicate untouchability distorts the Mahatma's role in Indian history, this perspective, taken together with the abundance of literature on Gandhi, reveals a lesser known aspect of the Untouchables' role in contemporary India.

Before discussing Gandhi's actions and Ambedkar's reactions to them, it would be well to look at the background and ideology of each of them. Gandhi's statements on untouchability have been collected in several small volumes: *Caste Must Go; All are Equal in the Eyes of God; None High: None Low; The Bleeding Wound!; My Soul's Agony; My Varnashrama Dharma; The Removal of Untouchability*, and others, which draw chiefly from his two newspapers, *Young India* and *Harijan*. Descriptions of his work, which sometimes included private asides as well as public pronouncements, have been written by his close associates about the Vaikam Satyagraha,[1] his experiences at the Round Table Conference in London,[2] his Communal Award fast[3] and the 1930s anti-untouchability campaigns.[4] Material on Gandhi has been taken from these works and the two other sympathetic but frank accounts of Tendulkar,[5] and Desai.[6]

Ambedkar's underlying beliefs and aims have been derived from his writings on caste,[7] his testimony to various British commissions, biographies in English[8] and Marathi,[9] and my own study of his life.

Mohandas Karamchand Gandhi (1869-1948)

At the beginning of his autobiography Gandhi identifies his caste as Bania (merchant) and states that for three generations his forefathers had not practiced the caste occupation, but had served as prime ministers in several princely states of the Kathiawad peninsula (now Gujarat). This was, and is, an essentially conservative region in its adherence to traditional patterns of social relations. Hindu and Jain merchant groups constitute an influential segment of the population. Vaishya, or Bania, castes are third in the traditional four-fold division of Hindu society, included with Brahman and Kshatriya among the twice-born. However, in Gujarat, probably more than in any other part of India, Banias are without peer in wealth, influence and piety. They tend toward orthodoxy. Gandhi's *jati*, the Modh Banias, outcasted him in 1888 upon hearing of his proposed trip to London for higher studies, and evidently never rescinded the proscription.

Gandhi's autobiography, which covers his life up to 1921, when he was fifty-two, contains only a few references to Untouchables or untouchability. The most striking reference is the story of his insistence on the admission of an Untouchable family to the *ashram* he had established near Ahmedabad in 1915. At the time of his assumption of leadership of the Indian National Congress in 1920, Gandhi made what seemed to be his first strong public statement on untouchability. They reflect his dual role as Mahatama and politician in Indian life, already apparent at that time. As politician, Gandhi said: "Swaraj is as unattainable without the removal of the sin of untouchability as it is without Hindu-Muslim unity" (*Young India*, 29 December 1920). As Mahatma Gandhi said: "I do not want to be reborn. But if I have to be reborn, I should be born an Untouchable...." (*Young India*, 27 April 1921). As both Mahatma and politician, Gandhi sought to weave the divergent interests in India into a unified opposition to the British, at the same time trying to pursue a course of reform without rending the social fabric of Indian society. In Dalton's words, "Indian society saw Gandhi, and Gandhi regarded himself, as occupying the peculiar position of a figure above the discord around him, and uniquely capable of harmonizing it".[10]

Gandhi inherited the Congress position on untouchability first recorded in a resolution in 1917 which urged "upon the people of India the necessity, justice, and righteousness of removing all disabilities imposed upon the Depressed Classes".[11] The Congress resolution seems to have been made in response to a meeting of the Depressed Classes in Bombay earlier in 1917 which asked for such a resolution, in almost the same wording, in exchange for support of the 1916 Congress-Muslim League constitutional scheme.[12] Gandhi's contribution to the position was to personalize it. Volunteers for the Non-cooperation Campaign in 1921 signed a pledge which placed responsibility on the individual: "As a Hindu I believe in the justice and necessity of removing the evil of untouchability and shall on all possible occasions seek personal contact with and endeavor to render service to the submerged classes".[13] This emphasis on the caste Hindu's obligations to the Untouchables remained a major tenet of Gandhi's teaching.

Gandhi's statements on the evil of untouchability were unequivocal from the first, although his views regarding other caste-based practices changed and grew less orthodox with the years. In 1920 he voiced moderate opposition to social intercourse between castes which some reformers advocated: "Interdrinking, interdining, intermarrying . . . are not essential for the promotion of the spirit of democracy" (*Young India*, 8 December 1920). Twenty-six years later, he said, "If I had my way I would persuade all caste Hindu girls coming under my influence to select Harijan husbands" (*Harijan*, 7 July 1946). Underlying Gandhi's change in attitude toward social practices was an unchanging belief in *varnashramadharma*, the divinely ordained division of society into four groups defined according to duty: Brahman, Kshatriya, Vaishya, Shudra. Although Gandhi castigated the contemporary Indian caste system with its superior and inferior divisions, he held to the end a belief in the traditional ordering of society for the preservation of harmony and the growth of the soul, and with it, traditional duties. "The Law of Varna prescribes that a person should, for his living, follow the lawful occupation of his forefathers", but with the understanding that all occupations are equally honorable: "A scavenger has the same status as a Brahmin"(*Young India,* 17 November 1927).

According to Gandhi, untouchability had no part in this divine ordering— the treatment of castes below the Shudra level as unclean was not only inhuman, but harmful to Hinduism. Gandhi described it at various times as a curse, an excrescence on Hinduism, a poison, a snake, a canker, a hydra-headed monster, a great blot, a device of Satan, a hideous untruth, Dyerism and O'Dwyerism, and the bar sinister. An Untouchable, wrote Gandhi, "should be regarded as a *Shudra* because there is no warrant for belief in a fifth caste" (*Young India,* 23 April 1925). While Shudras were created to serve the other three castes, their work was honorable. All varnas possess equality of status, but not equality of opportunity. "One born a scavenger must earn his livelihood by being a scavenger, and then do whatever else he likes. For a scavenger is as worthy of his hire as a lawyer or your President. That, according to me, is Hinduism" (*Harijan,* 6 March 1937).

Other early reformers, including Vivekananda and Dayanand Saraswati, espoused a similar conception of the ideal society as one composed of equal, harmoniously integrated Varnas. The belief that untouchability was a perversion of true Hinduism, and a view of the Untouchable as one deserving of Shudra status, was acceptable even to such an orthodox Hindu leader as B.G. Tilak. Shortly before Gandhi's assumption of leadership in the Congress, Tilak wrote, "It is a sin against God to say that a person is untouchable, who is not so to God Himself. ... Hinduism absorbed the Shudras, can it not also absorb the untouchables?"[14]

With his gift for symbolism, Gandhi selected the Bhangi, a scavenger caste of North India, to represent the problem of untouchability. Gandhi's abhorrence of untouchability, and his association of such practices with the sweeper caste, appear rooted in childhood experience. Although not mentioned in his autobiography, Gandhi's reactions to his family's sweeper at the age of twelve are recorded in an article that he wrote in *Young India,* 27 April 1921.

A Scavenger named Uka, an "untouchable", used to attend our house for cleaning latrines. Often I would ask my mother why it was wrong to touch him. If I accidentally touched Uka, I was asked to perform ablutions, and though I naturally obeyed, it was not without smilingly protesting that it should be so. I was a very dutiful and obedient child, and so far as it was consistent with respect for parents, I often had tussles with them on this matter. I told my mother that she was entirely wrong in considering contact with Uka as sinful.

Uka remained the symbol for Untouchables in Gandhi's mind. Scavenging and the Bhangi figure prominently in many of Gandhi's pronouncements and actions. He himself cleared a dirty latrine at the Calcutta Congress of 1901 and records it in his autobiography. He often used the metaphor of the mother's cleansing work for her child as a counterpart to the Bhangi's work for society. Sanitation work at Gandhi's ashrams was done by all members as a means for demonstrating the honorable nature of these essential duties. In later years Gandhi sometimes stayed in suitably cleaned Bhangi colonies. During the last days of his life, Gandhi even declared: "I would rejoice to think that we had a sweeper girl of a stout heart, incorruptible and of crystal purity to be our first President . . . assisted in the discharge of her duties by a person like Pandit Nehru".[15]

Although Gandhi was not the first to cry out against untouchability, he was the most prominent caste Hindu to proclaim that it was harmful to Hinduism, to make its removal a personal responsibility of the caste Hindu, to keep it before the public eye with passionate oratory and vivid imagery, and to found an organization for service to Untouchables. Perhaps as important as his ideology and his pronouncements was his personal example, from the beginning, of touching the Untouchable.

Bhimrao Ramji Ambedkar (1891-1956)

Ambedkar came from Western India, as did Gandhi, and was a London-trained barrister, as was Gandhi, but his caste, social background, and intellectual environment were very different. He was a Mahar, the largest Untouchable caste in the area now called Maharashtra, where this group constitutes about 10 per cent of the population. The Mahars were, in British administrative parlance, "inferior village servants", whose traditional duties involved the maintenance of streets, walls and cremation grounds, carrying messages, hauling away dead cattle, and similar menial and polluting tasks. However, the Mahars were not responsible for the cleaning of latrines or the removal of night soil. This work was and is done by Bhangis from North India and by Gujarati Untouchable migrants. During the nineteenth and early twentieth centuries, a substantial number of Mahars removed themselves from their traditional village servant role. The establishment of British rule in Bombay Presidency provided Mahars with the opportunity for service in the army, employment in cotton mills, ammunition factories, railroads, dockyards, construction work, and as servants in British homes. The 1921 Census records that only 13.5 per cent of the Mahar working force of nearly 300,000 were employed in their traditional occupation even though most Mahars maintained strong ties with their ancestral village.

The emergence of Mahar leaders and a new spirit of militancy in the nineteenth century was due in large measure to the influence of education acquired in the army[16] and in domestic service. In the twentieth century, leaders also emerged from the ranks of primary school teachers. Early efforts to legitimize Mahar claims to higher status were based on the assertion that their ancestors were of the Kshatriya varna (warrior class), a claim not uncommon among Untouchables elsewhere in India. This claim was advanced in petitions submitted to the British in the 1890s to protest the closing of Mahar enlistment in the army. Although army recruitment of Mahars was stopped at about the time of Ambedkar's birth in 1891, his father and grandfather served in the army, and his early education and environment were those of a child in army cantonment schools and pensioned soldiers' colonies. Despite this background, Ambedkar differed from previous Mahar leaders in that he never claimed high caste status for Untouchables, since such claims implied an acceptance of upper caste superiority, nor did he invoke another common claim--that Untouchables were pre-Aryan, the original settlers of the land. While Untouchables in Madras and the Punjab were to base their demands for separate political status on a claim to pre-Aryan origin, Ambedkar argued that the Untouchables' position in Indian society was of social, not racial, origin and therefore subject to change.

Ambedkar's views as to the origin of untouchability are presented in The Untouchables published in 1948, late in his political career. According to the account presented here, untouchability originated in the practices of separation and denigration imposed on those who remained Buddhists during an earlier period of renascent Hinduism. Despite the repressive role attributed to Hindus, Ambedkar's attitude toward Hinduism remained ambivalent for much of his life. In the early 1920s he participated in efforts at "Sanskritization" in which Untouchables imitated high caste religious ritual. But he soon found that the performance of Vedic style weddings, the donning of the sacred thread, and similar efforts to emulate upper caste ritual practice had little effect on the attitudes of others. Such innovations were dropped in the 1930s. However, from 1927 to 1935 Ambedkar helped organize campaigns to force the opening of Hindu temples to Untouchables. This also proved to be ineffective and in 1935 Ambedkar decided to reject all claims to Hinduism and to convert to another religion. At about this time, he presented in *The Annihilation of Caste* a list of reforms for Hinduism that appear naive and legalistic, based on abstractions rather than possibilities. The cardinal reforms listed were: there should be one standard book of the Hindu religion, acceptable to all Hindus; priests should receive their office not by heredity but by state examination; priests should be limited in number by law and should be subject to disciplinary action by the state.[17] Ambedkar's final resolution of the Untouchables' religious dilemma was adopted in 1956 when he converted to Buddhism in an attempt to link the Untouchables to the greatness of India's past while denying the contemporary concept of caste. This solution was in keeping with Ambedkar's pride in India's culture, a theme that appears intermittently throughout his writings, and his admiration of such religious reformers as the Buddha, Kabir, and Mahatma Phule.

Although Ambedkar experienced discrimination and humiliation during his youth, the Maharashtrian atmosphere of reform allowed him exceptional opportunities for education and later for leadership. As a bright Untouchable boy, and later as an educated, militant Untouchable leader, he was aided by caste Hindu reformers. The Gaikwad of Baroda, whose financial contributions to reformers and educators in Bombay Presidency were of considerable consequence, gave Ambedkar a stipend during his college days as part of the Baroda policy of educating Untouchables. Later the Gaikwad helped Ambedkar to go abroad for further education, and he obtained an M.A. and Ph.D. from Columbia University in New York, a D.Sc. from London University, and entrance to the Bar from Grey's Inn, London. Ambedkar returned to Bombay in 1923 to begin his organizational work among Untouchables, and soon came into close association with caste Hindus who encouraged his leadership. Many of his closest associates were high caste Hindus and they formed his intellectual circle at a time when there was no other Mahar who shared his intellectual interests. Caste Hindus also worked on the staff of Ambedkar's newspapers and labor unions, formed an inter-dining group of which he was president, taught in his educational establishments, and in 1936 they helped form his first political party, the Independent Labour Party. It was a Brahman, G.N. Sahasrabudhe, who backed Ambedkar in one of his most dramatic rejections of Hindu orthodoxy, the burning of the ancient law book, *Manusmriti*, in 1927 as a protest against traditional caste restrictions.

Ambedkar, therefore, did not find Gandhi's condemnation of untouchability radical; he was in close touch with reformers who not only condemned untouchability, but the Varna concept of caste as well, and who accepted his leadership in determining solutions to the problem. Not only as a highly educated Untouchable to whom pity was anathema, but also as a Maharashtrian reformer, Ambedkar found Gandhi's general ideology unappealing. Ram Joshi's later evaluation of the Maharashtrian urban intelligentsia's attitude toward Gandhian reform describes the milieu in which Ambedkar worked:

> They disdained Gandhi's traditional outlook and modes of behavi-our . . . . They considered his philosophy outdated and rejected his programme, which was based primarily on a concern for the rural masses . . . . In any case, they had no interest in a . . . drab reform programme which could neither stimulate their intellect nor excite them to revolutionary action.[18]

Ambedkar's programs were intended to integrate the Untouchable into Indian society in modern, not traditional ways, and on as high a level as possible. This goal stood in marked contrast to Gandhi's "Ideal Bhangi" (*Harijan*, 23 November 1936) who would continue to do sanitation work even though his status would equal that of a Brahman. Ambedkar's ideal for the depressed was "to raise their educational standard so that they may know their own conditions, have aspirations to rise to the level of the highest Hindu and be in a position to use political power as a means to that end".[19] Both reformers had a vision of equality, but for Ambedkar, equality meant not equal status of the *Varnas*, but equal social, political, and economic opportunity for all. Ambedkar planned his programs to bring the Untouchable from a state of "de-humanization" and "slavery" into one of equality through the use of modern methods based on education and the exercise of legal and political rights. At the same time, Ambedkar's modernizing ideology was tempered in practice by a clear perception of the tenacity of caste and tradition. He sought to awaken in the Untouchables an awareness of their debased condition and the common interests that would promote the unity needed for the development of effective organizations and mass action. For such reasons, Ambedkar advocated a separatist policy accentuating caste distinctions as an initial stage in creating a society in which identities would be unimportant.

Ambedkar's commitment to education as a major means for Untouchable advancement led him to initiate in the 1920s a program for the creation of hostels for Untouchable students. This effort resulted in the development of a system of colleges organized by the People's Education Society, founded by Ambedkar in 1945. While Ambedkar exhorted numerous conferences of Untouchables to expand their educational opportunities at every level, much of his own effort was aimed at producing highly educated men, capable of raising the image of the Untouchable through their ability to function at the highest level of Indian urban society. He also advocated the abandonment of customs and practices associated with the stereotype of the Untouchable, including the consumption of alcohol and carrion beef. Ambedkar's pronouncements on the need to live clean and moral lives sound very much like Gandhi's. However, Ambedkar's vision of the Untouchable's future role went far beyond that of Gandhi, or indeed that of any other Untouchable leader.

Ambedkar's political policies were developed in the light of India's democratizing political reforms. During his lifetime Ambedkar saw the representation of Untouchables in the Bombay provincial Legislative Council grow from one appointed member (granted in 1921 by the Montagu-Chelmsford reforms) to full-fledged elected representation based on a system of reserved seats. Achievements of this kind, founded on "protective discrimination" and western forms of government, supported Ambedkar's contention that political power must be assured to the Untouchable minority even if separatism was fostered by the granting of such power. This view, coupled with Ambedkar's firm belief in the power of representative political bodies to correct social and economic injustice, underlies many of the issues that arose between Ambedkar and Gandhi. Ambedkar's adaptation of western concepts to the Indian scene is also reflected in the terms he used to justify Untouchable political rights: democracy, fraternity, and liberty. In his Marathi speeches, Ambedkar conveyed the implication of these concepts in a single word, *manuski*, that was readily understood by the most illiterate Mahar villager. Although *manuski's* literal meaning is "human-ness", it serves to evoke feelings of self-respect and human attitudes towards one's fellow men.

In 1946, Gandhi said, ''I myself have become a Harijan by choice'' (*Harijan*, 9 June 1946). Ambedkar had no choice. His actions were molded not only by his own personal background and achievements, and the Maharashtrian thinking of his day, but also by his status as an Untouchable. The Untouchable caste he came from had begun social and political movements before he assumed a position of leadership. His contribution was to raise these attempts to a level of such effectiveness that the caste could achieve en masse a religious conversion, build a political party, and greatly increase its participation in education at all levels. Beyond his own caste, Ambedkar helped to shape the vast program of legal rights and safeguards for Untouchables which India developed. He directly influenced some other Untouchable castes through his conversion movement and his political parties, and indirectly affected many more. In his own person, as lawyer, writer, statesman, constitutionalist, he was an example to all India of what an Untouchable could become.

Ambedkar's Reaction to Gandhi

The Vaikam satyagraha of 1924-25 in Tranvancore state offered Gandhi his first opportunity to act publicly on behalf of Untouchables and produced Ambedkar's first public comment on Gandhian methods. Gandhi was not the initiator of the campaign to remove the prohibition against Untouchables' use of the roadway passing the temple at Vaikam, but he was in contact with campaign leadership and visited the area during the second year of the satyagraha to negotiate with temple and state officials.[20] The satyagraha for the use of the road was begun by several South Indian caste Hindus, a Syrian Orthodox Christian, and some followers of Sri Narayana Guru, the spiritual leader of a large and comparatively well-to-do Depressed Caste, the Ilavas. Although undoubtedly patterned after the Gandhian satyagraha method and supported by many Gandhians, the satyagraha was also an outgrowth to the Ilavas' own movement to gain political and religious rights. It came in the wake of the Ilavas' 1918 appeal to the Travancore government for the opening of state temples to all Hindus and their 1921 threat to convert in a body to Christianity.

Gandhi's negotiation with a Nambudiri Brahman trustee of the Vaikam temple at the time of the satyagraha, faithfully recorded by his

secretary Mahadev Desai[21] shows something of the temper of the orthodox at the time as well as Gandhi's method of persuasion:

> Gandhiji: Is it fair to exclude a whole section of Hindus, because of
> their supposed lower birth, from public roads which can be used by
> non-Hindus, by criminals and bad characters, and even by dogs and
> cattle?
>
> Nambudiri Trustee: But how can it be helped? They are reaping the
> reward of their karma.
>
> Gandhiji: No doubt they are suffering for their karma by being born
> as untouchables. But why must you add to the punishment? Are they
> worse than even criminals and beasts?
>
> Nambudiri Trustee: They must be so, for otherwise God would not
> condemn them to be born untouchables.
>
> G: But God may punish them. Who are we human beings to take the
> place of God and add to their punishment?
>
> N: We are instruments. God uses us as His instruments in order to
> impose on them the punishment that their karma has earned for
> them.
>
> G: But supposing the Avarnas outside varna, i.e., untouchables, said
> that they were instruments in the hands of God in order to impose
> afflictions on you? What would you do?
>
> N: Then the Government would stand between them and us and
> prevent them from doing. Good men would do so. Mahatmaji, we
> beseech you to prevent Avarnas from depriving us of our old
> privileges.

After a thorough discussion of the religious authority behind the prohibition against the Untouchables' use of the road, Gandhi made a last
proposal: "Would you accept arbitration? You appoint a Pandit on
behalf of the Satyagrahis, and the Dewan acts as Umpire. What do you
say to that?" No reply was recorded. Although the temple authorities
finally capitulated and the road past the temple was open to all (or moved

farther away from the temple--the denouement of the satyagraha is not clear), Untouchables were not allowed to enter the temple until 1936. At that time, coincident with another Ilavas threat to convert to Christianity, Travancore became one of the first states to enact a law opening its state temples to Untouchables.

Although the Vaikam satyagraha represents the only time Gandhi used non-violent direct action on behalf of Untouchables' rights, it foreshadowed many aspects of subsequent Gandhian activity: stress on the orthodox Hindus' inhuman treatment of Untouchables, attempts to secure voluntary lifting of the ban by changing the hearts of caste Hindus, and working within a Hindu framework of ideas. The temple trustees' negative response was also typical of later reactions to Gandhi's policies which often elicited bitter criticism from orthodox Hindus.

Ambedkar referred briefly to the Vaikam satyagraha in a speech that he delivered in 1924 to a provincial conference of the Depressed Classes. It was his first large public meeting after the completion of the London phase of his education, and also the founding meeting of his first organization, the Bahishkrit Hitakarini Sabha (Organization for the Welfare of the Excluded). At this time, however, Ambedkar spoke against conversion to another religion as a means of removing disabilities, and he stressed self-improvement, unity, and organization as the paths to a better life for Untouchables. He used the Vaikam satyagraha with its high caste participants as an example, not of caste Hindu sympathies, but of the political importance of the Untouchable:

> If we remain Hindus as we are, then the Aryan religion will persevere in this country. On the other hand if we become Muslim, then there well be a predominance of that foreign culture in India. If this were not so, the Brahmans would not have been ready to offer satyagraha for the untouchable class at Vaikam.

The following year the Bombay province Depressed Classes Conference, again with Ambedkar as president, heard Ambedkar present a more detailed analysis of the Vaikam satyagraha, which Gandhi had then joined. The address as a whole was still conciliatory in tone and more emphatic on internal reform than on changing Indian society, but there was no wholehearted support for Gandhi. Although Ambedkar stated that for Untouchables "the most important event in the country today is the satyagraha at Vaikam," he pointed out that after a whole year of protest there had been no result. He next spoke of Gandhi:

Before Mahatma Gandhi, no politician in this country maintained that it is necessary to remove social injustice here in order to do away with tension and conflict, and that every Indian should consider it his sacred duty to do so . . . . However, if one looks more closely one finds that there is a slight disharmony . . . for he does not insist on the removal of untouchability as much as he insists on the propagation of Khaddar [home-spun cloth] or Hindu-Muslim unity. If he had he would have made the removal of untouchability a precondition of voting in the party. Well, be that as it may, when one is spurned by everyone, even the sympathy shown by Mahatma Gandhi is of no little importance.

Ambedkar went on to note that the orthodox Brahmans at Vaikam had used scripture to justify their position to Gandhi:

This clearly indicates that either we should burn all these scriptures or verify and examine the validity of their rules regarding untouchability...and if we are unable to prove their falseness or invalidity, we are to suffer untouchability till the end of time! . . . Truly these scriptures are an insult to people. The government should have confiscated them long ago.[22]

Although Ambedkar did not completely reject Gandhi's support until their political battle over Depressed Class political rights in 1931, two remarks in the 1925 address portend his later actions. His scathing comment on Hindu scriptures culminated in a public burning of *Manusmriti* in 1927, and in 1935 Ambedkar announced his vow to leave Hinduism entirely and to convert to some other religion. Ambedkar's complaint that Gandhi had not required an oath of disbelief in untouchability as a precondition for membership in the Congress later turned to a wholesale condemnation of the Congress resolutions on the subject as hypocrisy.

Before Ambedkar's rejection of Hinduism in 1935, the Mahars made several attempts to gain religious and social rights by using the Gandhian technique of satyagraha, mass action without violence. A Depressed Classes conference was held in Mahad in 1927. During the course of that conference, a group of several thousand moved en masse to a tank in the Brahman section of the town, where the leaders of the procession stopped and drank water. After the conference, the tank was ritually purified by the townspeople. Later in the year Ambedkar called another conference in Mahad to reiterate the Untouchables' right to use the public water supply. It was at this second conference that the *Manusmriti* was publicly burned. This radical gesture was balanced by Ambedkar's decision to comply with a court injunction prohibiting further satyagraha for water rights. He preferred to fight a ten-year court case, which he won, rather than take to the streets again. In spite of the long delay in the resolution of this issue, the Mahars look upon the Mahad satyagraha as the beginning of their political awakening. The spirit and unity demonstrated in that first mass action became a Mahar legend. Some caste Hindus attended the conferences, but the burning of *Manusmriti* cost Ambedkar the approval of all but the most radical of his caste Hindu supporters.

The second Mahar satyagraha was initiated in 1929 in an attempt to gain entry to the Parvati Temple in Pune. This effort was also conducted in the Gandhian style, but it was not approved by Gandhi or the Congress. Untouchables from several castes led by a Mahar from Pune together with some Maratha and Brahman sympathizers joined in a four-month attempt to enter the gates of the complex on Parvati Hill. A song written by a Mahar for the satyagraha related that the marchers climbed the steps to the temple gates shouting the names of Lord Shankar, Shivaji Maharaj, Chokhamela and Dr. Ambedkar.[23] Gandhi's name was not mentioned, but the technique and inspiration for the satyagraha undoubtedly were drawn from Gandhi's teachings. Although Ambedkar's name was shouted by the marchers, he was not present.

The Anti-Untouchability Sub-Committee created by the Congress in March 1929 investigated the satyagraha. The committee, which included the Hindu Mahasabha leader Pandit M.M. Malviya and Jamnalal Bajaj, a Marwari businessman from Wardha who had built a Temple for Untouchables in his home district, expressed their disapproval of the satyagraha and recommended that the Congress should not support it. According to their report,[24] half a dozen temples had already been opened; negotiations with the temple trustees were being upset by the "atmosphere of bitterness and distrust" created by the satyagraha; and the "Bombay untouchable leaders . . . did not make too much of a fetish of non-violence." The latter criticism is inconsistent with another state-ment in the report that the Pune satyagraha observed "exemplary non-violence" in the face of attack.

Although there was no direct confrontation between Ambedkar and Gandhi on this issue, the failure of the satyagraha (Parvati Temple was not open to Untouchables until India's independence in 1947) and the lack of Congress support in an action performed according to Gandhian principles increased the distrust on the part of Ambedkar and his followers for the Congress and Gandhi. The last of the Mahar satyagrahas, held from 1930 to 1935 at Nasik, widened the breach.

This largest and longest satyagraha effort took place at the Kala Ram Temple in the important pilgrimage center of Nasik. Organized by Ambedkar and the local Mahar leaders, the Kala Ram Satyagraha involved thousands of Untouchables in intermittent efforts to enter the temple and to participate in the annual temple procession. As in the case of the Parvati satyagraha in Pune the attempt was unsuccessful. Here, too, opposition came not only from the orthodox Hindus but also from some local Congressmen. The outcome of the Kala Ram satyagraha, however, was not only further disillusionment with the satyagraha method and the attitude of the Congress, but also a rejection of Hinduism and a strengthening of the separatist political stance then developing among Untouchables.

In 1930, the first year of the Kala Ram satyagraha, Ambedkar appeared before a large conference of the Depressed Classes at Nagpur. Although he had helped to plan and had encouraged the Nasik satyagraha, he barely mentioned the Untouchables' attempt to enter the Kala Ram temple in his presidential address to the conference. Instead, he dwelt on political matters, Ambedkar had just been designated as one of the two Depressed class representatives at the Round Table Conference to be held in London, and he stated the position he would present to that august body in its deliberation on the future constitution of India. He held that only *swaraj* (independence) would bring the possibility of equality to the Depressed Classes, a position not before stated by an Untouchable leader. Ambedkar's option for independence, however, contained a proviso. He told his audience that while he agreed with Congressmen who said that no country was good enough to rule over another, he intended to tell the Congress "point blank" that the proposition does not end there and that it is equally true that no class is good enough to rule over another class.[25]

In this Nagpur speech, Ambedkar also indicated that he did not intend to press for a separate electorate for Untouchables, one in which they could vote for their candidates independently of the caste Hindu vote. This position differed from the plea for a separate electorate, similar to that won by the Muslims, advocated in 1928-29 by most of the Depressed Class groups in their testimony to the Simon Commission. Ambedkar, however, did ask for guaranteed rights, including "adequate" representation on all elected political bodies. This more moderate stance was still out of line with the Congress position. In 1928 the Nehru plan for government had rejected the idea of specific guaranteed rights for Untouchables at the same time that it abrogated the 1916 Congress-Muslim League agreement assuring communal representation for Muslims.

At the first Round Table Conference, held in 1930, which no Congressman attended because of the Non-Cooperation Movement, Ambedkar altered his moderate goal. Since his plea for adult suffrage had been rejected by the British, and the Muslim demand for separate electorates appeared unalterable, Ambedkar shifted his position and argued for separate electorates for the Depressed Classes for a ten-year period. Consequently, Ambedkar's political stance with regard to the Congress was stiffened considerably prior to his encounter with Gandhi at the second Round Table Conference held in London in 1931.

At the second Round Table Conference, Ambedkar confronted Gandhi, who not only refused to consider separate electorates for the Depressed Classes but also opposed any form of special representation involving reserved seats. The two men had met for the first time in Bombay just before the second Round Table Conference. Ambedkar's caste Hindu friends had arranged the meeting, but it did not lead to any understanding between the two. Ambedkar felt that he had been treated rudely, and Gandhi said later that he had not known Ambedkar was an Untouchable until the London Conference,[26] which implies that he knew little of Ambedkar's work in Bombay. This unsatisfactory meeting, and the basic disagreement between these leaders on the issue of special representation for Untouchables, made negotiation during the Round Table Conference sessions difficult. The situation was exacerbated by Gandhi's questioning of Ambedkar's bona fides: "I say that it is not a proper claim which is registered by Dr. Ambedkar when he seeks to speak for the whole of the Untouchables of India . . . . I myself in my own person claim to represent the vast mass of the Untouchables".[27]

After the third Round Table Conference, during which Gandhi was in jail, the British government announced a decision regarding representation which, it was hoped, would effect a compromise between the Congress and Ambedkar. This communal award of 1932 gave the Depressed Classes a double vote, one in a special constituency for a modest number of reserved seats, and another in the general electorate. Gandhi's response to communal award was to enter a "fast unto death' on 20 September 1932. On the first day of the fast, he wrote in a letter to

P.N. Rajbhoj, a Chambhar Untouchable from Pune:

> My fast has reference only to separate electorates . . . . I must say that
> I am not in love with the idea of Statutory reservation. Whilst it is not
> open to the same objection that separate electorate is, I have not a
> shadow of doubt that it will prevent the natural growth for the sup-
> pressed classes and will remove the incentive to honourable amends
> from the suppressers. What I am aiming at is a heart understanding
> between the two, the greatest opportunity of repentance and repara-
> tion on the part of the suppressers. I am certain that the movement
> is ripe for the change of heart among them. I would therefore favour
> widest possible franchise for the suppressed and establish a conven-
> tion between the two sections for securing proper election of
> representatives of the suppressed.[28]

This seems to be the voice of Gandhi speaking as Mahatma. A
somewhat more political motive for Gandhi's protest is indicated in the
report of a conversation between Gandhi and Sardar Patel a day after the
fast began. Gandhi's secretary, Mahadev Desai, recorded Gandhi's
comments:

> The possible consequences of separate electorates for Harijans [this
> must be Desai's editing--the word Harijan was not yet used by
> Gandhi] fill me with horror. Separate electorates for all other
> communities will still leave room for me to deal with them, but I
> have no other means to deal with "untouchables". These poor
> fellows will ask why I who claim to be their friend should offer
> Satyagraha simply because they were granted some privileges; they
> would vote separately but vote with me. They do not realize that the
> separate electorate will create division among Hindus so much that
> it will lead to blood-shed. "Untouchable" hooligans will make
> common cause with Muslim hooligans and kill caste-Hindus. Has
> the British Government no idea of all this? I do not think so.[29]

The British Government's response to Gandhi's fast was to declare
that a solution to the representation of the Depressed Classes had to be
settled within the Hindu community. Consequently, the man whose
leadership of the Depressed Classes was challenged by Gandhi in
London became the arbiter of Gandhi's fate. Ambedkar met with various
Hindu leaders under ever-increasing tension as Gandhi's condition

worsened. Since reserved seats had been unenthusiastically accepted by Gandhi in the period following his confrontation with Ambedkar in London, the issue was a separate electorate, a cause Ambedkar had adopted only the year before. Ambedkar drove a hard bargain, trading a separate electorate for a separate primary election plus a large increase in the number of seats reserved for Untouchables--from the seventy-eight given in the Communal Award to 148 seats.

In the ensuing years, neither caste Hindus nor Depressed Class politicians were happy about this agreement, called the Yervada or Poona Pact. Caste Hindus, particularly in Bengal, felt that reserved seats of the Depressed Classes unduly diminished the number of legislative seats available to Hindus in areas with a large Muslim population. Depressed Class leaders found the primary system to be expensive and unwieldy, and Ambedkar made at least one futile attempt to change it. Some Depressed Class leaders felt that the Congress did not nominate able and truly representative Depressed Class members for reserved seats. Although the Congress never formally approved the Poona Pact, it became, after the provision for a primary election was abandoned, the basis for all future elections.

The Poona Pact in itself accomplished little more than might have emerged from an earlier compromise, but the dramatic circumstances in which it was forged gave a great deal of publicity to Gandhi's concern for the Untouchable and to Ambedkar's leadership. Both men intensified their efforts to eliminate untouchability during the next two decades, each continuing to follow the line of action already established. Gandhi sought to change the heart of the caste Hindus by moral pressure within the framework of Hindu tradition. Ambedkar continued to work in the fields of education and politics in an attempt to gain legal rights for Untouchables in the secular world.

Among Gandhi's activities was the organization of a group devoted to the removal of untouchability. Formed in Bombay on 30 September 1932, it was first called the All India Anti-Untouchability League. Pandit Madan Mohan Malviya of the Hindu Mahasabha presided at the first meeting; the industrialist Ghanshyamdas Birla was named president, and the secretary was Amritlal B. Thakkar, a social worker who worked among the tribal peoples. Several Untouchables were on the central board, including M.C. Rajah of Madras, who in 1927 became the first Untouchable to serve in the central legislative assembly, Ambedkar, and Rao Bahadur Srinivasan of Madras. The latter was Ambedkar's fellow delegate to the Round Table Conferences. The name of Gandhi's organization was soon changed to the Servants of Untouchables Society. This title was then translated into Hindi as the Harijan Sevak Sangh, using the term Harijan (children of God) adopted by Gandhi as a new appellation for the Untouchable. The purpose of the society was to use peaceful persuasion to secure access for the Depressed Classes to all public wells, roads, schools, temples, and cremation grounds. Social reforms such as inter-dining and other caste-based practices were admittedly outside the scope of the new organization. Gandhi toured 12,500 miles over India from November 1933 to the end of July 1934, to preach against untouchability and to collect funds for the organization.

Although Ambedkar was a member of the first central board, his connection with Gandhi's organization lasted only a few months. While en route to the third Round Table Conference in 1932, Ambedkar wrote a long letter to the organization's secretary, A.B. Thakkar (a letter that Ambedkar claimed went unanswered), stating that he wanted the Anti-Untouchability League to be concerned primarily with civic rights and equal opportunity in economic matters and social intercourse.[30]

Ambedkar's view of the proposed goals of the League proved to be quite different from that of its founders. Ambedkar soon resigned, and other Untouchable members on the board seem to have disappeared quietly from the scene. In its form as the Harijan Sevak Sangh, the new organization was closed to Untouchable leadership. Gandhi defended this policy in response to criticism by explaining that it was an organization for penitents, for the expiation of the guilt of the caste Hindus. For this reason, Untouchables should advise, but were not to be the main actors.[31]

The years immediately after the Poona Pact were Gandhi's most intense period of work for anti-untouchability, but he failed not only to win the support of Ambedkar, but also to conciliate the orthodox Hindus. They took exception to his program and to his personal actions as well. An article vehemently critical of Gandhi for his temple entry campaign and also for his allowing the marriage of his son to a daughter of C. Rajagopalachari, a Madrasi Brahman, appeared in a Bombay journal, *The Indian Mirror* on 5 August 1933. This article included the accusation, expressed in a poem by Professor J. Mangiah, that Gandhi turned "good" Untouchables into malcontents:

Untouchables our folks are good,
Till Gandhi told them they were Gods
Content they were to faith they stood
To Congress lessons now each nods.

Sardar Patel, always the pragmatic advisor, told Gandhi during the Harijan campaign, "Why have you placed yourself between two stones? I keep telling you not to do so. Let the two stone grind each other. Why must you come in between?[32]

While the orthodox resented Gandhi's use of the word Harijan for Untouchables and rejected Gandhi's attempts at persuasion regarding the temple entry issue, educated Untouchables found the word Harijan patronizing and the results of the temple entry campaigns insignificant. Jagjivan Ram, a rising young Untouchable Congress politician from Bihar, described the Harijan Sevak Sangh as being erroneous in conception, faulty in emphasis, and halting in execution.[33] He addressed a spirited protest to Gandhi when Gandhi asked a Christian missionary to pray for the Harijans but not to try to convert them as they did not have "the mind and intelligence to understand what you talked . . . . Would you preach the Gospel to a cow?" (*Harijan*, 19 December 1936). Gandhi replied that no ill will was intended; for him the cow was a symbol of gentleness and patient suffering.[34] It was clear, though, that in Gandhi's concept of service to the suffering Untouchables, there was little room for the educated, politically conscious Untouchables pressing for civil rights.

Through the mid-1930s Gandhi continued his labors to exorcize the evil of untouchability by an arduous nine-month Harijan tour, a lengthy fast to purify his soul and to call attention to the existence of the blight of untouchability, and attempts to secure temple entry. During the same period Ambedkar moved farther and farther away from the possibility of cooperating with Gandhi's program based on religious reform or with Congress' political measures. In 1935, Ambedkar announced at Yeola, a town in Maharashtra near the site of the earlier struggle for temple entry at Nasik, that although born a Hindu, he would not die a Hindu. The following year, a conference of Mahars held in Bombay city passed a resolution to disassociate themselves from Hinduism by converting to some other religion. Ambedkar's plan provided that each Untouchable caste was to make its own decision. Although the idea was widely discussed among Untouchables in North India and in Travancore in the south, no caste other than the Mahars committed itself to leaving Hinduism en masse. The Mahars, however, did not implement their decision even though Christian, Muslim and Sikh religious leaders announced themselves ready to receive Untouchable converts. Ambedkar's 1935 conversion speech and the Mahar response to it bore every evidence of sincerity, but none of the existing religions satisfied

Ambedkar's criteria. Islam and Christianity were evidently disqualified because they were foreign and not Indian in origin. Sikhism was seriously considered, but there was no guarantee that the hard-won political rights of the Untouchables would be continued if they became Sikhs. Although Ambedkar was already attracted to the Buddhist past, there were no effective Buddhist organizations in India and little of the interest in Buddhism that was to appear in post-independence India.

The decision to convert may also have been postponed because of Ambedkar's intense political and administrative activity during the following decade. In 1937, his newly formed Independent Labour Party backed fourteen Scheduled Caste candidates for reserved seats and four caste Hindus for general seats in the Bombay Legislative Assembly. The party won eleven reserved and three general seats. (Two of the defeated candidates had contested seats in the area where the Mahad satyagraha had taken place ten years before.)

Although Ambedkar's party was successful in the election, its position as a small minority in a Congress-dominated assembly was very weak. The party was rarely successful in its areas of concern, chiefly labor and agricultural policies. In 1942, Ambedkar reformulated his political plans. He formed a new party, the Scheduled Castes Federation, and limited it to Untouchables in the hope of uniting all Untouchables in a new battle for political power. Ambedkar had been selected the same year to serve as the Member for Labour on the Viceroy's Executive Council, a post which gave him considerable power in formulating policy and granting patronage, but kept him from spending much time on party organization. His energies were devoted to administration on the highest governmental level and to writing a series of books on national problems and the position of the Untouchable.

It was during this period of the mid-1940s that Ambedkar launched his most vitriolic attacks on Gandhi. Ambedkar's personal political success, and the recognition accorded him as an able administrator, did little to assuage his anger. Although he recognized that the prospects for the Depressed Classes had been improved through the extension of educational opportunities and the reservation of government jobs, he was acutely conscious of the continuing disabilities that affected most Untouchables. Ambedkar's criticism was not of the orthodox Hindu, whom he had given up years before as hopeless, but of Gandhi and the Congress--those who would inherit political power in the impending withdrawal of British rule.

What Congress and Gandhi Have Done to Untouchables, first

published in 1945, contains Ambedkar's most impassioned criticism. It is basically a plea for a separate electorate for the Untouchable. Public statements, voting records, and numerous incidents showing the isolation and maltreatment of Untouchables are presented to support the contention that political separation from the Hindus in the electoral system is necessary for the attainment of Untouchable political rights. An indictment of Gandhian philosophy and action. is a major theme of the book. The Harijan Sevak Sangh is held to be a political charity, intended to bring Untouchables into the Congress camp. The temple entry campaign is criticized for its lack of success and the turning off and on of this issue to further Congress political interests. The *varnashrama-dharma* scheme is described as an unnatural ordering of society, impracticable and inhumane in its allocation of occupations by heredity. Gandhi's idea of ennobling the scavenging profession is viewed as "an outrage and a cruel joke". According to Ambedkar, "Mr. Gandhi's attitude is that let Swaraj perish if the cost of it is political freedom of the Untouchables".[35]

However, Ambedkar's words appear to have exerted little influence on the British. The Cripps Cabinet Mission, sent to India in 1946 to arrange the transfer of power to Indian hands, was more influenced by the failure of the Scheduled Castes Federation in the 1946 elections. Consequently, the British provided no special political rights for the Untouchables beyond reserved seats in the legislatures. Ambedkar's response to the Cripps proposal was to launch huge satyagraha demonstrations before the state legislatures at Pune, Nagpur, Lucknow, and in the industrial city of Kanpur from July to October 1946. This effort failed to move the planners of India's future.

After 1947

The creation of Pakistan in 1947 stilled the Muslims' demand for a separate electorate and eliminated the possibility that the Scheduled Castes might obtain such an award. Although Ambedkar's major effort on behalf of his community failed, his role as a national leader was recognized and enhanced by his election to the Constituent Assembly. Initially elected to this body in 1946 through the cooperative efforts of the Scheduled Castes and Muslim League in Bengal, after the partition of Bengal in 1947 he was continued in the same position by the Congress of Bombay -- evidently as a gesture of good will. In August 1947,

Ambedkar was named Law Minister in the first cabinet of independent India, while retaining his position as chairman of the committee responsible for drafting a constitution of the new nation.

The first years following Independence were a period of cooperation between politically conscious Untouchables and Congress Hindus. Ambedkar skilfully piloted the constitution through the Constituent Assembly. In doing so, he relinquished some of his radical ideas, such as the nationalization of agriculture, in order to create a constitution based on consensus. However, the refusal of the Congress leaders to support Ambedkar's Hindu Code Bill led him to resign from the cabinet in 1951. His resignation statement indicated frustration over Nehru's domineering leadership as well as India's treatment of Untouchables.

In the last years of his life Ambedkar devoted himself chiefly to his interest in Buddhism. In the months before his death in 1956 he took two actions based on his belief that separatist action on the part of Untouchables and other dispossessed groups was necessary for their eventual integration. He became a Buddhist on 14 October 1956, setting in motion - a conversion movement that was to encompass four million people. He also announced the establishment of the Republican Party, which was to be an instrument of political power for all the dispossessed, including the Scheduled Tribes, as well as the Scheduled Castes. His death left both new movements in the hand of those Untouchables most thoroughly organized by his work—the Mahars of Maharashtra.

Legacies of Leadership

Despite Ambedkar's criticism of Gandhi, and Gandhi's unwillingness to include such men as Ambedkar in the structure of his reform schemes, there were indications that each was conscious of the other's necessary place in any final solution of the problem of untouchability. Ambedkar recounted to reporters on the evening before his conversion to Buddhism that years before he had told Mahatma Gandhi, "I will choose only the least harmful way for the country" (*Nagpur Times*, 14 October 1956). On the other side, there is widespread belief on the part of many Mahars that Gandhi wanted Ambedkar to be Prime Minister. This is supported by a note in the *Illustrated Weekly of India* to the effect that if Gandhi had had this way, "B.R. Ambedkar, lifelong opponent of Gandhism, would have been even at the head of the state" (22 January 1950).

The paths of Gandhi and Ambedkar, while they often diverged, ultimately converged, forcing on the Indian conscience the problem of untouchability as an issue of national concern. Nurullah and Naik reinforce this view in their analysis of the influence exerted by these two men:

> Gandhiji's main work lay among the caste Hindus, and its greatness is to be measured by the extent of change brought about in the minds of the caste Hindus. But however painful, it is a fact of history that he did not have a very large following among the Harijans themselves. On the other hand, Dr. Ambedkar was Harijan by birth . . .and therefore was destined to be the leader of these people by virtue of his birth, complete identification with their cause and unequalled capacity . . . . In a way, his work was complementary to that of Mahatma Gandhi, although owing to differences of approach, he often came in conflict with Gandhiji and the Congress.
>
> The great service of Dr. Ambedkar to the cause is the awakening that he created among the Harijans. He gave them a leadership which they sadly lacked and which was very badly needed. He puts the problem of the Harijans before the country in its true perspective -- political, social and economic.[36]

There are no equivalents of either Gandhi or Ambedkar in India today, no famous Mahatma preaching that untouchability is a sin, no statesman-cum-partisan leader serving as an outspoken champion of Untouchables. Although Jagjivan Ram comes nearest to filling this latter role, he is primarily known as an astute politician. In a sense, the viewpoints of Gandhi and Ambedkar were amalgamated in such a way that political and social measures which Ambedkar would have approved are taken in the name of Gandhi. The scene described earlier in the Constituent Assembly illustrates this. Although the measure legally abolishing untouchability was adopted with cries of "Victory of Mahatma Gandhi!", Gandhi never advocated legal measures, feeling as he did that all change must come voluntarily from the heart. Yet such was his effect on the Hindu mind that the practice of untouchability is now considered, at least by the educated, as wrong, and uplift of the Untouchable to the level of others as good. In a speech to the Rajya Sabha, Prime Minister Indira Gandhi called for bringing "one of [Gandhi's] near dreams of reality" by giving education, employment, and land ownership to Harijans and ensuring "that people belonging to the Scheduled Castes and Tribes are put in positions of Authority where they can solve their own and others' problems'' (*Times of India*, 13 August 1967).

The vast machinery of protective discrimination for the Scheduled Caste was developed chiefly in the 1930s and '40s under the British, and legitimized psychologically by the Gandhian campaigns of the period. The post-Independence government adopted most of these measures and further refined and extended them. Benefits since accorded to Untouchables have included reserved seats in all legislative bodies, the reservation of Government jobs, aid to students through the college level, prizes to villages demonstrating equality, gifts of money for marriages in which one partner is an Untouchable, support for housing projects, and legal machinery for suits against discriminative practices. Such measures reflect the attitude and policies developed by the leaders and events of the past. They have also inhibited the emergence of a new Mahatma decrying passionately against remaining injustices, or the development of a separatist Untouchable leader capable of building a movement outside the wall of government privilege and patronage. These privileges have also walled off the continuing problems of the Untouchable from the Indian consciousness. Untouchability is news only when a government commission is appointed to investigate some aspect of the problem, or when a particularly dramatic event occurs, such as the burning of forty-two Untouchables in a hut in an east Tanjore district village during landlord-tenant conflicts (*Blitz*, 4 January 1969). Even public expressions of orthodox views are relatively rare as evidenced by the sensational news coverage given in 1969 to the Shankaracharya of Puri's public pronouncements in defense of untouchability.

While Gandhi may be credited with the general atmosphere of concern for the Untouchable expressed in India's official policies, efforts of the kind he most favored have diminished since his death. A continuation of the Gandhian tradition may be found in several voluntary agencies that maintain hostel and child-care centres for the Depressed Classes and seek to alter attitudes through propaganda. Vinoba Bhave, Gandhi's spiritual heir, initiated a voluntary land redistribution program that benefits some Untouchables through gifts of land to the landless.

Men like N.R. Malkani, a long-time Gandhian worker, have continued to labor for the Bhangi by working on the modernization as well as the humanization of scavenging.[37] However, such efforts have not received widespread financial support from private citizens. ''With the advent of freedom, the public response became somewhat cold and people began to argue (rightly or wrongly) that in a welfare state it was the State which should provide all the aid needed by such institutions".[38]

A continuing undercurrent of faith in the varna system appears to guide many social workers and reformers. K.K. Thakkar,[39] suggests that the Shudras should assist the three upper varnas who are credited with doing "constructive work". He tempers this view by advocating that varnas should be assigned on the basis of ability rather than birth. Dr. Pandharinath Prabhu of the Tata Institute of Social Sciences, in discussing caste and class at the seminar on "Casteism and Removal of Untouchability" in Bombay in 1955, reflected the views of Gandhi and other Hindu religious reformers in his conception of varna: "In fact, the entire Varna System is devised to co-ordinate and assemble the best and the utmost of group welfare, by yoking each section of the group to duties and responsibilities in terms of the efficiency of the specific work and service each of the sections is able to render unto the community life".[40] As in Gandhi's day, this approach has been more concerned with duties than with rights; it has not produced leaders from the ranks of the Untouchables; it has not offset the subtle discrimination felt by the educated Untouchable; it has little influence in most Indian villages where Untouchable living quarters, wells, and temples are still separate from those of caste Hindus.

Ambedkar's influence has also persisted. His ideas on political rights and privileges have been generally accepted by Untouchables. He himself still stands as an example of what an Untouchable can become. As late as the 1960s, the Scheduled Castes were still seeking self-respect by attempting to secure national recognition of his achievements. A "Charter of Demands" presented by the Republican party to the government in 1965 and backed by a satyagraha involving a third of a million people, headed its program with the demand that a portrait of Dr. Ambedkar be placed in the Parliament Building. (A statue of him has now been erected on that site). In 1969, three Swatantra Party Harijans not actually allied with Ambedkar's political movement undertook a fast in Ahmedabad to protest the absence of Dr. Ambedkar's portrait from the Gujarat Legislative Assembly.

In addition to the vital element of self-respect which Ambedkar engendered among Untouchables, his vision of progress though education and politics, rather than the Gandhian vision of a change of heart among caste Hindus, has come to inspire most Scheduled Caste leaders. However, these leaders and their followers are rarely united beyond their own regions. In general, they support the dominant party of the area--the Communist Party in Kerala, the DMK in Madras, the Congress in many provinces. Only in Maharashtra and portions of Uttar Pradesh has Ambedkar's Republican Party commanded any significant number of seats in recent elections.

Ambedkar's view that the problem of the Untouchable is economic, social, and political, as well as religious, widely prevails in India. The Untouchable who enters the modern sector of Indian society as school teacher, factory worker, or government servant, is comparatively free from earlier social disabilities. Even though there may be subtle discrimination in some areas, and a closed door in others, the educated Untouchable functions in a world where a concern with pollution is mitigated by other considerations. However, for the majority of Untouchables, who are landless villagers, the only open road to a higher economic and social status entails leaving the security of their village and somehow obtaining education. Gandhi may have softened the Hindu heart, Ambedkar may have awakened self-respect and interest in politics among Untouchables, but economic dependence upon others continues to restrict the upward movement of the Untouchable.

Notes

1. Mahadev Desai, *The Epic of Travancore* (Ahmedabad: Navajivan, 1937).
2. M.K. Gandhi, *The Nation's Voice*, edited by C. Rajagopalachari and J.C. Kumarappa (Ahmedabad: Navajivan, 2nd edn., 1947). This is a collection of Gandhi's speeches in England and Mahadev Desai's account of the sojourn--September-December 1931.
3. Pyarelal Nair (Nayyar), *The Epic Fast* (Ahmedabad: Mohanlal Maganlal Bhatt, 1932).
4. Rameshwari Nehru, *Gandhi is My Star* (Patna: Pustakbhandar, 1950).
5. D.G. Tendulkar, *Mahatma: Life of Mohandas Karamchand Gandhi*, Vol. I-VIII, (Bombay:Vithalbhai K. Jhaveri and D.G. Tendulkar, 1952).
6. Mahadev Desai, *The Diary of Mahadev Desai*, trans. from the Gujarati and edited by Valji Govind Desai (Ahemadabad: Navajivan, 1953). This is a record of Gandhi's life from 10 March 1932 to 4 September 1932-- a period of intensive concern with untouchability.
7. B.R. Ambedkar, "Castes in India--Their Mechanism, Genesis and Development," *Indian Antiquary*, XLVI, 1917, pp. 81-95; *Annihilation of Caste, with a Reply to Mahatama Gandhi* (Bombay: Bhusan P. Press, 1936); *What Congress and Gandhi have done to the Untouchables* (Bombay: Thacker, 2nd edn., 1946; first published in 1945); *Who were the Shudras?* (Bombay: Thacker, 1947, first published in 1946); *The Untouchables* (New Delhi: Amrit Book Co., 1948; 2nd edn., Lucknow, 1969).

8. Dhananjay Keer, *Dr. Ambedkar: Life and Mission* (Bombay: Popular Prakashan, 1962).

9. C.B. Khairmode, *Dr. Bhimrao Ramji Ambedkar*, Vol. I (Bombay: Y.B.Ambedkar, 1952); Vol. II (Bombay: Bauddhjan Panchyat Samiti; (1958); Vol. III (Bombay: Pratap Prakashan, 1964); Vols. IV and V (Bombay: Dr. Ambedkar Education Society, 1966, 1968).

10. Denis Dalton, "The Gandhian View of Caste and Caste after Gandhi, " in Philip Mason ed., *India and Ceylon: Unity and Diversity* (London: Oxford University Press, for the Institute of Race Relations, 1967), p. 170.

11. Quoted in B.R. Ambedkar, 1946, *op.cit.*, p.1.

12. S.Natarajan, *A Century of Social Reform in India* (Bombay: Asia Publishing House, 2nd edn., 1962), p. 148.

13. Pattabhi Sitaramayya, *The History of the Indian National Congress*, Vol. I (Bombay: Padma Publications, 1946, first published in 1935), p. 226

14. B.G. Tilak, "The Emancipation of the Untouchable", *The Hindu Missionary*, 42, 15 April 1918 (Bombay).

15. Pyarelal Nair (Nayyar), *Mahatma Gandhi: The Last Phase* (Ahmedabad: Navajivan, 1958), p. 228.

16. B.R. Ambedkar, 1946, *op.cit.*, p. 189.

17. B.R. Ambedkar, *The Annihilation of Caste* (Bombay: Bhusan P. Press, 1936).

18. Ram Joshi, "Maharashtra" in Myron Weiner ed., *State Politics in India* (Princeton: Princeton University Press, 1968), pp.194-95.

19. A.V. Thakkar, *Aboriginals Cry in the Wilderness: Their Education and Representation in Legislature* (Bombay: A.W. Thakkar, Servants of India Society, c.1945), p. 7.

20. Joan V. Banduvant, *Conquest of Violence: The Gandhian Philosophy of Conflict* (Princeton: Princeton University Press, 1958), pp. 46-52.

21. Desai, 1937, *op.cit.*, pp.17-21.

22. C.B. Khairmode, *Dr. B.R. Ambedkar*, Vol, *op.cit.*, pp.117-18.

23. Tulshiram Jamgekar, *Parvativaril satyagrahaca pawada* (Pune, 1930).

24. Indian National Congress; Anti-Untouchability Sub-Committee, *Report of the Work Done by the Anti-Untouchability Sub-Committee*, April-December 1929 (Jamnalal Bajaj, Secretary). Reported in the *Indian Annual Register*, 1929. Part II, pp. 276-80.

25. *Indian Annual Register*, 1930, Part II, p. 369.

26. Mahadev Desai, 1953, *op.cit.*, p. 52.

27. Indian Round Table Conference (Second - 1931 London), *Proceedings of the Federal Structure Committee and Minorities Committee* (London: H.M.S.O.,1932), p. 544.

28. Gandhi, *My Soul's Agony* (Ahmedabad: Navajivan, 1932).

29. Desai, 1953, *op.cit.*, p. 301.

30. Ambedkar, 1946, *op.cit.*, pp.134-41.
31. Ambedkar, 1946, *op.cit.*, pp. 142, 279-90; Pyarelal, 1958, *op.cit.*, pp. 667-68.
32. Kewal L. Panjabi, *Indomitable Sardar* (Bombay: Bhartiya Vidya Bhavan, 1962), p. 79.
33. Nalin Vilochan Sharma, "A Biography of Jagjivan Ram", in *The Working Man* (Patna: Jagjivan Ram Abhinandan Granth Committee, 1957) p. 107.
34. *Ibid.*, p. 83.
35. Ambedkar, 1946, *op.cit.*, p. 283.
36. Syed Nurullah and J.P. Naik, *History of Education in India* (Bombay: Macmillan, 1951), pp.723-33.
37. N.R. Malkani, *Clean People and Unclean Country* (Delhi: Harijan Sevak Sangh, 1965).
38. P.C. Dave, "Voluntary Organizations and the Welfare of Backward Classes", *Vanyajati*, XIV, pp.156-64.
39. K.K. Thakkar, in the *Indian Journal of Social Work*, Vol.17, No. 2, pp. 44-99.
40. Report of "Seminar on Casteism and the Removal of Untouchability", Delhi, 26 September-2 October 1955 (Bombay: Indian Conference of Social Work, 1955), p. 116.

Addendum to Part II

There have, of course, been many political developments since these essays were written in the 1960s and 1970s. A full analysis awaits the work of a political scientist, but these notes may be of interest now.

Ambedkar's Political Party

Prakash Ambedkar, Ambedkar's grandson, has moved from a quiet leadership of the Buddhist movement into the spokesman for the Bhartiya Republican Party, and for the first time a Brahman woman, Neelam Gorhe, has joined the ranks. R.S. Gawai, who inherited the following of the late Dadasaheb Gaikwad, is of this date (October 1989) the only elected Republican Party member of the Bombay Legislative Council, but continues to wield considerable influence. Girish Khobragade commands a third faction of the Party with a large following in eastern Vidharbha. B.C. Kamble of Bombay is still active, but without the power base of Ambedkar, Gawai or Khobragade. Two former Republican Party members, Dadasaheb Rupavate and N.M. Kamble, hold responsible positions in the Congress Party and continue to be spokesmen for

Ambedkar's ideals. In the North, Kanshi Ram has secured some success with his Bahujan Samaj Party, but his support in Maharashtra is not strong.

Dalit Panthers

The most interesting socio-political development among Ambedkar's followers is the rise of the Dalit Panthers, a militant group of young educated Buddhists formed in 1972. The Panthers offered a challenge to unite to the politicians in Ambedkar's movement and attempted to counter violence against Untouchables in the village. They also brought to public attention the emerging Dalit Sahitya, the literature of the oppressed, an important cultural contribution to Marathi literature. Now, in the late 1980s, the united power of the Dalit Panthers is much reduced by splits, but local efforts continue and the literary movement which accompanied the rise of the Panthers is still blooming. Ramdas Athvale of Bombay and Gangadhar Gade of Aurangabad lead an important faction of the Panthers. Jogendra Kavade of Nagpur speaks for unity among Dalits and Muslims. Arun Kamble of Bombay, a professor of Marathi, a dynamic speaker, and a critic of the Ramayana as anti-Dalit and anti-women's liberation, has brought his following into alliance with the Socialists (now in the Janata Party). Bhai Sangari leads a faction of the Dalit Panthers in Bombay in alliance with one of the founders, Namdeo Dhasal, still a formidable force as a recognized innovative poet. Raja Dhale, co-founder with Dhasal of the Panthers, has established a group called Mass Movement, and continues his artistic efforts and his translation of the Buddhist text, the *Dhammapada*. It is disunited but active scene! There is also a group of Dalit Panthers in Gujarat.

Political Events

Two events in the past ten years have demonstrated the continued prevalence of anti-Dalit violence, the power of united Dalits and the on-going importance of Babasaheb Ambedkar. An effort to re-name Marathwada University in Aurangabad in honor of Dr. Ambedkar in 1977-79 was a cause celebre for months. At first approved by the Maharashtra Legislature as a tribute to the man who had brought higher education to the backward area of Marathwada, the proposal was withdrawn in the wake of the most violent caste-based riots ever seen in Maharashtra. The issue now seems dead, but further politicized Dalits through a Long

March, a continued vigil and a great amount of publicity. A more effective effort concerned the "Riddles" controversy. The Maharashtra Government has sanctioned the publication of all of Dr. Ambedkar's writings, published and unpublished. A series of fourteen volumes was begun in 1979, edited by Vasant Moon with a distinguished editorial board of caste Hindus and Dalits. The fourth volume, published in 1986, was entitled *Riddles in Hinduism* and contained a long essay by Dr. Ambedkar, previously unpublished, which raised critical questions about the morality of some Hindu gods, especially Rama and Krishna. Hindu reaction secured the banning of the book, whereupon the largest *morcha* Bombay has ever seen, a procession which filled the broad streets of the city for miles, indicated the strength of the Dalits when united in common cause. The book has been available ever since; the first volume in the series is being reprinted in the quantity of 15,000; the Chief Minister of Maharashtra has contributed a preface to the continuing volumes in the series. The entire Riddles controversy is reported in Marathi in *Ridls* by Gulabrao Bagul (a pseudonym) (Nagpur: Saket Prakashan, 1989).

Additional Bibliography

Gandhi and Ambedkar

Specific analysis of the leadership of the two men appears in Vasant Palshikar, "Gandhi and Ambedkar", *New Quest*, 53 (September-October 1985); Trilok Nath, *Politics of the Depressed Classes* (Delhi: Deputy Publications, 1987); Hirendranath Mukherjee, *Gandhi, Ambedkar and the Extirpation of Untouchability* (New Delhi: People's Publishing House, 1982); and, in Marathi, G.B. Sardar, *Gandhi and Ambedkar* (Pune: Sugawa, 1987).

Interesting material from the Gandhi side of things includes: J. Bandhopadhyaya et al., *The Harijans* (Varanasi: Gandhian Institute of Studies, 1978); Dr. Z. Hasan, *Gandhi and the Harijans* (New Delhi: Shree Publishing House, 1986); and Mukut Behari Verma, *History of the Harijan Sevak Sangh 1932-1968* (Delhi: Harijan Sevak Sangh, 1971).

For biographical material which focuses on Ambedkar, see the list of books on Dr. Ambedkar at the end of this volume.

Studies of the Political Movement

For further analysis of the Ambedkar-led political movement, see Trilok Nath, *Politics of the Depressed Classes* (Delhi: Deputy Publications, 1987), which surveys the all India scene from 1927 to 1937; D.R. Jatava's *Dr. Ambedkar's Role in National Movement* (New Delhi: Bauddha Sahitya Sammelan, 1979); Barbara R. Joshi, *Democracy in Search of Equality* (Delhi: Hindustan Publication Corporation, 1982); and S.K. Gupta, *The Scheduled Castes in Modern Indian Politics: Their Emergence as a Political Power* (New Delhi: Munshiram Manoharlal, 1985), which gives a detailed treatment of the work of M.C. Rajah as well as Ambedkar. The most recent study is Joseph Benjamin, *Scheduled Castes in Indian Politics and Society* (New Delhi: Ess Ess Publications, 1989). There are many studies in Marathi, including one so unusual that it should be mentioned here: Urmila Pawar and Meenakshi Moon have done a study of women in the Ambedkar Movement entitled *Amhihi itihas ghadavla* (We made history too) (Bombay: Stri-uvac, 1989).

Studies of politics in other areas include T.P. Kamalanathan, *Mr. K. Veeramani is Refuted and the Historical Facts about Scheduled Castes Struggle for Emancipation* (Tiruppattur: Ambedkar's Self-Respect Movement, 1985); C. Parvathamma, *Politics and Religion* (New Delhi: Sterling, 1971); Shyamlal, *Caste and Political Mobilization: The Bhangis* (Jaipur: Panchsheel Prakashan, 1981).

Studies of Jagjivan Ram, a Scheduled Caste minister in the Indian Cabinet for many years and the most prominent Untouchable in the Indian National Congress, should also be checked.

Dalit Panthers and Marathwada Riots

Although much news has appeared in newspapers and journals, especially the *Economic and Political Weekly*, the only major analytical article is Jayashree B. Gokhale-Turner, "The Dalit Panthers and the Radicalisation of the Untouchables", in *The Journal of Commonwealth and Comparative Politics*, XVII:1 (March 1979), pp. 77-93. This lack will soon be remedied when Popular Prakashan in Bombay releases the Ph.D. thesis of Lata Murugkar, "Dalit Panther Movement of Maharashtra: A Sociological Appraisal" (Department of Sociology, University of Bombay, 1987). A selection of essays on the Dalit Panthers in Marathi appears in Sharnakumar Limbale, editor, *Dalit Panther* (Pune: Sugawa Prakashan, 1989).

B. Chinchunsure, *Rights, Social Equality and Riots. A Study with reference to the recent riots in Marathwada* (Bombay: Maharashtra Sarvodaya Mandal, 1978) is the most easily available printed source, although there is much information in journals and in mimeographed form.

III

RELIGION

The Revival of Buddhism in India*

The rebirth of Buddhism in India is perhaps best represented by two phenomena: the first is the count of 3,250,227 actual Buddhists in the 1961 Census; the second is the use of two Buddhist motifs as official symbols of independent India -- the *chakra* or wheel on the Indian flag and the lion capital of an Ashokan pillar.

The census figure of 1961 indicates that in the land of the Buddha's birth less than one per cent of the population is Buddhist; yet this is an enormous increase over the 1951 Indian Census figure of 180,823 Buddhists, most of whom were borderland hill peoples and other Asians living in India. The current count of over three million Buddhists represents a conversion movement begun in 1956, chiefly by Untouchables, 75 per cent of whom belong to the former Mahar caste of Maharashtra.

The use of the wheel and the lion capital by the Indian Government reflects not only its choice as a secular state of "neutral symbols", neither Hindu nor Muslim, but also acknowledges the importance of, and new intellectual interest in, the history of Buddhism in India. The history of the conversion movement and of the intellectuals' rediscovery of Buddhism go back less than 100 years, and they are unrelated -- except that renewed interest among intellectuals gave Buddhism the necessary prestige to serve as a base for converts from low status groups seeking a path that would lead to higher status and self-respect.

Buddhism seems to have been a living religion in India from the sixth century B.C. to the twelfth century A.D. There are problems enough sorting out facts from myth in its beginnings and spread, but its decline is even more of a puzzle. Gautam Siddhartha, the Sakya (or Shakya) prince who became the Buddha, was born in that remarkable sixth century B.C. which saw religious genius arise at many points in the great arc from Greece to China that was the civilized world. Buddhism, then, was only one of several heterodox movements in India, all of them a revolt in some way against the brahmanical ritualized orthodoxy of the time. From the beginning, man himself was the focal point of Buddhism. The gods,

---

*First published in *Asia*, 10 (Winter 1968). Slight corrections have been made.

rituals and whatever caste structure there was at the time were not so much denied as set aside in the emphasis on ethics, morality and the path to Nirvana. Equality in the body of monks, the Sangha, was offered to all, not just to those born in the priestly castes. The elements of humanity, gentleness and freedom from sacrifice and superstition, found in the life and teachings of the Buddha, formed the basis for the renewed interest in Buddhism which appeared in India 2,400 years later.

The spread of Buddhism from the third century on can be seen in its art -- those magnificent stupas and caves, some almost untouched by time, other in ruins, in the northwest, the east, the central and the west of India and as far south as Amravati on the river Krishna. The pillar and rock edicts of king Ashoka in the third century B.C. indicate the establishment of Buddhist precept over a great part of the subcontinent. Buddhism was carried through the mountain passes to Central Asia and China and by sea to Ceylon and Southeast Asia. However, even during the latter part of its spread east, and while foreign monks still came to India to gather scriptures and see the holy places, Buddhism as an institutionalized religion was losing ground in India. Many factors entered into its disappearance: destructive invaders -- probably White Huns -- leveled the Buddhist university of Taxila in the fourth century A.D.; Turkish conquerors, probably Muhammad Bakhtiar Khilji, razed the Buddhist university at Nalanda in the twelfth century. That Buddhism in India was unable to revive these institutions, or to continue after the twelfth century as an organized identifiable religion, can be attributed to its inward decline and to the absorptive power of the most syncretic of religions, Hinduism.

Although we know from its art and scriptures that Buddhism must have had widespread influence in India, it is impossible to determine how many Indians at any time actually considered themselves Buddhists. Brahmanical rites and thought were always powerful, and Hindu daily ritual was undoubtedly practiced throughout India during the Buddhist period. The *Mahabharata*, India's great epic, compiled during the centuries before and after the birth of Christ when Buddhist art flourished, does not mention Buddhism by name. The classical period of Hinduism, from the fourth to the sixth centuries A.D., *after* which the university at Nalanda was built, produced works which take fleeting notice of Buddhism (the gambler turned Bhikshu, almost a comic figure, in Shudraka's *Little Clay Cart* is an example). Hinduism not only continued, but absorbed many Buddhist practices and ideas. The Buddha was accepted as an avatar of Vishnu, a part of the Hindu pantheon but not widely worshipped, and it is only in this form that he appears after the twelfth century. In the south the color and warmth of devotional religion, *bhakti*, and the intellectual vitality of the *advaita vedanta*, preached by Shankaracharya in the eighth century, chipped away at the institution of Buddhism on both popular and philosophical levels. Buddhist concepts of non-violence and reverence for life were absorbed into Hindu *ahimsa* and vegetarianism. Hinduism in its varied forms, enriched by Buddhism, dominated India when the Muslim challenge appeared in the twelfth century. It may be that the remaining Buddhists on the periphery of the Hindu heartland -- in East Bengal and Sind -- became Muslim. But by the twelfth century the life of the great Sangha institutions, Buddhist art, the interpretation of Buddhist thought, even the knowledge of the Buddhist period, became lost to sight.

At the beginning of the nineteenth century, European scholars began the work of translation from Pali, Sanskrit and Tibetan, making possible the study of Indian Buddhism in the West. In 1837 an English official in India, James Prinsep, deciphered the script used on the Ashokan rock and pillar edicts, and recognition of the breadth and benevolence of that Buddhist king's rule came to both Europe and India. Alexander Cunningham, another Englishman, prepared the way for a revival of pilgrimage when he, using the seventh-century Chinese pilgrim Hsuan-tsang's travel book as a guide, identified various Buddhist holy places. Many scholars, working in Europe and never coming directly in contact with Indian life, contributed to an increasing knowledge of Indian intelligentsia.

However, it was Henry Olcott, a less orthodox personality, who most profoundly influenced the rebuilding of Buddhist institutions. Olcott, an American Civil War Colonel and one of the founders of the Theosophical Society, went to Ceylon in 1880 to help what he felt was submerged Buddhism. A young Sinhalese, David Hewavitame, joined the Theosophical Society there and after contact through the Society with Western Buddhist studies and Japanese Buddhism, conceived of a resurgent world Buddhism. Hewavitame became Anagarika Dharmapala (literally, the homeless protector of religion). In 1891, as a Buddhist bhikshu, he went to Bodh Gaya, the place where the Buddha had received enlightenment. He had set in motion an interest in Buddhism which led to the establishment of the Maha Bodhi Society of Calcutta. His focus was not on reinterpretation of the doctrine or on conversion but on securing recognition for Buddhism, its reputation and its still living institutions in Asia, and on restoring its pilgrim centres.

From the 1880s onwards, Indian scholarship, stimulated both by European studies in Buddhism and by a pride in Buddhism as part of Indian heritage, produced a steady flow of translations and interpretations, both in English and in some vernacular languages. The Buddhist Text Society was founded in 1892 in Calcutta, and Sarat Chandra Das and Satish Chandra Vidyabhushan (the first person to obtain an M.A. in Pali in 1901) worked under its auspices. In Western India, Dharmananda Kosambi worked both as a scholar and as one personally involved. He lived for a time in both Ceylon and Burma and, besides translating Pali works wrote on Buddhism in Marathi in a way that was both scholarly and persuasive. In South India the new interest in Buddhism seems to have penetrated below the intellectual level to become an interest of some lower caste groups. Buddhist temples started being built fairly early in the twentieth century in their quarters in Madras and in the Kolar Gold fields. In *The Essence of Buddhism*, published in 1907, P. Lakshmi Narasu, a Professor of Physics and Chemistry at Madras Christian College, predicted a popular revival of Buddhism in India. Buddhist themes entered literature and the arts, chiefly through the Tagores in Bengal. A number of reformers considered themselves Buddhists, although this was not accompanied with a concomitant rejection of Hinduism. This kind of interest is exemplified by A.R. Kulkarni, a Nagpur Brahman advocate who became interested in Buddhism as a purifying strand of Hinduism in the 1930s. In the 1940s he actually left his law practice to preach Buddhism, though without any implication of conversion. A few Indians, including some from the Arya Samaj tradition, became Buddhist monks; of these, Rahul Sankrityayan and Anand Kausalyayan combined Hindi literature with the propagation of Buddhism.

By 1947, knowledge and appreciation of the Buddhist period in Indian History had grown to the point where the *chakra* (the wheel of dharma) on the national flag and the lion capital found on an Ashokan pillar as a national emblem were acceptable to almost all Indians. By 1956 interest in Buddhism made the celebration of the 2,500th anniversary of the death of the Buddha an event on a national scale in India. A Buddha Jayanti celebration was observed in Delhi, a film on the life of the Buddha was produced, and a number of books on the Buddhist tradition and Buddhist art were published under Government auspices.

The year of the 2,500th anniversary of Buddhism in India also saw the beginnings of a conversion movement. The social movement of the Mahar caste, an untouchable caste of Maharashtra, which culminated in conversion, roughly parallels in time the revival of intellectual interest in

Buddhism, but it touches that revival chiefly through the figure of its twentieth century leader, Dr. B.R. Ambedkar. Ambedkar's own life reveals some of the factors that produced the Mahar upward movement. His father and grandfather had already broken away from the traditional position of the Mahar as a village servant by enlisting in the British army. Born into a family already urbanized and educated to some degree, Ambedkar's ability in school brought him to the attention of one of a number of caste Hindu reformers interested in the education of the lower castes -- the Gaekwad of Baroda. With the Gaekwad's financial aid and his own stubborn persistence, Ambedkar graduated from Elphinstone College in Bombay, the first B.A. among Untouchables in western India. He went on to secure an M.A. and a Ph.D. from Columbia University in New York, a D.Sc. from London University and was admitted to the Bar from Grey's Inn in London. Returning to India in the early 1920s, he was able to command an interest in education and in political action already present in the Mahar caste, bringing enough unity and organization into that group so that it was ready, almost en masse, to follow him into a political movement and a religious conversion in the mid-1930s.

1936 saw two significant developments among that strata of the Untouchables led by Ambedkar. The Independent Labour Party was formed by Ambedkar in Bombay to fight the elections of 1937. Although founded as a general party, it drew its strength from Ambedkar's own large caste. It represented an organized attempt to capture the political power that Ambedkar and other Untouchables had come to feel was necessary to secure their social rights. But while the political movement is important and interesting, it is the movement toward conversion that concerns us here. To gain special political and social privileges as the Muslim minority had and to prove that the Untouchables were a group separate from the caste-Hindu majority and had separate interests, it became essential for the Untouchable to politicize. This political motive was undoubtedly present in the 1930s decision to convert; but the personal need for self-respect was perhaps just as important, if not more so.

Conversion as a way out of the Untouchable status was not new in India. Islam, and more especially Christianity, drew large numbers of their converts from lower castes, and Sikhism in the twentieth century actively encouraged untouchable conversion.

Actually, conversion to Buddhism was not unknown, although its numbers in Madras and on the Malabar coast were small. The Madras Buddhists generally declared themselves Hindus, but in Cochin in 1931

the Census Commissioner reported 96 Buddhists, mostly educated
Malayali Iluvans, an Untouchable caste, who ''disgusted with the social
disabilities to which their caste is subjected within the Hindu fold, have
become Buddhist converts.... Though their numbers are so few as to be
altogether ignored, still, they point to a new tendency''. The influence for
conversion to Buddhism on the Malabar coast probably came from
Ceylon, rather than from the revived intellectual interest in Buddhism in
India itself. The Commissioner's comment, however, indicates the same
reason for conversion that a few years later affected the Mahars.

In 1935 Ambedkar announced his decision to leave Hinduism, but at
that time Buddhism was not seen as a viable alternative for the Mahars.
Ambedkar was aware of the increased intellectual interest in Buddhism.
He himself had received as an examination prize in 1907 a biography of
the Buddha in Marathi from its author, a Bombay school teacher. He had
been in correspondence with V.R. Shinde, a social reformer who was
interested in Buddhism, and who had founded a wide network of schools
and hostels for the Untouchables in the 1920s. Moreover, Ambedkar
named his new home in Bombay, built in 1934, Raj Griha, after the Bihar
city of the ancient Buddhist kings. But in spite of all this, when he
announced that he ''would not die a Hindu'' in 1935, he was not yet ready
to commit himself and his followers to Buddhism.

Ambedkar's personal conversion announcement in 1935 was followed in 1936 by a Mahar conference in Bombay. After an address by
Ambedkar, the conference as a whole declared its intention to converting to another religion. Portions of Ambedkar's impassioned plea for
conversion form a sort of litany, which in the printed version is lifted out
and placed in a poetry format. The passage begins:

> Religion is for man; man is not for religion
> (and continues:)
> If you want to gain self-respect, change your religion.
> If you want to create a cooperating society, change your religion.
> If you want power, change your religion.
> If your want equality, change your religion.
> If you want independence, change your religion.
> If you want to make the world in which you live, happy, change your
> religion...

The response to Ambedkar's plea to convert was positive, probably
because the Untouchable castes in the Bombay area had just gone
through some eight years of attempts to participate in Hindu festivals and

to enter Hindu temples without success. The 1935 announcement was made near Nasik, and many in Ambedkar's audience had undoubtedly participated in a five-year-long satyagraha (the word is borrowed from Mahatma Gandhi's non-violent technique, but Gandhi did not participate) to enter the famous Kala Ram Temple in Nasik, a pilgrimage city. Efforts to gain education, and efforts to secure political rights such as special representation in legislative bodies, had been fairly successful; however, efforts to claim religious rights had generally ended in failure. The idea of leaving Hinduism met with considerable approval among Ambedkar's own caste in western India and found echoes both in the south and north of India.

After the great conversion announcement of 1935-36, however, there was a hiatus of 20 years before Ambedkar's formal conversion to Buddhism took place. For the first few years, Ambedkar flirted with Islam, Sikhism and Christianity in an attempt to combine a personal need for self-respect, felt by many Untouchable groups, with an astute political move that would allow Untouchables more political power. Ambedkar personally felt Islam and Christianity to be "foreign religions", and his threatened conversion particularly to Islam, seems to have been more in the nature of a weapon to force recognition of the Untouchable needs from Hindus than a genuine interest. Sikhism was an Indian religion, and Ambedkar seems to have most seriously considered this avenue, but as a political expedient it was impractical. The appointment of Ambedkar in 1942 as Labour Member of the Viceroy's Executive Council, the highest position in Government to which any Untouchable had ever risen, and his subsequent place in the Constituent Assembly and in Nehru's first cabinet in independent India, gave such active rein to his political abilities that the religious question, except for his own personal interest, was left in abeyance.

During the time when Ambedkar was most active on the national scene, his personal interest in Buddhism increased. His college, established in 1946, was named Siddharth, the personal name of the Buddha, and a second College founded in 1951 was given the name of Milind, after the Greek king who converted to Buddhism. In 1948 Ambedkar republished P. Lakshmi Narasu's *Essence of Buddhism*, adding his own introduction, and the same year he also published his own study, *The Untouchables*, which theorized that Untouchables had been Buddhists who had been pushed aside from society when they fiercely clung to their religion, while there was a resurgence of Brahmanical Hinduism. In 1950 he visited Ceylon and in the same year began his own compilation of

Buddhist scriptures, *The Buddha and His Dhamma*, which was published in 1957. This volume contains his interpretation of Buddhism -- rational, moral, ethical and egalitarian, with little attention to contemplation and complete eradication of any mystical or magical elements. The actual conversion ceremony to Buddhism was held in 1956. Ambedkar by this time was an old man, in Indian terms, and so ill that he died only two months later. He took *diksha* from the oldest Buddhist monk in India before a large audience in Nagpur and set in motion the conversion process that brought over three million Indians into the Buddhist fold in the next few years. Most of the converts are former Mahars of Maharashtra, but small groups of new Buddhists exist in most other states.

Those involved in the intellectual revival of Buddhism in India have not been entirely happy about this actual conversion movement. The Maha Bodhi Society was represented at the Nagpur conversion ceremony and has from time to time carried articles in its journal about the movement (including one by Ambedkar in 1952). Although some Maha Bodhi monks aided in the conversion, several branches are not sympathetic to the conversion process. Nor can they be, since most Maha Bodhi members are caste Hindus whose leadership the new converts have rejected. The Government publication, *2500 Years of Buddhism*, edited by P.V. Bapat, which appeared in 1956, does not mention the conversion movement in its 1959 reprint. The conversion movement's insistence that Buddhism is separate goes against the general intellectual position found in S. Radhakrishnan's Foreword to the book. He writes, "The Buddha did not feel that he was announcing a new religion. He was born, grew up, and died a Hindu. He was restating with a new emphasis the ancient ideals of the Indo-Aryan civilization".

The newly converted Buddhists from the Untouchable castes cannot accept this position, for their conversion is a denial of their former position in the Indo-Aryan civilization. The conversion "oaths" devised by Ambedkar for the Nagpur ceremony not only contain positive statements about Buddhism such as, "I will follow the Eight-Fold Path of the Lord Buddha; I will have compassion for all living beings and will try to look after them", but include negative statements about Hinduism such as, "I will not regard Brahma, Vishnu and Mahesh as Gods nor will I worship them; I will never get any Samaskar performed by brahmans". This negativism, psychologically necessary to the differing social status of those in the converting group and the intellectual group, prevents any close cooperation.

Those of us who have worked on the Buddhist movement are often asked, both from Indians and Westerns: "It is just a political stunt"; "They aren't really Buddhists"? Our answers generally take the form of other questions "What possible political advantage does conversion offer"? Conversion to Buddhism immediately cuts off, except in Maharashtra where Buddhists are counted as "backward classes" deserving of governmental benefits, all those official, political and social privileges afforded by the Government of India to Untouchable castes. Ambedkar's delayed conversion came long after the period of combining the conversion idea with political expediency, and by then reference to conversion as a political threat had lost its significance. Instead, it had reference to the great Asian Buddhist world, the reputation of Buddhism as an important religion both in India and the West and the possibility of Buddhism as a moral force.

The answer to the question of "real Buddhists" seems to be, "What is a 'real' Buddhists"? Buddhism in Tibet, in Ceylon, in Burma, in Nepal, to name only those countries which are close to India, differs greatly, and each country has absorbed local cultural tradition. A Buddhism stressing rationality, morality and equality may be just as scripturally justifiable as any of its more established varieties. And even the place of Ambedkar as a Bodhisattva, a concept which sets the teeth of some Buddhists on edge, is justified by the concepts: "He actually *was* the bringer of Buddhism to his people". "Even the Buddha himself claimed to be no more than a man; why not a human savior"?

Perhaps a more valid question is, "What will be the lifespan of the current Buddhist movement"? There are signs which may give rise to a prediction that the new Buddhists will return to Hinduism at a somewhat higher level because of their emphasis on education and the purification of their living habits. There is among them the continuation of some Hindu ritual, especially among those who either are so well off economically and educationally that they have been able to integrate into modern, urban Hindu society, or so poorly off economically that they cannot afford to break the links with their Hindu neighbors.

However, there are also signs in the movement that point to the possibility of long-time continuation: the production of song literature, lives of the Buddha and translations of scripture in the vernaculars; the study of Pali, the Buddhist scriptural language, by young Buddhist college students and the teaching of Pali chants to groups at all levels; the celebration of Budha Jayanti with processions, speeches and drama all in the new tradition; the development of leadership, not so much in the traditional Sangha of monks as among young educated laymen; the presence of some 20 to 25 bhikshus -- English, Thai, Tibetan, Japanese, Sinhalese -- living or traveling in the centers of the new Buddhism, communicating belief and practice with varying degrees of success to those who call themselves Buddhists; pilgrimages, often by means of free passes by those who work on the railway, to the Buddhist holy places. Wherever it *is* financially or legally possible, Buddhist converts have built small *viharas*, Buddhist temples, or converted old temples into Buddhist centers, where an image of the Buddha (and a picture of Ambedkar) is installed, prayer or *vandana* meetings and public meetings are held, scripture and songs are heard, visiting bhikshus live and the nursery schools or the young men's student groups of the community meet.

Perhaps as important as any of these is a psychological change. Although *Bauddha*, the Marathi word now used for themselves by Buddhist converts in Maharashtra, is generally understood by others as a synonym for Mahar, the convert himself feels a release from the concept of pollution, a new freedom and self-respect.

There are few signs that today's Buddhist movement in India will produce the great art or the profound scriptures of its past days, but there is little doubt that the revival of Buddhism, both in its intellectual and conversion facts, has added a hopeful stress on equality and humanitarian behavior to the Indian scene.

For a more scholarly discussion of the pre-Ambedkar Buddhist revival see my "The Indian Rediscovery of Buddhism, 1855-1956", in A.K. Narain ed., *Studies in Pali and Buddhism* (New Delhi: D.K. Publishers & Distributors, 1979).

Religion and Legitimization
in the Mahar Movement[*]

The Mahar movement, more than other Untouchable caste movement to achieve upward mobility, may be seen as Western in its orientation. My own writings convey this impression. It is easy to see why: the methods used by the Western-educated Dr. B.R. Ambedkar, the unquestioned leader of the movement, seem modern -- governmental petitions and testimony, organized political parties, parliamentary procedures, mass contact through conferences and newspapers. The institutions created by the Mahars can all be named in English: the People's Education Society, the Republican Party, even the Buddhist Society of India. The rhetoric used also seems universal to all low-class movements: claim equality! agitate! educate! However, as I have turned my attention recently from the actions and the organizations of Dr. Ambedkar and the Mahars to what might be described as the inner aims of the movement, to its poetry, and to the mythic elements which bound the highly educated Ambedkar to the Untouchable masses, I have come to have new respect for the purely Indian (or purely Maharashtrian) and traditional elements of the movement. I now want to look from inside the movement, through its own documents, to see in what ways it attempted to legitimize higher status and new functions through religious sanctification or traditional legitimation. I will focus on six moments in time in the eighty-five years of the modern recorded history of the Mahars of Maharashtra.

The first is the 1894 petition of Gopal Baba Walangkar, a retired Mahar British army soldier, whose work is the first written record of new Mahar ambition in the nineteenth century. Its very existence indicates a change in the economic status of the caste, i.e., the fact that some Mahars had left the traditional position of the village servant for non-traditional occupations. The second document repeats the theme of the first: a plea for recruitment into the British army and the lower ranks of administration; it is the 1910 petition to the Government written by Shivram Janba Kamble, a Mahar butler in the Masonic Hall in Pune.

The next three documents are from the period when Ambedkar was the leader. The Mahad Conference of 1927, which is seen by many

---

[*]First published in *Religion and Legitimation in South Asia*, edited by Bardwell L. Smith (Leiden: E.J. Brill, 1978).

Mahars as the moment of their mass awakening, was called by Ambedkar after ten years of work through conferences, newspapers and parliamentary action. The conversion speech of 1935 announced Ambedkar's rejection of Hinduism and an end to the Mahar effort to force entrance into the institutions of Hinduism, although conversion to another religion was set aside for twenty years in favor of intense political, educational, and social activity. At the time of the third of Ambekdar's documents, the Buddhist conversion speech of 1956, such unity had been achieved that 75 per cent of the Mahars and a number of small groups outside Maharashtra followed Ambedkar into Buddhism, resulting in three million new Buddhists.

The final documents are current and consist of literature, the poetry and short stories of the Dalit school. This is the writing of the now-educated, highly politicized, still radical Mahar-Buddhist left; it constitutes both a new level of Mahar achievement and restatement of their basic aims.

From the very beginning of the Mahar movement, its leaders seem to have searched for legitimacy for a change in social position in five ways which could be classified as religious, or, more broadly, traditional:

1. Brahmanical approval of new status and function. In the Maharashtrian context, a Brahman must be seen as elite, as cultural and social arbiter, as well as ritual specialist.
2. Societal acknowledgement of a right to a place in religious activities on a level with clean castes.
3. Recognition of religious knowledge and purity of life.
4. Scriptural sanctification.
5. Justification by mythic history.

In examining the six documents, I have added the briefest of notes on the historical context of the material and have stressed the ways in which the document illumined the quest for legitimacy in one or another of these five ways.

The Walangkar Petition

Toward the end of the nineteenth century, recruitment of Untouchables from Maharashtra (Bombay Presidency) into the British army was stopped in favor of a "martial race" (chiefly from the Northwest) pattern of recruitment. For Mahars, who had been employed in the British army for a hundred years, this blocked one of their main paths of social advancement. A retired Mahar Havaldar, Gopalnak Viththalnak Walangkar, known as Gopal Baba, prepared a long petition for re-entry into the army and circulated it among the Untouchable pensioners. They were not ready for such unified action, however, and the petition was never signed and sent to the British Government. A handwritten copy which is bound together with a long poem by Pandit Kondiram, evidently a Mahar religious figure, is in the Khairmode Collection of Ambedkar material in the University of Bombay Library. (Ambedkar was a distant relative of Walangkar's and from the same Mahar army family background.) Newspapers of the 1890s confirm the authenticity of the document and report similar sentiments in Walangkar's public speeches.

Walangkar's main plea for the re-admission of Mahar, Chambhar, and Mang castes (all Marathi-speaking Untouchables) into the army was based on the proven worth of the "anarya" (non-Aryans) as military men. His rhetoric, however, also suggests an interesting pattern of legitimizing devices, and the accompanying poem further develops the Mahar position. Walangkar deals with the five legitimizing points in the following ways:

1. *Brahmanical approval*

Although there was high caste criticism of the treatment of Untouchables at this time and even the possibility that a sympathetic Brahman helped Walangkar write his petition, Walangkar's main effort is to question the origin of the high castes, and hence their right to discriminate, rather than to note the approval of the reformers among them. His sweeping judgments reflect a view of India's history as one of great mobility and change: Why should the opinion of the high castes count for so much, asks Walangkar, when the high caste people of the South were originally "Australian-semitic, non-Aryan and African Negroes"; when the Chitpavans were "Barbary Jews" shipwrecked on the coast who married low caste women and became Brahmans when they became rulers; when the Marathas themselves came to India as Turks? God has sent the British to rule, Walangkar claims, as punishment for these people's persecution of the Untouchable. In the tough language of the nineteenth century Maharashtrian reformers, Walangkar bypasses the need for Brahmanical approval by disparaging Brahmans, a position possible only so long as the British controlled the opportunities wanted.

2. *Rights in religious activities*

Walangkar does not concern himself with this. A newspaper report of another of his public protests (*Indu Prakash*, Bombay, 5 May 1890) notes his protest against Untouchables not being allowed to stay in *dharmsalas* (pilgrims' guest houses) but there does not seems to be any protest against Untouchables being debarred from temples and religious processions.

3. *Recognition of religious knowledge and purity of life*

Walangkar notes that even if a group stops eating beef for generations, they are still Untouchables. Sanskritization evidently brought no social reward. The poem attached to Walangkar's petition indicates why Walangkar did not belabor this point. In bitter, reproachful tones it notes the social consequences of the deprivation of the Untouchables: lice in women's hair, children playing in rubbish and dancing in *tamasha* (folk drama), men eating carrion, ignorance, humble faces, knowledge only of the demon gods, immoral *gosavis* (holy men). No claim to higher status on the basis of religious knowledge and purity of life among the masses could be made at this time. Internal reform must come first.

4. *Scriptural sanctification*

Walangkar asked the Brahmans, his petition states, five years earlier to prove the lowness of the Untouchable by religious scripture and to show how by religious remedies this lowness could be removed, but "none of the caste -- proud of their priests upto now, have proved our lowness". The poem of Pandit Kondiram is more radical. It ends starkly: "Burn these brahmanical scriptures".

5. *Mythic history*

Walangkar presents two contradictory myths in casual form to underwrite his plea for re-entrance into the army. The name of the group in whose name the petition was written is, in English, the Non-Aryan Group for the Removal of Wrongs. The position that Untouchables were the pre-Aryan peoples of India was accepted by movements in the South (*Adi-Dravida*, the first Dravidians) and in the North (*Ad-Dharm*, first religion). Such a concept legitimizes social protest by assuming that the

Aryan conquest, not inherent polluting qualities, reduced the Untouchable to a low status. However, in Maharashtra, this mythic history rationale was little used. Walangkar himself counters his own claim by asserting that the Mahars were former Kshatriyas, demoted during the Great Famine for eating forbidden food. A consistently satisfying mythic-history was not developed in the Mahar movement until Ambedkar's Buddhist conversion speech of 1956 but the *need* for such a mythic history is apparent at all levels of the Mahar movement.

The Walangkar petition and Pandit Kondiram's accompanying poem cannot be read as evidence of mass Mahar thought. Both were obviously far more radical statements than the majority of Mahars were prepared to make publicly. However, one can draw some general conclusions about the movement from these early protests.

First, Mahar leadership was more concerned about *function* than about ritual status. The right to have an opportunity to leave the traditional village Mahar duties of watchman, scavenger, message-bearer, etc. demanded that the ruling power provide opportunities to make that move. The right to have a new function, however, did involve legitimizing arguments both to the Government and to fellow Hindus. In the Walangkar petition, we see the Mahar avoiding a claim based on ritual purity to stress the view that high status groups have been low themselves in the past, that change has taken place in many periods of India's past, that the Mahar has just as much a right to change function as have high caste peoples. What is needed is good performance of that function and some sort of legitimizing mythic history to explain present low status and hence allow changes!

Later documents are more concerned with ritual status as the mass of Mahars reaches toward the lifestyle and values of the clean castes. However, this initial view of change in function as basic remains constant. It was the Mahar who had left the village function of, in British legal terms, "inferior village servant", who began the Mahar movement. As the movement progressed, not only did more Mahars enter non-traditional occupations (the mills, dock-work, construction, the railroad), but also those remaining in the village were urged to drop that aspect of their village function which was most polluting -- the eating of the carrion beef which it was their duty to drag from the village. The Mahar traditional occupation could not modernize although it could be stripped of polluting elements. It was up to the "new" Mahar, the Mahar who had left the village, to legitimize his new function, and then to try to extend that legitimacy and its consequent higher status image to his brethren still in the village.

Shivram Janba Kamble's Petition of 1910

Kamble's position as butler in the Masonic Hall in Pune illustrates another new Mahar occupation—that of the servant of the British. This kind of service allowed the Mahar to learn English as well as secure economic independence from village work, and, low as such service seems now, produced a number of Mahar innovators in the past. Kamble's group were those who had become urbanized and worked as semi-skilled labor, as well as a few old retired soldiers of Walangkar's breed. His petition, although it is also a plea for re-admittance into the army and opportunities for service in the lower reaches of Government administration, is far more sophisticated than Walangkar's. It was sent to the Earl of Crewe, Secretary of State for India in London, from the Conference of the Deccan Mahars and may have helped, along with war-time necessity, in the creation of a Mahar labor force as an adjunct to the army during World War I. Looking at the Kamble petition through the same five foci as we did Walangkar's petition indicates that the basic matter of *function* still predominates (Navalkar, 1930).

1. *Brahmanical approval*

Kamble notes the anti-untouchability stance of several Brahman reformers and political leaders. Here the elite rather than the ritual status of the Brahman is important, but it must be remembered that in the Maharashtrian context, social elite are Brahman, thus inextricably mixing ritual and social status. Kamble also rests his case on the fact that the British parliament now contains groups who, "only a quarter of a century ago, were regarded as but Mahars and Paryas by the more educated and affluent classes of their nation", thus extending the concept of radical change in history from the Indian to the European milieu.

2. *Right to religious activities*

Since Kamble's petition is directed very consciously to the British, this element does not enter into the document. Kamble's own activities, however, included a sustained attempt in 1929 to enter Parvati Temple in Pune. This satyagraha failed completely in the face of obdurance and violence. However, Kamble's efforts to force entrance of Untouchables into tea shops in Pune indicated that an attack on this aspect of ritual pollution in the urban areas could be successful.

3/4/5. Purity of life, scriptural sanctification, mythic history

Kamble's position on these matters cannot be gleaned from the petition. A suggestion that Kamble attempted to use mythic history is in the title of a newspaper that he founded in 1909, *Somwanshiya Mitra*, friend of the Somwanshi. Somwanshi is a sub-caste among the Mahars; it also is a major mythological division of Hindus into "the race of the moon" in contrast to "the race of the sun". Kamble used the word Mahar in calling caste conferences as early as 1903 and was far more caste-based in his activities than either Walangkar before him or Ambedkar after him. It seems to me that in his use of *Somwanshiya* he is linking the Mahars to a mythic past, important chiefly to Rajputs, and hence suggesting a Kshatriya linkage. Kamble worked with a retired Mahar army man in his various campaigns in Pune and he often held meetings at the foot of the Koregaon monument, a pillar erected to commemorate the war heroes during the British defeat of the Peshwa in 1818 which lists many Mahar names. Kambles's stress on the militant Mahar past indicates a basic Kshatriya mythic history.

The Mahad Conferences of 1927

B.R. Ambedkar appeared publicly on the Bombay scene in 1918, when he testified at length to the Southborough Commission. This testimony, however, was mid-point in his advanced education. After graduating from Elphinstone College, he had studied at Columbia University and gone on to England to do a D.Sc. from the London School of Economics and thereafter to enter the Bar. Returning in the early 1920s, he used the same methods as Kamble, conferences and newspapers, to build group unity, served as a legislator (as a nominated Untouchable representative) in the Bombay Assembly, and began to push at a much greater pace the demands for opportunities for employment in the British administration, the schools and the police. The Mahad Conference of 1927 was one of the many he called, but its drawing power and its actions created the numbers and the news which made it a landmark.

The Kolaba District Depressed Classes Conference (note that the name Mahar is not used) met at Mahad, a small town south of Bombay. The site was chosen on the basis of an invitation by the caste Hindu reformer who headed the Municipality and who was a friend of Ambedkar. The speeches and resolutions of the first conference were similar to those of other conferences. After the meeting, several thousands marched to a pond in the high caste area of Mahad and the first to arrive drank the water from the tank. This action incited such violence that the Untouchables had to hastily withdraw for fear of their lives. A second conference was called later the same year to protest against the ritual cleansing that the Mahad pond had undergone, and it was at this meeting that the Mahar path of radical protest was begun and the ancient law book, *Manusmriti*, which condoned untouchability, was burned.

In terms of the five point rubric used previously, the conferences' speeches and actions yield these positions:

1. *Brahmanical/elite approval*

A number of Brahmans keen on social reforms and high caste non-Brahmans were among Ambedkar's followers. One had invited Ambedkar to use Mahad as a site for a conference; a Brahman proposed the resolution to condemn the *Manusmriti*. Ambedkar did not ask for Brahmanical sanction for change in any ritualized way. He did, however, use all the support he could muster from the elite for his program, maintaining his hold on the reins of power and delegating certain responsibilities to these radical reformers. In addition, Ambedkar himself *appeared* as one of the elite; his speech, dress, presence, educational background and aggressive temperament were all similar to those of Maharashtrian Brahman elite. It might be said that by the time of the Mahad Conference, Ambedkar himself had assumed an elite function -- as teacher, writer, legislator--without, of course, elite or clean-caste ritual status. Using what radical brahmanical approval was available to him, Ambedkar was beginning to reject any sort of orthodox legitimization. He both served as a source of charisma for his own caste and as an enabling device in governmental circles. Ambedkar's "westernization" could also be called "brahmanization" in a broad cultural sense, and this met some ideal goal current among his people, binding them to him.

2. *Right to religious activities*

The Mahad satyagraha was for the right to use the common water tank, but it was the fear of the higher caste population that the Untouchables would enter the temple that had triggered the attack, according to reports. Temple-entry was in the air and the Mahars were soon to make three organized attempts at Amravati, Pune and Nasik. They had already made an unsuccessful attempt to take part in a Ganpati procession in

Bombay. Ambedkar was never especially concerned with ritual rights, but it is clear that those who followed him expected that participation in institutionalized Hindu activities would be a consequence of their activities and self-improvement.

3. Recognition of religious knowledge and purity of life

Ambedkar did not try to claim that the heterodox religious practices of the Mahars were worthy of respect, nor did he for long encourage Sanskritized religious practices. As a student at Elphinstone College in Bombay he had attempted to study Sanskrit, but objections by the teacher forced him to take Persian as his second language instead. I have no doubt but that had he been able to master Sanskrit, he would have added that source of religious knowledge effectively to his own elite image. Deprived of that skill, he devoted his energy in encouraging "purity of life" among his followers. At the Mahad conference he asked all those who attended to take a vow to renounce the eating of carrion and reinforced this attempt to remove the basic root of Mahar pollution by asking caste Hindus to bury their own dead cows and the Government to prohibit by law the eating of carrion! He also asked his listeners to "improve the general tone of our demeanour, *re-tone our pronunciations* and revitalise our thoughts". Women in special meetings were asked to dress like caste Hindu women, to send their children to school, not to feed their husbands if they were drunk. Internal attempts at reform, now much stressed by the Mahar movement, fit very well into M.N. Srinivas' rubric of Sanskritization, but note here that the emphasis is on elements which are social rather than ritualistic.

4. Scriptural sanctification

The high point of the second Mahar Conference of 1927 was the ceremonial burning of the *Manusmriti*, an act recalled with shock by caste Hindus even today. Within a few years, Mahatma Gandhi was to challenge anyone to find justification for Untouchability in the scriptures, but the Mahars had already asked the question, had found evidence of scriptural legitimization of their untouchability, and rejected it.

5. Justification by mythic history

Ambedkar used neither the pre-Aryan nor the former-Kshatriya myths. Possibly he felt that a pre-Aryan claim would set the Mahars aside as a separate race, and he had seen permanent racial division in America during his student years. As for claiming Kshatriya status, the clean caste Maratha community had fought that battle for years with a much more viable argument of past kings and Rajput linkages. During his Mahad speech, Ambedkar hinted at a time when "we, who are condemned as Untouchables, were much advanced, much ahead in education compared with communities other than the advanced classes. This part of the country was then pulsating with the action and authority of our people" (Keer 1962: 69-70). His reference is not clear but the need for a mythic past, however, is clear, and when Ambedkar had developed a view of the Mahar past which would both explain the caste's low position and justify its current struggle for empowerment, it became a vital part of his message.

The Conversion Speech of 1935

By the mid-thirties, the Mahars had been involved in six years of futile temple-entry struggle; they had also been involved in agitation for political rights which had won them reserved places in the legislature which would insure representation even beyond their numbers. It seems to me that the conversion speech can be seen in two lights: one is the genuine anguish which Ambedkar felt as a Hindu who polluted other Hindus; the other is the glow of political success and the hope that the threat of conversion, which would cut down the numbers of Hindus in the numbers game of separate electorates vis-a-vis Muslims, would act as a catalyst to force Hindus to open up in the religious field from political motives. The mood of the speech is best expressed by a short quotation:

> Because we have the misfortune of calling ourselves Hindus, we are treated thus. If we were members of another Faith, none would dare treat us so. Choose any religion which gives you equality of status and treatment. We shall repair our mistake now. I had the misfortune of being born with the stigma of an Untouchable. However, it is not my fault; but I will not die a Hindu, for this is in my power. (Ambedkar, 1936)

The analysis of the conversion announcement involves only one of my five points, that of the need for an acknowledgment of religious rights. It is this element of legitimization that Ambedkar was trying to force. The religious rights he saw as necessary to underwrite the Mahar claim to equality must be gleaned not only from his speeches but also from his reaction to the responses which followed (The Depressed Classes, 1935).

Although individuals among the Mahar community protested, no Mahar group rejected the idea of conversion. The *Manusmriti* was burned again, this time near Nasik, the site of a five-year temple entry satyagraha. Groups from outside Maharashtra, chiefly in the North and in the Kerala area, picked up the conversion refrain, but Ambedkar did not use this response to organize a massive movement. Caste Hindus also responded. Pandit Madan Mohan Malaviya offered to fund a special ritual ''with which all disabilities would go except dinner and marriage''. Dr. Kurtakoti, the Sankaracharya of Karwar Math, offered to found a new sect with equal status to other sections of Hinduism. To these overtures, Ambedkar answered with a clear view of what he meant by religious equality: K.K. Sakat, an Untouchable who was an exemplary Hindu, should be elevated to the position of Sankaracharya for a year and so acknowledged by Chitpavan Brahmans; Hinduism should be changed from a "religion of rules" to a "religion of principles", and the necessary changes would involve: (1) one standard book of Hindu religion, (2) no hereditary priesthood, but an examination system open to all, (3) state permits required for priests, (4) a limit by law on the numbers of priests, (5) state supervision of the priest's morals, beliefs and worship. No Hindu, however interested in reform, indeed no realist, could accept these dicta. Hinduism would have to entirely change its character. But Ambedkar's point is that the Mahar here himself claims the right to earn Brahmanhood.

Ambedkar dallied with the Muslims, Christians, Sikhs, Buddhists and Arya Samajists who were interested, for one reason or another, in the possibility of a Mahar conversion to their numbers. For a while, he seemed to lean toward Sikhism, but then dropped the whole idea when it became clear that after conversion they could not carry the new political privileges of the Untouchables into a new religion. The Mahars, however, never again returned to a group movement for Hindu religious rights.

The Buddhist Conversion of 1956

Twenty years after the Mahar Conference on conversion, Ambedkar was at last ready to announce a new religion. An old man, sick with diabetes and with less than two months to live, he took *diksha* (conversion) from the hands of the oldest Buddhist monk in India under the hot October sun in Nagpur. The following day he converted the half-million of his followers who had responded to his call to convert.

Ambedkar had been interested in Buddhism since the early 1930s; by 1956 Buddhism had become not only an intellectual passion but a more viable new religious home for those who found sanction within Hinduism for their new role and function. In Buddhism, Ambedkar had found an Indian, not a foreign, religion which could legitimize the claims of the Mahar. The nature of the Buddhism which he initiated may be seen in his conversion speech; in *The Buddha and His Dhamma* (1957), Ambedkar's rationalized life of the Buddha and explanation of his teachings; in the twenty-two "Buddhist Oaths" which constituted part of the conversion ritual (see Appendix); and in the small number of practices Ambedkar was able to develop before his death.

Opting out of Hinduism might seem to obviate the need to legitimize through the five ways I have used to analyze all other documents. Looking at the conversion through these lenses, however, does show that the acceptance of Buddhism in some ways tracks closely with previous Mahar efforts.

1. *Brahmanical or elite approval*

By choosing Buddhism, Ambedkar leapt over the necessity of eliciting approval. Buddhism itself is egalitarian, and by 1956 Buddhism as a religion was respected although not much practiced in India. The symbols of independent India, the wheel on the flag and the lion pillar, were Buddhist or from Buddhist times. Two important neighbors, Burma and Ceylon, which Ambedkar had visited to experience living Buddhism, were Buddhist countries. Several important scholars, chief among them Dharmanand Kosambi, a Maharashtrian, were doing research on Buddhism and a few Indian intellectuals (Rahul Sankrityayana, Anand Kausalyayan, Kashyap) had become Buddhists out of conviction. Ambedkar stressed the respect in which Buddhism is held in the world in his conversion speech: "Even today, 2500 years afterwards, all the world respects the principles of Buddhism". "Only one name is proclaimed throughout the world, and that name is Buddha".

2. *Religious rights*

Ambedkar made it clear that the Buddha's message was equality.

"In the Buddhist religion, 75 per cent of the Bhikshus were Brahman; 25 per cent were Shudra and others". Ambedkar did not set in motion a way to develop a Sangha; he actually only began the institutionalization of the conversion. It is as if he made a gift of Buddhism to those who had followed him along the educational and political paths he opened, wiping away the stigma of religious inequality by presenting a way to say with inner certainty, "I am equal; I do not pollute". The Buddhist's Oaths which are reproduced in the Appendix illustrate the way in which Ambedkar combined the rejection of specific Hindu beliefs with an acceptance of Buddhism. The rather crude negative oaths seem to have been essential to inculcate the sense of psychological freedom from pollution that the Mahar had never been able to gain within the confines of Hinduism.

3. *Recognition of religious knowledge and purity of life*

Throughout his conversion speech, Ambedkar told little stories which reinforced all the long years of striving to purify Mahar practices. A Brahman had asked him, "Why do you throw away 500 rupees profit every year from hide, hoof and meat when you are so poor"? and Ambedkar had told him, "You have many dependents. Why don't you remove the dead cattle and get the profit? I myself will give you 500 rupees on top of that". He used another homily to reiterate the need to maintain the dignity of women: In the locality of prostitutes in Bombay, the women rise in the morning and say, "Suleman, bring bread and a plate of minced meat". The Depressed Class sisters do not even get ordinary chutney-bhakri. However, Ambedkar said, they live with dignity; they live piously. The point is clear; the Mahar, now Buddhist, life is to be pure by both Hindu and elite standards. The Buddhist newly converted said Ambedkar, must bring honor to Buddhism, whether he is an educated or an illiterate man.

Ambedkar's conversion speech simplifies Buddhism. It is in no way a scholarly analysis of religious knowledge Mahars would then be expected to exhibit. It must be understood, however, that education had been a major tenet of the movement from its earliest days. In his speech Ambedkar assumes that the Mahar will value education; he refers often to his own school days and his own learning. He states that it is his duty to lead his people "to a stage of full knowledge" and that he is writing a book which will help them to achieve this end. The speech of 1956 stresses good behavior. In the colleges he had established, Ambedkar had

instituted departments to teach Pali and it is clear that he expected those
who became highly educated to master the source of Buddhist religious
knowledge. At this time the emphasis is still on gaining religious
knowledge and establishing purity of life, not on securing
acknowledgement of those accomplishments.

4. Scriptural sanctification

Obviously the scriptural sanctification required here is in Buddhism.
In his speech, Ambedkar talks of an argument with Mahatma Gandhi
over *chaturvarna* (four-fold caste hierarchy) in which he asked, "who
created the *chaturvarna* and who will end it"? and Gandhi can give no
answer. Ambedkar then added that Marxism is not enough to remove suffering. No "scripture" sufficed for Ambedkar save the Buddha's
teaching of equality.

5. Justification by mythic history

Ambedkar had already developed his theory that Untouchables had
been Buddhists cast aside as India became re-Hinduized in his book, *The
Untouchables: Who were they? and why they became Untouchables*. In
his speech at the time of conversion he stated that during the Aryan
harassment of the Nag people, Agastya Muni helped one Nag man to
escape. "We spring from that man". The Nag people then met Gautam
Buddha and "spread the teaching of Bhagwan Buddha all over India".
The city of Nagpur was chosen for the conversion because it was the city
of the Nags. In his speech, Ambedkar does not fully develop his theory,
nor does he belabor this point. In the Mahar mind, however, the idea was
quickly assimilated. The Mahar as former Buddhist, persecuted because
he had clung to his Buddhism, was now returning to his old faith.
Ambedkar had given a fully satisfactory explanation of the low status and
a justification for a claim to a respected place in Indian society.

The analysis ought to end here with a note comparing Walangkar's
original statement of Mahar aims and Ambedkar's concluding message
for his poeple. The Mahar, now Buddhist, movement is still dynamic,
however. Buddhism has not proved to be a panacea. *Bauddh*, in Marathi,
means Mahar. As a Buddhist, he has a sense of psychological freedom,
a satisfying mythic history, and full rights within a respected world religion. But although many of the old practices of untouchability are gone,
the Buddhist still suffers from poverty, from some discrimination, and

from the violence which erupts when he oversteps his place in the village. In the last three years the movement has developed another aspect, that of *Dalit* politics and *Dalit* literature. *Dalit* means broken, "reduced to pieces", oppressed or low. It avoids the ritual pollution connotations of the word Untouchable but unmistakably refers to that group.

Dalit Panthers, Dalit Literature

Dalit literature, that is, writing which is considered genuine literature rather than folk-protest poetry and "movement" literature, may be said to have begun in the late 1950s with the short stories of Shankarrao Kharat, who wrote movingly of his childhood as a village Mahar (Miller, 1972). A lawyer and former Vice-Chancellor of Marathwada University, Kharat produced books within the movment: an edition of the letters of Ambedkar, the story of the Buddhist conversion. He also produced short stories which had to be considered as genuine evidence of creativity in the strong Marathi literary tradition. Since that time, a fairly steady flow of short stories and poetry and a series of Buddhist and Dalit Literacy Conferences have resulted in what must be called a significant new school of Marathi writing, that of Dalit Literature. Acknowledgment of the worth of this writing is evidenced in the 25 November 1973 supplement of the *Times Weekly*. Dileep Padgaonkar's introduction to this special issue on Dalit Literature states: "Its immense merit is to have effectively rebelled, in life as in letters, against the middle-class Hindus who have monopolised cultural expression".

Accompanying the tough, realistic, unorthodox literature, a new socio-political movement has surfaced; it was organized in 1972 as the Dalit Panthers. The first of the new Mahar Buddhist writers, Shankarrao Kharat, is not part of this movement, but most of the recently acknowledged young writers are. The Dalit Panthers reject the compromising ways the political party Ambedkar had established came to adopt. Their methods (calling for a boycott of an election, marching on a village where a caste Hindu who raped a Buddhist girl was not brought to justice) are outside normal politics. The Panthers, however, do not reject Ambedkar or Buddhism, and although their loyalty to his teaching, if not his organizations, is mixed with a vague Marxism, they feel the new thrust of his movement.

The rhetoric of the Dalit Panthers returns to the days of Ambedkar's exhortation to his followers to be defiantly strong, even to the time of Walangkar's disparagement of Brahmans, of belief in the possibility of radical change. Ambedkar once told his people, "Become the ruling community", a slogan I have seen painted on the walls of a tiny library built in the 1930s in a Mahar city slum. A pamphlet of the Dalit Panthers states, "We do not want a little place in the Brahman Alley. We want the rule of the whole land". The poetry returns to the tough, bitter tone of the poem of Pandit Kondiram which lay, unpublished, in the personal library of Ambedkar along with the Walangkar petition of 1894. One example is Arun Kamble's *The Life We Live*, translated by Gauri Deshpande in the *Times Weekly Supplement* of 25 November 1973:

> If you were to live the life we live
> (them out of you would poems arise).
> We: kicked and spat at for
>   our piece of bread
> You: fetch fulfillment and
>   name of the Lord.
> We: down-gutter degraders
>   of our heritage
> You: its sole repository
>   descendants of the sage.
> We: never have a paisa to scratch our arse
> You: the golden cup of offerings in your bank.
> Your bodies flame in sandalwood.
> Ours you shovel under half-turned sand.
>
> Wouldn't the world change, and fast,
> If you were forced to live at last
> This life that's all we've ever had?

Another poem by Kamble, *Speech*, translated by Gauri Deshpande in the same *Times Weekly* supplement, also contrasts the Mahar-Brahman images:

> Bone-chewing granpus
> at burning ghat
> permanent resident
> of my own heart
> with weight of traditon
> behind his back
> yells, "sadding bastard, I tell you,
> Stutter with *our* tongue"!

> Picking through the vedas buttering his queue
> Brahmin teacher at school
> bellows, "speak my pure tongue,
> whoreson".
>
> Now, you tell me which
>   speech
> am I to tongue?

Here is the defiant Mahar, the Buddhist free from the psychological burden of pollution, bitter about both past and present but still proud of being what he is, and proclaiming both bitterness and pride in the Brahman's own tongue, i.e. sophisticated literature.

What dimension does the new school of Dalit Literature add to the Mahar movement? What new demands are made and what sorts of legitimation are sought for them? Walangkar's petition to re-enter the army was met in 1942 by the establishment, at Ambedkar's urging, of a Mahar Regiment as a proud unit of the Indian army. Kamble's urging that the Mahar be accepted into the lower ranks of administration and police was met by the legal provision that a percentage of all governmental positions be reserved for the Scheduled Castes. Ambedkar's secular demands have been met, at least in theory, by the constitutional outlawing of any act of discrimination against Untouchables; his religious demands were obviated by the Buddhist conversion, and for those who did not convert there has been a general opening of Hindu temples, at least in urban areas. What still burns is the general poverty level of most Scheduled Castes; sporadic but often intense enforcement of traditional subservience—at times violent—in the rural areas; subtle indications of inferiority in the cities—and something that can only be described as a lack of recognition of *manuski*, the full humanity of the Untouchable.

Looking at the Mahar story, it seems as if religious legitimation of their upward movement has been unimportant. The great changes wrought have come by secular government fiat or economic opportunity. But Hinduism is more than a religion, and its hierarchy of social groupings has been correlated not only with status but also *function*. When one studies the Mahar movement as a group change in function, it becomes clear that the simple view of education and urbanization equaling modernization is not good enough. One must look at the nature of the function the Buddhist leadership now performs not only in terms of occupation but in terms of the traditional caste structure of Maharash-

tra. And one must consider this caste structure in order to understand why
all Ambedkar's efforts, and those following him, failed to build a class
movement, an organization of the Depressed Classes and the exploited in
general, and has remained limited to the Mahars (and to smaller groups
of other castes in areas outside Maharashtra).

Given this view, one asks: what new function could a Mahar Untouchable have whose traditional role was to serve the village as remover
of pollution, low-status functionary in the bureaucratic system, enter-
tainer in folk-music and folk-drama, and, of course, agricultural labor?
When he becomes highly educated, urbanized, politicized, he does not
yearn for the land (which he has never owned in viable quantities); he has
no artisan skill; he has no instinct for trade (no Marathi-speaking caste of
any size has entered this field); he can only fill the traditional social role
of the Maharashtrian Brahman: the administrative echelons and the
cultural establishment. Entering government service has been encouraged by special-privilege acts of the Government of India; filling a
cultural role has been on the Mahar's own initiative.

What seems to be happening today is that the Mahar as "Brahman"
is seeking and winning societal approval for a cultural *function*: the
creation of literature, which has a meaningful high status value in
Maharashtrian society. And the approval must come from the cultural
establishment, which is still largely Brahman. As Dileep Padgaonkar,
quoted earlier, has said, the Dalit writer has "effectively rebelled, in life
as in letters, against the middle-class Hindus who have monopolised
cultural expression". Though the Village enemy may well be Maratha,
whose caste dominates the land agriculturally and politically, the ideological enemy, the "mirror-image" in Arun Kamble's poems, and in
many others, is still the Brahman. And yet paradoxically the very poets
who translated the Dalit literature in the Special Issue of the *Times
Weekly* are Brahman!

But all the years of effort have still left the bulk of the Mahars, now
Buddhists, in the village. What is especially interesting in the Mahar
movement is its leadership: for however elite they themselves may have
become, the Mahar leaders have sought to extend the legitimacy won in the
exercise of their new function to those still caught in the lower reaches
of society. This cohesiveness is what has made the Mahar struggle in
Maharashtra a movement of different quality than that of other Untouchables' efforts toward higher social status. The tie of the Dalit poets
with the Dalit Panthers is not a coincidence. The new Mahar, the
Buddhist, the poet, with his new "tongue" proclaims the human worth
of all his fellows.

Appendix

Buddhist's Oaths

1. I will not regard Brahma, Vishnu and Mahesh as Gods nor will I worship them.
2. I will not regard Rama and Krishna as Gods nor will I worship them.
3. I will not accept Hindu Deities like Gauri, Ganapati, etc., nor will I worship them.
4. I do not believe that God had taken birth or incarnation in any form.
5. I do not believe that Lord Buddha was the Incarnation of Vishnu. I believe this propaganda as mischievous and false.
6. I will never perform any Sharaadha* nor will I offer any Pinda.**
7. I will never act against the tenets of Buddhism.
8. I will never get any SAMSKAAR performed by Brahmins.
9. I believe in the principle that all are equal.
10. I will try to establish equality.
11. I will follow the Eight Fold Path of Lord Buddha.
12. I will follow all the ten Paramitas of the Dhamma.
13. I will have compassion on all living beings and will try to look after them.
14. I will not lie.
15. I will not commit theft.
16. I will not indulge in lust or sexual transgression.
17. I will not take any liquor or drink that causes intoxication.
18. I will try to mould my life in accordance with the Buddhist preachings, based on Enlightenment, Precept and Compassion.
19. I embrace today the Bauddha Dhamma discarding the Hindu Religion which is detrimental to the emancipation of human beings and which believes in inequality and regards human beings other than the Brahmins as low born.
20. This is my firm belief that the Bauddha Dhamma is the best religion.
21. I believe that today I am taking New-birth.
22. I solemnly take oath that from today onwards I will act according to the Bauddha DHAMMA.

Sabbe Satta Suknee Hontu

---

*A ceremony after the death of the man in Hinduism.

** Handful rice offered in the name of the deceased.

References

Ambedkar, Bhimrao Ramji, *Mukti Kon Pathe?* (What Path Freedom) (Bombay: Bharat Bhushan Printing Press, 1936).

―――― *Annihilation of Caste with a Reply to Mahatama Gandhi* (Ambedkar: Ambedkar School of Thought, 1945, 3rd edition, First published in 1936).

―――― *The Untouchables. Who were they and why they became Untouchables* (New Delhi: Amrit Book Co., 1948).

―――― "Report of Dr. Babasaheb Ambedkar's Speech in Nagpur" in *Prabuddh Bharat*, Translated by Rekha Damle and Eleanor Zelliot from the Marathi (27 October 1956).

―――― *The Buddha and His Dhamma* (Bombay: Siddharth College, 1957).

The Depressed Classes, "Bombay Depressed Classes Decision" in *The Depressed Classes: a Chronological Documentation.* Part I (Ranchi: Rev. Fr. J. Jans S.J., Catholic Press, 1935). Part II - Part VII (Kurseong: St. Mary's College, 1935-37, published in one volume).

Dhananjay Keer, *Dr. Ambedkar, Life and Mission* (Bombay: Popular Prakashan, 1962, 2nd edition).

Robert J. Miller, and Pramod Kale, "The Burden on the Head is Always There" in J. Michael Mahar ed., *The Untouchables in Contemporary India.* (Tucson: University of Arizona, 1972), pp. 317-590.

H.N. Navalkar, [petition] "To The Right Honourable The Earl of Crewe" in *The Life of Shivram Janba Kamble and Brief History of Poona Parvati Satyagraha* (Pune: S.J. Kamble, 1930), pp. 142-57.

M.N. Srinivas, "Sanskritization in *Social Change in Modern India* (Berkeley: University of California Press, 1966), pp. 1-45.

Times Weekly Supplement, "Special Issue on Dalit Literature" (Bombay, 25 November, 1973).

Gopalnak Viththalnak Walangkar, "To His Excellency the Commander-in-Chief of Bombay Presidency, at Poona, from the Anarya Doshpariharakham at Dapoli", 1894. *Manuscript* translated by D.R. Maheshkar with accompanying *pad* by Pandit Kondiram in the Khairmode Collection of the University of Bombay Library.

Note: This English version of the 22 oaths has been taken, without correction, from a pamphlet published by the Buddhist Society of India, New Delhi, no date.

Eleanor Zelliot, "Buddhism and Politics in Maharashtra" in Donald
E. Smith ed., *South Asian Politics and Religion* (Princeton:
Princeton University Press, 1966), pp. 91-212.
———— "Dr. Ambedkar and the Mahar Movement", Unpublished
Ph.D. dissertation submitted to University of Pennsylvania,
1969.
———— "Learning the Use of Political Means: The Mahars of Maha-
rashtra", in Rajni Kothari ed., *Caste in Indian Politics* (New
Delhi: Orient Longmans, 1970), pp. 29-69. Also in this volume.
———— "The 19th Century Background of the Mahar and Non-
Brahman Movements in Maharashtra", in *The Indian Eco-
nomic and Social History Review*, Vol. 8, No. 3, 1970).
———— "Gandhi and Ambedkar: A Study in Leadership" in J. Michael
Mahar ed., *The Untouchables in Contemporary India* (Tucson:
University of Arizona Press, 1972), pp. 69-95.

The Psychological Dimension of the Buddhist Conversion*

The psychological impact of Buddhism, the matter of changed identity, cannot be judged by visible signs. One way of gauging it is from Buddhist literature, writings and songs. A song of Waman Kardak reads:

Here there is no caste, no useless black-white splits,
My Gautam Buddha loves each one.
The door is open for all -- Shudra, Chandala, Weaver,
    Gardener, Brahman, Fisherman, all merge
    in the triad of Buddha, Sangha, Dhamma.
There are no separate paths, all are brothers.
There is no pollution, no harassment,
    in Buddha's religion.
There is no shelter for hypocrisy
    in the place of my Buddha.
There are no gods; there is no fate,
    no deed binding one to a fatal direction.[1]

In his article on this singer, Gangadhar Pantavane writes, ''Bhimrao (Ambedkar) has placed us in the lap of a life-giving religion and so has awakened psychological independence . . . . This is the religion of Gautam, who with love won the world, and the spine of this religion is humanity''.

For Waman Kardak, an uneducated but highly skilled and professional performer, and for Gangadhar Pantavane, a Professor of Marathi in Milind College (now in Marathwada University), a writer and an editor, the profoundly satisfying psychological meaning of the conversion is clear. The same sense of pride in Buddhism, and in the same degree the love and respect for Babasaheb Ambedkar, is found in the numerous folk songs current in the Buddhist community. A more

---

*Only the final portion of this paper, originally published in G.A. Oddie ed., *Religion in South Asia* (New Delhi: Manohar, 1977), has been included in this volume.

sophisticated school of writing, a new development called Dalit Literature, is more concerned with the injustices still visited upon the lower castes than with religion, but even here, two of major leaders of this literary movement and its concurrent social arm, the Dalit Panthers, support the idea that conversion brought psychological freedom. Namdev Dhasal, a forceful poet and once the major figure in the Communist faction of the Dalit Panthers, is reported as having said, in an interview,

> Conversion to Buddhism . . . freed the scheduled castes from mental and psychological enslavement . . . . Religion (has) an attraction for the common man and it was not easy to change his attitude toward it . . . (The Buddhists have) liberated themselves from old ideas of karma and destiny and from worship of Hindu gods. To the extent this facilitated their adopting rational attitudes to their condition in society, the chances of their actively striving to change their conditions were better.[2]

The leader of the non-communist, "Ambedkar" faction of the Dalit Panthers, Raja Dhale, takes a more personal view. To him, Buddhist conversion is simply the turning again of the wheel of Dhamma, the return to the Untouchables' former identity. Buddhism is for all; it is relevant, consistent, complete. But if a Buddhist does not himself turn the wheel of Dhamma by his own thought, he becomes an Untouchable again.[3] There is little Buddhism in Raja Dhale's political or literary writing, but it seems clear that the conversion is a necessary part of his own identity.

My own observations among the Buddhists, which have tended to be primarily of educated Buddhists, support the view that psychological freedom from the sense of being a polluting person is a major achievement of the Buddhist conversion. A recent article in the *Times of India* confirms my conclusions: "They (Buddhists) seem to have got rid of their age-old inferiority complex. They have a fresh sense of identity and a newly acquired confidence. What is more, the youth among them have completely shed the superstitions that had cramped their existence and have adopted a more rational view of life".[4]

The same article reports an interview which explains why more visible Buddhist ritual cannot be reported as concrete evidence of new belief. One of the educated Buddhists interviewed notes that "the grip of blind dogmas and superstitions has been loosened to a great extent". But he fears that the vacuum will be filled by Buddhist religious rituals. He hopes, ''that the new class of rational Buddhist youths would not allow this to happen''. In other words, the very sort of replacement of Hindu processions, yatras, festivals and temple life which might involve the Buddhist masses in visible Buddhist practice is discouraged by educated Buddhists.

In spite of a thousand possible examples of new thought and new life, it must be said that the mass of Buddhists in the slums of cities, or the landless in the rural area, live in much the same fashion as the desperately poor in any culture. It is difficult here for new Buddhist identity to produce a new Buddhist morality or a new Buddhist life-style. What has happened is that even in areas where observers report ''no change at all'', one finds that Buddhists no longer carry out what they feel are ritually submissive, degrading, or impure duties; that some young people, far more than in other Untouchable and backward communities, become educated; and that Buddhists do not participate in the Hindu public practices so long denied them, not now out of prohibition but out of a sense of separateness.

What, then, has the Buddhist conversion done? It has given devout and religiously-minded Buddhists a field of religious investigation which is both highly respected for its wisdom and insight and totally free from caste bias. For those in need of a myth to explain their Untouchable status (and they are not a few), it has given a new identity as former Buddhists, reduced to a low status for their very loyalty to religion rather than because of sin. It has given strong Buddhist communities a new set of religious ideas, a thought-provoking image, a series of occasions around which to rally which have no historic overtones of caste hierarchy. It has freed the Mahar from any sense of inferiority, suspicion that any ill-treatment is justified, and although this belief in the equality of men was a part of the Mahar movement from its initial stages, it seems to have taken a conversion to a new identity to undergird this tenet.

The rationale for the conversion was psychological and the benefits have been psychological, but it is clear that this is not enough. The conversion has one facet of a multi-level effort. Economic improvement for the masses, freedom from village harassment and urban prejudice, room at the top for the ambitious and the able -- all this must come through some other path. The conversion seems to have helped to create the will to probe every possible means, and it has created the means to preserve group unity. This separatism has been decried as self-defeating to Buddhists, since their future lies in integration with the total Indian community. Separatism, however, has marked all movements of an inferior group for equality. It seems to be an essential psychological weapon in the maintenance of the group unity necessary for organized effort. And in choosing Buddhism as the vehicle for separatism, Ambedkar committed his people to a wholly Indian, basically non-violent, rational, potentially creative way.

Notes

1. In "Waman Kardak" by Gangadhar Pantavane, *Amrut*, Vol. 23, No. 9, October 1975. Translated by Eleanor Zelliot with Vidyut Bhagwat.
2. *The Economic and Political Weekly*, Vol. VIII, Nos. 31-3, p. 1398.
3. Raja Dhale, *Dr. Ambedkarance Dharmaparivarthan ki Yugaparivartan Dhamma Chakra*, 14 October 1975, Nasik District Branch Dalit Panthers.
4. "Neo-Buddhists in Maharashtra -- Conversion has Helped" by Arun Sadhu, *Times of India*, 15 November 1975.

Tradition and Innovation in Contemporary Indian Buddhism: Activities and Observances*

The contemporary Buddhist conversion movement in India arose neither from a missionary enterprise which carried its own organizational structure and leadership nor from the Buddha-ization of a highly developed existent religious structure. Unlike any other mass conversion in history, this new religious movement was almost completely on its own. The massive conversion which began in 1956 largely affected low castes, particularly the Mahars of Maharashtra, who had been involved for decades in battle for political, social and religious rights. Buddhism was chosen as the religion of conversion because of its qualities of rationality, equality and intellectual creativity -- because it offered a way out of the psychological imprisonment of the Hindu caste system. Buddhism as an organized religion, however, was almost non-existent in India at that time, and the ex-Untouchables who chose to convert had to create leadership, structure, religious observances and activities from very indirect models, and what they created had to be a religion that would fit their own needs.

The leader of this conversion movement, Dr. B.R. Ambedkar, had been interested in Buddhism most of his adult life. He had read books on Buddhism which had become a minor part of India's discovery of her own past in the twentieth century; he had met some of the men who had, as individuals, become interested in Buddhism; he had traveled to Ceylon and Burma to see living Buddhism in Buddhist countries; and he had written *The Buddha and His Dhamma*, a rationalized life of the Buddha and a selection of texts, chiefly from Pali sources. Moreover, he had prepared his followers psychologically for a conversion from Hinduism from 1935 on, beginning with his own statement that he ''would not die a Hindu''. But the conversion was held suddenly, dramatically and

*This is part II of the article which was first published together with Part I: Beliefs and Views, by Joanna Rogers Macy, in A.K. Narain ed., *Studies in History of Buddhism* (Delhi: B.R. Publishing Corporation, 1980).

without much organizational preparation on 14 October 1956, and within two months of it Ambedkar was dead. He had died a Buddhist, and he had set in motion a movement that soon involved over three million people. But although the inspiration of Ambedkar's own example and his invitation to others to follow him were powerful directives, the organization of the new religion was at a bare minimum.

The structural and leadership elements developed during the long struggle for social and political rights and for educational opportunities were pressed into service to provide the thrust and direction of the religious movement. Without the living example of a Buddhist society before them, the "new Buddhists"[1] had to create a meaningful religious life from the sources available to them: Dr. Ambedkar's precepts, traditional Buddhism as they understood it from the texts, and non-Indian Buddhists with whom they came in contact. Most importantly, they had to build that Buddhist society in the light of the needs of the Buddhist converts, most of them from formerly Untouchable castes, in the context of a dominant Hindu society.

Now, twenty years after the conversion, the movement has slowed in garnering numbers.[2] There were 180,823 Buddhists in India in 1951, before the conversion; 3,250,227 Buddhists in 1961, and 3,812,325 Buddhist in 1971, according to the Indian Census. The great bulk of the Buddhists are in Maharashtra, 3,264,000 Buddhists, but there are sizable numbers in urban centres outside that state: 10,000 in Andhra Pradesh, 81,800 in Madhya Pradesh, 14,100 in Karnataka, 87,00 in the city of Delhi, 8,400 in Orissa, 1,300 in the Punjab, 3,500 in Rajasthan, 1,100 in Tamilnadu, 42,200 in Uttar Pradesh and 39,600 in West Bengal.[3] There is no single leader, there is no overall organization, but there is flourishing, creative, controversial Buddhist society which has evolved patterns of Buddhism both innovative and traditional.

My purpose in this paper is to look at some of the visible elements of contemporary Buddhist society in India, i.e., the place of Dr. Ambedkar in their activities and observances; the buildings that house Buddhist activities; the leadership which teaches, preaches and conducts ritual; the sorts of public holidays and festivals which are observed. The Buddhist tradition, the Mahar tradition and the surrounding Indian tradition all have marked the practices of the Buddhist converts. Much that seems innovative to the Buddhist tradition will be found to be a necessary carry-over from the convert's past or an almost unconscious response to the prevailing Indian (largely Hindu) present. My observations were made in three separate year-long visits to India, 1964-5, 1971 and 1975-6. My perspective is limited to Maharashtra, although much of what I observed would also be found among Buddhist groups in a number of cities outside that state.

The Role of Babasaheb Ambedkar

The presence of a picture of Dr. Ambedkar in all Buddhist *viharas* and at all Buddhist functions seems to set the Indian Buddhists apart from the main Buddhist tradition. The inclusion of "Babasaheb" Ambedkar as an object of reverence is the most visible innovation in the practice of contemporary Buddhists in India. The Buddha and Babasaheb in plaster, stone, poster-art and painting, in song and drama and story, seemingly of near-equal importance, rarely one without the other, are continual evidence that contemporary Indian Buddhism proudly combines its own tradition with that of the main Buddhist tradition. Ambedkar is neither worshipped nor prayed to nor, of course, is the Buddha. No *puja* is performed, no *navas* (vows) are made to either figure, so their functions are not those of a Hindu god. But at every occasion, both figures are garlanded, the Buddha first; incense is lit; and Bhagwan Gautam Buddha and Parampujya Dr. Babasaheb Ambedkar are addressed before the speaker acknowledges the Chairman of the function and "Brothers and Sisters".

Efforts have been made to place Dr. Ambedkar in the traditional Buddhist framework. Some Buddhists acknowledge Dr. Ambedkar as Bodhisattva in recognition of his role in bringing modern Indian converts into Buddhism, i.e., as a savior. This use has been justified by, at least, one traditionally trained Theravada Buddhist bikshu. Other Buddhists reject the Bodhisattva concept as Mahayana Buddhism, which they see as inferior to the rational, non-supernatural, humanity-centered religion they believe the Buddha taught. Another broadly accepted way of honoring Ambedkar is to add the diminutive of his first name, Bhimrao, to the list of refuges, i.e., *Bhimam saranam gachchami*, so that the "Three Jewels" become four:

I go for refuge to the Buddha;
I go for refuge to the Dhamma (doctrine)
I go for refuge to the Sangha (order of monks)
I go for refuge to Ambedkar.

These efforts to honor Dr. Ambedkar within the framework of the

Buddhist tradition are an affront to some outside the conversion movement. Those who understand the importance of Dr. Ambedkar in the earlier struggle for political, social and religious rights are more charitable in accepting the continuing homage paid to him. That homage can best be understood by reference to the Indian tradition of the *guru* (teacher or master), a concept most explicit in Hinduism but also found in heterodox sects and in secular life in India. The use of the term "Bodhisattva", the inclusion of Ambedkar as a refuge, is an attempt to use Buddhist concepts for the basic Indian idea of the need for a teacher to show the way to religious insight and personal freedom. The old practice of *guru-shishya* (master-pupil) is often expanded in modern India to a generalized acceptance of the importance of one special person-- parent, teacher, ideal, hero-- as a chief inspiration in life. The key is that the guru figure is the one who brings his disciple into self-realization, into freedom, i.e., the man who "saves" him.

Ambedkar himself claimed that he had three gurus: The Buddha, the fifteenth century iconoclastic saint-poet Kabir, and the nineteenth century radical social reformer, Mahatma Jotiba Phule. In turn, his followers feel that he has been responsible for almost all the educational, social and political progress in their lives and in addition has shown them the way to a religion which is both honorable and honored, a religion which negates the religious concepts that made them untouchable in the eyes of society. Many feel that Ambedkar has quite literally saved them, and often highly educated Buddhists feel more strongly about Ambedkar as guru than those who have not benefited so much from the movement.

Ambedkar is by no means a guru in the way that Maharshi Mahesh Yogi or Bhagwan Shree Rajneesh or any of the many contemporary cult figures are gurus. He is a guru in a less specific but totally Indian way. One's guru does not need to be saintly in character or religious in profession; he needs only to be the one who points toward enlightenment. The picture of Dr. Ambedkar, usually clad in a blue business suit, a book in his hand, a fountain pen in his pocket, placed beside the picture of the yellow-robed Buddha, makes clear the very human sort of guru he was.

One of the many contemporary songs sung to folk tunes or film music by Buddhist singing groups illustrates the combination of social and religious enlightenment Ambedkar represents:

He gave us the conversion at Nagpur
He threw his light in the darkness

He never was the slave of anyone
He showed us the way of Buddha
He gave us salvation.[4]

The importance of this concept is also expressed in a more sophisticated way by Namdeo Dhasal, a political radical and a poet of the new
Dalit school of literature, which is chiefly composed of educated Buddhists. In this excerpt from one of Dhasal's poems, "they" refers to the
forefathers of today's ex-Untouchables; "fakir" is used in Marathi for a
Muslim saint, and Dhasal has used it here probably to avoid a reference
to Hinduism:

Turning their backs to the sun, they journeyed through centuries;
Now, *now*, we must refuse to be pilgrims of darkness
After a thousand years we were blessed
with a sunflower-giving fakir;
Now, *now*, we must like sunflowers turn our face to the sun.[5]

Whether he is called Boddhisattva, a refuge, a guru or a fakir,
Ambedkar is honored as the one who in his lifetime showed the way and
who continues after his death to be seen as the wisest and most inspiring
of men.

The Vihara -- Meeting-place for Buddhists

The new buildings dedicated to the Buddhist religion in Maharashtra as
well as the old buildings converted to Buddhist use are called *viharas*, the
technical term for the residence of the Buddhist monks. The words for
temple in Marathi, *deul* and *mandir*, are studiously avoided, and the only
term for a gathering place in the old Buddhist tradition seemed to be
vihara. The need of today's Buddhists, however, is not so much living
quarters for bhikshus as a meeting place for the laity, a place where the
image of the Buddha can be kept, the community can gather for lectures
on Buddhism or for *vandana*,[6] and children can be instructed. As in the
case of other lay elements in Buddhist structure, there was no living
model for the place of gathering of the Buddhist community available in
India, and so the multipurpose *vihara* came into being.

The *vihara* is most often a plain rectangular structure, embellished,
where possible, with architectural detail from the most accessible models
of Buddhist structures: the caves of Ajanta and the stupa of Sanchi. These

buildings are newly built whenever the Buddhists of some locality have the money and the cooperative spirit to create a symbol of their newly accepted faith. In many villages, the *caudi* (community hall) of the old *Maharwada* (the quarters of the Mahar, somewhat removed from the village proper), does double service as community meeting room and center for Buddhist activities. I have seen few Hindu temples converted to Buddhist use, probably because few were completely in the hands of those Mahars who converted.

No one has undertaken the immense amount of travelling over Maharashtra and in the cities of the Buddhist conversion elsewhere to record the presence of *viharas*, nor is there any organizational record, since the building of a Buddhist center is an entirely local matter. The ones I have seen range from a small community shrine, large enough only to accommodate a statue of the Buddha, in the slums of Delhi, to a large building with an elaborate stupa on top in Pulgaon, Maharashtra, where Buddhists constitute a large, economically secure, factory-worker community. Most *viharas* serve the Buddhist community in several ways. Daily or weekly *vandana*, memorial services and meetings for religious observances are held in the *viharas*, although few are large enough to accommodate all Buddhists in the locality and great occasions require that a pavillion be erected near the *vihara*. Many *viharas* are used for educational and social as well as religious purposes. In some, there are rooms for visiting or resident bhikshus. Others combine a room for the image of the Buddha with a room for a pre-school or a kindergarten. Such a *vihara* was dedicated in Wardha in May 1976. Residents of the area, many of them casual labor on the railway, collected money for some twenty years and then built a small building. The lower room is a *balwadi* (children's school) dedicated to Mahatma Phule; above, underneath a Sanchi-like dome, is a small room dominated by a Buddha image brought from Thailand and a photograph of Dr. Ambedkar, with quotations from both the Pali scriptures and Dr. Ambedkar painted on the walls.

The *vihara* of Buddhists today is not an imitation of a Hindu temple. There is no *pujari* or ritual priest, there is no stream of individual worshippers paying homage to the image. The *vihara* serves chiefly as a symbol of the community's faith and as a center for the community to gather as Buddhists. And since knowledge is seen as a Buddhist virtue, both Buddhist and secular education can easily be combined with its religious function.

The Leadership of the Buddhists

At the time of the conversion in 1956, there were few Buddhist bhikshus in India, and none who spoke Marathi as their native tongue. The oldest Buddhist Bhikshu then in India, Mahasthaveer Chandramani of Burma, came to Nagpur for the initial conversion ceremony and gave Dr. Ambedkar *diksha*. From then on, anyone who had converted to Buddhism during the mass meetings at Nagpur could convert others, and the stress was on the individual's commitment in a public ceremony. Another huge ceremony was held in Bombay ten days after the death of Ambedkar in December 1956, and here Bhikshu Anand Kausalyayan, a Hindi-speaking monk, initiated thousands into the new religion through the use of the Three Jewels (or three refuges) and the oaths of declaration of acceptance of Buddhism. There were few trained bhikshus available for *diksha* and teaching, however, and the burden of leadership in the early days of the movement fell upon the political leadership from Ambedkar's Republican Party. Religious conversion from the hands of political leaders may have seemed strange to outsiders, but for those in the movement, these were the men who knew them, who had worked with Ambedkar, who had long ago given up Hinduism as a religion of inequality and superstition.

Another group of leaders soon rose at the local level. These were the students -- young men and a few women trained in the colleges that Ambedkar had founded. Some had studied Pali, all had sought out some knowledge of Buddhism in the intense and joyful early days of the conversion. They conducted marriages and memorial services in a simple ritual devised by Ambedkar, founded classes for children and study groups for adults, joined in Young Men's Buddhist Associations and women's service groups. They published pamphlets on Buddhism in Marathi, wrote songs to be sung in community meetings, and, whenever they could, found a traveling Buddhist bhikshu or an educated sympathetic Hindu to speak on Buddhist ideology at public meetings.

The overall organization of the Buddhists in India was less effective than that at the local level. The Buddhist Society of India, centered in Bombay and led by Dr. Ambedkar's son, Yeshwant Ambedkar, was established by Dr. Ambedkar in 1955. Theoretically the center of Buddhist activities, the Buddhist Society of India has given little direction to the movement, and the ties between the center and its local branches are very loose. The center was dominated by political leaders, and as factions began to appear in Ambedkar's party, they affected the religious organization also.[7] The non-political leadership which arose on the local level could not effect a strong central leadership, but neither could the lack of a center affect the vitality of the new movement. The Buddhist Society of India has now completed the Dr. Ambedkar Memorial Shrine, a multipurpose *vihara* on the seashore at Shvaji Park in Bombay, the site where Dr. Ambedkar was cremated. The *viharas* in the towns and villages of Maharashtra, however, reflect local commitment and local leadership.

Now, after twenty years, it seems clear that Buddhism in India will continue its strong emphasis on the laity and lay leadership. It is still the lay leadership that performs most of the teaching and preaching, writes most of the religious material which continues to flow from the movement, collects the money and plans the *vihara*. But there are increasing numbers of Marathi-speaking bhikshus, appearing it seems not so much from the need of the community as out of their own individual commitment to Buddhism. Some go to Bodh Gaya or some other Buddhist center in North India for training, a few to Thailand, and a few others to Ceylon. One young man is now in Japan with the Nichiren sect. Most of the Marathi-speaking bhikshus are young and highly educated; many are working on doctoral degrees in Pali, archaeology or some other field related to the Buddhist past. The only Maharashtrian center for the training of bhikshus is that at Nagpur under the care of Bhandant Anand Kausalyayan, a former Punjabi Hindu who became a bhikshu in Ceylon in 1930. The Ven. Kausalyayan moved to Nagpur in 1970, has built a home and training center on the grounds where the 1956 conversion took place, and has educated dozens of young men, about fifteen of whom have been ordained as bhikshus.

The function of the bhikshu among the Buddhists in Maharashtra seems to be primarily teaching, although it seems also true that the very presence of a bhikshu is an important symbol of the identity of a Buddhist group. I have met many sorts of bhikshus during my visits to India. In the 1960s, the Ven. Sangarakshita of England and Kalimpong devoted half of each year to teaching in Maharashtra and Gujarat. He preached many sermons, his English being interpreted into Marathi by one of the young Buddhist students, and he also conducted *samnera*, a period of ten days or so in which Buddhist laity lived as monks. A Thai bhikshu, Vivekananda, also traveled widely in Maharashtra, giving simple lectures on Buddhist morality. A number of Thai bhikshus study at the University of Poona or Deccan College in Pune, and some of these establish working relationships with Maharashtrian Buddhists, particularly in Buddhist

Sunday schools for children, but none are in India permanently. Some Tibetan monks have moved through Maharashtra, but those I met knew no English, Marathi or Hindi and so served the community by making clay images of the Buddha and reciting some texts in hastily learned Pali. In 1975 a Tamil-speaking Bhikshu was teaching meditation and performing some medical service both in Bombay and in the railroad porters colony in Pune. Singhalese, Burmese and Japanese bhikshus have been of service to the community at various times, their effectiveness dependent upon their ability to communicate and their attitude toward the still generally economically and socially depressed community.

The appearance of Marathi-speaking bhikshus with roots in the community may create a situation in which religious leaders become more essential to be community. However, to be effective, they will have to be highly educated, able to preach and teach, totally ethical, willing to be completely identified with the community, and free from any political ambition.

Such a sangha is now emerging, but there are not enough bhikshus to serve each Buddhist community. And along with the appearance of Marathi-speaking bhikshus, the creative lay leadership continues to function. Three examples will serve to indicate its direction: two dedicated professors teach Pali to over 2000 students at the complex of colleges in Aurangabad established by Ambedkar, and are deeply involved in plans for a Buddhist center, with a resident bhikshu, which will reach far beyond the student body. Another striking example is that of a young woman in Pune who combines works as a clerk in a government office with study for a law degree. She performed so well in a class taught by Thai Bhikshus in her community that she was sent to a Buddhist conference in Thailand. Since her return she has participated in numerous weddings, funerals and other ritual occasions, leading the Pali *vandana* and giving talks on Buddhism. A third example of lay leadership is the most ambitious of all. Waman Godbole, one of the planners of the Nagpur Conversion in 1956, called an All-India Buddhist Dharma Conference in Nagpur in December 1975. Eight bhikshus from many traditions and hundreds of lay leaders particiapted in the conference, with tens of thousands coming to the public sessions and taking part in processions. Godbole hopes for a structured organization that will unify all Buddhists in India. He recognizes that it took twenty years to plan such a conference, however, and is content to work slowly and patiently to build a functioning umbrella Buddhist organization. Godbole is a well-educated Buddhist layman who continues with his railway job to support himself and who has not married in order to devote his life to the movement.

Leadership among Buddhists in Maharashtra has had to emerge out of a vaucum over the last twenty years. The Buddhist leaders are not related to the old Mahar religious leadership, which in any case lost its importance when Ambedkar's movement became committed to leaving Hinduism in the 1930s. The new Buddhist leader, whether a member of the sangha or a lay person, is effective only if he or she can share a knowledge of Buddhism and if he or she is committed to the service of the community.

The Holy Days of the Maharashtrian Buddhists

The four great observances of the contemporary Buddhists in India-- Dhamma Diksha Day, Buddha Jayanti, Ambedkar's death memorial day, and Ambedkar Jayanti-- reveal their determination to preserve hard-won glory of their past as well as to state their commitment to Buddhism. The anniversary of the day of the conversion, 14 October, is celebrated as Dhamma Diksha day. Those who can, return to the field in Nagpur where the 1956 conversion was held for a great ceremony; others hold local observances of varying sorts. In Aurangabad, the Buddhist caves just outside the city are the focus of a procession, Pali *vandana* and later games for the children, while speeches and song services are held in the colleges. Buddha Jayanti, the day of observance of the Buddha's birth, has been observed since 1950, when Ambedkar arranged for the celebration as a public occasion in Delhi. The Jayanti is a time for speeches, music, drama on Buddhist themes and occasionally a solemn procession.

Ambedkar's death anniversary, 6 December, is a time for quiet and sorrowful gatherings, and talks or music by one of the many singers or singing groups in the community predominate. Ambedkar's birth anniversary, 14 April, on the other hand, is a noisy and joyful occasion. Here the borrowings from the processions found in Hinduism, Islam and Jainism are clear. As in the Muslim Moharram or the Hindu Ganapati festival, local groups form committees which plan their contribution to the citywide procession. In Pune, the central point is the statue of Dr. Ambedkar near the railway station, and groups of dancing, shouting youngsters and older men march from their scattered localities to Ambedkar Square. The Maharashtrian dance game *legim* is often played by the marchers, as in the Ganapati festival, although the Buddhists have at least one girls' group, which the Hindus do not. One group rented the city zoo's elephant in 1976 to carry Ambedkar's photograph in the procession, but generally the marchers try to out-do each other in spirit rather than constructing elaborate floats.

A Jayanti held at the Aundh Road Buddhist locality near Pune illustrates the mood of this day. Dozens of boys and a few older men drummed and danced their way the twenty miles to Ambedkar Square and back. A meeting then began at about 9 o'clock that night, presided over by one of the exhausted participants. Speeches were made by a young Marathi-speaking bhikshu from another slum locality in Pune, a Maratha caste convert to Buddhism who had just attended a Buddhist conference in Thailand, and this American scholar who is considered an authority on Ambedkar's life. The speeches were followed by a local drama group. Every social group, male and female, and every political faction in the locality was invited to participate in an effort to unite the community, and no outside political leaders were asked to attend. The events of the day reached the children, the young people and the adults of the community in one phase or another. The procession was sheer fun, the speeches of the Bhikshus and the Buddhist converts contained heavy doses of ethics and morality, and the drama provided both entertainment and a glimpse of the Buddhist past.

While these observances bear some resemblance to Hindu or other Indian holy days or festivals, particularly in the idea of the public processions and the exhibiting of the photographs of the "gurus", the Buddha and Dr. Ambedkar, they are unlike Hindu occasions in their emphasis on teaching and their rationality. There is no one astrologically timed sacred moment, no one hallowed sacred space. There is no need for a religious figure to give an auspicious presence, blessing or rite. There is no spirit-possession, no religious ecstasy. These four observances are times for community spirit, for education, for remembrance.

The innovations of the contemporary Buddhist movement in India represent those elements in the past of the Buddhists which are important to their present progress: the work of Dr. Ambedkar, their social unity in the face of continued prejudice and occasional violence, their rejection of Hinduism as a religion of inequality, irrationality and superstition. Nevertheless, there is also some retention of Hindu or Indian elements among the modern Buddhists-- the guru idea, the public processions, the days honoring the birth or death of great men. It must be remembered that the Buddhists of India are a minority in a dominant Hindu society, and as

in the case of other minorities-- Muslims, Christians, Sikhs and Jains--
the ways of showing identity, loyalty and group spirit which are a part of
Indian culture have colored Buddhist celebrations.

The outward symbols of traditional Buddhism most stressed are those
which carry inner meaning of the conversion: honor, equality, rationality,
humanism. The image of the Buddha used is a simple one; he is the
enlightened one, not a god. The study of Pali is important not only as the
language of the Theravada texts but as a symbol of commitment to the
Buddhist world. Pali ritual phrases are used in group performance of
vandana, partly to produce a moment of group unity and party to show that
this is the holy language of Buddhism, as Sanskrit is the holy language of
Hinduism. The Buddhist art and holy places of the past are honored by
contemporary Buddhists as proof of past greatness and part of their own
heritage. The decorated caves of Ajanta, Elora, Aurangabad, Nasik and
Junnar are visited with reverence and awe, and many make pilgrimages to
Sanchi, Sarnath or Bodh Gaya.

Along with the amalgam of traditional Buddhism, the Mahar past
and the socio-religious practices of Hindu society in general, the Buddhists of India seem to have created some new and interesting developments on their own. The multipurpose *vihara* and the initiative and
responsibility of the lay leader are the most striking of these. Wherever
it has gone, Buddhism has adapted itself to the needs of the surrounding
culture. The contemporary Buddhists of India are not an exact copy of
Singhalese, Burmese, Thai, Cambodian or Japanese Buddhists. As in
those societies, Buddhism has retained some of its ancient lineaments
while allowing those who claim commitment to it to change it in accordance with their own needs.[8]

Notes

1. The Indian press and many Westerners use the term "Neo-Buddhist" for
   the converts to Buddhism in the Ambedkar movement. The Buddhists
   themselves point out that the words "Neo-Muslim" or "Neo-Christian"
   are not used, and they find "Neo-Buddhist" a patronizing and unacceptable
   term.
2. Growth among Buddhists in the last decade has shown a 17 per cent
   increase, in contrast to a 24 per cent increase for Hindus, 31 per cent for
   Muslims, 32 per cent for Sikhs and 33 per cent for Christians. Buddhists
   claim that many outside Maharashtra would convert but for the fact that they

lose their privileges as the Scheduled Castes (scholarships, reserved government jobs and other benefits) upon conversion, except in the State of Maharashtra.

3. These figures, which have been rounded to the nearest hundred, are from the *Census of India* 1971. Series 1, Paper 2 of 1972: Religion. I have omitted those areas where numbers of Tibetans obviously account for Buddhist figures, but some refugees and some carry-over Buddhist groups in Bengal and Orissa may account for several thousands in these figures.

4. From "Majha Bhimraya" (My Bhim, the King), a song collected by Russ Geyer for an undergraduate research paper on the songs of the Buddhists, Pune, 1969.

5. From "Atta" in *Golpitha* by Namdeo Dhasal (Pune: Nilkanth Prakashan, reprint 1975).

6. *Vandana* is defined in Molesworth's dictionary as "adoring, worshipping, rendering reverence or homage", and is used in place of the words describing Hindu prayer or ritual, *prarthana* or puja. *Vandana* generally consists of the *trisharana* and other Pali Buddhist textual material.

7. Some political leaders have done yeoman work in the promotion of Buddhism: Dadasaheb Gaikwad has built a complex of schools and a *vihara* in Nasik and D.T. Rupavate in Ahmadnagar; B.C. Kamble and his followers have been active in Buddhist teaching; R.D. Bhandare has kept his interest in Buddhism even after leaving the Republican Party for the Congress, and I am told he is responsible for the translation of the *Tripitika* into Hindi by the Government of Bihar. Nevertheless, the factions among the political leadership have resulted in factions among local Buddhists, and there is now an attempt to place Buddhist activities and organizations in a totally non-political context.

8. For further reading, see Adele Fiske, "Scheduled Caste Buddhist Organizations" in J. Michael Mahar ed., *The Untouchables in Contemporary India* (Tucson: University of Arizona Press, 1972); the work of D.C. Ahir, the major writer of the movement in English, particularly *India's Debt to Buddhism* (New Delhi: Maha Bodhi Society of India, 1964) and *Buddhism in Modern India* (Nagpur: Bhikku Niwas Prakashan, 1972); and two of my articles, "Buddhism and Politics in Maharashtra" in Donald E. Smith ed., *South Asian Politics and Religion* (Princeton: Princeton University Press, 1966) and "The Psychological Dimension of the Buddhist Movement in India" in G.A. Oddie ed., *Religious Conversion and Revival Movements in South Asia in Medieval and Modern Times* (Delhi: Manohar, 1977). Also see the Bibliography at the end of this section for more recent publications on the Buddhist conversion movement.

Buddhist Sects in Contemporary India:
Identity and Organization*

The 1971 Census recorded the number of Buddhists in India as 3,812,325, i.e., less than one per cent of the population but a startling increase over the number of Buddhists noted in 1951. All but a few hundred thousand of these Buddhists have been converted since the 1956 Buddhist conversion of Dr. B.R. Ambedkar, an ex-Untouchable leader, and around eighty-five per cent of the contemporary Buddhists live in the State of Maharashtra, Ambedkar's home territory. The 1971 figure represents a 17.025 per cent increase over 1961, less than any other religious group in India, but the Buddhist movement is still very much alive. This article will deal chiefly with the identity and organization of the recently converted Buddhists, with a few notes on the other Buddhist groups now in India, for example, the Tibetan refugees and the Buddhists of Bengal.

An estimate of the number of Tibetans in India ranges around 100,000, chiefly in refugee settlements in Mysore, Assam, West Bengal, Madhya Pradesh and Himachal Pradesh. The Dalai Lama is the spiritual head of these Buddhists, and the monastic system is preserved through training centers for monks at Dharmshala in Himachal Pradesh[1] and at Mundgod in Karnataka. The Buddhism prevalent in old Tibet is preserved as much as possible by the refugees, and the resettlement of most Tibetans in groups in specific localities works toward the retainment of their culture.

There is little contact between Tibetan Buddhism and those converted since 1956, and little expectation of future interaction. Language is one basic problem, the form of Tibetan Buddhism another. One instance of interaction illustrates this: I met two Tibetan monks living in the guest room of a very simple *vihara* in a very small poor Buddhist community outside Pune in Maharashtra. They had been there several

---

*First published in Peter Gaeffke and David A. Utz eds., *Identity and Division in Cults and Sects in South Asia* (Philadelphia: South Asia Regional Studies, 1984).

weeks, had learned enough Pali to chant some formula familiar to the Maharashtrian Buddhists, and were making plaster Buddha images from molds they had brought with them to repay the hospitality they were given. No other communication was possible, and I expect the connection did not last long. Robert and Beatrice Miller have told me that a young Buddhist boy from Maharashtra was taken to Dharmshala by Tibetans for training in the 1960s, but was returned home as he was too immature.

Tibetans are invited on the rare occasions when Buddhists in Maharashtra call for an All-India Buddhist conference. But it is unrealistic to expect the two groups to find much common ground. The Tibetan identity is all-important to the refugee Buddhists; they have little to gain from integration with a group of very low social and economic status. On the other hand, the recently converted Buddhists have no monastic or even priestly tradition; respect for leadership is based on the teaching ability of the bhikshu, and only secondarily on his institutional role.

The second group of older Buddhists in the subcontinent is almost equally removed from the mass of Buddhists in Maharashtra in terms of distance, language and organizational structure.* These are the Bengali Indian Buddhists (as distinct from Burmese Buddhists living in Bengal and Bangladesh) who have retained their identity as Buddhists from pre-Muslim times, and have undergone a revival in the mid-nineteenth century which reintroduced Theravada Buddhist ideas, practices, and training for bhikshus. These Buddhist remnants exist in Orissa, Bengal and possibly Assam, but the largest number live in the district of Chittagong, now in Bangladesh. The 1970 Chittagong Census count of Buddhists is near 80,000, most of them Barua Magh, a reference to the ancient center of Buddhism in Maghada, i.e., "the great Maghadas".

Something of a reformation began among these Bengal Buddhists who were almost submerged in Hinduism in 1856 when a Burmese bhikshu stopped by in Chittagong on his pilgrimage to Bodh Gaya and stayed there for two years to preach Theravad Buddhism to those he saw as corrupted Buddhists. Coincident with this, a young Barua Magh had discovered Theravada Buddhism through a Singhalese in Calcutta, and after his ordination as a bhikshu in Ceylon ordained in turn a new generation of Bengali bhikshus. The revival has produced schools and large-scale Buddhist festivals in Chittagong, and in Bengal a number of

---

*However, I recently (1989) found a young Bengali bhikshu conducting Pali Vandana in a small *vihara* behind the government employees' quarters in the Bandra East locality in Bombay.

scholars. The most famous, B.M. Barua, dominated Pali and Buddhist scholarship in Calcutta for twenty-five years.

Although there is some contemporary study of the Eastern Indian Buddhists by Heinz Bechert[2] and others, the fullest report on the organization of the Buddhists of that area available to me now is that of the *Chittagong Gazetteer*, and since it repeats in large part the information given in 1908 Gazetteer, I will not venture to comment on the current organization beyond saying that it seems to depend upon the Sangha and upon popular festivals organized around holy places in the Chittagong region.

The identity and organization of the Buddhists in India whose conversion stems from the Ambedkar movement is a complex matter. The current life of the movement is based on local organizations and leadership, and its current creative edge is often the work of a single man. A great deal can be said, however, about what Buddhist identity means to the mass of these Buddhists, and scattered impressions of Buddhist organizations reveal a pattern which probably holds throughout Maharashtra and in the larger cities of India.

The Census figures on Buddhists in India probably indicate the minimum number. Only in the state of Maharashtra do Buddhists qualify for the government benefits of "compensatory discrimination" (the phrase is Mark Galanter's) which means scholarships, aid in housing and reservation of jobs in government organizations to ex-Untouchables. In other states, religious conversion means the cutting off of all these privileges, and in Maharashtra itself, the benefits at the Central Government level are not available to Buddhists. Consequently, only those who are financially secure or extraordinarily committed can afford to register themselves as Buddhists.

At its simplest, the identification with Buddhism of both official and non-official Buddhists is twofold: identity with one of India's greatest cultural periods, and, perhaps more important, identity with an anti-caste religion of rationality and egalitarianism. An interesting, if not numerically significant, group of Indians looked at Buddhism in this light before Dr. Ambedkar's conversion. Tagore and Nehru were among them, along with a number of high caste Hindu intellectuals. Dharmanand Kosambi, Rahul Sankrityayan and Jagdish Kashap (respectively, Pali scholar, writer, and founder of the revived Nalanda University, as well as the uncle of A.K. Narain) were also members of the Sangha, at least for a time. Several hundred lesser figures also became Buddhists or extolled that religion as the purest form of Hinduism.[3] Curiously enough, there

were also at least two low-caste movements toward Buddhism, one in
Madras and one in Rajasthan, which have not been recently
investigated.[4]

The identification with Buddhism on the part of low-caste converts
involves more than an intellectual attraction, however; it contains a large
component of psychological freedom. A well-known Buddhist lawyer,
writer and government official, Shankarrao Kharat, stated this simply
and strongly:

> I have accepted the Buddhist Dhamma. I am a Buddhist now. I am
> not a Mahar, nor an Untouchable, nor even a Hindu. I have become
> a human being. I have now become equal with high-caste Hindus. I
> am equal with all. I am not lowborn or inferior now. With the
> acceptance of Buddhism my Untouchability has been erased. The
> chains of Untouchability which shackled my feet have now been
> shattered. Now I am a human being like all others. I am no longer the
> slave and menial servant of high caste Hindus. I will never again
> accept servile labour from the high caste Hindus. I have become
> independent. I am now free. I have become a free citizen of inde-
> pendent India.

One also senses the great sense of psychological freedom in the
hundreds of songs written by amateur musicians and sold in cheap paper
pamphlets at any gathering of Buddhists. One such song by a Buddhist
from Akola in Maharashtra who uses the pen name "Dinbandhu",
brother of the poor, "The Hindu faith, the hateful faith--we threw it out",
and includes such lines as:

> The rope of slavery has been broken.
> We'll rise up to the heights of the sky;
> Our deeds will make the world seem small.

Another song by a professional folk musician, Waman Kardak, recounts
the events of the conversion day, 14 October 1956, in Nagpur with this
chorus:

> We have thrown away the rags
> which never did cover our shame.

and ends, "The humble were freed from the valley of Untouchability".
The sense of inner freedom, however, is only partially meaningful in

outer matters. While it can give the ex-Untouchable greater ambition and great courage, it does not create much difference in the minds of non-Buddhists. *Bauddh* or *Nav-bauddh* (new Buddhist, a term the Buddhists themselves reject) in Maharashtra is a synonym for Mahar, since the vast majority of the converts were from that caste. The ex-Untouchable does not reach a position of equality automatically with conversion, but it does affect his attitude toward himself and his rights.[5]

In addition to the sense of release from being untouchable, there is a sense of belonging to a great past, an identity that supersedes current low status. There are many ways for the Buddhist convert to express this identity. Chief among them is to claim, as Ambedkar did in *The Untouchables* (New Delhi: Amrit Book Company, 1948), that Untouchables had been Buddhists in an earlier period, and indeed the very reason for their untouchability was that they, as staunch and recalcitrant Buddhists, had refused to join the Hindu revival of the middle ages. Few Untouchables have ever used the *karma* theory of past bad deeds to explain their low status; almost all untouchable myths of origin all over India use some ancestral error, usually based on good intentions, to account for their despised place, or claim pre-Aryan status, or ex-Kshatriyahood. The theory of previous Buddhist identity fits well into the untouchables' need for an honorable past, a cultural heritage that can be claimed with pride, and even the unlettered find this mythic background comforting.

There are an astonishing number of visual and verbal references to the Buddhist past within the current movement. Pali is taught in all the colleges founded by Dr. Ambedkar and his followers, and studied by literally thousands of students. Local groups teach Pali chants to children in a sort of Buddhist Sunday School, and I have at times sat as long as forty minutes at a stretch listening to little ones reel off seemingly endless scripture. Whenever possible, architectural features from Buddhist structures, usually the caves at Ajanta or the stupa at Sanchi, are worked into school buildings or the *viharas* erected by local groups. Some Buddhists go on pilgrimage to Bodh Gaya, Sarnath or Sanchi; a great many visit the caves of Ajanta and Ellora. Actually, a good many of the guides and the guards at the caves are Buddhists, since the position is one for which there are reserved places in the government scheme, and these guides at times act as if they truly owned the caves, treating them as if they were contemporary places of special holiness. Buddhist caves at Aurangabad, Junnar and Nasik are used as sites for festival occasions such as the celebration of the Buddha's birth by local Buddhists. The Buddha Jayanti is observed in all local Buddhist groups, and while it is not quite the popular and exuberant festival of Ambedkar's birth, it can be a very impressive occasion in the cities.

Much of the expression of a relationship with the Buddhist past is in literature. A Buddhist from Maharashtra oversaw the publication of the *Tripitika* in Hindi while he was Governor of Bihar. A Buddhist from Nagpur took upon himself to publish an archaeologist's findings on the location of Kapilavastu. Another Maharashtrian Buddhist published a well-received novel about the Buddha's wife, and a Pune based Buddhist playwright (a government servant) has written a play based on the conversion of a courtesan by the Buddha.

Perhaps even more interesting are the subtle ways in which Buddhist concepts are used by the writers in the contemporary Dalit Sahitya (literature of the oppressed) movement in Marathi, a recent phenomenon that has given birth to a whole new school of literature.[6] There is no such straightforward exultation of Buddhism as in the popular song literature; indeed, some of the best-known writers, such as Baburao Bagul, never mention Buddhism, although he has told me that it was the conversion to Buddhism which freed the ex-Untouchables to write! But where a reference to Buddhism does enter, it is obviously a profoundly meaningful part of the writer's mental resources. Daya Pawar's poem on the Bodhi Tree, the tree under which the Buddha was sitting when enlightenment came, appears in an autobiography which barely mentions Buddhism otherwise:

I have seen this tree choking with grief
Its roots are deep like a *bodhi-tree's*
But the bodhi tree, at least, flowered.
This tree is scorched in all seasons.

The sorrows that try to burst through every vein
The leaves fallen off like leper's fingers...
What is this disease? To bough after bough
        is tied a prop.
It bears death-like tortures, because it cannot die.
I have seen this tree choking with grief.

(Translated by Priya Adarkar in her presentation of excerpts from *Balut*, by Daya Pawar, translated as "For Them the Chaff: The Dalit Story" in *Imprint*, January 1980.)

Another poem by Daya Pawar uses the figure of Angulimal, a bandit of exceptional cruelty who was converted by the Buddha, as metaphor for the society of today:

O Siddhartha,
You made a tyrant like Angulimal tremble.
We are your humble followers.
How should we confront this ferocious Angulimal?
O Siddhartha,
If we fight tooth and claw,
Try to understand us.
Try to understand us.

(The full poem, translated by Vidya Dixit, Jayant Karve and Eleanor Zelliot, appears in the *Bulletin of Concerned Asian Scholars*, X:3 (1978, p. 3, and in section IV of this volume). The same figure of Angulimal is used in a totally different way by the prize-winning Buddhist poet, Tryambak Sapkale (who is also a train conductor on the Dhond-Manmad line in Maharashtra), who sees himself turned into Angulimal by society.

All these things help to build the kind of proud cultural past that few Untouchable groups can claim. They are part of what Richard Lambert once called "the vital dimension of self-respect" which is an essential element in any egalitarian social movement. Dr. Ambedkar dedicated his book, *The Untouchables*, to the Untouchable Bhakti saints, Nandnar, Ravidas and Chokhamela, the group that represented about the only claim to cultural contribution the Untouchables ever had. The Buddhist past which he opened up to his followers in the year of his death is an even deeper mine of riches, an endless source of meaningful imagery and a claim to a proud heritage.

It is clear that the identity of the Buddhists converted in Ambedkar's movement goes beyond caste identity, but it is still clearly bound up to that movement. A few Buddhists go to international conferences on Buddhism or on world religions, but for most identity is still in the context of the Hindu world, and when they stretch beyond this, it is through a very personal understanding of the meaning of Buddhism for them as individuals.

The full range of Buddhist organizations in India includes as much variety as the ways of identification with Buddhism, and is less easy to generalize about. No one knows the exact extent of organized groups among the Buddhists in India, not even in Maharashtra. Activity is almost entirely on the local level, there is no effective overall organization and there are few people who travel widely enough to know the developments in more than one area. My notes on organization are not comprehensive; rather I will try to use examples to point up the nature of institutions and leadership among the Buddhists.[7]

Two, perhaps, three, organizations in Maharashtra aspire to guide the Buddhist movement. Dr. Ambedkar himself founded the Buddhist Society of India before the conversion, but left no ongoing structure. Its leadership passed into the hands of Ambedkar's son, an ineffective and somewhat tragic figure, who was the token head until his recent death. The Society has achieved the building of the Dr. Ambedkar memorial Shrine on the seashore in Shivaji Park, Bombay, an expensive and gaudy affair that serves both as shrine and, it was hoped, a place for bhikshus to stay. Local societies often call themselves Buddhist Society of India groups, but there is no direct link with, certainly no guidance from, the central organization. Another group in Bombay, guided by members of the Peoples Education Society which manages the colleges begun by Ambedkar, undertakes a certain amount of organization. Calling themselves the Bauddha Mahasabha, the group has translated into Marathi and published Ambedkar's *The Buddha and His Dhamma*. [8]

A more ambitious organization is that of Waman Godbole in Nagpur. One of the planners of the conversion in Nagpur in 1956 (an occasion which drew perhaps as many as a half-million people and was organized in five weeks), Godbole, called an All-India Buddhist Dharma Conference in 1975. Eighty-five bhikshus and hundreds of laymen from many Buddhist traditions, including the Tibetan and Bengali, attended, and the name of a Barua can be noted as a Vice-President of the conference. The Dalai Lama, however, was unable to come. Godbole has plans for slowly building an organization that will unite all Buddhists in India, standardize *viharas* and increase conversions. He is a well-educated layman who continues his railway job to support himself and who has not married in order to devote his life to the movement. He says that it took twenty years to plan the Dharma conference and is willing to plan for another twenty to achieve some further results.

It is often said that Buddhism is a monastic religion. What then of the Sangha among the Buddhists of India? Needless to say, there is no centrally-trained, well-organized group in Maharashtra. There are perhaps eighty bhikshus functioning in one way or another in the State and in a few other areas of India, representing many traditions and many countries. The largest group, perhaps fifteen to twenty, has been trained by Anand Kausalyayan, a former Punjabi Hindu who became a bhikshu in Ceylon in 1930, and moved to Nagpur in 1970, supporting himself by heading a Hindi language promotion organization. The bhikshus trained by Kausalyayan tend to be Marathi-speakers who also take degrees at Nagpur University, often even a Ph.D. in Pali or archaeology, fields which can be related to the Buddhist past. Kausalyayan also conducts classes in Buddhism for groups of young men.

Other Marathi-speaking bhikshus have been trained in Thailand, Bodh Gaya, or a center in Yeotmal (about which I know little). Besides perhaps 25 or 30 bhikshus from Maharashtra itself (probably ex-Mahars, although no one who has become a bhikshu will talk about his former caste), there are a dozen other varieties of bhikshus in Maharashtra alone: a Japanese rather unwillingly serving Buddhists from the locality at the Worli Buddhist temple in Bombay built by the Birlas; an enthusiastic Nichiren Japanese bhikshu using his drum in lieu of English or Marathi to communicate in Nagpur; a Tamil-speaking bhikshu who has a dispensary in the slums of Pune and teaches meditation in several places; several Singhalese bhikshus, at least two of whom have stayed in Maharashtra for years; Thai bhikshus studying at Deccan College or the University of Poona who work with Buddhist groups in Pune, and bhikshus and *Shramanera* from England.

The Buddhist establishment from England offers the most unusual solution to the problem of the leadership of Buddhists in India. Work among the new converts began shortly after the conversion ceremony with bhikshu Sangarakshita, an English Buddhist convert, who conducted training sessions and often went with a Thai bhikshu to both urban and rural groups. With a base in Kalimpong, Sangarakshita visited the Buddhists of Maharashtra and Gujarat several months of each year in the 1960s. Very recently, he has returned from a new center in England to the area, establishing one of his English converts, a robed but not ordained Buddhist, in Pune to teach Buddhism. Lokamitra (friend of the people) lives in Buddhist housing colony, holds classes in Buddhism in Pune and publishes a Marathi periodical. The goal of the group is to educate, and the establishment of a Sangha is not seen as necessary or desirable.

Can Buddhism function as a lay religion? Are a large group of bhikshus necessary for the continuance of the conversion movement and the education of the converts? There is some evidence that Dr. Ambedkar distrusted the Sangha. On a visit to Ceylon some five years before the conversion, he criticized the Sangha to its face for its lack of response to people's needs, and at a meeting in Sarnath, he again attacked the members of the Sangha from various countries for "parasitical behavi-our''. As he himself said, it was a ''grave omission'' in Buddhism to have an initiation into the Sangha and not into the Dhamma itself, and for his own conversion and that of his followers in 1956, he initiated such a ceremony.

If an example of a ''leaderless'' religious organization in Maharashtra can be stretched a bit, it can show how such a religious group can function and flourish. The Bhakti movement which had included the saints Ambedkar revered is still strong and vital in Maharashtra after 700 years. It has no clear leadership patterns, but it does have a series of ''texts'', including songs, which are sung in local groups, a yearly pilgrimage to Pandharpur, and standards of morality accepted by all. The single outward sign of a *warkari* is a necklace of tulsi beads. The temples at Pandharpur and at lesser sites such as Alandi and Dehu do have temple priests-- these, however, are not *warkaris* or members of the sect, and it is not necessary to enter the temple, only to make the group pilgrimage. Local leadership, the tradition, and the songs are what hold the group together. (See G.A. Deleury, *The Cult of Vithoba*, (Pune: Deccan College Postgraduate and Research Institute, 1960). Many contemporary Buddhists, and a few scholars, think the Bhakti movement has strong connections with Buddhism, and that the image of Vithoba at Pandharpur is brought from an earlier Buddhist holy center. But that argument is not the point here; rather it is that the foci of the contemporary Buddhist movement consist of somewhat the same things: local leadership, the Ambedkar tradition, the songs, festivals and rituals developed by the contemporary Buddhists.

The continuance, growth and creativity of the current Buddhist movement, unless it should develop a Sangha more quickly than now seems possible, is dependent upon lay leaders, usually based in a close-knit locality. In larger cities all over India Buddhist groups include members from a number of ex-Untouchable castes, drawn together as educated men and women in a search for a new religious ethos, but in Maharashtra itself all but a handful of the Buddhists share the Mahar past. Two instances of local leadership which resulted in impressive achievements during the past five years illustrate the way in which Buddhism is organized in Maharashtra.

In Aurangabad, a college educated Buddhist with a clerk's job at one of Ambedkar's colleges has supervised the building of a small *vihara* which serves chiefly as a meeting place for the teaching of children and for speeches by passing dignitaries in a locality that is totally Buddhist. The *vihara* is simple; the gates which set it off from the crowded slum street use a wrought-iron design based on the Bodhi Tree which is both unique and quite beautiful. In Wardha, where railway labor gathered pennies for 20 years, another educated Buddhist with a senior level railway job has designed and constructed a *vihara* which houses a preschool for children and, also has a small domed room, Sanchi style, for pictures of Ambedkar and the Buddha, a Buddha image, and scriptures inscribed on the wall. Neither of these *viharas* had a bhikshu in residence, although in both cases the local community would have welcomed one who was dedicated to teaching them.

Like the *warkari* or Bhakti tradition, the Buddhist movement also has its festival days which are celebrated by the entire community. Ambedkar's birth and death days, Buddha Jayanti, and the anniversary of the conversion on 14 October are the most important of these, and they are observed in such a way as to involve the whole community and to make a statement to the outside world. But unlike the *warkari* tradition, the Buddhist movement in Maharashtra has no place, no Pandharpur, no physical center. Nothing in the present or past Buddhist tradition in Maharashtra offers such a center, not even the Ajanta and Ellora caves, which are government-owned. The "physical" center continues to be Babasaheb Ambedkar, and the attempts at centers build on this fact. The Bombay center is built on the site where Ambedkar was cremated. Kausalyayan's center in Nagpur is on the ground where the mass conversion took place in 1956. A visionary Buddhist in Nagpur has grand, rather impractical plans to build a training center for bhikshus at Mahu in Madhya Pradesh, the birthplace of Babasaheb Ambedkar.

Dr. Ambedkar serves as a focal point both for the illiterate and, even more profoundly, for the educated. He fills three traditional ties of loyalty: the planner for progress: social, political and religious; the guru, i.e., the one who showed the way; and, in Buddhist terminology, a Boddhisattva. The idea of the business-suited, bespectacled, often impious Ambedkar as Boddhisattva sets some Buddhists' teeth on edge, but in terms of bringing the masses into Buddhism, in "saving" them from the world's evils, he fulfilled the role of Boddhisattva as modern Buddhists in Maharashtra understand it. The idea was actually conceived by Kausalyayan, an ordained bhikshu since 1930, and his teaching included a quadruple "refuge": I take refuge in the Buddha, I take refuge in the Sangha, I take refuge in the Dhamma, I take refuge in Bhim (Bhimrao Ramji Ambedkar.) *Bhimam saranam gachchami* can still be heard at the end of the Pali *trisaranam* chant in many places.

But in spite of the inspiration of Ambedkar's writings, the use of the other material on Buddhism, chiefly in Marathi, and the energy of local leadership, there is a great sense of need for teachers among Maharashtra's Buddhists, and a continual search to find ways to create a Sangha. Almost immediately after the conversion, six or eight boys were sent to Ceylon for training. They returned in a few months, troubled by teasing on what seems to have been a caste basis in the Buddhist schools. Tibetan monks took a village boy with them on one of their journeys through the state, and his parents gladly let him go, but he was returned within a year for being too young. Nichiren monks took a Nagpur boy to Japan, with his parents' full blessing, and there seems to be a real sense of service in this training effort. Pictures of the boy in his *shramanera* robes, and in his Japanese baseball suit, are sent periodically to the parents.

Basically, however, there is no traditional base for a priesthood or a Sangha among the ex-Untouchables of Maharashtra. The Hindu situation before the conversion was even more amorphous and confused than the current Buddhist structures. *Gosavis, potrajas,* an occasional *warkari* leader, children dedicated to the god Khandoba, *devrishis* there were, but no priestly class or access to the Brahman priests, and certainly no tradition of celibate scholarship and piety. It seems wasteful to many for an intelligent, highly educated young man to do work that will not aid in his family's growth nor his family's future. And bhikshus who are not intelligent, moral, well educated and totally dedicated are not acceptable to the community!

The pattern of organization that prevails now will probably hold for years: young men and women conducting *vandana* (Buddhist "prayer"), training schools, song festivals, etc. in their localities; older men who have raised their families turning to the building of *viharas,* the translation of books and texts, attendance at Buddhist conferences. An occasional bhikshu may visit; the wealthier and most committed localities may be able to arrange for a resident monk's presence. Literature at all levels: translation of Pali and English books into Marathi, the production of popular songs, the creation of new material from Buddhist imagery, will continue at an increased pace. Babasaheb Ambedkar will continue to be the centre and the inspiration. It may be enough. At the very least, the Buddhist movement has added new dynamism, new forms of organization and new movements of creativity to the social movement Dr. Ambedkar set in motion some sixty years ago. And it is very conscious of its newness and its needs. Just a year and a half ago, I was rocked out of my bed in a Buddhist locality in Nagpur at 5:30 in the morning by Pali chanting played over a loudspeaker at a decibel not even a Carleton student stereo could achieve. I protested: do the Muslims and Sikhs living on the fringes of the Buddhist area want to hear this public proclamation of your religion? My Buddhist host said: the community needs this at this stage. Perhaps later there will be better ways to inform ourselves about Buddhism.

Notes

1. Pradyumna P. Karen, *The Changing Face of Tibet* (Lexington: The University Press of Kentucky, 1976), pp. 58-9.
2. Heinz Bechert, "Contemporary Buddhism in Bengal and Tripura", *Educational Miscellany*, IV. 3 & 4 (Dec. 1967-March 1968), pp. 1-25.
3. Eleanor Zelliot, "The Indian Rediscovery of Buddhism, 1855-1956" in A.K. Narain ed., *Studies in Pali and Buddhism* (New Delhi: D.K. Publishers' Distributors, *1978*)
4. Adele Fiske, "Scheduled Caste Buddhist Organizations", in J. Michael Mahar ed., *The Untouchables in Contemporary India* (Tucson: University of Arizona Press, 1972).
5. S.K. Thorat, "Passage to Adulthood: Perceptions from Below", in Sudhir Kakar ed., *Identity and Adulthood* (Delhi: Oxford University Press, 1979).
6. Eleanor Zelliot, "Dalit--New Cultural Context of an Old Marathi Word", *Contributions to Asian Studies* XI, 1978 (1978a).
7. See also Owen M. Lynch, *The Politics of Untouchability* (New York: Columbia University Press, 1969).
8. B.R. Ambedkar, *The Buddha and His Dhamma* (Bombay: Siddharth College Publication I, 1957).

Tibetan Buddhists in India

Beatrice D. Miller, "Lamaist Laity and Sangha in West Bengal, India", *Religious Ferment in Asia*, Robert J. Miller ed. (Lawrence: University Press of Kansas, 1974).
Office of Tibet. Report. 1969.

Bengali Buddhists

Sukomal Chowdhury, "Renaissance of Buddhism in Bengal in the Modern Period", *Maha Bodhi*, 79, 1971, pp. 410-19.
Hara Prasad Sastri, *Discovery of Living Buddhism in Bengal* (Calcutta: Sanskrit Press Depository, 1897).

The Contemporary Buddhist Movement in India

D.C. Ahir, *Buddhism in Modern India* (Nagpur: Bhikku Niwas Prakashan, 1972).
————— "80 Years of Buddhism in India", *Maha Bodhi*, 79 (1971), pp. 219-21.

Iravati Karve and Hemlata Acharya, "Neo-Buddhism in Maharashtra", *Journal of the University of Poona*, Humanities Section, 15 (1962), pp. 130-33.

Joanna Macy, and Eleanor Zelliot, "Tradition and Innovation in the Contemporary Buddhist Movement in India", *Studies in the History of Buddhism*, edited by A.K. Narain (Delhi: B.R. Publishing Corporation, 1980).

Beatrice Miller, "Revitalization Movements: Theory and Practice, as Evidenced Among the Buddhists of Maharashtra", in M.C. Pradhan et al. ed., *Anthropology and Archaeology: Essays in Commemoration of Varier Elwin* (London: Oxford University Press, 1969).

Eleanor Zelliot, "The Psychological Dimension of the Buddhist Movement in India", in G.A. Oddie ed., *Religions in South Asia* (New Delhi: Manohar, 1977).

————— "Religion and Legitimation in the Mahar Movement", in Bardwell L. Smith ed., *Religion and Legitimation in South Asia* (Leiden: E.J. Brill, 1978). And in this volume.

For recent sources, see the bibliography at the end of this section.

The Buddhist Literature of Modern Maharashtra*

Introduction

The Buddhist literature of Maharashtra is only thirty years old, stemming from the conversion of Dr. B.R. Ambedkar on 14 October 1956, in Nagpur. Bhimraọ Ramji Ambedkar,[1] born into the Untouchable Mahar caste, had announced that he would leave Hinduism way back in 1935, after a series of temple entry and political frustrations. But he continued his remarkable career as educator, writer, lawyer and statesman without actual conversion until near the time of his death in December 1956. Such was his prestige, however, and so well prepared were his followers, that more than four million converts to Buddhism have followed in his footsteps. The great majority of these are in Ambedkar's own area of Maharashtra, and among his own caste of Mahars, but a sizeable group comes from the urban areas of other states in India[2] and there are even a few high caste Hindu converts to Buddhism, drawn to that religion from the period of the rediscovery of Buddhism in India.[3]

An impressive range of material on Buddhism has been produced by Ambedkar's movement, although its content is very uneven. I have first discussed Ambedkar's writings, translations from Pali, and the most meaningful work of earlier Buddhists. The following four groupings of Buddhist literature reveal the special nature of this Buddhist conversion and cast light on the way in which Buddhists think of themselves. I have arranged the literature, most of it in Marathi, to express what seem to me

---

*Maharashtrian Buddhists dislike the term 'neo-Buddhist', finding it a form of condescension as they do Gandhi's term for Untouchables, Harijan (people of God). Therefore, neither of those terms has been used here, but rather Buddhist; ex-Untouchable (untouchability having been made illegal in practice by the Constitution of independent India); the governmental term Scheduled Caste; or Dalit (oppressed), the all-inclusive word now current.

This article was first published in " 'Minorities' on Themselves", in Hugh van Skyhawk ed., *South Asian Digest of Regional Writing*, Vol. II (1985), (Heidelberg, 1987). A few deletions and additions (indicated by square brackets) have been made.

to be the most important thrusts of the conversion movement: (1) guides
to ritual and practice and histories of the conversion; (2) literature on the
history and legends of Buddhism; (3) songs about Dr. Ambedkar and the
conversion; (4) creative literature by Buddhists of the educated elite.

Dr. Ambedkar's Bible; Other Buddhist Writings; Translations

The study of Pali, translations from Pali scriptures, and the reprinting of
literature written by earlier Indian Buddhists, all reinforce the idea that
today's Buddhists are part of the classical Buddhist tradition, dormant
but not dead during the previous millennium. In 1948, long before the
conversion, Dr. Ambedkar expressed the idea that Untouchables had
been Buddhists in the past. They had been pushed aside when neo-
Brahmanism rose to engulf Buddhist tradition and reassert militant Hinduism. This premise is accepted without question by present Buddhist
converts from low-caste communities. It has proved to be a very
satisfactory explanation of untouchability and a very meaningful way to
develop pride in one's past. Though it is not explicated in literature, the
idea of a proud Buddhist past underlies the current attitude toward Pali,
Buddhist literature, and Buddhist art. The importance of this theory can
be seen in the choice of Nagpur, home of the Nagas, early followers of
the Buddha, as the base of the conversion movement in 1956. The discovery of a major Buddhist site at Pauni, near Nagpur, several years ago, was
hailed with delight by Buddhists.

The Pali scriptures, rather than the Sanskrit scriptures of Mahayana
Buddhism, are used in the current movement. Dr. Ambedkar felt that the
Pali tradition was purer and more rational; it is also more logical that
rebels against Brahmanism would want Pali rather than Sanskrit as their
religious language, and so in the Bible of the movement, Dr. B.R.
Ambedkar's *The Buddha and His Dhamma* (Bombay: Siddharth Publica-
tions, 1957), stories from the Pali scriptures as well as interpretations of
Buddhism from a rational, humanistic viewpoint dominate.

Even though Ambedkar's book is basic to the movement, a Marathi
translation did not appear until 1970. Vasant Moon of Nagpur published a
Marathi analysis in 1960, and Anand Kausalyayan published a Hindi
translation of the book in 1961, with notes on the Pali sources, which
Ambedkar had not felt necessary to publish. The stories and the moral
interpretations found in *The Buddha and His Dhamma*, however, circulated
widely from the beginning of the conversion movement. The book is arranged in almost biblical fashion, with every verse numbered. The life and

teachings of the Buddha are spelled out in very simple fashion, and Ambedkar's interpretation is humanistic and rational -- no mythic material is included. The final chapter, "The Man who was Siddharth Gautama", lays emphasis on the Buddha's humanity, compassion, and sense of equality. In the sections on the Buddha's thought, the ideas of transmigration of soul, of rebirth according to past deeds, and of the individual soul (*atman*) are rejected as not being part of the Buddha's teaching, as also is, of course, the Hindu concept of *chaturvarna* (four fold caste structure).

Although Ambedkar's book is clearly most important, a number of other Buddhist interpretations are much used in the movement. Dharmanand Kosambi (1876-1948), a Brahman scholar who became a Buddhist early this century, published *Bhagwan Buddha*, a life of the Buddha, which stresses rationality, and which Ambedkar undoubtedly read; it has been reprinted at least twice since its initial publication in 1940. Kosambi's *Buddha, dharma ani sangha*, which appeared in 1910, is in its fifth printing and is widely distributed in Buddhist book stores. The Maharashtra State Literature Committee, a body that feels considerable responsibility to represent all Marathi-speaking groups, has reprinted Kosambi's *Buddhalilasarasamgraha*, which first appeared in 1914. A Buddhist in Pune told me that he felt Kosambi's *Hindi samskrti ani ahimsa* (Culture and Non-violence), which appeared in 1935, was one of the most important books for a Buddhist.

The work of other earlier Indian Buddhist converts is also important, although none were from the Untouchable community or from Maharashtra. Bhikshu Anand Kausalyayan, who established a Buddhist training centre in Nagpur after the conversion, has published nineteen books and pamphlets in Hindi, a language understood throughout eastern Maharashtra. Rahul Sankrityayan (1893-1963) is popular among younger left-wing Maharashtrian Buddhists who can read his Hindi works. *The Essence of Buddhism* by P. Lakshman Narasu, an early Tamil-speaking Buddhist, was republished by Ambedkar himself, and seems to be known to all English-educated Maharashtrian Buddhists, but has not been translated into Marathi.[5]

A very new group of Buddhist literature stems from an English bhikshu, Sangarakshita, who lived in India for twenty years and worked closely with the early conversion movement. Within the last few years, Sangarakshita's young English Buddhist converts have established centers for teaching and publishing in Pune, Bombay, and Ahmedabad, and a retreat near the ancient Buddhist cave at Bhaja, and their many

publications are readily available. A magazine appears monthly in
Marathi, and a great many pamphlets in Marathi and English are
published. A sizeable group of highly educated Marathi-speaking lay
leaders do almost all the teaching within this movement.
Translations from Pali had appeared within the community even
before much education in Pali language was available. D.P. Ranpise in
Pune secured the help of a sympathetic Brahman Pali scholar, P.V.
Bapat, to publish some work in Pali and Marathi shortly after the
conversion. A number of translations of the *Dhammapada*[6] have appeared, and the Hindi translation of the *Milinda panha* by bhikshu
Jagdish Kashyap, an early high caste convert to Buddhism, was trans-
lated into Marathi by Haribhau Pagare and published in Bombay in 1961.
Some Buddhists own the *Tripitaka* in Hindi, a massive work undertaken
by the Bihar Government, I am told, under the direction of R.D.
Bhandare, a Buddhist from Maharashtra who was then Governor of
Bihar.

Pali is very important in the conducting of life-passage rituals among
today's Buddhists, and in the *vandana* (Buddhist prayers) that take place
in the *viharas* across Maharashtra. It is also important as a subject taught
in the vast complex of colleges established by Ambedkar and by his
followers. Given the stress, it is strange, that more Pali scripture does not
appear in Marathi translation. It is also perhaps a bit unexpected that
more of the basic English works on Buddhism have not been translated
into Marathi. It is almost as if the movement finds its intellectual
understanding only in the work of those who, like Ambedkar, Kosambi
and Sangarakshita, know how to relate Buddhism to the hopes, dreams,
and social conditions of the lowest of the castes in the Indian system.

Guides on Buddhist Ritual: Studies of the Meaning of Conversion

Since classical Buddhism in India left life-passage rituals in the hands of
the Hindus, today's Buddhists have had to invent their own marriage and
naming ceremonies, their own funeral rites, their own patterns for holy
days. Ambedkar was aware of the need for Buddhist ritual, and prepared
twenty-three oaths which were to be taken as part of the conversion to
Buddhism. These promises are a mixture of declaration of faith in
Buddhist principles and rejection of Hindu gods and social systems.[7] No
more elaborate conversion ceremony has been devised. As on the first
mass conversion day in Nagpur on 15 October 1956, would-be Buddhists
still recite the oaths and are given *diksha* by either a bhikshu, if one is

available, or by a lay Buddhist.

Ambedkar also prepared a little guide to Buddhist ritual, but this has been superseded by a great many other manuals and guidebooks. Typical of these is the *Bauddhasamaskar-path* of V.R. Ranpise, which was first published in 1957, and was in its fourth edition by 1964, having reached a total of 10,000 copies. Its title might be translated "Readings in the Practice of Buddhism", since that is the thrust of the pamphlet. The Pali chants heard all over the Dalit areas of the Maharashtrian world, "*namo Buddhaya*", "*saranattaya*" (The Three Refuges), and the "*panch-shila*" (The Five Moral Vows) begin the pamphlet. *Vandana* or prayer-meditations on the Buddha, the *dhamma*, and the *sangha* follow, together with prayers for protection. The *Jayamangala-atthagatha* (The Eight Auspicious Sentences), *Maha-mangala-sutta* and the *Ratanasutta* follow, with a Marathi translation. A long section on ceremonies--for weddings, deaths, entering school and other occasions -- comes next, with considerable attention to who may be called an *upasak*, a lay member, and what standards of conduct must be followed by one who leads. A list of Buddhist names for boys and girls is included. The pamphlet ends with ways to observe the various *purnimas* (full-moon days), and the various holidays such as Diwali and Holi associated with Hinduism.

Probably no religious conversion ever began with as much emphasis on the laity. Even now, thirty years after the conversion, there are not nearly enough trained bhikshus in many communities, and given the pressure on young men to help their families, the life of an indigent ascetic may be one that few are able to take. The creativity of the movement still lies with local lay leaders, and their degree of devotion and inventiveness determines the practice of their localities much more than any action by the Buddhist Society in Bombay, or the center established by Waman Godbole in Nagpur, important though these centers are. The number of inexpensive pamphlets that are produced locally to aid Buddhist practice is not so large as the number of song pamphlets intended for the spreading of the message or the celebration of various holy days, but it is impressive.

There are also histories of the conversion itself, and the events and circumstances that led up to it. Shankarrao Kharat, a highly respected author, produced the first of these with *Da. Babasaheb Ambedkarance dhammantar* (Dr. Babasaheb Ambedkar's Conversion), published in Pune in 1966, and three professors from Dr. Ambedkar College at Mahad published a *Nagpurchi dhamma kranti* (the religious revolution of Nagpur) in 1981, which indicates the perception of the conversion as a revolution. D.L. Ramteke, a Maharashtrian Buddhist, has attempted a history of Buddhism as well of the conversion in an English work, *Revival of Buddhism in Modern India* (New Delhi: Deep and Deep Publications, 1983), which is the most ambitious effort to date to present the entire movement to non-Marathi speakers. All of these stress the social significance of the conversion, and although Ramteke devotes the latter part of this book to the ideals of Buddhism, it is the social ethics of Buddhism that are stressed.

Although I have not made a close study of the Buddhist periodicals which appear in Marathi,[8] such as *Dhammarajya*, published in Pune, I have a feeling that many issues being discussed among Buddhists do not appear in them. Many ponder what the Buddhist response can and should be to the violence that is increasingly used against them. Having denied the validity of caste, some see a conflict in accepting the benefits given on a caste basis, albeit to a caste that has suffered discrimination. Some wonder if Buddhist philosophy is too passive, not militant enough for an oppressed group. Others wonder how Buddhism can be made a uniting rather than a separating factor in India today. The training of bhikshus, and the necessity for bhikshus, is another issue which the community seems not to want to discuss in print. Perhaps, anything smacking of criticism is seen as better discussed verbally than in public.

The great flood of confessional literature in Christianity which delineates the meaning of that faith has some counterpart in Marathi, but is also not well developed. A sensitive essay entitled "Passage to Adulthood: Perceptions from Below" by a young Buddhist, S.K. Thorat, appeared in *Identity and Adulthood*, edited by Sudhir Kakar (Delhi: Oxford University Press, 1979). The autobiography of Daya Pawar, *Balute* (a gift in kind for hereditary work: the Mahar was a *balutedar* in the village community), was published by the Bombay Granthali Prakashan in 1978 and won much attention, but Pawar's insight on the conversion is not as startlingly meaningful as on his life as an Untouchable. The publishing of autobiography has now become a major trend among Dalit writers, but the preoccupation is still the struggle for *manuski* (human dignity) with Buddhism being accepted as a necessary but unexplained part of that struggle for those writers from a Mahar background. True, confessional religious literature is not part of the Hindu religious tradition, and perhaps one should not expect it; and perhaps it is significant that the closest thing to an accounting of the conversion process is in K.N. Kadam's *Buddhism as Rationalism and Humanism*, a set of essays written between 1950 and 1981 and published in mimeograph form for private circulation-- and Kadam was educated in Jesuit schools!

The History and Legends of Buddhism

Interest in the Buddhist past is very high among today's converts, and the re-telling of the legends of Buddhism takes many forms. Two books in Marathi tell of pilgrimages to Buddhist holy places all over India. V.R. Ranpise published *Baudhairnchi Bharatatila pavitra tithakshetre* (The Holy Places of the Buddha in India) in Pune in 1962, and the following year L.N. Ankush Guruji published *Majhe Bauddha tirthatana* (My Buddhist Pilgrimage) in Bombay: both are sizeable pamphlets intended to serve as guides as well as notes on the author's experiences. Two other publications deal with pilgrimage places in a rather unexpected manner. Chandrabhan Kisan Naranavare, known as "Chandranag" of Nagpur, has published a pamphlet intending to prove that the hill of Ramtek north of Nagpur was originally a Buddhist place. M.D. Panchbahi published *Kapilavastu*, a scholarly work by K.M. Srivastava of the Archaeological Survey of India, when he feared that interpretation of the site of the Buddha's birth would not be published officially.

At least two Ph.D. theses on the Buddhist past reflect the writer's own religious concerns. B.R. Kamble's *Caste and Philosophy in Pre-Buddhist India* (Aurangabad: Parimal Prakashan, 1979) is a contribution to the ongoing debate about the relationship of the sixth century Hinduism to Buddhism. Bhau Lokhande produced "The Influence of Buddhism on Marathi *Sant*-Literature" for his Nagpur University Ph.D. in 1975-76, and this discussion of the importance of Buddhist thought to the dominant bhakti cult in Maharashtra has been published in Marathi as *Marathi Santa sahityavara Bauddha dharmacha prabhava* (Nagpur: Ashok Prakashan, 1979).

Histories that are not original scholarship are also important. D.C. Ahir, a Hindi-speaking Buddhist from Delhi, includes among his many books one called *India's Debt to Buddhism* (New Delhi: Maha Bodhi Society of India, 1964), a title which reflects the sentiment of the Maharashtrian Buddhists about the importance of the Buddhist past.[9] M.S. Moray, a Marathi-speaking Buddhist employed in government service in Gujarat, has published the *History of Buddhism in Gujarat* (Ahmedabad: Saraswati Pustak Bhandar, 1985) and has earlier published three books in Marathi which retold the stories of the Chinese travelers to India and the early history of Buddhism in Maharashtra as outlined by

R.G. Bhandarkar and B.G. Gokhale. Moray writes about the past but is very conscious of the present: "Let us again, therefore, give India that glory which was its during the Buddhist period".

Buddhist legends and stories are presented in many ways. A very respectable novel on the life of the Buddha's wife, Murlidhar Bhosekar's *Siddhathachi Yashodhara* (Pune: Ravind Prakashan, 1975) was well received, and he thereafter published another, *Kapilvastucha raj kumar* (the Prince of Kapilvastu) in 1977. Sugandha Shinde of Nagpur published a children's story of the life of the Buddha, and a play on Amrapali. B.S. Shinde's *Vasavadatta*, a play about the courtesan who became a Buddhist nun, has been presented in Pune with a cast from a Buddhist locality, and Shinde has more recently formed a *Dalit Rangabhumi* (Dalit Theater Company), which has great interest in performing plays on classical Buddhist themes as well as modern problem theater.

Buddhist stories and legends which contain social messages are most popular, stories in which untouchability is ignored, in which courtesans become respected nuns, in which princes give up their thrones for the good of the common man. Classic tales are adapted for amateur theater in many localities, just as classic Buddhist architecture is adapted for *viharas* and Buddhist school buildings. In Buddhism, ex-Untouchables may lay claim to a proud past, and the importance of justifiable pride to an oppressed people cannot be overstressed.

The Songs of the Buddhist Movement

Perhaps the best way to understand what the conversion means to the unsophisticated masses is to look at the song literature of the Maharashtrian Buddhists. Sold in cheap pamphlet form at all Buddhist occasions--the birth and death anniversaries of Dr. Ambedkar, the Buddha jayanti (birthday), the anniversary of the conversion ceremony in Nagpur-- these songs reflect a popular, unsophisticated celebration of Buddhism, with "Babasaheb" Ambedkar given prime attention as the savior of his people. Some of the following translations were made by somewhat educated converts, and I have let their sometimes inaccurate but touching English stand since the originals are not available to me.[10] It should be understood that "he" and "Bhim" refer to Bhimrao Ramji Ambedkar.

Rajananda Gadapyle in *Jagati pramjota* (The Awakened Torch of Life), written shortly after the 1956 conversion, touches on a number of themes:

> The light of enthusiasm is spread everywhere
>   and the teaching of Buddha is happy.
> The evil days of slavery are gone
>   and the sorrowful songs are gone.
> Bhim gave us the great hymn *Buddham sarnam gachchami*
> (I Go for Refuge to the Buddha)
>   and by attaining the perfection of this hymn
>   we become the riders of our own chariot.
> The torch of revolution is burning in every heart.
> A Buddhist life is smitten with humanity.
> He turned the wheel of revolution.
> He died the maker of an age.
> All the ten directions give praise,
> India gives praise.

Dinbandhu, the pseudonym of an Akola-based writer, dwells chiefly on the theme of release:

> The Hindu faith, the hateful faith-
>   We threw it out!
> Today we took the Buddha's way.   (Chorus)
> Today we cut the bonds of slavery,
> Today is the joy of victory,
> The old religion lies in pieces,
> The new religion is ever new joy.
> Every drop of blood is fired up today!
>
> Come on, let's tell all the world,
> Let's tell the sun, the moon, the stars,
>   the rivers, mountains, corners of the earth,
> Say: listen, hear this voice,
> New religion, new birth today is ours!
>
> Who is Untouchable now?
> Who is Chandal, the Atishudra?
> Bhimrao gave the gift of life,
> He turned cow dung into gold,
> He showed the path of peace and equality!

An unknown poet in a song recorded by an American student puts the Buddhist message this way:

> Neither todays nor yesterdays.
> Neither war nor brutality.
> This is a religion of socialism, this Buddhism.

Another anonymous poet transposes a Buddhist precept into simple language:

> In Buddhism first comes the duty.
> Mere speech is not religion,
> Otherwise life would end in madness.
> If you do not behave as you talk
> What sense is there?

Ranu Bhima of Pune refers to the past, as do many of the songs, claiming the glory of earlier Buddhism as his own:

> Bring to this country once again
> The blessed name
> Which made land of thy birth sacred
> To all the distant lands!
> Let the great awakening under the Bodhi tree
>   be fulfilled.
> Let the open doors that are barred
>   and the resounding conch shell
> Proclaim thy arrival at Bharat's gate.
> Let, through innumerable voices,
>   the gospel of an unmeasurable love
>   announce thy call.

Another song from the same source refers to the train, a reflection of the importance of the railroad in bringing Mahars from the villages to service on the tracks in the 19th and early 20th centuries, the first step toward freedom from village servitude:

> Bhim's train has come, has come . . . ring the bell.
> It is in India, and the Untouchables are sitting in it.
> There are tracks of touchability . . . tell, o please tell.

The tracks should come together . . . tie them, o please tie them.
The main station is Delhi. We must go there.
Lord Buddha is the Ticket Master . . .

The way in which Bhimrao Ambedkar and the Buddha are linked, and the
way in which Buddhism must be related to the ongoing struggle of the ex-
Untouchables for equality, is shown in a touching and rather unusually
pacifistic song recorded in the Nagpur area.[11]

Bhimjayanti and Buddhajayanti are celebrated.
Buddha gave the message of peace to the world
And Bhim gave us the *Panchashila*.
Following the advice of the *Panchashila*
We gave up the language of revolution
And made our enemy our friend.

Waman Kardak, the best known and the most sophisticated of the folk
poets, summarizes the social meaning of the conversion in his song,
"14th October", the day on which Ambedkar himself converted:

We have thrown away the rags
which never did cover our shame . . . (Chorus)
The drum of bravery was beaten;
The frame of *chaturvarna* was broken.
Bhim's promise to himself was fulfilled
The humble were freed
        from the valley of untouchability.[12]

Dalit Sahitya and Buddhist Literature

Stress on education, a passionate desire to make their suffering understood, and an intense need to contribute to culture has produced a school
of literature in Marathi called Dalit Sahitya--the literature of the oppressed. Probably the single most important development in Marathi
literature in the past ten years, Dalit Sahitya seems to be only marginally
concerned with the Buddhist conversion. I asked Baburao Bagul, a
powerful short story writer, about this, and he answered simply that
something must be completely absorbed and understood before it can be
written about. He also added that the Buddhist conversion set the
Untouchable free to be creative! An example of this point can be found

in a folder entitled "Buddhist Revolutionary Poems", published privately in Bombay in 1980, which begins with a quotation from P. Lakshmi Narasu's *The Essence of Buddhism,* about the relation of Buddhism and aesthetic aspirations and closes with a note that the poetry manifests "the Buddhist way of righteousness", although Buddhism is not specifically mentioned in the poems themselves. The pamphlet was published by Ashok Chakravarti and collected, translated and edited by Gautam Shinde, which seems to be a joint Bengali-Maharashtrian as well as a high-caste-Buddhist venture.

The poet Daya Pawar who has recently won considerable honor and fame for his autobiography, *Balute,* has used Buddhist symbols and concepts in at least three poems. A rather bitter poem which appears in the English translation of excerpts from *Balute* by Priya Adarkar (*Imprint*: January 1980) begins with:

> I have seen this tree choking with grief
> Its roots are deep like a bodhi-tree's
> But the bodhi tree, at least, flowered
> And this tree is scorched in all seasons.

[The other Buddhist poetry in this essay has been published in full in III:5 (*Buddhist Sects in Contemporary India: Identity and Organization*) and IV:2 (*India's Ex-Untouchables: New Past, New Future, the New Poetry*) and so is not reproduced here.]

A particularly touching short story in this Buddhist literary tradition is one entitled *Ani Buddha marun padla* (And the Buddha Died), in Arjun Dangle's collection *Hi bambhavarachi manasa* (Pune: Mangova, 1979). A young Buddhist student attempts to get the Buddhists in his village to let the Untouchable Mangs (traditional enemies of the Untouchable Mahars, the caste which became Buddhist) use their well. He refuses to give money to help build a Buddhist temple when they will not. But then his father dies, and since he must have help with the funeral, he agrees to contribute. Then, as he looks down at his dead father's face, he sees the Buddha has died.

Perhaps it is fitting that we end with a story written by a highly educated Buddhist about village Buddhists, and that the sophisticated work of the poets here balances the exuberant but unsophisticated folk songs given earlier. Today's Buddhists are both illiterate and highly educated, they are village labourers and professors in universities, their social class varies enormously, but they are bound together by a common belief that the Buddhist conversion has freed them, and that the way taught them by Bhimrao Ambedkar is the only way for them to possess full human rights, human dignity, and pride in what they are.

Notes

1. The fullest biography of Dr. Ambedkar is still Dhananjay Keer's *Dr. Ambedkar: Life and Mission* (Bombay: Popular Prakashan, 1971, 3rd edition). All of Dr. Ambedkar's shorter writing will eventually appear in the *Dr. Babasaheb Ambedkar Writings and Speeches* series edited by Vasant Moon under the sponsorship of the Education Department, Government of Maharashtra. [Thus far, ten volumes have appeared -- the first in 1979.]

2. See Owen Lynch, "Dr. Ambedkar -- Myth and Charisma" and Adele Fiske, "Scheduled Caste Buddhist Organisations" in *The Untouchables in Contemporary India,* J. Michael Mahar ed. (Tucson: University of Arizona Press, 1972) for notes on Buddhists outside Maharashtra. D.C. Ahir of New Delhi is probably the most prolific writer from India's Buddhist community today in English. Jullundar in Punjab, has a major Buddhist publishing center under the leadership of L.R. Balley and Bhagwan Das.

3. I have described the pre-Ambedkar interest in Buddhism in "The Indian Rediscovery of Buddhism, 1855-1956" in A.K. Narain ed., *Studies in Pali and Buddhism* (Jagdish Kashap Memorial Volume) (New Delhi: D.K. Publishers' Distributors, 1978).

4. Dr. B.R. Ambedkar, *The Untouchables* (New Delhi: Amrit Book Company, 1948).

5. P. Lakshmi Narasu (1860-1935), was evidently of a low caste, but not an Untouchable. A professor at Madras Christian College, he advocated conversion to Buddhism as an antidote to the caste system. *The Essence of Buddhism,* first published in 1907, was again published by Thacker and Company with an introduction by Ambedkar in 1948, and republished in Delhi by the Bharatiya Publishing House in 1976.

6. The *Dhammapada* seems to be by far the most meaningful of the Buddhist scriptures to the new Buddhists. I know of at least six translations, one of them in the traditional *ovi* meter of Marathi folk poetry, and another in the *abhang* genre used in the all important saint-poet literature of the bhakti movement in Maharashtra [One of the founders of the Dalit Panthers, Raja Dhale, is now translating the *Dhammapad.*]

7. I have reproduced the Buddhist's oaths in my article "Religion and Legitimation in the Mahar Movement", in Bradwell L. Smith ed., *Religion and Legitimation of Power in South Asia* (Leiden: E.J. Brill, 1978) and in this volume.

8. The number of publications is impressive, and at times it seems there is a journal in each town, if only for a short while. Among the more unusual journals, which deal with Buddhism as well as other issues are *Asmitadarsh*, an excellent Dalit literary journal published by Gangadhar Pantawane in Aurangabad, and *Outcry*, a periodical published in English by the Dr. Ambedkar Mission, a group of staunch Buddhist migrants in Toronto, Canada.

9. Another interpretation of the contemporary Buddhist view of history by a non-Maharashtrian convert is by W.R. Vijayakumar, "A Historical Survey of Buddhism in India" in T.S. Wilkinson and M.M. Thomas eds., *Ambedkar and the Neo-Buddhist Movement* (Bangalore: Christian Institute for the Study of Religion and Society; Madras: Christian Literature Society, 1972).

10. Three young undergraduate students in the Associated Colleges of the Midwest's India Studies Program during the last fifteen years have collected Buddhist songs, many of them gleaned directly from singers during Buddhist occasions. I regret that I cannot credit James H. Fisher, Russell Geyer, and John A. Luke more specifically for the songs they have provided.

11. Indira V. Junghare, "Songs of the Mahars: An Untouchable Caste of Maharashtra India", *Ethnomusicology*, XXVII, 2, 1983, p. 290.

12. Published in *Watchal* (Movement) (Prabhodan Prakashan, Aurangabad, 1972). The full poem is translated by Jayant Karve and Eleanor Zelliot in Peter Gaeffke and David A. Utz eds., *Identity and Division in Cults and Sects in South Asia* (Proceedings of the South Asia Seminar, University of Pennsylvania, 1980-81) (Philadelphia, 1984), p. 108.

Addendum to Part III

Literature in Marathi produced by Buddhists has increased vastly since this research was done. My general categories still seem valid, however, and the interested Marathi reader should scan the shelves of Nimjibhai's Book Store in Dadar, Bombay, the book kiosk run by the Trilok Mahabauddh Sangha in front of the Ambedkar statue in Pune or the book stores of Nagpur to find the full range of Buddhist material.

Material in English has also appeared recently. D.C. Ahir in Delhi has added *Dr. Ambedkar on Buddhism* (Bombay: Siddharth Publication, 1982) as a major work to his long list of publications. Two works on the Maharashtrian movement, although not by Indians, should be consulted as literature from inside the Buddhist movement: Sangarakshita, *Am-*

bedkar and Buddhism (Glasgow: Windhorse Publications, 1986) and Terry Pilchick, *Jai Bhim: Dispatches from a Peaceful Revolution* (Glasgow: Windhorse, and Berkeley: Parallax Press, 1988). An interesting collection is *Ambedkar and the Neo-Buddhist Movement*, edited by T.S. Wilkinson and M.M. Thomas (Madras: Christian Literature Society, 1972).

A work by a Russian scholar, *Religion in Indian Society: The Dimensions of 'Unity in Diversity'* (Bangalore: Sterling, 1989) offers a very interesting look at the Buddhists of India in the context of the whole society.

Other interesting material on religion and conversion includes V.T. Samuel, *One Caste, One Religion, One God: A Study of Sree Narayana Guru* (New Delhi: Sterling, 1977), which offers the contrast of a low class Kerala movement; Walter Fernandes, *Caste and Conversion Movements in India* (New Delhi: Indian Social Institute, 1981); Sipra Bose Johnson, "New Buddhists and Black Muslims: A Comparative Analysis of Two Religions of Protest" in Tai S. Karg ed., *Nationalism and the Crises of Ethnic Minorities in Asia* (Westport: Greenwood Press, 1979); Mark Juergensmeyer, *Religion as Social Vision: The Movement Against Untouchability in 20th Century Punjab* (Berkeley: University of California Press, 1982); Satish Kumar Sharma, *Social Movements and Social Changes: A Study of Arya Samaj and Untouchables in Punjab* (Delhi: B.R. Publishing Corporation, 1985); and Devendra Swarup ed., *Politics of Conversion* (Delhi: Deendayal Upadhyay Research Institute, 1966).

In the last *Census of India* (1981), Paper No. 3 of 1984, the Buddhist population reached 4,719,028, a decal growth less than that of Hindus. Of these, 3,209,752 were rural, 1,510,044 urban. Other statistics indicate the continued interest in Buddhism as established by Babasaheb Ambedkar: it is estimated that 15 lakh people came to the Diksha Bhumi (Conversion ground) in Nagpur this October on the anniversary day of the conversion to Buddhism. Another million are expected to come to the Ambedkar memorial in Shivaji Park, Bombay, on 6 December, the day of his death. Buddhists from the outlying areas stay in various Buddhist *viharas* in the city, often camping with only a canvas roof for shelter, the week of Ambedkar's death day observances.

A parallel movement among Christians is best understood through *Towards a Dalit Theology*, edited by M.E. Prabhakar (Delhi: Indian Society for Promoting Christian Knowledge, 1989). The newest study of the Buddhist movement deals with art forms: Gary Michael Tartakof "Art and Identity: The Rise of a New Buddhist Imagery", *Art Journal* 49:4 (Winter 1990).

IV

DALIT LITERATURE

Dalit -- New Cultural Context
for an Old Marathi Word*

dalit: 1. Ground. 2. Broken or reduced to pieces generally.
Molesworth's Marathi-English Dictionary, 1975 reprint of 1831 edition.

In the early 1970s, two Maharashtrian movements achieved enough prominence to be noticed by the English language press--the Dalit Panthers and Dalit literature. By substituting the word "Black" for "Dalit" the reader can immediately understand that a phenomenon comparable to the American Black Panthers and Black literature has surfaced among the lower castes in social and literary affairs in western India. Like the American movements, the Dalit Panthers and the Dalit school of literature represent a new level of pride, militancy and sophisticated creativity. The Marathi word *dalit*, like the word Black, was chosen by the group itself and is used proudly; and even in the English press, the unfamiliar Marathi word had to be used. None of the normal words--Untouchable, Scheduled Castes, Depressed Classes, Gandhi's euphemism, *Harijan*--had the same connotation.[1] *Dalit* implies those who have been broken, ground down by those above them in a deliberate and active way. There is in the word itself an inherent denial of pollution, *karma*, and justified caste hierarchy.

The *Times Weekly Supplement* of 25 November 1973 contained the first significant analysis of Dalit literature in English, together with translations of poetry, stories and essays, and it remains the best introduction in English to this school of literature. The *Supplement* also included news of the Dalit Panthers, a militant organization founded by two writers, Namdeo Dhasal and Raja Dhale, in April 1972 and already famous for its celebration of "Black Independence Day" on 15 August of that year, the Silver Jubilee of India's Independence, and for its mass physical reaction to violence against Untouchables or Buddhists in the

---

*First published in *Contributions to Asian Studies*, XI, 1978; reprinted in *Contemporary India* (Pune: Continental, 1982). A few changes and deletions have been made. New material is added in an Addendum.

villages. In 1974, however, the Panther leadership split, and with the prohibition of demonstrations under the Emergency in 1975, the organization plummeted into near obscurity as quickly as it had risen into the limelight. [For current Panthers, see Section II Addendum.] It will not concern us much here, except as an example of the extreme militancy, commitment to action and profound bitterness of many of the Dalit writers.

The Marathi press had taken notice of the new school of literature four years earlier with the publication of the editorial in the 1969 Diwali issue of *Marathwada*, published from Aurangabad. The lead editorial presented the issue as ''A Discussion: The Literature of the Dalit: Consciousness, Direction and Inspiration'', with a drawing of the Buddha placed beside the title to indicate the debt of the movement to the conversion of Untouchables, largely from the Mahar caste, to Buddhism. Articles by M.N. Wankhade, a Buddhist who had received his Ph.D. in Literature from Indiana University; Baburao Bagul and Daya Pawar, both Buddhist writers; and Janardan Waghmare, a caste Hindu professor who studied Black literature for his Ph.D. thesis, as well as essays by several well-known Marathi critics were included, together with poems and stories from Buddhists such as Keshav Meshram, Shankarrao Kharat and Sukharam Hivrale and from other lower caste writers, including P.M. Shinde, who were associated with Dalit literature, along with the work of some of the most prestigious writers in the Marathi literary establishment. The Diwali issues of Marathi magazines are highly popular and widely circulated, and the dedication of a large part of its Diwali number by *Marathwada* to the Dalit movement meant that Dalit literature had arrived on the Marathi literary scene. For the first time since the seventeenth century, a school of accepted Marathi literature had arisen from a non-elite group.

The clearest definition of *dalit* in its contemporary usage I have seen comes from a letter written to me by Gangadhar Pantawane, a Professor of Marathi at Milind College now at Marathwada University in Aurangabad and founder-editor of *Asmitadarsh* (mirror of identity), the chief organ of Dalit literature:

> To me, Dalit is not a caste. He is a man exploited by the social and economic traditions of this country. He does not believe in God, Rebirth, Soul, Holy Books teaching separatism, Fate and Heaven because they have made him a slave. He does believe in humanism. Dalit is a symbol of change and revolution.

The key here is a radical rejection of the religious legitimization of poverty and untouchability by those who have suffered from either, a criteria which pretty well limits the true Dalit writer to a former Untouchable who has embraced Buddhism, i.e., a member of Mahar caste who rejected Hinduism in the movement led by Dr. B.R. Ambedkar and joined the Buddhist revival started in 1956, or a low-caste Marxist. The Marxist, however, would define Dalit in terms of class, generally including women, tribals, workers and agricultural laborers. There is a Marxist impact on the Dalit school: two of the best known writers are Communists, not Buddhists: (the late Annabhau Sathe, an Untouchable Mang by birth, is usually counted among Dalit writers, while Narayan Surve, an abandoned orphan and hence casteless, is more often thought of as a proletarian poet than a Dalit writer, but his tone is much the same as that of many Dalit poets); some major Buddhist writers are interested in Marxist economic thought or in the Hindi *Samantar* (parallel) litera-ture, which seems Marxist; and an exceptionally able Buddhist poet, Namdeo Dhasal, combines Buddhism and Marxism, and indeed the split in the Dalit Panthers was to some degree due to Dhasal's Communist con-nections. The history of the Dalit literature movement and its themes, however, is much more profoundly a part of the Mahar movement and the Buddhist revival. Dr.Ambedkar, the hero of the movement and the guide to Buddhism, wrote off Marxists as "a bunch of Brahman boys" and avowed that Buddhism contained all the economic and social help necessary. The Pantawane definition of *dalit* will serve for most of the writers I will discuss.

While Dalit literature or, in Marathi, *Dalit sahitya*, as a school, a self-conscious movement, is a product of the 1960s, individual writers from among the Untouchables appear in the fourteenth century and again in the Mahar movement which began in the late nineteenth century. In the long history of Marathi literature before the 1960s, only one school of acknowledged writers included members of the lower castes -- that of the Bhakti (devotional religion) saint-poets. Popular entertainment-- *lawani* (ballads), *pawada* (panegyric poetry) and folk-dramas called *tamasha*[2]-- undoubtedly was produced by low castes, but was anonymous and never considered respectable literature. The Bhakti movement, begun tradi-tionally by Dnyaneshwar in the thirteenth century, was joined by saint-poets from almost all Marathi-speaking castes, including the Mahar poet Chokhamela. Two of the most popular Bhakti saints are the Shimpi (tailor) Namdeo, a contemporary of Chokhamela in the fourteenth century, and the last and greatest of the saint-poets, the Maratha-Kunbi[3]

Tukaram in the seventeenth century. Dnyaneshwar himself was an outcaste Brahman and another major figure in the Bhakti pantheon, the saint, Eknath of the sixteenth century, kept his Brahmanical standing only by virtue of miracles performed with the help of Vithoba, the God of the Bhakti movement.

The Maharashtrian Bhakti movement, like Bhakti movements throughout India, was anti-orthodox, inclusive of both women and Shudras, and based on the experience of God rather than on traditional piety or formal ritual. Its radical stance and its inclusiveness, however, were largely confined to the religious plane, and little action for social equality came from it.

Chokhamela himself occasionally protested about his caste. One *abhanga* ends:

In the beginning,
    at the end
    there is nothing but pollution.
No one knows anyone who is born pure.
Chokha says, in wonder,
    who is pure?

But in other *abhangas*, Chokhamela credits his low birth to past sins. Contemporary Buddhists are interested in the Bhakti movement, and indeed it is one of the few places where they can find a rationale for pride in their past. Bhau Lokhande of Nagpur wrote his doctoral thesis on the influence of Buddhism on the saint-poets, and several articles in *Asmitadarsh* discuss the attitudes and effect of Namdeo, Tukaram and others. Many believe that there was a connection between Buddhism in Maharashtra and the Bhakti movement, but the general stance of dalit writers, however, is to mourn that even the compassionate saint-poets upheld social distinctions, and that their compassion had little effect.

Throughout the period of *pandit* poetry following the Bhakti period and during the British period in Maharashtra, 1818-1947, the field of literature was dominated by the literate Brahman. There was some concern even in belles-lettres for the problems of the lower castes, beginning in the late nineteenth century at about the time the Mahars were beginning to speak for themselves. Marathi's first major modern poet, Keshavsut (K.K. Damle, 1866-1905) wrote poems entitled "Labourer" and "A Worker Forced to Starve". In "New Soldier" he wrote,

> Neither a Brahman, nor a Hindu, nor am I of any sect,
> Only those who have fallen circumscribe the universe.

and in "The First Question of the Untouchable Boy" he states at the end, after a Mahar child's mother has explained to him that the Brahman boy cursed him because "we are low and they are high",

> How would she know
> that highness in this world is built
> on sin and glory on
> the degradation of others.[4]

Brahman reformers, chiefly M.G. Ranade and G.G. Agarkar, were writing at the same time as Keshavsut, and it was also in the last decade of the nineteenth century that documentation for a vigorous Mahar movement appears. An ex-soldier, Gopal Baba Walangkar from the Mahar caste, presented his demands for better treatment of Untouchables and an Untouchable poet, Pandit Kondiram, wrote bitterly of the condition of Untouchables, ending his long unpublished poetic complaint with an injunction to burn the Brahmanical scriptures! Earlier in that same century, a Mali (gardener) reformer, Jotibha Phule, had begun the Satya Shodak (truth-seeking) movement to attempt to reduce Brahman influence on the lower castes. Phule backed his preaching with such concrete action as a school for Untouchables and one for women, and seems to have been the first to use the word *dalit* in connection with caste in the term *dalitodhar* (uplift of the depressed). Indeed the second half of the nineteenth century was full of protest and reform, but only Keshavsut among the literary figures put social consciousness into poetry. And for the next several decades, no proper literature reflected the increasing dynamism of the Mahar protest. As Pantawane writes, "Only one Keshavsut has given expression to the outburst of social greed".

The twentieth century saw the full blooming of the modern Marathi novel, a great emphasis on short stories which still continues, and several schools of poetry. It also saw the blossoming of the Mahar movement into a full-scale effective protest of social, religious and political disabilities, but there was little connection between Literature (with a capital L) and the progress and increasing vocality of the Mahars. Kisan Fagoji Bansode of Nagpur, one of the most important pre-Ambedkar leaders, did write poetry which was collected and published after his death by his son. The newspapers of Dr. Ambedkar, the only highly educated Untouchable, which began in 1920, occasionally contained poems and stories, but these were generally read only by those in the movement. Ambedkar's stress, however, was not only on equality in religion and power in political but also on education and cultural creativity. Most of the creativity took the form of material for the movement-- *jalsa* (a singing--message-performance), songs, poems, polemics, dozens of newspapers and although nothing that was considered Literature by the literary establishment appeared, a regard for literature, the habit of writing and a host of educated young people were well established by the time of the Buddhist conversion in 1956.

It is strange that this dynamic movement brought forth no response from Marathi writers. There is no Marathi equivalent to Mulk Raj Anand's *Untouchable,* or Sivashankar Pillai's *Scavenger's Sons,* and certainly nothing as historically important as Harriet Beecher Stowe's *Uncle Tom's Cabin.* The reason probably rests in Marathi literature's commitment to realism, which meant that writers, if they wrote about social matters, wrote about what they actually knew--middle class marriage, the position of women, the problem of widowhood, or the independence movement.

This is not to say that there was no mention of the Untouchable. S.M. Mate, a professor of Marathi in Pune, wrote his first two books on the problems of the Untouchable. *Asprishyavicar* (thoughts on Untouchables) appeared in 1922 and in 1933. Mate coined a new word, *asprishata* (the untouched rather than the untouchable) in his book *Asprishatanca prashna* (the question of those who are untouched). In the intervening period he devoted so much personal attention to the Untouchable community that he became known as "Mahar Mate". In 1941, a collection of short stories entitled *Upekshitance antarang* (the mind of the neglected) appeared. Mate was in touch with Dr. Ambedkar in the 1920s and I have seen a copy of one of Ambedkar's speeches with a note to Mate on it asking for the latter's comment. However, Mate seemed to be too radical for the establishment and not radical enough for the Mahar movement. Known primarily as a social thinker and essayist, rather than as a literary figure, he is somewhat neglected today by the Dalits and the high castes alike. I asked the Buddhist Baburao Bagul about him, and Bagul replied, "Mate was sympathetic but he showed the customs of the Untouchables as if they were 'these strange ones' ".

Another Brahman writer with great social concern was Sane Guruji

(1899-1950), still revered as a Gandhian reformer. In a very influential book, *Shyamci Ai* (Shyam's mother) which appeared in 1935, Sane Guruji's short stories taught courage, compassion and universal love as the true religion. In the story entitled "Devala Sari Priya" (all are dear to God), Sham's mother tells him that he must help an old Mahar woman, and that she will gave him a bath afterward so that others will not criticize him. "To God all forms seem pure. He took the form of a fish, a tortoise, a boar, a lion. The meaning of that is that to God all forms are holy. God is in the body of the Brahman, the fish, even the Mahar...". Sane Guruji put his beliefs into action and is credited with the opening of the chief Bhakti pilgrimage place, the temple at Pandharpur, to Untouchables in 1948. His courageous satyagraha at the temple door, however, took place after the Mahars had vowed to leave Hinduism, and today his pity is totally unacceptable to the Dalit school.

The rural school of writers, chiefly Vyankatesh Madgulkar and Shankar Patil, do use figures from the lower castes among their characters, but neither makes untouchability a major point of concern. Madgulkar's dispassionate, sharp-eyed objectivity prevails even in his novel on the anti-Brahman riots of 1948 which profoundly affected his own family, and obviously he was not one to present an emotional protest of the Untouchables' condition. Madgulkar's superb stories, however, do reveal much of the life of the village Mahar, and I will compare one with the work of a Buddhist writer of rural short stories later in this article.

While the Marathi literati did not write about the Mahar movement, many did (and still do) give support to it. Among the names of those who either were marginally associated with Ambedkar or, in the current period, helpful to contemporary Dalit writers are some of the best known writers in the Marathi establishment: P.K. Atre, Mama Warerkar, Kusumagraj, D.K. Bedekar, G.T. Madkholkar, Durga Bhagwat, Vijay Tendulkar, Dilip Chitre, Bhalchandra Nemade. But the literary establishment has generally left the passionate description of Mahar life to the Untouchables themselves. Only recently have the city slums figured in fiction, and one of the best of this *genre*, Janavant Dalvi's *Chakra* (wheel), was described by a Marathi critic as the work of an "outsider writing for outsiders".[5]

The "insiders" began their serious work in the late 1950s. Although most of the writers have come out of the Buddhist movement, one of the earliest, Annabhau Sathe, who belonged to the Untouchable Mang caste, was deeply influenced by Communism. Although he dedicated one book to Ambedkar and had before his death close connections with Buddhist

writers, Sathe's best known novel was not concerned with protest but
with the Mang as hero. *Fakira* deals with the anti-British revolt of the
Mangs and other low castes in the nineteenth century. A short story,
"Savala Mang", which presents the Untouchable as a Robin Hood, is
available in English.[6] At about the same time, Shankarrao Kharat's very
different short stories began to be published; "Manuskichi Huk" (the cry
of humanity) appeared in P.K. Atre's journal, *Navayug*, in 1958. Kharat's
book depicting the lives of all the "servants" of the village, *Bara
Balutedar* (the twelve Balutedars) appeared the same year. Kharat was
very much a part of the Ambedkar and Buddhist movements, serving as
editor of one of Ambedkar's newspapers for a time. And although he and
Sathe were the only even moderately well-known writers of the time,
there was enough interest in writing for a Maharashtra Dalit Literature
Conference to be called by Buddhists in 1959.

In the sixties, the flow of Dalit literary writing increased. Conferences were held almost every year; *Asmitadarsh*, a journal devoted to
literature in contrast to the more general magazines of the movement,
was founded by Professor Pantawane at Milind College in Aurangabad,
one of the colleges formed by Ambedkar and the name Dalit Sahitya
achieved the status of a genuine school of literature with the
Marathwada issue of 1969. In the 1970s, individual volumes of poetry
began to appear: Cokha Kamble's *Pimpalpan* (leaf of the pimpal tree),
with an introduction by Durga Bhagwat, who was soon to be President of
the Maharashtra Literary Conference; Namdeo Dhasal's *Golpitha* (a
slum area of Bombay), with an introduction by the dramatist Vijay
Tendulkar; Waman Nimbalkar's *Gaokushabaheril Kavita* (poetry from
beyond the village boundary); Daya Pawar's *Kondwada* (cattle pen);
Trymbak Sapkale's *Surung*. All were published by the Maharashtra
Buddhist Literature Committee, Asmitadarsh Press, or the Marxist
Magova Press, with the exception of *Golpitha*. All were well printed and
bound and most accompanied by vivid modern art--a far cry from the
cheap pamphlets sold at the movement's meeting. Gangadhar Panta-
wane's books of essays, *Mulyavedh* (the preception of value) appeared in
1974, and a volume of biographical sketches of "opposition writers",
including Annabhau Sathe, the folk-singer Waman Kardak, an early
Nagpur writer N.R. Shende, Kisan Fago Bansode, the early Pune leader,
Shivram Janba Kamble, Shankarrao Kharat and Bandhu Madhav (Modak),
a writer of the 1930s, which appeared earlier in the popular monthly
Amrit will soon be published. The work of the proletarian poet, Narayan
Surve, began to appear on standard M.A. reading lists in Maharashtrian

universities. Baburao Bagul's volumes of the 1960s were printed, his, novella, *Sud* (revenge), appeared, and Keshav Meshram's work was published. As the volumes appeared, Marathi criticism followed-- praising, scorning, serious, frivolous. Dalit literature was to be found in every bookstore in the Marathi-speaking area, and had become unmistakably part of the Maharashtrian literary scene. The 1974 survey of regional literature in the Sahitya Akademi's *Indian Literature* included Vasudha Mane's piece on "Recent Marathi Writing", which began

In a Society which is still caste-ridden, the new crop of writers belonging to castes and classes which were traditionally outside the pale of literature so far, has attracted attention during the past few years in Marathi literature. They come from backward rural areas, from slums in industrial towns and many of them hail from families of labourers and menials. They come with experiences hitherto unknown and unimagined by the most sympathetic and observant of writers in the traditionally literate classes. They come with a language and expression which has trampled all conventions.[7]

The discussion of themes and expression in Dalit literature which follows is a very personal one. During a recent Sabbatical year in Pune, I read and translated as many poems, stories and essays as I could, with the help of Rekha Damle, Vidyut Bhagwat and Jayant Karve, in the time left from work on another project. I met many of the major writers; attended the Dalit Literature Conference in Nagpur and the Buddhist Literature Conference in Bombay, both in 1976; and checked meanings of words and phrases with Buddhist friends who dropped by. My expertise, however, is in the history of the Mahar and Buddhist movements; literary criticism is not my forte, and I here apologize for misunderstandings or for omitting significant work. I have tended to take my examples from several published volumes rather than search through Marathi magazines, and I have chosen themes which interest me most as a historian rather than attempting a literary analysis based on all Dalit literature.

The Life of the Lowly

There is, of course, a focus on the life of the lowly in Dalit literature. The style and content vary, however, from the suffering tinged with hope of the village Mahar in Shankarrao Kharat's stories to the gaunt, stark brutality of life in the Bombay slums described by Baburao Bagul in prose and Namdeo Dhasal in poetry. To take Shankarrao Kharat first-- he is himself the son of a village Mahar who did the work delicately described in British records as that of the "inferior village servant"-- cutting wood, carrying messages, bringing fuel to the burning ground, working on other's lands, dragging out dead cattle. Kharat managed an education, however, and had a degree in law. His childhood experience and the life he saw in the slums are the subjects of his fictional writing, although he does have other books on Buddhist and Ambedkarian subjects and is writing a history of the Mahars. His first book, *Bara Balutedar*, took all twelve village servants as subjects for stories, not only the Mahar, and he has continued to deal with characters from many different communities, generally the lower orders, in a dozen volumes.

Three stories translated by Pramod Kale in Robert Miller[8] represent Kharat's treatment of the Untouchable. In "The Burden", a Mahar *kotwal* refuses the help of an educated Mahar who has returned to the village, saying "You felt my pain and that's why you held the umbrella over my head in this soaking rain. It's all very well. You may hold the umbrella over my head now. But what about tomorrow. Rain is there. Heat is there. The burden on the head is always there. Yes". In "The Town Crier's Call", the Mahar village servant has to go out to drum and announce the need for all villagers to come to be inoculated by the visiting doctor, even though he himself is so sick he falls, vomits and dies as he attempts to shout and drum. In "Inside the Village Womb", an educated Mahar, returning to his village, remembers himself as a school boy following his father on his humiliating round of duty, and runs from the now "tumble-down houses, that empty chavadi, that collapsed shop ... wet with perspiration". In an as yet unpublished (in English) story, "Potraj" (the servant of the cholera goddess), a Mahar school boy outwits the villagers who demand that he take his father's place in placating the goddess by arranging a "miracle". [See Addendum].

A Mahar story by the Brahman Vyankatesh Madgulkar is included in the same Robert Miller article[9]. Many of the same themes that Kharat uses enter Madgulkar's story, "Nirvana"--the separate quarters of the Maharwada at a distance from the village; the distinct greeting *johar*, used by Mahars to higher castes; the traditional duties; the lack of true communication between Untouchables and caste Hindus--but the figure of the old Mahar who alone does not convert to Buddhism and who dies trying to perform his duties for the uncaring village is an unlikely subject for a Dalit writer. Old mad Bavarya is honored after his death by the caste Hindus for his loyalty; the Dalit writers, including the gentle Kharat, would say that honor must come in life and that true honor is not possible without change. Pantawane has put it this way, "In short, the Dalit story's essence is not individual commitment, but social commitment". The city world of the Dalit is most cruel in the poetry of Namdeo Dhasal and Baburao Bagul's prose. To set the stage, let me quote from Vijay Tendulkar's introduction to Namdeo Dhasal's *Golpitha*, in part because Dhasal's poetry is far too complex for me to even start to translate (Tendulkar himself lists twenty-six words and phrases he could not understand.) [See Addendum]. Tendulkar, perhaps the best known of the contemporary Marathi dramatists, writes:

In the calculations of the white collar workers, "no man's land" begins at the border of their world, and it is here that the world of Namdeo Dhasal's poetry of Bombay's Golpitha begins. This is the world of days of nights; of empty or half-full stomachs; of the pain of death; of tomorrow's worries; of men's bodies in which shame and sensitivity have been burned out; of overflowing gutters; of a sick young body, knees curled to belly against the cold of death, next to the gutter; of the jobless; of beggars; of pick-pockets; of Bairaga swamis; of Dada bosses and pimps; of Muslim tombs and Christian crosses; of film star Rajesh Khanna and the gods on the peeling wall above the creaking bed; of a hashish cot and a beautiful child asleep on the edge of that cot and a tubercular father employed at a cat-house nearby still cherishing the ambition that his child may become a "sharif", a gentleman; of hermaphrodites; of home-brew liquor; of records of philosophical Quwali; and of hot sticky blood running at the price of water at any moment; of steaming tasteless cups of bright red tea; of smuggling; of naked knives; of opium ... Dhasal's Golpitha, where leprous women are paid the price and fucked on the road, where children cry nearby, where prostitutes waiting for business sing full-throated love songs, from where one cannot run to save his life, or if he runs, he comes back--that Golpitha. Mercy-grace- peace do not touch Golpitha. Dhasal says, here all seasons are pitiless, here all seasons have a contrary heart.

Tendulkar's view through Namdeo Dhasal's eyes is more complete, more picturesque, less personal, than that of the true insider. Baburao Bagul's story of Bombay, "Death is Getting Cheaper"[10] is as violent and as stark; his characters are Christian, Muslim, Maratha, Madrasi, Mahar, all in one way or another defeated by hopeless poverty, crushed by the system, but they are real people and one cares about them. In "Lutalut" (the looter looted), prostitutes quarrel, and the air around them is heavy with vulgarity and violence [See Addendum]. But Bagul himself is not at all a defeatist. He has written, "Dalit Sahitya is not a literature of vengeance. Dalit Sahitya is not a literature which spreads hatred. Dalit Sahitya first promotes man's greatness and man's freedom and for that reason it is an historic necessity".[11] He told the Dalit Literature Conference held in Nagpur in 1976, "Anguish, waiting, pronouncements of sorrow alone do not define Dalit literature. We want literature heroically full of life for the creation of a [new] society".[12]

Perhaps the contrast between Bagul, the man of hope, and Bagul, the writer of stark despair, can be explained by yet another quotation. Daya Pawar's report on the 1976 Dalit Literature Conference quotes Bagul this way[13]:

Even if democracy has been placed over government power, even if Manu has been thrown into darkness, he did not die. He is living today in books, in holy scripture, in temple after temple. He lives in mind after mind. The structure of society he created is what we have today. He is so great that society's arrangements are under his control. And only his loving people are at the center of power. So in India at this time there are two worlds, two powers, two life traditions, two scriptures. He who wants victory, he who wants influence, must take a role in determining the future. We must bring our role to completion with literature and art.

It seems to me Baburao Bagul's purpose is to present the world of the lowly in all its harshness in order to make the middle class understand. Heroism and hope come in facing and acknowledging what is, in order that something better may be created.

The Speech of the Dalit

Dalit writers at times use speech from the Mahar past or the city slum present that is incomprehensible or offensive to the high caste reader. This may be in part simply a new trend in Marathi literature; the non-Dalit novels *Chakra* by Jayavant Dalvi and *Vasunaka* by Bhau Padhye were considered by many to the obscene.[14] But it is true that some words and images genuinely represent the Mahar past. Dhasal most of all, but also many other writers, use phrases that the average city dweller does not understand. There seems to be a certain pride in this, a lack of the sense of dual pressures of speech depicted in a poem of Arun Kamble which appeared in the *Times Literary Supplement* Dalit issue, translated by Gauri Deshpande:

Bone-chewing grampus
at the burning ghat:
permanent resident
of my own heart:
with the weight of tradition
behind his back
yells: Saddling bastard
I tell you,
stutter with our tongue!
Picking through the Vedas,
buttering his queue,
the Brahmin teacher at school
bellows: Speak my pure tongue
whoreson!

Now you tell me which speech
am I to tongue?

The Dalit poet makes an effort to use images as well as words which come from his own experience. In his introduction to a collection of poems, *Kondwada*, Daya Pawar reflects on his growth as a poet. At first, after his move to the city, he wrote romantic poetry, and then when he realized that he was being untrue to both past and present, that he had no acquaintance with the "holy gourd" he had used as an image, that his beloved slept on the ground and had no pillow to stain with tears, he stopped.

My uneasiness grew. I was not satisfied with the kind of poetry that I had published. I read poetry continually from the collections of respected Marathi poets. Mardhekar is understood to be the sculptor of the new poetry. At that time I was not touched by Mardhekar's poetry nor did he seem to me to be different. Men had been made insects by the machine age, so he thought, but the machine age had not touched me. Actually we were waiting for the machine age. We were convinced that our salvation was in the machine age. I thought that the angry generation coming after Dilip Chitre was controlled by "form". I thought their poetry was vapid, caught in a tangle of images, and I could not write such poetry. I think it well that I did not get a B.A. or M.A. in Marathi at a university. Otherwise I would have written such flaccid poetry swollen with images. Muktibodh, Vinda Karandikar, Kusumagraj--I liked the progressive thought in their poetry. I was mute until the poetry collections of Narayan Surve, *Thus I Am Brahma, My University*, appeared. Surve's writing style, his straightforward language, told me much . . .

Nevertheless, few Dalit poets apart from Dhasal, break many Marathi poetic convention. I could wish for some experimentation in carrying over the "low" Mahar cultural tradition of the past, of *tamasha*, of *jalsa*, but this is found only in the comparatively unsophisticated poetry of the folk-poet, Waman Kardak (1972). Pawar has written, in prose, more vividly than any other Dalit writer of the cultural influences of his childhood--the difference between the music and literature in a Brahman and in a Mahar home, his father's band, his boyish imitations of *tamasha*, the mime and music of the nomadic Rayrandi who stayed in the Maharwada, the *jalsa* groups inspired by the Ambedkar movement who would sing such things as "The child of a Mahar is very, very clever; in all the world you will not see his like. Come on, look up, look up!" But even Pawar does not use these rhythmic influences in his poetry.

True, there is no Freud, or T.S. Eliot fallout in Dalit poetry. But only the subjects, a certain straightforward quality, the attitudes, some special words, and the references to history and myths from a dalit point of view, mark Dalit poetry as *dalit*--not its inherent structure.

Interest in Black Literature

Dalit writers are extremely interested in Black American literature and see their own movement as a parallel phenomenon. Gangadhar Panta-wane began his major essay on Dalit literature[15] with a quotation from James Baldwin in English: "Our humanity is our burden, our life, we need not battle for it; we need only to do what is infinitely difficult--that is accept it". Janardan Waghmare has written extensively of the possible comparison between Black and Dalit, pointing out that although the Black was brought to America from Africa, the Dalit was born in his own country,

> He may have been an heir of this country but he could not claim his heritage. . . . So Ambedkar said, "Gandhiji, I have no homeland. . . . Baburao Bagul says,

> Those who by mistake were born here
> should themselves correct this error
> by leaving the country! Or making war!

> . . .The words *a peculiar institution* describe the untouchability created by the caste system. . . . The Negro should not change the colour of his hide, nor the Untouchable his caste.There is no difference between the *place* of the Negro in America and the step or level of the Untouchable in India. And so for a long time both were caught in the whirlwind of self-denigration and self-hatred.Both were confined in the prison of fatalism. To prolong this imprisonment, the whites found authority in the Bible's myths and symbols, and the clean castes in the Vedas and Manusmriti.*

There is an occasional reference to the Black world in Dalit literature, such as in Daya Pawar's poem entitled "Harlem," which is a love poem to his wife with full realization of the life-destroying world around them. There seems, however, to be no imitation of Black literature and its two strongest fields, autobiography and drama, are not yet developed in Dalit literature [See Addendum]. A Buddhist amateur playwright, however, B.S. Shinde, who has previously produced plays based on Buddhist legends with an amateur caste in the off-hours of the prestigious Bal Gandharva theatre in Pune, is fascinated by James Baldwin's *Blues for Mr. Charlie* and would like to do a Marathi version of it. But the chief influence of American Black literature is as support, as proof that a group similar to the Dalit can become militant, can become creative, and can progress in a hostile society.

---

*Words originally in English italicized (Waghmare, 1974).

Anti-Traditionalism

This section on anti-traditionalism might as well be started off with lines
from the most condemnatory of the poets, Namdeo Dhasal. Even the best
of orthodoxy is unacceptable to him:

> Their traditional pity is no better than
> the pimp on Falkland Road.[16]

and even well wishers get no sympathy:

> The very intelligent people. . .
> those who don't even know
> the darkness under their asses
> they should poke their noses
> like fifty-cent prostitutes
> even today
> at men who are burning ![17]

Daya Pawar is equally condemnatory, though less scurrilous, in
"Sanskriti"(culture)[18]:

> In hut after hut, total darkness.
> Then the siren went off.
> From the fourteen story Damodar
> comes--what's this--a gleam of light.
> What do you say:
> They've got a permit for light.
> Sh! Sh!
> Don't peep into their windows
> They've taken shelter under their beds.
> Generation after generation
> has arranged the plastic pastime
> of that Great Divine Culture.
> Now then they
> stuff balls of cotton in their ears.
> In huts after hut, whimpering,
> the weeping of a broken heart
> *disturbs* their peaceful life.
>
> (words originally in English italicized)

And in "He Mahan Desha" (O great country)[19] , he ends:

O great country
how can you be called great?
You don't see the charred waste burning at your feet.
Like Nero you play the sarangi
and sing sweetly of the Himalayas.

Manu, the Brahmanical law-giver, is seen as the arch enemy. Indeed the earliest recorded modern Mahar poet, Pandit Kondiram, cried out for the burning of the Brahmanical scriptures way back in the late nineteenth century. The *Manusmriti* was actually burned at the Mahad Conference of the Depressed Classes in 1928, at the hands of a Brahman who worked closely with Dr. Ambedkar. It was a gesture which shocked (and still shocks) many pious Hindus. Waman Nimbalkar uses the image of burning in a reversed way in "Itihas" (history) which begins[20]

O heirs of Manu! For millennia we have watched our own
naked evening. In half a dozen huts on the village
boundary our countless bodies have been burning, set
afire by your feeble thoughts.

(translated by Graham Smith and Eleanor Zelliot)

Shashikant Lokhande puts it this way[21]:

When you try to heat the bread of your sweat or pull up
the lungoti of your pain they slash at your buttocks,
yours breast, your hand, they bind on your neck the
burden of Manusmriti.

Daya Pawar, in "Ye Hemangi" (come, gold-skinned one), is more optimistic[22]:

By the mixture of our blood
Manu's wall will be demolished brick by brick.

The great Hindu epics are seen quite differently from the Dalit viewpoint. *The Mahabharata* calls up not an image of heroism and performance of duty but the figures of Karna, the illegitimate son of Kunti, who was scorned by his Pandava brothers for his unknown parentage,[23] and Eklavya, the low born, who cut off his thumb at the command of the guru he had followed from afar, lest he might triumph over the guru's favorite, Arjuna, in archery. *The Ramayana* evokes the image of Shambuk, who was killed because he heard the Vedas, not the models of the perfect king Rama and the perfect wife, Sita. Eklavya and Shambuk as archetypal symbols of suffering appear in dozens of poems, though these references to minor epic characters are often tucked in the poetry without explanation, as in Waman Nimbalkar's "Kavita" (poem) which ends with a reference to the Buddha through the use of one of his names, Tathagatha, and to Eklavya as an oath of resolve[24] :

Gathering the sky in my eyes,
I cast my glance forwards,
-- and so on to Tathagatha.
On the horizon I will erect
the rainbow arch of mankind.
I am conscious of my resolve.
The worth of the blood
of Eklavya's broken finger --
This is my loyalty.
I will not barter my word.
I stand today at the very end
of the twentieth century.

Tryambak Sapkale also uses the image of Eklavya as strength:

Round earth.
Steel oar
in my hand
but no oarlock?
O you ideal disciple
Eklavya!
Give me
your slashed finger
for support.

Waman Nimbalkar[25] expresses the attitude toward the epics in general:

O Gods of Words!
You have created great epics--

those eating gold, walking with the wind,
wearing gold-bordered cloth--
heaps of words were dampened
in leaves, flowers, fragrance,
the intoxication of Madira.
This dire, crushed life of the
outskirts of the village
never became the subject of your poetry.

Even the beloved Maharashtrian saint-poets are not free from scorn in the poetry of the Dalit. Daya Pawar's poem "Pay" (legs or feet) refers to the Rig Vedic hymn of creation, the story of Eknath giving water to a donkey, and the legend of Dnyaneshwar, who produced the sacred Vedas from the mouth of a bufallo to show that these sacrosanct texts should not be confined to the high castes. The imagery of "Pay"[26] shows Hindu culture as a pyramidical structure, crushing those on the bottom, and ends:

The legs of those born from the feet
were snapped like green buds.
Everyone says: "The safety of the pyramid is worth fifty
legs. O come on, bear a little pain".
They paint the pyramid's pinnacle.
Your name is not mentioned.
Someone cuts the ribbon.
The pitchers of Ganges water come and are poured
into the mouth of a donkey.
If the water vessel is filled, they say,
Dnyaneshwar's buffalo will come!

But the picture is not entirely negative. Even in the same poet one can find both condemnation of Hindu culture and the demand for a place in it. Daya Pawar in the introduction to the collection which contains the above poem wrote: "I am intensely conscious of the chasm in Indian cultural life. If my poetry is sacrificed for the removal of cultural duality, then that's all right. I came to that conclusion and I wrote:

Like the elephant leading the charge
on the pike-studded doors of the fort,
let us die laughing".

Tryambak Sapkale puts it another way in a poem addressed, as I read it, to Mother India[27] :

Your whole life you were simply a woman;
You never became a mother.
Your hunger for motherhood
I can satisfy
Would you be a mother?
I am ready to be adopted.

and ends his collection[28] with an exquisitely wrought poem so simple it is difficult to put into interesting English:

Don't despair.
This day will depart too.
Now, this day is pregnant with day.
Our day is not far away.
Look, from the day is born the day.

And Waman Kardak, the folk poet, sings: "We will burn, but we will light the earth"!

The Use of the Mahar Past and Buddhist Tradition

The way in which Dalit writers evoke their own past, the references to "Babasaheb" Ambedkar and to Buddhism, the use of recent events, are the most interesting themes at least as far as the historian in me is concerned. Although most of the poets are educated, many are city-dwellers, and some have entered at least the lower reaches of middle-class comfort, the Mahar past is not far from even the young generation. Arun Kamble's poem, translated by Gauri Deshpande in the 1973 *Times Weekly Supplement*, is addressed to the Brahman:

If you were to live the life we live
(then out of you would poems arise).
We: kicked and spat at for our piece of bread.
You: fetch fulfillment and name of the Lord.
We: down-gutter degraders of our heritage
You: its sole repository and descendants of the sage.
We: never have a paisa to scratch our arse

You: the golden cup of offerings in your bank.
Your bodies flame in sandalwood
Ours you shovel under half-turned sand.

Wouldn't the world change, and fast,
if you were forced to live at last
this life that's all we've ever had?

Although the Brahman, as originator and protector of the caste hierarchy,
is still the arch-enemy to the Dalit, the dominant agricultural caste, the
Marathas, who are far more closely associated with the village Untouchable, are also seen as tormentors. Prahlad Chendwankar's poem, translated by Gauri Deshpande in the *Times Weekly Supplement*, attacks the
Maratha headman, the Patil:

When Patil sent
for me, I went
"Siddown", said, yet
ground was wet.

Threw at my head
torn sacking jute
still there I stood
quite mute.

Patil cracked betelnut
yelled, 'why aint this runt
bloody scum, dancing on boards
to fill its gut'.

Paunch-scratching, spewed
forth filth-abuse
I went on standing mute
rooted still within my boots.
Wonder now, why did I stand
hadn't eaten no fodder
at his father's hand.

Dr. B.R. or Babasaheb Ambedkar receives much less direct attention
in sophisticated Dalit literature than in the movement literature. [See

Addendum]. Often the reference is to a 'sunflower-giving *fakir*', our *sannyasi*, or to the sun which has set. J.V. Pawar, in a poem which appeared in *Magowa*, uses the image of the conference at Mahad in 1928, which many see as the turning point in Ambedkar's movement, to turn from despair to militancy:

> Even the sea has a shore.
> Why doesn't my grief have limits . . .
> A mantra was given to start some Mahad . . .
> I have become an ocean.
> I stand erect, I roll like the ocean,
> I have started to build your tombs . . .

The literature which does deal directly with Ambedkar and the conversion to Buddhism seems less sophisticated, more in tune with the earlier movement literature. A rather charming story by Waman Howal in the Diwali issue of *Asmitadarsh* in 1974 illustrates this. In "Angara" (sacred ash), an old Mahar village *devrishi* is converted to Buddhism and gives up all his magic. But when pressed by the villagers, he rather scornfully throws ordinary ash from his stove on the sufferer, and laughs quietly underneath his moustache. It is doubtful if a story like this would be accepted by any but the journals associated with the Ambedkar movement. [Later: I am now not sure about this point.]

A recent novel on the life of Buddha's wife, *Yasodhara*, by a Buddhist has been well received by the Marathi press, but most Dalit writers deal as obliquely with Buddhism as they do with Ambedkar. I asked Baburao Bagul for an explanation, and he said something to the effect that experience must be completely absorbed and understood before it can become literature. He also stated that Dalit literature began with the Buddhist conversion, that only that release from the psychological imprisonment of untouchability freed the poet, the writer, to create. Daya Pawar's poem "Jhad" (tree)[29] places this belief in the symbolism of Hindu and Buddhist trees:

> This tree I saw mangled with sorrow
> had roots as deep down as the Bodhi-tree's.
> But the Bodhi-tree flowered,
> and this tree through all seasons was barren.

Recent violent events involving Buddhists and the Dalit are quite often used as subjects for poetry. The Worli riots of 1974 which saw Dalit Panthers and Buddhists opposed to their Maratha neighbors and the police evoked a long poem from Daya Pawar.[30] It ends with the image of a soldier of the Mahar Battalion (founded at Ambedkar's plea in 1942) lying in his Worli room filled with tear-gas:

> Mahar-Battalion Kamble, legs lost in service,
> stares in the dark with gas-burned eyes.
> Who did I fight for there on the border?
> Why was I crippled for this country?
> The question pierces like the scream from the soul.
> Now his hand gropes near the pillow
> for the long-missing gun.

The blinding of the Buddhist Gawai brothers in January 1975, during a dispute with Marathas in a village, brought forth a bitter poem from the usually gentle Sapkale[31] which has been translated by Vidyut Bhagwat:

> The other day I heard your speech--
> you condemned America
> for bombing Vietnam--
> Workers of the World unite
> you roared.
> The next day your brothers
> condemned Russia
> and wept for the Hungarians
> Gawai brothers lost their eyes.
> not a tear I saw
> in your eyes.
> No protest meetings.
> Just a small news in a couple of dailies
> and everything is so peaceful! Quiet! Quiet!

Such internal matters as splits and quarrels among the Buddhists themselves also receive attention. The most explicit example I have seen is from the folk-poetry of Waman Kardak. I heard him sing this song at the Nagpur Dalit Literature Conference, and the young Dalit Panthers in the front rows of the audience demanded that he sing it over and over again, hardly letting him stop for breath. "Bhim" in the poem is a reference to Ambedkar through a shortened version of his name, and

"Mother Bhim" follows an old Marathi convention of feminizing a deity or a saint to evoke the sense of creation and protection:

> All are children of Mother Bhim.
> I weave the garland of unity.
> Build this nest again.
> Oh become a friend of Waman.
> On the stem of the heart
> engrave the name of Bhim,
> live happily here in unity.

Do Dalit Writers Protest too much?

That headline is from the *Times of India*, 30 May 1976, and although the news story itself is sympathetic, the editorial lead reads: "It is inevitable for early Dalit literature to have given expression to the torments of an oppressed people. But the note of continued protest and indignation is beginning to pall, . . . and writers should give a new direction to the Dalit literature movement". Most Dalit writers would not agree. One of the best received poems spoken in an open session at the Nagpur Dalit Literature Conference contained these lines:

> In a song full of hope in the evening
> there is no meaning.
> This is a time to breathe battle!

It was recited by the late Mina Gajbhiye, a very young woman, and so far the only feminine poet highly regarded in the new Dalit school. [See Addendum]. But there are also signs of new sorts of creativity. At the same time that the Dalit school appeared, a Mahar poet who does not belong to the Dalit school, who writes brilliant lyric and nature poetry, who refuses to mention caste, achieved status as a major Maharashtrian poet using the pen-name of "Grace". The urge to creativity is there among the formerly inarticulate lowly. Their voices may find different instruments in the future, but they will not be stifled.

Notes

1. "Downtrodden" is a fairly accurate translation of *dalit*, but "downtrodden Panthers" and "downtrodden literature" seem ridiculous in English and

carry none of the dignity and pride of the Marathi word.

2. There has been a government-sponsored revival of *tamasha* in the post-Independence era, and some *tamasgirs* are well known. Indurikar (Dadu Raghu Sarode), a Mahar, won a Sangeet Natak Akademi Award for Tamasha in 1973.

3. Tukaram was probably a member of the Kunbi agriculturalist caste which in the twentieth century has become completely united with the Marathas.

4. I have used Shahane's translations of these two fragments of Keshavsut's poems (1974, pp. 20-1) but have made two changes in accordance with my reading of *Keshavsutanci Kavita* (Bombay: Keshavsut Janmashtabdi Samaroh Samiti, 1967).

5. Shantra Gokhale, *Chakra* [review], *Indian PEN*, 41; 8, 1975, pp. 16-18.

6. Beatrice Miller, "The Man Inside", J. Michael Mahar ed., *The Untouchables in Contemporary India* (Tucson: University of Arizona Press, 1972), pp. 361-73 includes Annabhau Sathe's "Salvala Mang").

7. Vasudha Mane, "Recent Marathi Writings", *Indian Literature*, XVII: 4, 1974, pp. 98-103.

8. Robert J. Miller, and Pramod Kale, "The Burden on the Head is Always There", J. Michael Mahar ed., *The Untouchables in Contemporary India* (Tucson: University of Arizona Press, 1972), pp. 317-59. (Includes three stories by Shankarro Kharat, one by Vyankatesh Madgulkar).

9. Ibid., pp. 34-59.

10. Baburao Bagul, "Death is Getting Cheaper" translated by Vidyut Bhagwat and Eleanor Zelliot from "Maran Swast Hot Ahe", *Vagartha*, 12, 1976, pp. 18-31.

11. Baburao Bagul, "Dalit Sahitya: Mansachya Mahatice, Mansachya Muktice" (Dalit literature: man's greatness, man's freedom), *Asmitadarsh*, VI: 1, 1973, pp. 56-57.

12. Vidyut Bhagwat, "Dalit Sahitya Samelanatla Don Diwasaca Anubhav" (two days experience of the dalit literature conference), *Maharashtra Times*, 28 January 1976, Bombay.

13. Daya Pawar, "Dalit Sahitya Samelan" (Dalit Literature Conference), *Lalit*, XIII, 3, 1976,   pp. 22-4.(a)

14. Mahadeo L. Apte, Contemporary Marathi Fiction: Obscenity or Realism"? *Journal of Asian Studies*, XXIX: 1, 1969, pp. 55-66.

15. Gangadhar Pantawane, *Mulyavedh* (the perception of value) Aurangabad: Asmitadarsh Prakashan, 1974).

16. Namdeo Dhasal, *Golpitha* (Poona: Nilkant Prakashan, 2nd edition, 1975).

17. Gangadhar Pantanwane, Ibid., p. 114.

18. Daya Pawar, *Kondwada* (cattle pen) (Pune: Magova Prakashan, 1974).

19. Ibid., pp. 31-2.

20. Waman Nimbalkar, *Gaokushabaheril Kavita* (poetry from beyond the village boundary) (Aurangabad: Asmitadarsh Prakash, 1973).

21. Gangadhar Pantawane, Ibid., p. 116.

22. Daya Pawar, 1974, Ibid., p. 22.
23. There have been two popular plays and a novel in Marathi on Karna in the last few years. Establishment literature, however, sees Karna as an intriguing individual; Dalit literature sees him as a tragic victim of the social hierarchy.
24. Waman Nimbalkar, "Poem", translation of *kavita* by Graham Smith, *Vagartha*, 12, 1976, pp. 32-33.
25. Gangadhar Pantawnae, 1974, Ibid., p. 116.
26. Daya Pawar, 1974, Ibid., p. 40.
27. Tryambak Sapkale, *Surung* (Aurangabad: Asmitadarsh Prakashan, 1976).
28. Ibid., p. 48.
29. Daya Pawar, 1974, Ibid., p. 35.
30. Ibid., pp. 58-60.
31. Sapkale, Ibid., p. 40.

Bibliography

Cokhamela, *Cokjamela Abhanga Gatha* (Bombay: Balkrishna Lakshman Pathak, 1950).

Waman Kardak, *Watcal* (movement) (Aurangabad: Prabodhan Prakashan, 1972).

Daya Pawar, "Four Poems" translated by Graham Smith, *Vagartha*, 12, 1976, pp. 34-35.(b)

J.V. Pawar, "Udhanloy" (I have become an ocean), *Magova*, I, 7-8, 1972, p. 62.

Sane Guruji, *Shyamci Ai* (Pune: Pune Vidhyarthi Prakashan, 1971, reprint of 1935).

V.A. Shahane, "Realism in Marathi Creative Literature", Carlo Coppola ed., *Marxist Influence and South Asian Literature*, Vol. II, (East Lansing: Asian Studies Center, Michigan State University Press, 1974), pp. 17-29.

Times Weekly Supplement, 25 November 1973, Bombay.

Janardan Waghmare, "Nigro Wangmay va Dalit Wangmay" (Negro Literature and Dalit Literature), *Asmitadarsh*, VII, 1, 1974, pp. 41-46.

Eleanor Zelliot, "Buddhism and Politics in Maharashtra", in Donald E. Smith ed., *South Asian Politics and Religion* (Princeton: Princeton University Press, 1966).

See also Jayshree B. Gokhale-Turner, "Bhakti or Vidroha: Continuity and Change in Dalit Sahitya", in *Tradition and Modernity in Bhakti Movements*, edited by Jayant Lele (Leiden: E.J. Brill, 1981).

India's Ex-Untouchables: New Past, New Future and The New Poetry

Part I*

Since the conversion to Buddhism in 1956, the ex-Untouchable Mahar caste of Maharashtra has entered upon an extraordinary literary movement that has made a major contribution to Marathi literature. *Dalit sahitya* (the literature of the oppressed) includes short stories, novels and drama, but has been most effective in poetry and autobiography. The following poems reflect something of my theme, ''new past, new future'', in that they refer either to the proud Buddhist past of India, re-interpreting it for today's needs, or to the conflict between the past tradition and the contemporary movement.

The first two poems deal with the legendary figure of Angulimal, a ferocious robber converted by the Buddha. Daya Pawar sees Angulimal as the symbol of the fierce society around him; while in the second poem, Tryambak Sapkale takes a diametrically opposite view of the figure of Angulimal, and sees himself *becoming* the violent man who wore his victims' fingers in a garland around his neck.

Siddharthanagar

O Siddhartha![1]
The town of your name[2]
in this twentieth century
has been struck by the tyrannical plough of power.
Each hut
is uprooted like a worthless stone.

Over the sign board with your name on it
a police van was driven.

---

*Hand out prepared for a talk at the Asia Society, New York, 1985.

Clothing, mats in each hut --
the huge earnings of umpteen generations --
scattered by police clubs.
A bunch of naked little children,
screaming and moaning, came onto the road.

--Hey, call that woman in Delhi!
--Oh, someone phone the minister!

--Oh, isn't it nice, dear.
--That hell in front of our apartment is going away --

These were the shouts heard in the air.
Before their eyes the surrounding land was cleared.
In air conditioned glass apartments
power has taken the pose of the three monkeys
If anyone asks, the sahib has left town --
that message has been left with his Personal Assistant.

O Siddhartha, did you know
a project is going on to change the hearts
of the bandits in Chambal valley;
and here in the cultured world
white collar inhumanity has reached a peak.
Your Anand and Sariputra,[3]
see, see -- shelter under someone's awning.

-- Let's go, take out five rupees each,
Let's take a march to the center of power. --
Those gangsters, living under your name,
have come.[4]

O Siddhartha,
You made a tyrant like Angulimal[5]
tremble.
We are your humble followers.

How should we confront
this ferocious Angulimal?
O Siddhartha,

If we fight tooth and claw,
Try to understand us.
Try to understand us.

by Daya Pawar
translated by Vidya Dixit,
Jayant Karve, Eleanor Zelliot
published in *Bulletin of Concerned
Asian Scholars*, X:3 (1978)

Angulimal

When I came into this world
I was crying.
The world was laughing.
Two hands caressed me
on the back, on the stomach.

When I was crawling
I used to fall
then get up with
the little fingers of hands
to support me.

When understanding came
I cried.
The world only laughed.
Two hands raised the whip
to my back, my stomach.

As I ran through this
bounteous, plentiful land
my feet burned
I ran yelling for life
hoping to meet some saint like Eknath.[6]

I met quite a few who reverenced Eknath.
They were engrossed
in their kirtan.
My cry did not
enter their hearts.

Even the Sahara
has an oasis.
I ran in search of
something like an oasis.

I tried to catch hold of this turning world.
My hands were brushed off.
I fell.
The world laughed.
pointing its fingers at me.

Tears dried
Feet froze.
Gathering all strength
I laughed at this world
Ha . . . ha . . . ha . . . ha . . .
The world trembled
at my laugh.

Hey, I said, how come
you rabbits, spawn aren't laughing anymore?
Those fingers that were pointed at me
will become fingers in the garland around my neck.

Angulimal.
I am Angulimal...
I am Angulimal...

by Tryambak Sapkale,
translated by Jayant Karve and Eleanor Zelliot in
Surung (Aurangabad: Asmitadarsh Prakashan, 1976)

In a third "Buddhist Poem", Daya Pawar rejects the classical
images of the Buddha for one walking through the Bomabay slums:

Buddha

I never see you
In Jetawana's garden
Sitting with closed eyes

In meditation, in the lotus position;
Or
In the caves of Ajanta and Elura
With stony lips sewn shut
Taking the last sleep of your life.
I see you
Walking, talking,
Breathing softly, healingly,
On the sorrow of the poor, the weak;
Going from hut to hut
In the life-destroying darkness
Torch in hand,
Giving the sorrow
That drains the blood
Like a contagious disease
A new meaning

from Daya Pawar's Introduction to
his book of poems, *Kondwada* (cattle pen)
translated by Eleanor Zelliot,
Vidyut Bhagwat and Jayant Karve
(Pune: Magova Prakashan, 1974)

The next group of three poems deal with the Mahar's village past, where his traditional work was to serve the village, especially the village headman or Patil. Note that Arun Kamble is bitter in "The Life we Live", but funny in "Speech". While much of the literature is bitter, a strain of humor and optimism runs through the work of almost every poet. [See "Dalit -- New Cultural Context for an Old Marathi Word" for Arun Kamble's poems, omitted here to avoid duplication.]

Narayan Surve is not a Mahar, but a casteless orphan from the streets of Bombay. His poem, "For I am Brahma" expresses beautifully one of the themes of Dalit literature -- the betrayal of high Hindu concepts by the facts of India's social reality.

For I Am Brahma[7]

I will protect all that belongs to Brahma,
all that is Brahma.
I'll undo the knot of time.

I'll bring the world to my door,

where it will frolic like a child.
I'll play lagori with the sun.

I'll tie up big clouds like cows outside my house.
I'll milk them to fill pots with ambrosia.

I'll hold the wind in my yard,
where it will spin like a top.
I'll raise the rooftops of heaven.

I'll straighten out the bending sky,
single-handed
and punish whoever bent it in the first place!

The mole's mountain, the mountain's mole --
they're both inside of *me*.

For I am Brahma. I hold the world together --
I, the helpless one,
      without even a room to call my own.

                    by Narayan Surve, *Aisa ga mi bram!*
               translated by Jayant Karve and Eleanor Zelliot
                          with the assistance of Pam Espeland
                    (Bombay: Popular Prakashan, 1976 (1971))

The final two poems are by Namdeo Dhasal, the most innovative,
prolific and difficult of all the Dalit poets. Images torn from all aspects
of the Bombay life around him tumble through his work, from the
grossest sexual images of the prostitutes' area near his childhood home
to the fragments of sophisticated Bombay intellectual life which impinge
on the fringes of his world. The last of these two poems reflect the respect
and adulation even a fiercely individualistic writer like Dhasal gives to
Dr. Ambedkar, "Babasaheb", the long-time spokesmen for Untouchables in India. The images in this one range from the railway line on
which nineteenth century Mahars worked as gangmen to the universities
(and Ambedkar founded several colleges), from the echo of Krishna as
the charioteer of Arjuna in the *Bhagvad Gita*, to an echo of the Lord's
prayer. Nothing is sacred to Dhasal, except possibly his own creative gift
and the memory of a man who believed in the creative powers of his own
Untouchable people.

Poverty as My Own Independent Piece of Land

Destiny willing, the form may change or may not.
Even then poverty itself is my own independent piece of land
And as I cultivate it my days rise
And my days fall . . .
Earlier men could have been wretched slaves . . .
I refused to make compromise with the later feudal lords
My limbs of a forest were fostered by geometric contagion
Drenched me in gentle innocence
I am the headless body of a rat with a pyramid rising above me
Meat and fish
Rice and eggs
Bootleg liquor and the flowers of white champak
Kisses, embraces, coital postures, jewels,
And beds, and a house with a leaking roof,
And the rhythm of a lullaby.
I am squeezed: in my yearning
Feminine beauty flowers
The Mona Lisa painted by Leonardo da Vinci
In the service of A-B
Rain driving down in sheets, a dying cigarette,
a dehydrated dancing girl,
Contrasting color harmony
I too have poverty as my own independent piece of land . . .

by Namdeo Dhasal in *Golpitha* (a slum area of Bombay),
translated by Dilip Chitre and published first in *Times Weekly*, 25
November 1973,
(Pune: Nilkanth Prakashan, 1975).

From Dr. Ambedkar

You are the one
Who dances from shrub to shrub like the butterfly
Of the new year and emits rays of light.
Who goes on expanding like the railway lines
Who unnerves the foundations of universities
who travels from freedom to freedom.
You are the only one, charioteer of our chariot
Who comes amongst us through fields and crowds,
And protest marches and struggles.

Never leaves our company
And delivers us from exploitation
You are the one
The only one.

Namdeo Dhasal, in *Golpitha*,
translated by D.B. Karnik
(Pune: Nilkanth Prakashan, 1975).

PART II -- MORE DALIT POETRY*

ONE DAY I CURSED THAT MOTHER-FUCKER GOD

One day I cursed that mother-fucker God.
He just laughed shamelessly.
My neighbor -- a born-to-the-pen Brahman -- was shocked.
He looked at me with his castor-oil face and said,
"How can you say such things to the
Source of the Indescribable,
Qualityless, Formless Juggernaut?
Shame on you for trying to catch his dharma-hood
in a noose of words".

I cursed another good hot curse.
The university buildings shuddered and sank waist-deep.
All at once, scholars began doing research
into what makes people angry.
They sat in their big rooms fragrant with incense,
their bellies full of food,
and debated.
On my birthday, I cursed God.
I cursed him, I cursed him again.
Whipping him with words, I said
"Bastard"!
"Would you chop a whole cart full of wood
for a single piece of bread?
Would you wipe the sweat from your bony body
with Your mother's ragged sari?
Would Your wear out your brothers and sisters
for your father's pipe?

---

*Poetry and a brief statement on Dr. Ambedkar prepared for a Conference of American Blacks and Indian Dalits sponsored by the Minority Rights Group and held in New York City in 1984.

Would you work as a pimp
to keep him in booze?
Oh Father, Oh God the Father!
You could never do such things,
First you'd need a mother --
one no one honours,
one who toils in the dirt
one who gives and gives of her love".

One day I cursed that mother-fucking God.

Keshav Meshram, in *Vidrohi kavita* (Poetry of Protest),
translated by Jayant Karve and Eleanor Zelliot with Pam Espeland
(Pune: Continental Prakashan, 1978)

You Wrote from Los Angeles

"In the stores here, in hotels, about the streets,
Indians and curs are measured with the same yard-stick;
'Niggers' 'Blacks'! This is the abuse they fling me
And deep in my heart a thousand scorpions sting me".
Reading all this, I felt *so damn good*!
Now you've had a taste of what we've suffered
In this country from generation to generation . . .

Daya Pawar, in *Kondwada* (cattle-pen),
translated by Graham Smith
(Pune: Magowa Prakashan, 1974)

Mother

Just as the day sank down and the dark's kingdom came
We would sit at the door with no light in the hut.
In house after house the lamp would be lit,
The fire would be started, bhakri kneaded,
From somewhere the smell of lentils, of wange,
Would hit our noses. In our stomachs all was darkness.
And a stream of tears would flow from my eyes.
The darkness was split, a dull shadow came toward us.
As she walked, the burden on her head shook, shifted.

Dark, dark slender body--this was my mother.
Drudged in the woods for sticks from morning on.
All we brothers, sitting, waiting, watching, for her.
And if she didn't sell the wood, all of us slept hungry.
One day something happened, how, we never understood.
Mother came, foot wrapped, blood flowing down.
A huge black snake had bitten her, two women said.
It showed its hood, struck, then slowly crawled away.
Mother was laid on the mat, the charmed cord tied, the mantras said,
    the village vaidya came.
Day went, and as it went, life went from her body.
Our wailing broke out, became thin in the air.
Mother had gone, leaving her children in the wind.

My eyes seek my mother. I still grieve.
I see a thin vendor of wood. I buy her sticks.

> Waman Nimbalkar, *Gaokusabaheril Kavita*
> (Poems from Outside the Village)
> translated by Vidyut Bhagwat and Eleanor Zelliot
> (Aurangabad: Asmitadarsh Prakashan, 1973).

Revolution

We used to be their friends
When, clay pots hung from our necks,[8]
Brooms tied to our rumps,
We made our rounds through the Upper Lane
Calling out "Johar Maybap".

We fought with crows,
Never even giving them the snot from our noses
As we dragged out the Upper Lane's dead cattle,
Skinned it neatly
And shared the meat among ourselves.
They used to love us then.
We warred with jackals-dogs-vultures-kites
Because we ate their share.

Today we see a root to top change
Crows-jackals-dogs-vultures-kites

Are our closest friends.
The Upper Lane doors are closed to us.

"Shout victory to the Revolution"
"Shout victory" [But]
"Burn, burn those who strike a blow at tradition".

Arjun Dangle, *Chavni Halte Ahe*
(The cantonment has begun to move),
translated by Jayant Karve and Eleanor Zelliot
(Bombay: Karmavir Prakashan, 1977)

I Don't Get Angry

I don't get angry; this is my sin.
Who can I blame, tell me, who can I blame?

The village is the same, the villagers are the same.
When my Bhim was alive, they used to tremble.
King Bhim went away, cowardice came.

Even though I met with cruel hard times
Bhim was with me, my head was held high.
But today, I have diminished the Bhim in me.

Here, there, they strip naked my mothers, my sisters.

I don't get angry, I don't get angry.
Today I see my own honour dishonoured.

My own daughter's virtue is looted in public,
my eyes look on, my body shakes,
cowardice grows from my helplessness.

My brother is burned alive in my hut.
What happened, what did not, doesn't go in the book.
Today I myself wipe out the marks my feet have made.

Every day the axe falls on my people.
My hunger, my dead will, are guests in my house.
I am cowed and that doubles the torment.

I was a lion's cub, now I'm a lamb's tail.
The people are wolves; who'll hunt the wolves?
My blood does not boil like King Bhim's did.

A new Peshwai has come, grinding me underfoot.
I don't get angry, I don't get angry.
With my own hands, I've burnt my everything to ash.

> Waman Kardak, *Watcal* (On the Road), translated by Jayant
> Karve and Eleanor Zelliot (Aurangabad: Prabodhan Prakashan,
> 1972). This song of a popular Dalit folk singer recalls the days
> of the active movement under the leadership of Dr. Bhimrao
> Ramji Ambedkar, lovingly called Bhim. Although Ambedkar
> died in 1956, his memory serves as an inspiration in a thousand
> ways.

Primal Bond

From what generation to what generation
is this journey?
And I'm like this:
when I contain all brightness and all darkness
why do I bear this dead skin,
these sighs?
From under what seer's beard
came this insomnia,
this hypnotic coma
embracing Time?
And this face of mine, found in an excavation,
is faithful to what connection?

. . . and this flock of white swans
flying up in the sky
this burning vineyard of skinless grapes
what place should be set afire?
In what kitchen was this body made --
a "pure" one?
and this flock of white swans . . .
All this as if fused together.

How much this romantic nonsense:
". . . I want to paint your picture
I want to sing you a poem
I want to fill my eyes with you
I want to marry you."
Go on walking around with sun flowers
and then quench their sun faces.
You are from that ageless tradition.
But how can I call you a poison girl?[9]
Why are you faithful to
that skeleton from an excavation?

Turn your dust smeared face this way
and salvage these lives.
A stone lying in the bazaar.[10]
I don't know why, girl
but I see in you an ancient skeleton
thousands of years old,
found in an excavation . . .
The primal bond of the universe
which blesses the phenomenon
of procreation
is forming in you.

Arun Kamble, in *Vidrohi kavita* (Poetry of Protest),
edited by Keshav Meshram,
translated by Jayant Karve and Eleanor Zelliot
(Pune: Continental Prakashan, 1978).

The Gods of Ochre

All that was yours was devastated
so the Gods of the Godhouse
who pitted fate on your forehead
were flung into the little stream.

Ten heads turned in ten directions
like the festival play of Bohad.
Why did the thirty-three crores of Gods
dancing arrogantly in the back alley
come to life again?

Lighting the torch in broad daylight,
brandishing weapons in eight hands,
panting with bloody tongues,
they beat the drums of tradition.
You say you want to flee
this ghost-ridden town!
Oh yes, but how can you run far enough?
You may go anywhere, but wherever you step
you will stumble over the ochre-colored gods.

> Daya Pawar, *Kondwada* (cattle-pen),
> translated by Jayant Karve and Eleanor Zelliot
> (Pune: Magowa Prakashan, 1974)

Empty Advice

This country which demands
A pot of blood
For a swallow of water
How can I call it mine
Though it gives the world
The (empty) advice of Peace.

> Pralhad Chandwankar, in *Audit*
> translated by Jayashree Gokhale-Turner
> (Bombay: Abhinav Prakashan, 1976)
> Parenthesis is in the original.

I Have Become the Tide

As the sand soaks up the water at the shore,
so my great sorrow.
How long will it be like the sand?
How long will it cry out because of it's obstinate wish to exist?

As a matter of fact, it should have been in tide like the sea.
Much would have been gained by beating up the drawfs around here.
Even the sea has a shore; why doesn't my grief have limits?
Why didn't those who squeezed oil from the sand[11]
have any inkling of sorrow?

The wind that blows every day
that day yelled in my ear
  "women stripped"
  "boycott in the village"
  "man killed"
As it spoke, it told me a mantra: "Make another Mahad"[12]
My hands now move toward the weapon on the wall.
I am now the sea; I soar, I surge
I move out to build your tombs.
The winds, storms, sky, earth
Now are all mine.
In very inch of the rising struggle
I strand erect.

                              J.V. Pawar, in *Virodhi kavita* (*op.cit.*),
                      translated by Jayant Karve and Eleanor Zelliot.

THREE POEMS BY NAMDEO DHASAL*

Amber/Sky Alchohols in the Glass

My everything amber/sky alcohols in the glass[13]
    let breath reel stagger
    "lover
    I swear I don't get love"[14]
Let snake-vines keep the beat move shake
    the raga of gutter-ganges
Let the donkey under your skin bray
Let flow the pain, the dark serpent, the charging boar
    let your balls sizzle
    an honest beast in your torch[15]
    now is yours
Sell cheap faith-in-Christ, family-plan your vulgarity
    kick this heavenly virtue, this fatherly atrocity
    this poor promising puking lamb
Crumpled-paper-Pandurang-dindi goes on singing[16]
    winding

---

*These three poems by Namdeo Dhasal are from *Golpitha* (Pune: Nilkanth Prakashan, 1975) and were first published in English in the *Journal of South Asian Literature*, XVII, 1, 1982. The translations are by Jayant Karve and Eleanor Zelliot, with the assistance of A.K. Ramanujan.

The sweet notes flute
Juhu beach fragranced
a quarter jingle jangles
daughters wed between their thighs
Uncle Uncle Little Star
    strumming
        the delicate guitar of impurity
Listen to the dainty ankle bells

Your future is yours alone
Police: pot belly: muck around: a thousand day's night
count every yard
everything's hard
//Bitter fate// O Allah cork the bottle
O Allah fit a loop
The sin of your Diwali
itches a lot
silly malang raise the palang[17]
the chillum is sticky the hands-feet are numb
fix a dose: play hide-and-seek
let's roll and rub like Mira[18]
chutney
ghutney
the share depends on the size of the brood
ungrateful bastard
bread-breaking auntie
in what situation did you drop your calf
Phebriks itch
your mate
abracadabraca
skeleton in petticoat
prayers to himself for his own realm that's allowed
the full glass vomits fragrance
grance
muck
in dreams
in liquor
in the glass
come come come come God

crush the frogs in the earthenware pot
blow out the lamp
of the umpteen generations
suck, drool over the pelvic bone
my essence droops drunken
    why pull it up
for every one in front of everyone the wine filled glass

Their Eternal Pity

Their eternal pity -- no taller than the pimp on Faulkland Road.
No pavilion put up in the sky for us.
Lords of wealth, they are, locking up light in those vaults of theirs.
In this life carried by a whore, not even sidewalks are ours,
Made so beggarly it is nausea to be human,
Cannot fill our shrivelled gut even with dirt.
Each new day just supports them as if bribed --
not a sigh slips through the fingers of day's plenty as
we are cut down.

Leaving the House

As you leave the house, the doors should be left as they are.
We have avatared
to cover your white white forehead with kum-kum.
Tell me I'm yours. Say I'm yours.
Why don't you say somethin'? Why don't you say somethin'?
Look, we've brought this brand new slate with us.
Give me an answer: answer me; give, I say.
Prostitutes multiply: question mark question mark question mark
Slums multiply: question mark question mark question mark
Hunger death multiply: question mark question mark question mark
Beggers multiply: question mark question mark question mark
Men without work: question mark question mark question mark
multiply
Why do questions multiply, multiply: questions:
Why wasteland: why more wasteland?
You are silent   you will be given only three minutes
You are silent

                     speak
                speak speak
           speak speak speak

O.K.
We're turning our backs on you right now.
Right now we're becoming assassins,
taking off even the doors as we leave,
running war-tanks over you.
Spit on you; I spit on you: Spit! Spit! Sky. Us. Sky. Us.

Ambedkar: 1980

1.
You died, but didn't cease to be.
Like us, you slept with your wife
You brought forth children, but didn't let them flap in the wind
While we grew up like this, like that, somehow, anyhow
But our children
will never dare deny your affection
Academician/technician/politician/scientist
philosopher
These men will define you any which way
But you lived like a man
There was no acting in it
No dramatics.
No imitation, no imitators.
Now this is old stuff,
that they wouldn't touch us when they gave us water
Now this is old stuff,
that they made us sit outside the school on the veranda
Now this is old
that they wouldn't let us see
the black and white feet of Vithoba[19]
Now they and we are all alike
This world's socialism
This world's *communism*
and all those things of theirs
We've put them to the test
and the implication is this
Our shadow can cover our feet.[20]

2.
I've cursed you too, but
you gave us the tongue
I've even sunk you in the water, but
you gave the water[21]
We've done things to you, even so,
anything can be done to you
But the question remains of my loyalty
my honesty
Who are you?
Who were you?
Whose are you?

3.
The times are wholly yours[22]
yet your people are unhappy.
A fakir can be Prime Minister here
but not a Mang or a Bhangi.[23]
In front of the chair, the Parliament's value is less
In front of the law, the prostitute's value is less
One thing I saw in all this
the wheel of seasons came to us equally
You like the wheel were equal to all

4.
It was a Friday
An arithmetic book a slate
and one piece of chalk
mother with eagerness brought from the bazaar
She was very tired that day
In the light of the brass lantern
she made me massage her hands and feet.
Then she said,
"Baba - until I fall asleep
take a look at this book
I never learned
but you do this
To start your education
make B for Babasaheb.
He was far more beautiful than Lord Ganesh.

So don't trace
Shri Ganesh.[24]
The lord of the people is never ugly
He is from among men
True/Holy/Beautiful
Babasaheb Ambedkar
is true, holy, beautiful
Otherwise this book has no meaning."

5.
While I write all this at night
it's three o'clock
Though I want to have a drink
I don't feel like drinking.
I only want to sleep peacefully
and tomorrow morning see no varnas.[25]

Words in English in the original Marathi version are italicized.

By Namdeo Dhasal,
translated by Asha Mundlay and Laurie Hovell,
with Jayant Karve and Eleanor Zelliot.
From *Tuhi iyatta kanchi*
(Bombay: Ambedkar Prabodhini, 1981)

Dr. Bhimrao Ramji Ambedkar (Babasaheb) 1891-1956

Dr. Ambedkar, or Babasaheb Ambedkar, is the key figure in the Untouchable movement in India. He dominated every aspect of social,
political and religious efforts for equality throughout most of his adult
life, and is seen today as inspiration for progress and growth. Among his
legacies are the Republican Party, a political party which speaks for the
dispossessed (or *dalit*); a network of schools and colleges under the
People Education Party; a Buddhism conversion movement which now
includes over four million Buddhists; and a literary movement which is
a new force in Marathi literature and growing now in the Kannada and
Gujarati language areas of India.

Babasaheb Ambedkar was born in Mhow, where his father was a
school-teacher in an Army normal school, following a long-time trend of
members of the Untouchable Mahar caste of joining the British army to
escape from their traditional lowly work in the villages. The family

moved to Bombay to allow Bhimrao, their fourteenth child, a good education, and he fulfilled his promise by graduating from Elphinstone College. The Gaekwad of Baroda, a reformist non-Brahman prince, sent him to Columbia University in New York, where he got a Ph.D., and Ambedkar, with the help of another reformer, Chhatrapati Shahu of Kolhapur, went on to London to pass the bar from Grey's Inn and get a D.Sc. from the London School of Economics. Returning to India to stay in 1923, Ambedkar began his life work of educating, agitating and organizing for equality.

The hallmarks of his career may be seen in a few of his many activities: *Mooknayak* (Voice of the Dumb), the first of many newspapers; the Mahad conference, the largest and most important of many conferences, marked by an effort to drink water in a Brahman locality and by burning the classical Hindu law book, the *Manusmriti*, which delineated the restrictions on Untouchables; the Nasik satyagraha in the early thirties to enter the temple; the declaration in 1935 that he "would not die a Hindu," which set in motion the movement that eventually resulted in conversion to Buddhism. Along the way he established hostels and schools which culminated in a huge independent system of colleges. He founded political parties which, if not always successful, thoroughly politicized the Untouchables throughout Maharashtra and in urban centers throughout India. He wrote continually, not only about the problems of Untouchables but also about Indian economics, the prerequisites for democracy, and the problem of the Pakistan movement. He taught at Government Law College, served as a member of the Bombay Legislative Council, testified to every Government commission investigating the matter of franchise and to the Round Table Conference in London and effectively demanded "compensatory discrimination", -- reserved places for Untouchables in every Government body to insure them their rights. In the euphoria of Independence he was chosen chairman of the Drafting Committee for the Indian Constitution and in that position and also as Law Minister in Independent India's first cabinet, had a large part in creating contemporary India's legal system. He resigned in 1951 over the slowness of the law in dealing with the problems of India's lower classes and its women.

Ambedkar's conversion took place in October 1956, two months before his death, and was followed by mass conversions to Buddhism in Maharashtra and in several cities in India. Since his death, the educational and religious movements he set in motion have continued strong. The governmental commitment to accommodate Untouchables (now ex-

Untouchables since the practice of untouchability was made illegal in the Constitution of India) has resulted in a strong and creative middle class, although no such opening to all castes has been required of private business. His political party has been divided by factionalism and is at a low ebb, but such organizations as the Dalit Panthers, born in 1972, in protest both against violence in the villages and political ineffectiveness, rise from time to time to express political and social grievances. The most recent movement to carry on Ambedkar's dreams is the literary movement, Dalit Sahitya, which exprsss both protest and the joy of creativity. Dalit literary conferences, the journal *Asmitadarsh*, and the newly created Dalit Rangabhumi (Theater of the Oppressed) have made an indelible impression on the Marathi literary establishment, indeed have created another channel for the movement to call for humanity, the rights of all men, and the worth of all human beings.

Every seventh human being is an Indian; every seventh Indian is an ex-Untouchable. India has done much for her minorities, probably as much as any country in the world with the possible exception of the U.S.A., but new violence and continued discrimination mark the present scene. Ambedkar's American experience seems to have marked him in giving him an unshakable faith in democracy, in encouraging a pragmatic, many-faceted approach. His movement has much in common with the American Black movement, and both Black literature and the militancy of the Black Panthers have influenced his followers. This first attempt to bring together involved Indians and involved Americans may result in further creative efforts to bring equality to all humans.

Notes

1. Siddhartha: a name of the Buddha.
2. A slum area of Bombay named Siddhartha Nagar, inhabited chiefly by Buddhists and low-caste Hindus.
3. Two of Buddha's disciples.
4. Politicians who collect money to protest slum clearance but do nothing.
5. A robber converted by the Buddha.
6. Eknath, a sixteenth century Brahman saint-poet in the Bhakti (devotional religion) tradition, ate with Mahars and cared for a Mahar thief out of his great compassion for all classes of men.
7. Brahma refers to the Upanishadic concept that ultimate reality, *brahman*,

as the same reality as a human soul, *atman*, and the two are known to be one when complete understanding is achieved.

8. In the Peshwai days of the eighteenth century, Untouchables wore pots around their necks to keep their spit from polluting the ground and brooms to obliterate their footprints. The Untouchable Mahar caste used a greeting, Johar Maybap (Hail Mother-and-Father) which differed from those used by high caste Hindus, and among his traditional duties was the hauling of cattle carcasses from the village. The ending of the poem is ironic: Shout victory to the revolution is a quotation from a well-known Brahman poet; but while the elite call for revolution, those who revolt are burned.

9. Poison girls refers to an ancient story that women were fed poison until they could kill anyone who slept with them while tolerating the poison themselves.

10. Stone in the bazaar refers to the classical story of Ahilya, turned to stone by a curse and awakening only to the touch of Rama's foot.
The translator's interpretation of this poem is that it is addressed to a Brahman girl who represents India's classical tradition.

11. The Brahman poet Waman Pandit wrote: If you try hard enough, you can squeeze oil from the sand.

12. Mahad: site of Ambedkar's first satyagraha in 1928, and later the site of the burning of the *Manusmriti*.

13. Dhasal uses the Sanskrit word "sky", *ambar*, and clearly seems to be making a play on the English word "amber". He makes a verb of the Marathi noun for "alcohol", *daru*, which is as ungrammatical in Marathi as it is in English.

14. These italicized lines are in Hindi, probably from a film song.

15. Literally, "let your eggs sizzle, *andi* (eggs) can also be vulgar word for testicles; since the entire poem is oriented to sex, we have translated it in sexual terms; "torch" here clearly means "penis".

16. *Pandurang-dindi*: a procession of pilgrims to the annual pilgrimage to Pandharpur, centre of the famous Bhakti sect.

17. *Malang*: a Muslim holy man; *palang*: a bed.

18. Mira: Mirabai, the Rajput princess and saint-poet whose songs to Krishna are popular throughout all of Northern India.

19. Vithoba is the God of the important Bhakti (devotional religion) sect of Maharashtra. Untouchables numbered among the pilgrims and even were saint-singers in the 700-year old tradition, but until Independence in 1947 were never allowed inside Vithoba's main temple at Pandharpur.

20. In the past, an Untouchable's shadow was held to be polluting. Therefore, at high noon, when the shadow was covered by the feet, an Untouchable could enter the village. Dhasal in his maverick political career has joined both the communists and socialists, as well as the Congress Party, and implies here that all these political groups still hold the now ex-Untouchable as defiling.

21. After the festivals of the gods Ganesh and Durga, the clay images are sunk in the water to symbolize the end of a cycle and a new beginning.

22. Dr. B.R. (Babasaheb) Ambedkar was Law Minister in Independent India's first Cabinet as well as chairman of the Drafting Committee of the Indian Constitution. India probably has more "protective discrimination" laws in terms of Reservations in educational institutions and in government jobs than any other country, and has outlawed the practice of Untouchability as well. Discrimination, however, continues.

23. A Mang is a Maharashtrian Untouchable caste, traditionally held to be socially and ritually inferior even to Dhasal's own Mahar caste. A Bhangi is a member of the very large scavenging caste of the North.

24. Children traditionally start learning the alphabet with the symbol for Shri as an auspicious practice. Shri Ganesh is the Lord of all beginning enterprises. Also known as Ganpati, he is the elephant-headed god.

25. *Varna* is the traditional fourfold caste system, consisting of Brahmans, Kshatriyas, Vaishyas, all twice-born and allowed to read the Vedas, and the rest of mankind, Shudras. Individual Indian castes probably number in the tens of thousands, and are generally placed in one or another of the varnas. Reformers such as Mohandas Gandhi rejected the idea of an Untouchable class and repudiated the individual castes (jatis) but held to the broad varna system of social organization.

Further Reading

Eleanor Zelliot, "Dalit Sahitya -- The Historical Background" in *Vagartha*, 12, 1976 (New Delhi).

——— "Dalit -- New Cultural Context of an Old Marathi Word" in *Contributions to Asian Studies*, XI, 1978 (Leiden).

——— and Gail Omvedt, "Introduction to Dalit Poems" in *Bulletin of Concerned Aisan Scholars*, X:3, 1978.

——— and Philip Engblom eds., "A Marathi Sampler", *Journal of South Asian Literature*, XVII:1, 1982.

——— "The Revival of Buddhism in India" in *Asia*, No. 10, Winter, 1968.

The Folklore of Pride: Three Components of Contemporary Dalit Belief*

The Hindus wanted the Vedas and they sent for Vyasa who was not a caste Hindu.

The Hindus wanted an Epic and they sent for Valmiki who was an Untouchable.

The Hindus wanted a Constitution, and they sent for me.

Dr. B.R. Ambedkar (*Marathi*, 1978, p. 25)

Do Dalits have a culture of their own, a counter culture or a parallel culture to the "Great Tradition"? Is their culture a "Little Tradition" waiting to be absorbed into the Sanskritic tradition of India, a concept defined by Redford (1956) and applied to India by Singer (1958)? Or is their culture a pale reflection of high caste culture (Moffatt 1979)? Dr. Ambedkar's startling claim, quoted above, could be read several ways, but it seems to suggest most boldly a claim to a tradition, a culture, which is in itself both Great *and* a creative, contributing, essential factor in the all-Indian culture. This is perhaps a fourth way of looking at the culture of the Dalits, a word I use because ex-Untouchables and other low castes involved in a contemporary cultural movement identify themselves as *dalit*--ground-down, downtrodden, oppressed, not as Untouchables, Scheduled Castes, or Harijans.

An early challenge to the Little-Great Tradition theory came in Robert J. Miller's "Button Button..." article (Miller, 1966), a provocative essay based on the folklore of the Mahars, the caste at the heart of the Dalit movement. Other work supporting this idea of a different set of cultural attitudes among low status groups is to be found in Juergensmeyer (1980) and most recently has appeared in the Ph.D. thesis of

---

*To appear in Gunther D. Sontheimer ed., *Folk Culture, Folk Religion and Oral Traditions as a Component in Maharashtrian Culture* (Proceedings of the Third Maharashtrian Conference, held in Heidelberg in 1986).

Vincentnathan (1988). The case for a widespread counter culture has been carried farthest in David Lorenzen's "Traditions of Non-Caste Hinduism: The Kabir Panth" (Lorenzen, 1987). He also summarizes the opposing view "from the top down" found in the influential work of Dumont (1972). Another dimension of Untouchable cultural creativity is encountered in the new research on the songs and epics of the Untouchables themselves, a genre well represented by the "crying songs" of an Untouchable caste described for the first time in a recent article by Egnor (1986).

In this essay, rather than entering directly into this debate, I want to examine the folklore of the Dalits through the current "folklore of pride", some of the beliefs of the Dalits in Maharashtra. It is now virtually impossible to recreate the older folk culture of the Mahars. Bhimrao Ramji Ambedkar (1891-1956) not only served as chairman of the Drafting Committee of the Constitution of independent India, as he notes in the quotation above, he also changed the lives of many Untouchables in India in the realms of religion, education, politics and cultural life. The movement he led from 1920 until his death brought about increased education, political representation, a widespread conversion to Buddhism and a literary flowering (Zelliot, 1977). It also created a new Dalit folklore which has in many ways replaced or adapted the traditional folklore of the Untouchables who were influenced by his movement. Since I am dealing with the folklore of a self-conscious group, the Dalits, rather than a traditional caste, I will simply state that Dalits feel they do have and have had a culture of their own, in no way inferior to anyone else's tradition.

The folk beliefs of today's Dalit centre around three ideas:

(a) the idea that they are and were creators of culture, an idea expressed graphically in the Ambedkar quotation which begins this article.

(b) the idea that they were "Lords of the Earth", the original inhabitants of their areas shunted aside by the Aryan invaders; corollary with this is a disbelief in hereditary pollution and purity, a disbelief in karmic rebirth.

(c) the idea that they were and are a militant people, with heroes who used their strength in a self-sacrificial way for their people.

While my chief references for these beliefs are current in the area of Maharashtra, similar ideas may be found in the folklore of other ex-Untouchable groups in other areas of India, and I will explore those when relevant. Not much is left of the traditional system of beliefs among the Mahars, but those past beliefs will be referred to as they can be reconstructed from older people's memories and such sources as the Gazetteers and the Tribes and Castes volumes of Bombay and the Central Provinces which deal at length with Mahars.

Dalits as Creators of Culture

The Dalits of Maharashtra have in the past twenty years created a school of literature, Dalit Sahitya (Zelliot, 1976; 1978a; 1978b; *A Marathi Sampler*, 1982, pp. 93-101; Dharwadker, 1989), which has changed the face of Marathi literature and inspired similar literary creativity in Gujarat and Karnataka. Among their many themes is an occasional reference to the epics, often identifying the creators as low caste, even Dalit, as does Ambedkar in the quotation above. Along with this belief is a sense that Mahars have *always* been contributors to culture. Daya Pawar, an important contemporary Dalit writer, in particular holds this opinion, and quotes a Marathi proverb to show acceptance of the idea of Mahar gifts (Pawar, 1974, p. 2):

In the Brahman house--writing
In the Kunbi house--grain
In the Mahar house--singing

Pawar mourns the loss of the "great cultural treasure" the Mahars could have had if the kind of music his father and those who visited his home made had not been considered "debased" by other castes.

It is clear that Mahars did have a place in the cultural life of traditional Maharashtra. Even though it is the Untouchable Mang caste which most often is described as "village musicians" in the *Gazetteers*, Mahars seem to have been the chief musicians and actors in *tamasha*, the folk drama of Maharashtra. We do not know if Mahars had a part in creating *tamasha*, which was a recognized form by the sixteenth century and at its height under the Peshwas in the eighteenth century, but we know they dominated the field. The revival of *tamasha* in the late nineteenth century is credited to a Brahman, Patthe Bapu Rao, together with his "beautiful Mahar consort" Pawala (Abrams, 1974). *Tamasha*, however, was considered vulgar by the twentieth century Mahar reformers, and the low status of *tamasha* women countered an image of progress, so that village drama was frowned upon by Dr. Ambedkar. Nevertheless, Dadu Indurikar, also known as Indu Mahar, was until very recently a sterling example of *tamasha* art (Pranjpye, 1971). And some of the skills of *tamasha*, although not its earthy, even vulgar humor were continued in *jalsa* groups which traveled the countryside singing the message of Ambedkar's movement in the 1930s.

There are other suggestions that Mahars may have had special musical gifts. The *Thana Gazetteer* notes that Mahars refused to play music for the Muslim Muharram procession since the Muslim refused to let the image of Vithoba be carried through the streets at the same time (1882, p. 524), which implies a public music tradition. Converted Christian Mahars had special music duties during the feast of Mount Mary in Bandra and played the reed pipes and drum at weddings (Fernandes, 1927, 53). The *Khandesh Gazetteer* reported that the Mahars are "fond of music, playing a one-stringed instrument *tuntune*, a lute *vina*, a tambourine *daf*, and a small drum *dhol*", 1880, p.119). However, Mahars had no such overweening musical duty as the *pariah* of Madras, whose very name means drum.

Other Untouchable groups have claims to cultural achievement. Many of the Bhangi caste of the North call themselves "Valmiki", tracing their lineage to the author of the *Ramayana*, supposedly an outcaste and a criminal before his conversion by the inadvertent repetition of the name of Rama. There seems to have been no building of literary tradition based on this claim, but an effort of the much-scorned Bhangi sweepers to elicit pride for self-improvement (Kolenda, 1960). (The recognition of Vyasa, son of a Brahman sage and a fishergirl, supposed author of the Vedas and of the *Mahabharata*, as a fellow Dalit is found, however, only among the contemporary Dalit intellectuals and does not seem to be traditional). A poem by Daya Pawar illustrates the way in which a modern poet thinks of Valmiki as a betrayer of his low-caste identity. (Pawar, 1976, pp. 34-5). His reference to Shambuk relates to the story of Rama's punishing the Shudra Shambuk for hearing the Vedas:

Oh Great Poet

Oh Valmiki
Should you sing the praises of Ramarajya
Because you're the great poet of poets?
Seeing the heron's wounded wing

Your compassionate heart broke out in lament.
You were born outside the village
In a shunned neighborhood . . .
      where misery itself was born
Never festooned with fruit or flower . . .
The dejected faces . . . furrowed with care
Is it true you never heard
Their lament as they cried for liberation?
One Shambuk of your own blood
Caught fire, rose in anger.
On great poet,
Singing the praises of Ramarajya,
Even there the icy cliff of inhumanity towered up.
Oh great poet,
How then should we call you a great poet?

"Dalit culture" has now become something of a fashionable article
of faith. The Dalit Voice, an English weekly from Bangalore, claims from
time to time that Devadasi culture, which includes the classical dance
from Bharata Natyam, is a Dalit form of creativity. The June 1986 issue
of Religion and Society, a scholarly journal published from Bangalore by
the Christian Institute for the Study of Society and Religion, is entirely
devoted to Dalit culture, Hindu as well as Christian. Even more striking,
however, are the ways in which today's Dalits encourage cultural creativity. The poem by Daya Pawar on Valmiki both indicates a belief in the
Dalit creative past and is itself an act of creation. Since the early 1970s,
short stories, a few novels, much poetry and most recently autobiography
have flowed from Dalit pens in great quantity.
    Dalit theater followed close on the heels of Dalit poetry and short
stories, and Dalit Rangabhumi, the first Dalit theater, which was based in
Pune, has been followed by dozens of others, both in Maharashtra and
outside the state. The Delhi-based Ahwan Theatre, a Cinema and Mass
Media group has "definite plans to provide extensive exposure to the rich
cultural heritage and traditional Dalit and folk arts of the country".
(Ahwan brochure, 1987). The first two plays of Ahwan Theatre were a
Hindi play entitled Devadasi and a Hindi translation of Langston
Hughes' Mulatto. The Ahwan group has also attempted to help the Bhats,
puppeteers originally from Rajasthan who are counted among the Sched-
uled Castes. The Bhat puppeteers traveled to Wahsington D.C. during the
Festival of India celebrations, but are now back in their Delhi slum,

trunks filled with magnificent puppets, but with no change in their economic or social status.

Several Dalit drama conferences have been held, and it is said that there are now more than forty Dalit theatre groups. Many write their own plays, a few adapt plays from the American Black theatre, some revive the arts of *tamasha*. B.S. Shinde of Pune, founding father of Dalit Rangabhumi, has written plays based on Buddhist themes and a drama built around the legendary Mahar hero, Amrutnak.

There seems to be no end to new Dalit cultural creativity. Dalit women in Bombay organized the Dalit Stri Samwadini (Dalit Women's Dialogue) in 1986, probably the first women's literary conference in Maharashtra. A Dalit art exhibition was held in Nagpur in connection with the Asmitadarsh literary conference in 1979, and an all-India art conference was called in Hyderabad in 1987. Some Dalits believe that the sculptors of the classic period of Indian art were an Untouchable caste.

The Lords of the Earth/The Sons of the Soil

One of the most common beliefs among Untouchables all over India is that they were the original inhabitants of the land. The Ad-Dharm movement of the North rose and fell in the 1920s and 1930s as it attempted to list Untouchables as those of the "original religion", separate (and pure), in the Punjab and United Provinces Censuses (Juergensmeyer, 1982); and in the Adi-Dravida movement of Tamilnadu (Pandian, 1899: Barnett, 1976; Kamalanatha, 1985), the claim to "original Dravidian" status is still somewhat important as the designation of some groups of Untouchables in the South.

In Maharashtra, the idea that the Mahar was the original settler is one of the most persistent images among Mahars, Dalits *and* Buddhists. The Mahar was called *dharnice put* or *bhumiputra*, Marathi and Sanskritized Marathi terms for "sons of the soil". Many educated Mahars know that scholars such as John Wilson (1857, p. xxiii) and R.E. Enthoven (1922, p. 401) believed that the very word Maharashtra was derived from "the country of the Mahars", although most Indian scholars denied the claim vehemently. Irawati Karve stressed the identification of the Mahar with all areas of Maharashtra, reporting that on the eastern edge of Vidarbha where Hindi speakers are mixed with Marathi, a Mahar told her proudly, "Wherever you find Mahars, there is Maharashtra" (Karve, 1959). A rather unflattering folk saying implying that nothing is perfect,

"Wherever there is a village, there is a *maharwada*," is also a recognition that Mahars were probably the only caste to be found in every village in the entire Marathi-speaking area. Some of the traditional duties of the Mahars also lend credence to this belief, especially their position as "authorities in all boundary matters"(Enthoven, 1922, p. 416). What is most interesting about the Mahar case is that Dr. B.R. Ambedkar, the still all-important Mahar leader, opposed any idea that Untouchables were a separate race from other Indians. In his earliest testimony to a governmental commission, Southborough Committee gathering evidence in 1918 for the Montagu-Chelmsford Reforms, he argued in a most sophisticated manner that Untouchables deserved a low franchise and a large communal representation in the popular assemblies because there was no "like-mindedness", no "endosmosis" between Touchables and Untouchables (The Reforms Committee (Franchise) 1919, pp. 729-39). Other Untouchable petitioners argued for separate electorates, pre-Aryan status, recognition as non-Hindu. But Ambedkar's words are somewhat ambiguous; they recall his student days at Columbia University where he wrote for a sociology seminar that caste divisions were "an unconscious growth in the life of a human society under peculiar circumstances", not a command of a Supreme Authority (Ambedkar, 1917). The implication seems to be that separation caused by human society could be replaced by unity and fellow feeling if that human society so chose. Ambedkar's hesitancy to use any "original people" or "pre-Aryan" formula was not shared by his followers; the idea of the "Lords of the Land" persisted. In the end the ambiguity of ideas about Mahar origins was resolved by the conversion to Buddhism.

Maharashtrian Dalits (and some caste Hindus) accept wholeheartedly Ambedkar's final solution to the problem of origins and the relationship of Untouchables to the Hindu religion. Untouchables had been Buddhists, he claimed, loyal to their religion and pushed to the outskirts of the village when Brahmanism won out over Buddhism well over a millennium ago (Ambedkar, 1948). The Mahars had been proud Buddhist Nagas, Ambedkar said, at the 1956 conversion ceremony to Buddhism in Nagpur, a city chosen for the event as not only an active center of the Mahar movement but as the "city of the Nag people" (Ambedkar, 1969). The status of Buddhism past and present links the ex-Mahar to a rich heritage, one which encompasses art and egalitarianism, rationality and humanism, and is also part and parcel of an all-India heritage. The Buddhist identity encompasses the "Lords of the Earth claim", the idea of past creativity, and the disbelief in pollution or *karma* as the cause of Untouchability.

Just as Ambedkar's final message to his people, the 1956 Buddhist conversion speech, stated a belief in an origin that was both a proud claim to a past and a denial of the whole theory of pollution, so the earliest Mahar document of the modern period propounded a belief in origins which inherently denied hereditary untouchability. The petition for re-admission into the army prepared by Gopal Baba Walangkar in 1894, now in manuscript form in the Khairmode Collection of the Bombay University Library, is from the "Non-Aryan" group for the removal of wrongs, but claims Kshatriya status in the body of the document. This ambiguity is resolved by a sweeping and scornful history of everyone's origins: high-caste people from the South were "Australian-semitic non-Aryans" and African Negroes; Chitpavan Brahmans were "Barbary Jews"; The high caste Marathas' forebears were "Turks" (Walangkar, 1894). In other words, almost everybody was "non-Aryan"; most Indians were something else at one time! Clearly belief in a hereditary hierarchy based on pollution is denied in this account.

The need to be recognized as a separate (and separated) yet not inherently inferior people has been met in many ways by various Untouchable and low-caste groups. An idea first promulgated by Mahatma Phule in the nineteenth century Maharashtra (O'Hanlon, 1986, p. 136) was that the low caste possessed a king, Bali, who represented pre-Aryan religion and culture brought low by the Aryan invasion. The Bali theme seems to have been dropped very early on by Phule's own Shudra groups, Malis and Marathas. Ambedkar never referred to such a myth at all. However, Bali is still a current theme in the recreation of some Dalits' cultural past. A recent article tells how "the Great Dalit Emperor" Bali, out of a misplaced faithfulness to his oath, lost the land of Untouchables to the wily Aryan dwarf, Waman (Rai, 1989, pp. 15-16, 18).

A natural part of the "Lords of the Earth" theme, but also independent of it, is a total rejection of the idea of hereditary pollution. The myths of origin of Untouchable castes almost always refer to a sort of cosmic (or comic) accident or some mistaken act of goodwill, not a polluting occupation or a sinful past life. One such myth from the past will serve to illustrate the hundreds that have been recorded (Roberston, 1939, p. 74):

Mahars are descended from one of the four sons of the cow, The mother asked her sons how they proposed to honor her after her death. Three of them said that they would give her divine honors. The fourth answered her that as she had borne him in her body, so would he carry her in his. The other sons were astounded at his impiety, and they exclaimed *maha ahar,* that is, great appetite. The name, Mahar, thus clung to him and his descendants; for he and they have kept the vow until this day in their eating of beef.

Although the origin myths differ, the attitude that pollution is not a hereditary factor has been found among Untouchables by almost all those who have studied an Untouchable community closely, beginning with Kolenda's pioneering work on Untouchable sweepers in a North Indian village (1964). One of the recent and most thorough is Vincentnathan's study of a group that calls itself Harijan in the South (1988). The rejection of the idea of pollution may be much older than the modern period. A classic statement was made in the fourteenth century by the Mahar saint-poet Chokhamela who asked:

> In the beginning, at the end,
> There is nothing but pollution.
> No one knows anyone who is born pure.
> Cokha says, in wonder, who is pure?
>
> *(Abhanga* 11)

In this *abhanga,* Cokhamela speaks the mind of the modern Dalit, seeming to suggest a coherent tradition of belief, or disbelief, over six centuries.

A Militant People

Buddhists though they may be, contemporary ex-Mahars are very proud of their military record. Mahars had guard duties in the days of Shivaji's seventeenth century kingdom. They were in the Birtish army and marines almost from the initial days of any British military force. The cancellation of Mahar recruitment in the late nineteenth century as the British leaned more and more on "martial" races brought the first Mahar protest, Gopal Baba Walangkar's petition for reinstatement. The return of the Mahars to the army came in an impressive way during World War II when the Mahar Machine Gun Regiment was formed in 1942 at Kampti near Nagpur, and three battalions later in the year at Belgaum, Kampti and Nowshera (Thorat, 1954). The creation of these units in the name of the Mahar caste was Ambedkar's contribution, possible since he served on the National Defence Council and then as Labour Member of the Viceroy's Council. It seems to me clear that army recruitment was not the only reason for the creation of the Mahar Regiment. Surely the building of pride in the past, and hence the present, was part of the motive. The Regiment still exists, still bears the name Mahar, although other castes and religions serve and have been part of the unit from the beginning.

The cap of the Mahar Regiment when it was founded bore the word "Koregaon" and a symbol of a pillar. The final battle of the British with the Marathas was fought at Koregaon, a village near the Maratha capital of Pune, in 1818. In commemoration of that historic event, a pillar was erected, and the names of those who died in the battle engraved upon it. Many of those names end in *nak*, the designation of a Mahar. There is no agreement on the meaning of the suffix *nak*. Some derive it from *naik* (leader). Others believe it is a derivation of *nag* (the Naga people). Either definition is satisfactory to the Mahars; either supports an origin of distinction and militancy.

Since Independence the Government has dropped identifications with the British army such as Koregaon pillar insignia. However, the mythic quality of the Mahar military past is seen in the fact that the Dalit Panthers, a militant group formed in the early 1970s to fight injustice and protest against atrocities, meets every year at the Koregaon pillar. Dalit Panthers from Pune ride on bicycles to Koregaon village and gather at the pillar to pay their respects to past heroes and to gain inspiration from the Mahar military past.

In his article on the Mahar tradition, Robert Miller (1966) uses the legend of the Mahar hero Amrutnak as an example of a tradition which is one of the many unrelated to the Brahmanical system, as a denial of the idea of *one* Great Tradition. The story of Amrutnak is one of heroism and self-sacrifice. The handsome warrior volunteered to rescue the queen of Bedar, lost during an attack on a hunting expedition. Before going on his long journey, all the way to Kabul on his wondrous Ablakha horse, Amrutnak gave a small box into the hands of the sultan for safekeeping. After many adventures, he brought back the Begum, but was met with gratitude tinged with hostility because of the days and nights he had spent alone with the Queen. "Amrut laughed and reminded the king about the small box", which contained proof of the Queen's chastity and Amrutnak's ultimate sacrifice. In return for his self-castration and his bravery, Amrutnak requested fifty-two rights for his people, the Mahars. The poem celebrates not only Amrutnak but his people: "Great Great are the Mahars . . . Mahars are known for their bravery during wars, protecting their empire, keeping their sword always active" (Khairmode, 1961).

The Amrutnak story was published in 1929 by an educated Mahar, C.B. Khairmode, and reprinted in 1961 after the Buddhist conversion by

S.T. Savant, who was a Buddhist convert. There is no reference to it in any *Gazetteer*, nor does it seem to have been sung by any group preserving Mahar epic literature. Whatever its provenance, the Amrutnak story enlarges on themes of militancy and self-sacrifice which is documented in the Mahar tradition. Robertson tells a similar story of an unnamed watchman who castrated himself lest a Moslem king doubt his Queen's chastity, adding that the Mahar received not only fifty-two rights but the name *mahavira*, great hero, which in time became "Mahar" (Robertson, 1938, pp. 72-3).

The idea that the fifty-two rights of the Mahar, a traditional number involving such perquisites as the clothes of the corpse and grain at certain times, were won by a Mahar for his people is present in a number of myths. The *Akola Gazetteer* tells of Dego Mego, who had the power of commanding rain, and so he secured "definite and enforced payments" of rights of Mahars when he brought a grievous famine to an end (*Gazetteer*, 1910, p. 119). *The Tribes and the Castes of the Central Provinces* tells the story of Mayo beheaded while singing the praises of Vishnu so that a tank of water stopped leaking, and so winning the reward that his people should not be compelled to live at a distance from the towns nor to wear a distinctive dress (Russell, 1916, p. 144).

Along with the Dego Mego story in the Vidarbha area is a common myth of five brothers, or a reference directly to the Pandavas, an association repeated in the apparatus and speech of the *potraj*, the servant of the epidemic goddess, Mariai, who was almost always a Mahar and who seems to have been a village phenomenon all over the Marathi-speaking area. This Pandava connection, however, was not appropriated for use in the modern period, and no reference appears in the work of those who strove for greater unity and militancy. The Mahar seems to have had a variety of myths from which to chose, but in the contemporary period preferred to base his idea of a militant past either on the historic record or a quasi-historic figure, rather than on legendary ancestors or an origin myth of great antiquity. [Professor Dattatreya Punde has shown me a handwritten manuscript of the "Pandhava Pratap", the deeds of the Pandhavas, copied out with care and style by a Mahar in the nineteenth century.]

What seems to be missing in Maharashtra is the quantity of poems, ballads, even epics in other language areas which are associated in some way with Untouchables. Blackburn has recorded astonishing tales of Untouchables as heroes, Brahmans becoming Untouchables (Blackburn, 1978). Welbon has recorded the touching Chandala's song of devotion

(1982). Rogair found a group of Untouchables in Andhra who had preserved the oral tradition of a major epic (1982). There is an ever increasing record of tales, most of them from the South, in which Untouchables figure prominently. We are left with questions: Are there unexplored areas in which traditions are shared? In which caste epics interpenetrate each other? In which both Untouchables and caste Hindus act in heroic ways? The folk literature of Maharashtra area has barely been scratched; no one has yet suggested the creative connections of Untouchables with other castes as Shulman has in the Tamil tradition (Shulman, 1984, 1985).

However partial this view of Dalit folklore in contemporary Maha - rashtra, it can at least be said that the folk ways of the past persist into the present. The current folklore of the Dalits, self-conscious and changed though it is, seems clearly related to much of the past, and seems to relate to timeless need. In the person of Dr. B.R. Ambedkar, whose words began this essay, the Dalits today have a hero of extraordinary propor- tions, one who is seen as militant, as self-sacrificing, as creative and as the revealer of the truth of Dalit origins in the proud Indian past.

References

Tevia Abrams, "Tamasha: People's Theatre of Maharashtra State, India", Ph.D. dissertation submitted to Michigan State Univer- sity, 1974.

Bhimrao Ramji Ambedkar, "Castes in India -- Their Mechanism, Genesis and Development", *Indian Antiquary*, IX. VI, 1917, pp. 81-95.

———— *The Untouchables* (New Delhi: Amrit Book Company, 1948).

———— "The Great Conversion", in Bhagwan Das ed., *Thus Spoke Ambedkar*, Vol II (Jullundar City: Bheem Patrika Publications, 1969).

Marguerite Ross Barnett, *The Politics of Cultural Nationalism in South Asia* (Princeton: Princeton University Press, 1976).

Stuart H. Blackburn, "The Folk Hero and Class Interests in Tamil Heroic Ballads", *Asian Folklore Studies*, 37, 1978, pp. 131-49.

Sir Patrick Cadell, *History of the Bombay Army* (London: Longmans, Green and Co, 1938).

Chokhamela, *Chokhamela abhang gatha* (Bombay: Balkrishna Laksh- man Pathak, 1950) (in Marathi).

THE FOLKLORE OF PRIDE 329

Vinay Dharwadker, "The Future of the Past: Tradition, Modernization, and the Transforming of Two Indian Traditions", Ph.D. dissertation submitted to University of Chicago, 1989, Ch. II.

Louis Dumont, *Homo Hierarchicus* (Chicago: University of Chicago Press, 1970).

Margaret T. Egnor, "Internal Iconicity in Paraiyar 'Crying Songs'", in Stuart H. Blackburn and A.K. Ramanujan eds., *Another Harmony: New Essays on the Folklore of India* (Berkeley: University of California Press, 1986).

R.E. Enthoven, *The Tribes and Castes of Bombay*, Vol. II (Bombay: Government of Bombay, 1922, Mahar, pp. 401-18).

Braz A. Fernandes, *Bandra: Its Religious and Secular History* (Bombay: author, 1927).

Gazetteer of the Bombay Presidency, Vol. XII: *Khandesh*. Edited by James M. Campbell, General Editor (Bombay: Government Central Press, 1880).

———— Vol. XIII: *Thana*. Edited by James M. Campbell, General Editor (Bombay: Government Central Press, 1882).

Gazetteer of the Central Provinces and Berar, Vol. A: *Akola District*, Edited by C. Brown and A.E. Nelson. (Calcutta 1910).

Mark Juergensmeyer, *Religion as Social Vision: The Movement against Untouchability in 20th Century Punjab* (Berkeley: University of California Press, 1982).

T.P. Kamalanathan, *Mr. K. Veeramani is Refuted and the Historical Facts about Scheduled Castes Struggle for Emancipation* (Tiruppattur: Ambedkar's Self-Respect Movement, 1985).

C.B. Khairmode, *Amrutnak* (Pradna Publishing Company, 1961, first published in 1929) (In Marathi).

Pauline Kolenda, "Changing Religious Practices of an Untouchable Caste" in *Economic Development and Cultural Change*, VIII, 3, 1960, pp. 279-87.

———— "Religious Anxiety and Hindu Fate", *Journal of Asian Studies*, XXIII, 1964, pp. 71-81.

David N. Lorenzen, "Traditions of Non-caste Hinduism: The Kabir Panth", *Contributions to Indian Sociology* (N.S.), 21.2, 1987, pp. 263-82.

A Marathi Sampler, *The Journal of South Asian Literature*, XVII, 1982, pp. 48-63, 93-101.

M.O. Mathai, *Reminiscences of the Nehru Age* (New Delhi: Vikas, 1978).

Joan P. Mencher, "The Caste System Upside Down, or the Not-so-Mysterious East", *Current Anthropology*, 15, 4, 1974, pp. 469-93.

Michael Moffat, "Harijan Religion: Consensus at the Bottom of Caste", *American Ethnologist*, 6, 1979, pp. 244-60.

Robert J. Miller, "Button, Button . . . Great Tradition, Little Tradition, Whose Tradition?" *Anthropological Quarterly*, 39, 1, 1966, pp. 26-42.

Rosalind O'Hanlon, *Caste, Conflict and Ideology: Mahatma Jotirao Phule and Low Caste Protest in Nineteenth-century Western India* (Cambridge: Cambridge University Press, 1985).

T.B. Pandian, *Slaves of the Soil in Southern India and Pandian and the Pariah* (Amsterdam, 1899).

Sai Pranjpye, "Dadu Indurikar", *Times Weekly*, 24 October 1971, p. 7.

Daya Pawar, *Kondwada* (Pune: Magova Prakashan, 1974, Introduction (In Marathi).

—— "Four Poems", translated by Graham Smith. *Vagratha*, 12, pp. 34-5.

Sq. Ldr. P. Shivaprasad Rai, "Bali Chakravarti, The Great Dalit Emperor, Killed by the Wily Vaman", *Dalit Voice*, January 6-21, 1989, pp. 15-16, 18.

Robert Redford, 1956, *Peasant Society and Culture: an Anthropological Approach to Civilization* (Chicago: University of Chicago Press).

The Reforms Committee (Franchise), *Evidence taken before the Reforms Committee*, 2 Vols (Lord Southborough, Chairman) (Calcutta, 1919).

Religion and Society, "Culture, Counter-culture and Dalits", XXXIII, 1986, p. 2 [See especially A.M. Abraham Ayrookuzhiel's article "Religion and Culture in Dalits' Struggle for Liberation"].

Alexander Robertson, *The Mahar Folk* (Calcutta: Y.M.C.A. Publishing House and Oxford University Press, 1928).

Gene H. Rogair, *The Epic of Palnadu: A Study and Translation of Palnati Virula Katha* (New York: Oxford University Press, 1982).

R.V. Russell, *The Tribes and Castes of the Central Provinces of India*, Assisted by Hira Lal, Vol. IV (London: Macmillan, 1916).

David Shulman, "The Enemy Within: Idealism and Dissent in South Indian Hinduism", in S.N. Eisenstadt et al. ed. (Berlin, New York and Amsterdam: Mouton, 1984).

The King and the Clown in South Indian Myth and Poetry (Princeton: Princeton University Press, 1985).

Milton B. Singer ed., *Traditional India: Structure and Change* (Philadelphia: American Folklore Society, IX, 1959, p. XXII, Preface).

Major General S.P.P. Thorat, *The Regimental History of the Mahar MG Regiment* (Dehradun: The Army Press, 1954).

Lynn Vincentnathan, "Harijan Subculture and Self-esteem Management in a South Indian Community", Ph.D. dissertation submitted to University of Wisconsin-Madson, 1988 (summary given in "Harijan Concept of Person and Ideology: Cultural Strategies for Self-esteem", paper presented at the 17th Annual Conference on South Asia, Madison, November, 1988).

Guy R. Welbon, "The Candala's Song", in Guy R. Welbon and Glen E. Yocum eds., *Religious Festivals in South India and Sri Lanka* (New Delhi: Manohar, 1982, pp. 77-100).

Eleanor Zelliot , "Dalit Sahitya -- The Historical Background", *Vagaratha*, 12, 1976.

――― "The Leadership of Babasaheb Ambedkar", in B.N. Pandey ed., *Leadership in South Asia* (New Delhi: Vikas, 1977).

――― (a) "Dalit -- New Cultural Context of an Old Marathi Word", *Contributions to Asian Studies*, XI, 1978, pp. 77-90.

――― with Gail Omvedt, (b) "Introduction to Dalit Poems", *Bulletin of Concerned Asian Scholars*, X, 3, 1978, pp. 2-10.

――― "Chokhamela and Eknath: Two Bhakti Modes of Legitimacy for Modern Change", *Journal of Asian and African Studies*, XV, 1-2, 1980, pp. 136-56.

Addendum

One more example of pride in the military past of the Mahars: A portion of Ardythe Basham's Ph.D thesis from the University of British Columbia has been edited by Bhagwan Das and published as a pamphlet, *Untouchable Soldiers: The Mahars and the Mazhbis* (Bangalore: Ambedkar Sahitya Prakashan, 1980).

Addendum to Part IV

There have been very interesting developments in Dalit Literature in the past few years. The movement has spread south to Karnataka and north to Gujarat and there is now serious and important Dalit fiction and poetry in Kannada and Gujarati. In Maharashtra, the very areas in which I reported little progress have become among the most active. Beginning with Daya Pawar's autobiography *Baluta*, there has been a steady stream of pioneering autobiographies from Mahars, Buddhists, Chambhars, "De-notified tribes", and other Dalits. Several of these are prize-winning volumes; all add new dimensions of life to Marathi literature. In the past three years, two barely educated women, Bebi Kamble and Shantabai Kamble, have published their life stories. Women's poetry is also becoming important, and there are now, at least, six or seven published women Dalit poets. A Dalit Women's Literary Conference, probably the first women's literary organization in Maharashtra, was organized in 1986.

Theatre called Dalt Rangabhumi, has also spread from its inception in Pune to a number of cities in the state and to Delhi. Social themes, Buddhist legends and historical incidents such as the reaction to Untouchable conversion to Islam at Meenakshipuram in Madras are subjects which have been staged.

What is still missing is criticism and translations into English. I did a brief historical background to Dalit Sahitya in *Vagartha*, 12, 1976, an issue which also contained the Baburao Bagul's story and Waman Nimbalkar's poems. The Marathi Sampler Issue of the *Journal of South Asian Literature*, XVII, 1, (Winter/Spring 1982), which I edited with Phillip Engblom, contains Baburao Bagul's "Looter Looted" and Shankarrao Kharat's "Potraj", a critical essay on Namdeo Dhasal by Dilip Chitre, and translations from Dhasal, Daya Pawar and Trymbak Sapkale. The translations from Dhasal were done with the help of Jayant Karve, an exceptional ex-Pune Brahman whose command of various forms of Marathi speech penetrated the special language of Dhasal. Laurie Hovell, who first met Dhasal as an undergraduate student in India in 1982, has published some of his poetry in *Translations* (1968) and given a talk on his work at the Wisconsin South Asia Conference, Madison, 1988. We can expect a full-fledged article soon. Dilip Chitre has made a documentary film on Dhasal.

A Ph.D. dissertation from the University of Chicago, Vinay Dharwadker, "The Future of the Past: Tradition, Modernization and the Transforming of two Indian Traditions" (1989), deals extensively with Dalit literature in the context of modern Hindi and Marathi literature. When it is published, it should be consulted as a sophisticated analysis of the Marathi Dalit sahitya.

A Seminar on Dalit Literature in Marathi and Gujarati was held in February 18-20, 1988 by the Centre for Social Studies in Surat with over fifty scholars and writers in attendance. Papers, chiefly in English, were circulated in mimeographed form.

The first collection of the varied choice of the Ambedkar Movement has appeared in Barbara Joshi ed., *Untouchable* (London: Zed Press, 1986). Many of the pieces come from the Minority Rights conference of 1984 held in New York City for which the preceding selection of Dalit poetry was prepared.

* * *

A representative selection of Dalit poetry, short stories, essays and auto-biography appears in *Poisoned Bread*, edited by Arjun Dangle (Hyderabad: Orient Longman, 1992).

Select Bibliography

Biographies of B.R. Ambedkar
(Together with significant short articles and pamphlets)

B.K. Ahluwalia, and Shashi, *B.R. Ambedkar and Human Rights* (New Delhi: K.K. Publishers, 1981).

D.K. Baisantry, *Dr. Ambedkar, a Pioneer of Labour Welfare* (Jalandhar: Buddhist Publishing House, 1982). Pamphlet.

Chandra Barill, *Social and Political Ideas of B.R. Ambedkar* (Jaipur: Aalekh Publishers, 1977).

Raju G. Ganni, *The Life of Dr. B.R. Ambedkar* (Hyderabad: Babasaheb Dr. Ambedkar Memorial Society, 1979).

Daya Ram Jatava, *Political Philosophy of Dr. Ambedkar; Social Philosophy of B.R. Ambedkar* (Agra: Phoenix Publishing Agency, 1965).

K.K. Kavlekar, and A.S. Chausalkar, eds., *Political Ideas and Leadership of Dr. B.R. Ambedkar* (Pune: Vishwanil Publications, 1989).

Dhananjay Keer, *Dr. Ambedkar: Life and Mission* (Third edition: New Delhi: D.K., 1987; Second edition Bombay: Popular Prakashan, 1962; First Edition: 1951). Also in Marathi and Malayalam.

Dinkar Khadbe, *Dr. Ambedkar and Western Thinkers* (Pune: Sugava Prakashan, 1989).

Chandeo Bhavanrao Khairmode, *Da. Bhimrao Ramji Ambedkar* (in Marathi) 1st volume: 1952; 9th volume: 1988. Various publishers, the most recent, Maharashtra Rajya Sahitya ani Sanskriti Mandal, Bombay).

W.N. Kuber, *Dr. Ambedkar: A Critical Study* (New Delhi: People's Publishing House, 1973). Also *B.R. Ambedkar*, Builders of Modern India Series, New Delhi: Government of India, 1978).

C.H.J. Jacob Lobo, *Dr. B.R. Ambedkar: The Champion of Social Democracy in India* (Bangalore: Hilerina Publishers, 1984).

G.S. Lokhande, *Bhimrao Ramji Ambedkar: A Study in Social Democracy* (New Delhi: Intellectual Publishing House, 2nd revised edition, 1982; first published in 1977).

Hoti Lal Nim, Compiler, *Thoughts on Dr. Ambedkar* (Agra: Siddhartha Educational and Cultural Society, 1969).

A.M. Rajasekhariah, *B.R. Ambedkar: The Politics of Emancipation* (Bombay: Sindhu Publications, 1971).

G. Ganni Raju, *The Life of Dr. B.R. Ambedkar* (Hyderabad: Babasaheb Dr. Ambedkar Memorial Society, 1979).

Jeanette Robbin, *Dr. Ambedkar and His Movement* (Hyderabad: Dr. Ambedkar Publishing Society, 1964).

G.N. Sharma, and Moin Shakir, "B.R. Ambedkar" in *Politics and Society* (Aurangabad: Parimal, 1976).

R.D. Suman, *Dr. Ambedkar: Pioneer of Human Rights* (New Delhi: Bodhisattva Publications, 1977).

T.K. Tope, *Dr. B.R. Ambedkar, A Symbol of Social Revolt* (New Delhi: Maharashtra Information Centre, 1964). Pamphlet.

J.A.M. Bamfield, Bhagwan Das, D.R. Jatav, D.K. Baisantry, L.R. Balley, *Thoughts on Dr. Ambedkar* (Jalandhar: Bheem Patrika Publications, 1972).

A. Varadarajan, *Dr. B.R. Ambedkar and Popular Sovereignty* (Dharwad, 1982). Pamphlet.

Studies of the Reservation Policy and Social Mobility

There have been a flood of books on the first of these areas since my basic bibliography on Untouchability was published in the classic J. Michael Mahar ed., *The Untouchables in Contemporary India* (Tucson: University of Arizona Press, 1972). The following list notes some of the more general and more recent literature as well as current statements of theory.

Pratap Agarwal, *Halfway to Freedom* (New Delhi: Manohar, 1983).

C.L. Anand, *Equality, Justice and Reverse Discrimination* (New Delhi: Mittal, 1987).

Suma Chitnis, *A Long Way to Go: Report on a Survey of Scheduled Caste High School and College Students in 15 States of India* (New Delhi: Allied, 1981).

I.P. Desai, Ghanshyam Shah, etc., *Caste-Conflict and Reservation* (Surat: Centre for Social Studies, 1985).

Vasant Deshpande, *Towards Social Integration: Problems of Adjustment of Scheduled Caste Elite* (Pune: Shubhada Saraswat, 1978).

Charence J. Dias, *The Quest for Equality: Protective Discrimination or Compensatory Justice, Ethical Dilemmas of Development in Asia* (Lexington: D.C. Heath, 1983).

Marc Galanter, *Competing Equalities: Law and the Backward Classes in India* (Berkeley: University of California Press, 1983).

Dilip Hiro, *The Untouchables of India* (London: Minority Rights Group, 1982, 2nd edition).

Harold R. Issacs, *India's Ex-Untouchables* (New York: Harper and Row, 1974, first published: 1965). Still a classic.

N.D. Kamble, *Poverty Within Poverty* (New Delhi: Sterling, 1979). A classic from within the movement.

R.S. Khare, *The Untouchable as Himself* (New York: Cambridge University Press, 1985). A penetrating attempt to allow various levels of Untouchables to speak for themselves.

Dinesh Khosla, *Myth and Reality of the Protection of Civil Rights Law: A Case Study of Untouchables in Rural India* (Delhi: Hindustan Publishing Company, 1987).

R.K. Kshirsagar, *Untouchability in India: Implementation of the Law and Abolition* (New Delhi: Deep and Deep, 1986).

Joseph Mathew, *Ideology, Protest and Social Mobility: A Case Study of Mahars and Pulayas* (New Delhi: Inter-India for Indian Institute for Regional Development Studies, Kottayam). Caste studies across regions.

Haroobhai Mehta, and Hasmukh Patel eds., *Dynamics of Reservation Policy* (New Delhi: Patriot Publications, 1985). Many opinions.

Michael Moffatt, *An Untouchable Community in South India: Structure and Consensus* (Princeton: Princeton University Press, 1979). The chief explication of Dumont's theory of hierarchy as inevitable and acceptable in India.

Prabhati Mukherjee, *Beyond the Four Varnas: The Untouchables in India* (Shimla: Indian Institute of Advanced Study; Delhi: Motilal Banarsidass, 1986).

K.S. Pandhya, and Jayashree Mahapatra, *Reservation Policy in India* (New Delhi: Ashish, 1988).

Y.A. Parmar, *The Mahyavanshi: The Success Story of a Scheduled Caste* (Delhi: Mittal, 1987).

M.E. Prabhakar, ed., *Towards a Dalit Theology* (Madras: Published for the Christian Institute for the Study of Religion and Society and the Christian Dalit Liberation Movement by ISPCK, 1988).

Ishwari Prasad, *Reservation: Action for Social Equality* (New Delhi: Criterion Books, 1986). Dedicated to Lohia.

Sunanda Patwardhan, *Change Among India's Harijans* (New Delhi: Orient Longman, 1973). A pioneering comparison of several castes' progress in the Indian city of Pune.

Jagjivan Ram, *Caste Challenge in India* (New Delhi: Vision Books, 1980).

Nandu Ram, *The Mobile Scheduled Castes: Rise of a New Middle Class* (Delhi: Hindustan Publishing Corporation, 1988). Excellent bibliography.

Ramashray Roy, and V.B. Singh, *Between Two Worlds: A Study of Harijan Elites* (Delhi: Discovery Publishing House, 1987).

Satish Saberwal, *Mobile Men: Limits to Social Change in Urban Punjab* (New Delhi: Manohar, 1989).

Sachchidananda, *The Harijan Elite* (Faridabad: Thomson Press, 1976. The initial statement of alienation; see Singh and Sundaram for another view.

D.N. Sandanshiv, *Reservations for Social Justice: a Socio-Constitutional Approach* (Bombay: Current Law Publishers, 1986).

Vimal P. Shah, and Binod C. Agarwal eds., *Reservation: Policy Programmes, Issues* (Jaipur: Rawat, 1986).

B.A.V. Sharma, and K. Madhusudhan Reddy, *Reservation Policy in India* (New Delhi: Light and Life, 1982).

M. Showeb, *Education and Mobility among Harijans* (Varanasi: Gandhian Institute of Studies; Allahabad: Vohra Publishers and Distributors, 1986).

Parmanand Singh, *Equality, Reservation and Discrimination in India: A Constitutional Study of Scheduled Castes, Scheduled Tribes, and Other Backward Classes* (New Delhi: B.R. Publishing Corporation).

Sheo Swarath Singh, and S. Sundaram, *Emerging Harijan Elite: A Study of Their Identity* (New Delhi: Uppal Publishing House, 1987). The case for the majority not breaking ties.

Shoran Singh, *The Scheduled Castes of India: Dimensions of Social Change* (Delhi: Gian Publishing House, 1987).

A.K. Vakil, *Reservation Policy and Scheduled Castes in India* (New Delhi: Ashish, 1985).

See also the bibliographies after the chapters in Section I, and at the end of Section II, III and IV.

A special note should be made of the only collection of essays on various aspects of Dalit Life by Dalits themselves: Barbara R. Joshi ed., *Untouchable* (London: Zed Press, 1986. Every author represented was touched in some way by the Ambedkar movement.

A new series of volumes on Maharashtra should be consulted for a broad picture of European-Indian cooperative scholarship on the area. A Maharashtra conference at the University of Toronto in 1985 resulted in two volumes edited by Milton Israel, N.K. Wagle and Donald Attwood and published by the Centre for South Asian Studies, University of Toronto, 1987. A Conference at Heidelberg in 1988 on folklore and literature will result in a volume to be edited by Gunther D. Sontheimer. A third conference with a theme of women was held in 1991 at the Arizona State University under the guidance of Anne Feldhaus, and a fourth at S.N.D.T. Women's University in Bombay with Meera Kosambi in charge.

The study of the Ambedkar movement is greatly facilitated by the publishing of all his work in volumes entitled *Dr. Babasaheb Ambedkar: Writings and Speeches*, edited by Vasant Moon and published by the Education Department of the Government of Maharashtra. The series of sixteen volumes was begun in 1979 and to date 13 volumes have been published.

Index

Ad-Dharm movement of North, 322
Adi-Dravida movement of Tamil Nadu, 322
Agarkar, Gopal Ganesh, 43, 271
Agarkar, Gopal Krishna, 68
Agastya Muni, 210
Agricultural castes, 33-47
Ahir, D.C., 255
Aiyyavaru, Ramayya Vyankayya, 37
Ambedkar, Dr. Bhim Rao, 10, 11-12, 13, 24, 33, 34, 36, 44, 45 46, 53,-73, 79-117 (*passim*), 155-177, 191-214, 218, 222-226, 235, 237, 239, 241, 242, 243, 245, 249, 256, 259, 261, 269, 272, 273, 274, 280, 281, 283, 287, 289, 298, 299-300, 310-312, 317, 318, 319, 320, 323, 324, 325, 328; American experience of, 79-85, 314; and Mahatma Gandhi, 150-177; and mystic past, 57-59; Bible, other Buddhist writings, translations, 250-252; conversion of 12, 313 -conversion speech of (1935), 206-207; guiding principles of, 61-62; image of, and Mahar stereotype, 59-61; leader, religion, political party, 144-145; leadership, politics and education, 70-72; leadership completion of myth, 72-73; leadership of, at Mahad Conference, 67-70; leadership of, Southborough testimony and its ramifications, 64-67; Movement, 333, 339, political party of, 179; presided over a meeting at Trymbak (1929), 11; reaction of, to Gandhi, 160-172; rebel, 128-136; Republican Party of, 140-144; role of, 224-226; sketch of, 312-314; study in America, 79-85
Ambedkar, Prakash, 179
Ambedkar, Savita, 84
Ambedkar, Yashwant, 228
America; American Blacks, 82 - American Black movement, 314; American Black theatre, 322; Negroes of, 81, 82, 281; Negro Slavery, 82 Black American literature, 280-281, 314
Angulimal, 295-296
Ankush Guruji, C.N., 255
Apte, Hari Narayan, 43, 64
Arya Samaj, 47, 190; Arya Samajists, 207
Asmitadarsh Literary Conference (1979), 322
Assam, 235, 236
Atre, P.K., 140, 273, 274
Backward Classes, 112, 114, 127, 137, 140
Bagul, Baburao, 240, 268, 272, 275, 277, 278, 288, 332
Bagul, Gulabrao, 181
Bahishkrit Hitakarini Sabha (Depressed Classes Association) (*See also* Depressed Classes), 101, 162
Bahujan Samaj, concept of, 43

Bahujan Samaj Party, 179

Balu, P., 104

Bansode, Kisan Fagoji, 10, 56, 57, 63, 65, 70, 87, 95, 96, 101, 128, 271, 274

Bapat, P.V., 194, 252

Bapu Rao, Patthe, 319

Barshi Conference of (1924), 68

Barua, B.M., 237, 242

Bedekar, D.K., 273

Bengal, 135, 236; Bengal Buddhists, 236-237

Bhagwad Gita, 22

Bhagwata Purana, 15

Bhagwat, Durga, 273, 274

Bhagwat, Vidyut, 275, 289, 297, 302

Bhakti movement, 3, 8, 9, 12, 15, 26, 42, 73, 244, 269, 270; Bhakti school, democracy of, 9; Bhakti sect in Maharashtra, 26; Bhakti tradition, 22

Bhalekar, Krishnarao Pandurang, 37

Bhandare, R.D., 116, 252

Bhandarkar, R.G., 42-43, 64, 256

Bharatiya Janata Party, 179

Bhima, Ranu, 258

Bhole, R.R., 106

Birla, Ghanshyamdas, 168

Black Panthers, 314

Boad outcastes, 111

Bole, S.K., 98

Bombay, 45, 135, 251; Bombay Legislative Council, 66, 67, 98, 106; Bombay Province Depressed Classes Conference, 162; violence in 109

Bose, Subhash Chandra, 102

Brahmanism, 72, 137, 250, 323; Brahmanical system, 326

Brahmans, 3, 9, 23, 24, 37, 38, 39, 40, 41, 42, 45, 46, 47, 57, 64, 93, 100, 154, 163, 200, 211, 327; Brahmanical elite approval, 199, 202, 204; reform association of, 44

Brahmo Samaj, Bengal, 47

Buddha, 72, 157, 187, 188, 190, 192, 195, 208, 210, 218, 224, 226, 227, 233, 236, 239, 240, 245, 251, 259, 288, 296-297; refuge to, 136-140; temple to, 13

Buddha Jayanti, 190, 195, 231, 256

Buddhism, 12, 13, 72, 114, 117, 126-145, 173, 198, 203, 209, 210, 221, 222, 233, 235-247, 269, 276, 313, 318, 323; Buddhist conversion, 33, 115, 117, 126-127, 136, 138, 139, 141, 151, 187, 190-195, 207-211, 213, 219, 222-233, 249, 261, 293, 326-327 - Ambedkar's conversion speech 206-207; justification by mythic history, 210, recognition of religious knowledge and purity of life, 209, religious rights, 208, scriptural sanctification, 210, studies of meaning of, 252-255; history and legends of, 255-256; psychological impact of, 218-221; revival of, 187-196; social significance of, 139

Buddhist: All-India Buddhist Conference, 236; All-India Buddhist Dharma Conference (1975), 230, 242; Buddhist and Dalit Literacy Conference, 211; Buddhist caves, Aurangabad, Junnar and Nasik, 239; Buddhist Council, 72; Buddhist Literature: Dalit Sahitya and 259-261, Buddhist Literature Conference, Bombay, 275, Buddhist Literature of Maharashtra, 249; Buddhist Mahasabha, 242; Buddhist movement, 273 - songs of, 256-259; Buddhist ritual, guides on, 252-255; Buddhist Society of India, 197, 228; Buddhist tradition, use of Mahar past and, 286-290; Worli Buddhist temple,

Bombay, 243
Buddhists, 12, 13, 59, 71, 72, 86, 116, 117, 126-145, 187-196, 198, 207, 208, 210, 214, 219, 220, 224, 227, 229, 231, 232, 233, 235-247, 250, 252, 267, 270, 288, 289, 322, 325, 332; All-India Buddhist Dharma Conference, Nagpur, 230, 242; identity and organisations of converted, 235-247; leadership of, 228-231; Maharashtrian, holy days of, 231-233; Neo-Buddhists, 233; Vihara-meeting place for, 226-227; Young Men's Buddhist Association, 228
Burmese Buddhists, 233, 236
Cabinet Mission, 109
Cambodian Buddhists, 233
Cannon, Edward, 84
Caste system, 9, 24; traditional legitimization 43
Chakravarty, Ashok, 260
Chamars, 101, 106, 107 Conference (1939), 107; of North, 56; of Chattisgarh, 33, 57; of Maharashtra, 13 of Uttar Pradesh, 93 (Chambhars) 332
Chandaseniya Kayastha Prabhu (C.K.P.), 44, 45, 106
Chandramani, Mahasthaveer of Burma, 228
Chandwankar, Prahlad, 287, 306
Chavan, Yeshwantrao, 117
Chokha, 22
Chokhamela, 3-13, 14, 15, 26, 38, 42, 56, 59, 73, 93, 96, 128, 164, 241, 269, 270, 325
Chokhamela Hostel, 10, 56
Chokhamela Libraries, 56
Chokhamela Reform Society, 10, 93
Chokhamela Vidyawardah Mandal, 10
Choksey, R.D., 88
Chiplunkar, Vishnu Krishna, 61
Chitre, Dilip, 273, 280, 299, 332

Chittagong, 236, 237
Christianity, 61, 126, 134, 160, 162, 171, 191, 193, 207, 233, 254
Communal Award of (1932), 104, 105, 132, 152, 166, 168
Communism, 137, 142, 273; Communist Party of India, 142, 143, 176; Communists, 142
Congress (Indian National Congress), 33, 44, 53, 66, 69, 98, 101, 103, 104, 107, 109, 111, 112, 113, 114, 115, 116, 117, 118, 130, 133, 136, 140, 141, 142, 143, 153, 155, 163, 164, 168, 172, 173, 176, 179; Congress-League Plan, 66; Congress-League Scheme for self-rule, 66; Congress-Muslim League agreement, 166; Congress-Muslim League Constitutional Scheme, 153
Cripps, Sir Stafford, 108, 109; Cripps Cabinet Mission, 172; Cripps Proposals, 109, 172
Cunningham, Alexander, 189
DMK, 176
Dalai Lama, 235, 242
Dalit art exhibition, Nagpur, 322
"Dalit Culture:, 321
Dalit folk beliefs, 318-328
Dalit folklore, 317-328
Dalit literature, 211-214, 219, 267-339; Dalit Literature Conference, 211, 275, 278, 314; life of lowly in, 275-278; Seminar on Dalit Literature in Marathi and Gujarati (1988), 333
Dalit movement, 317
Dalit Panthers, 179-180, 211-214, 219, 267, 289, 314, 326; Black, 314
Dalit poetry, 293-314
Dalit Rangabhumi, 314, 321, 322, 332
Dalit Sahitya, 180, 240, 319, 332; and Buddhist Literature, 259-261
Dalit Stri Samwadini (Dalit Women's Dialogue), 322

Dalit women, 322; Dalit Women's Literary Conference, 332
Dalit theater, 321-322
Dalit writers, 273-290; speech of Dalit, 278-280
(The) Dalit Voice, 321
Dalits: as creators of culture, 319-320; Dalit Life by Dalits, 338, in Maharashtra, 318; interest in Black American literature, 280-281; Lords of the Earth/Sons of the Soil, 322-328; Maharashtra Dalit Literature Conference, 274; of Gujarat and Karnataka, 71; "Original Dravidians", 322-328
Dalvi, Janavant, 273, 278
Damle, Krishnaji Keshav, 42
Damle, Rekha, 275
Dangle, Arjun, 260, 303
Das, Sarat Chandra, 190
Dayanand Saraswati, 154
"De-notified tribes", 332
Deorukhakar, B.J., 104
Depressed Classes, 45, 61, 67-70, 95, 97, 99, 100, 111, 117, 128, 129, 130, 131, 132, 134, 153, 160, 162, 163, 165, 166, 171, 175, 207, 209, 214, 267, 283; Central Provinces Depressed Class Association, 101; All India Depressed Class Conference, Nagpur, 58, 67, 105, 108; Depressed Class Associations of Bombay, 104, 106; Depressed Classes Institute, 68, 103; Depressed Class Mission, Pune, 63, 133; Depressed Class Mission Society, 66; Depressed India Association, 96, 97, 99; Kolaba District Depressed Classes Conference, 203; of Bombay State, 97; of Punjab, 33; reaction of Depressed Classes to Simon Commission, 101; uplift of, 133
Desai, Mahadev, 161, 167

Deshpande, Gauri, 212, 279, 286, 287
Dewey, John, 80, 83, 84, 97
Dhale, Raja, 180, 219, 267
Dhamma Dikhsa Day, 231
Dharwadker, Vinay, 332
Dhasal, Namdev, 24, 180, 219, 226, 267, 269, 274, 276, 277, 278-279, 280, 282, 298, 299, 307, 312, 332
Dhulia Satyagraha, 116
Dixit, Vidya, 241, 295
Dnyaneshwar, 4, 10, 22
Eastern Indian Buddhists, 37
Education, 62, 71-72, 90; University Reforms Commission, 66; Wardha Scheme of Education, 107
Eknath Maharaj, 3, 13-27, 270
Enthoven, R.S., 322
Feldhaus, Anne, 339
Franchise Committee (Southborough), 66, 96
Gadapyle, Rajananda, 256
Gadge Maharaj, 12, 25
Gadhe, Gangadhar, 180
Gaikwad, B.K. (Dadasaheb), 45, 106, 116, 117, 131, 144, 179
Gajbhiye, Mina, 290
Gajendragadkar, Justice P.B., 9
Gandhi, Mahatma, 24, 60, 61, 64, 69, 73, 82, 84, 103, 104, 105, 111, 132, 152, 155, 193, 216, 267, 281; and Ambedkar, 150-177
Gandhian Satyagraha method, 160
Gawai, G.A., 10, 65, 94, 96, 97, 98
Gawai, R.S., 179
Gholap, D.D., 98
Gholay, V.R., 37
Ghodbole, B.G., 256
"Great Tradition", 317
"Harijan", term, 150
Harijans, 10, 60, 73, 108, 153, 167, 169, 170, 174, 317; Harijan Sevak Sangh 105, 108, 170, 172; Harijan Temple Entry Bill, 107
Hindu Code Bill, 112, 136, 173

Hindu Mahasabha, 105, 164, 168
Hindu-Muslim unity, 103, 150, 163
"Hindu Raj", 133
Hindu temples, 130, 157, 193
Hinduism, 47, 61, 69, 70, 94, 95, 110,
  114, 126, 130, 131, 133, 137, 139,
  154, 155, 156, 157, 163, 170, 188,
  189, 192, 193, 198, 207, 208, 226,
  228, 231, 232, 236, 237, 249, 269
Hindus, 61, 91, 93, 97, 98, 104, 132,
  133, 134, 138, 156, 161, 165,
  167, 168, 169, 171, 173, 181, 191,
  206, 214,; Caste Hindus, 61, 65,
  73, 88, 91, 100, 105, 106, 110,
  113, 130, 131, 139, 157, 160,
  168, 191, 194, 205, 276
Hivrale, Sukhram, 268
Iluvans, 192
Independent Labour Party, 70, 83, 106,
  107, 134, 135, 158, 171, 191
Indian Social Conference (1895), 43
Islam, 61, 107, 126, 134, 171, 193, 231,
  332
Jadhav, Bhaskarrao (B.V.), 37
Jadhav, D.G., 106
Jagjivan Ram, 174
Jalgaon Satyagraha, 116
Jana Sangha, 143
Japanese Buddhists, 233
Jatavas, 127
Jaya Prakash Narayan, 79
Jayakar, M.R., 110
Jedhe, Keshavrao, 101
Johar bharuds, 15-20
Johar poems, 15-20
Jinnah, M.A., 135
Joshi, Barbara, R, 333, 338
Joshi, M.M., 98
Joshi, S.M., 140
Justice Party in Madras, 101
Kabir, 11, 22, 72, 157, 225
Kabir Panth, 58, 93, 318
Kadam, K.N., 254
Kajrolkar, N.S., 112

Kakar, Sudhir, 254
Kala Ram Satyagraha, 165
Kala Ram Temple, Nasik, 94, 165, 193
Kale, Pramod, 276
Kolhapur, 60
Kamble, Arun, 180, 212, 214, 279,
  286, 305
Kamble, B.C., 112, 115, 179
Kamble, B.R., 255
Kamble, Bebi, 332
Kamble, Cokha, 274
Kamble, N.M., 179
Kamble, Shantabai, 332
Kamble, Shivram Janba, 36, 41, 63,
  65, 91, 92, 99, 128, 197, 274;
  Petition of (1910), 202-203
Karat, Shankarrao, 211
Kardak, Waman, 218, 238, 259, 274,
  280, 286, 289, 304
Karve, Iravati, 8, 26
Karve, Jayant, 241, 275, 295, 296, 297,
  298, 303, 304, 305, 306, 307, 312
Kashyap, Jagdish, 208, 237, 252
Kausalyayan, Anand, 190, 208, 229,
  242, 243, 250, 251
Kavade, Jogendra, 180
Keer, Dhananjay, 135
Keluskar, K.A., 137
Khairmode, C.B., 326
Kharat, Shankarrao, 238, 253, 268, 274,
  275, 276-277
Khobragade, B.D., 116
Khobragade, Girish, 179
Khoti Abolition Bill, 107, 110
Kirloskar Brothers, 37
Kolaba District Depressed Classes
  Conference, 203
Kondiram, Pandit, 199, 200, 201, 202,
  271, 283
Kosambi, Dharmananda, 190, 208, 237,
  251, 252
Krishnajee, Subhedar Bahadur Ganga-
  ram, 36, 91-92
Kshatriyas, 22, 43, 57, 58, 91, 93, 154,

201
Kulkarni, A.R., 190
Kulkarni, Datta J., 25
Kumbhar, Dhondiram Namdeo, 37
Lingayats, 103
Lingu, P. Rajanna, 37
Little Great Tradition, 317
"Little Tradition", 317
Lohia, Rammanohar, 140
Lokhande, Bhau, 255, 270
Lokhande, N.M., 37
Madgulkar, Brahman Vyankatesh, 273, 276
Madhav, Bandhu, 274
Madhya Pradesh, 127, 235, 245
Madkholkar, G.T., 273
Madras, 135, 238; "Adi" - Dravida in, 57; Non-Brahman movement of, 33
Maha Bodhi Society, Calcutta, 189, 194
Mahad Conference, 67-70, 100, 104, 203, 206, 283, 313
Mahad Satyagraha, 100, 164, 171
Mahapati, 22-23
Mahar Battalion, 289
Mahar elite, 36
Mahar movement, 10, 24, 33-47, 57, 197-214, 269, 271; brokers, 44-46; communication and, 46; essential factors in the processes, 34; for religious rights, 9-10; grievances understood by both elite and mass, 38; leadership released from traditional service, 34-38; legitimization, 41-44; traditional role of Mahars, 34-38
Mahar myths, 58
Mahar political movement, 100
Mahar Regiment (Mahar Machine Gun Regiment), 92, 213, 325-326
Mahar Satyagraha(s), 10, 110, 164
Maharashtra, 3, 9, 15, 22, 33-47, 235, 237, 238, 239, 240, 241, 242, 244,

245, 246, 270, 293, 313, 318-328, 332; Bhakti (devotional religion), 44; Bhakti movement, 270; Bhakti sect in, 4, 26; Bhakti tradition, 22; Brahmans, 40; Buddhism and politics in, 126-145; Buddhist Literature Committee, 274; Buddhist literature of, 249-261; Buddhist holy days of, 231-233; Dalit Literature Conference, 274; Dalits in 318; Literary Conference, 274; Mahars of, 53-73, 86-188; Maharashtra Conference, University of Toronto (1985), 339; reform movement in, 47
Mahars, 3, 4, 11, 12, 13, 15, 16, 18, 34-38, 43, 45, 46, 47, 106, 126, 127, 133, 134, 135, 137, 138, 139, 141, 155-156, 163 170, 173, 191, 192, 194, 197-214, 243, 249, 258, 260, 273, 276, 298, 317, 318-328, 332; Conference (1936) speech to, 12; Conference of Deccan Mahars, 91; difference between Mahars and other untouchable castes, 62-64; economic opportunities presented to, 89; in early twentieth century, 62-64; in Junnar, 38; in Poona, 10; justification by mythic history, 205-206; mythic history, 200-201; myths of origin and heroism, 54-55; of Maharashtra, 33-47, 53-73, 86-118, 222; purity of life, scriptural sanctification mythic history, 203; recognition of religious knowledge and purity of life, 205; scriptural sanctification, 205; stereotype, Ambedkar's image and 59-61; traditional role of, 34-38; use of Mahar past and Buddhist tradition, 286-290
Malaviya, Pandit Madan Mohan, 164,

168, 207
Malkani, N.R., 175
Mane, Vasudha, 275
Mangiah, J. 169
Mangs, 106, 107
Manu, 283
Manusmriti, 69, 100, 164, 204, 207, 283
Marathas, 37, 39, 41, 43, 44, 46, 57, 58, 66, 97, 99, 101, 103, 206, 287, 289
Marathi Bhakti tradition, 15
Marathi Literacy Conference (1977) Pune, 25-26
Marathi Sahitya Sammelan, 25
Mate, S.M., 272
Meshram, Keshav, 268, 275, 305
Maurya, B.P., 116
Mehta, Ashok, 113, 141
Miller, Beatrice, 236
Miller, Robert, 276, 317,
Moon, Vasant, 181, 250, 339
Moonje, B.S., 105
Montagu, Edwin, 45, 65
Montagu-Chelmsford Reforms, 37, 64-65, 81, 96, 98, 159, 323
Moray, M.S., 255
Muddiman Committee, 98
Muknayak, newspaper, 11, 130, 313
Mundlay, Asha, 312
Muslim League, 109, 135, 172
Muslims, 97, 104, 132, 134, 136, 142-143, 191, 206, 207, 233, 247; demands of, for Pakistan, 110
Nagpur, 57, 70, 72, 102, 103, 114, 126, 133, 135, 137, 142, 165, 194, 228, 231, 240, 242, 243, 245, 246, 249, 250, 251, 252, 253, 256, 259, 270, 271, 325, 327; Buddhists, 71; Conference, 68; Conversion, 230; Dalit Literature Conference, 275, 289, 290; violence in, 109
Namashudras of Bengal, 33
Namdeo, 4, 269, 270

Nandnar, 59
Naarahari, 22
Narain, A.K., 237
Naranavare, Chandrabhan Kisan, 252
Narasu, P. Lakshman, 137, 190, 193, 251
Narayana Guru, Sri, 160
Nasik, 104; Nasik Satyagraha at Kala Ram Temple, 69, 94, 95, 110, 116, 130-131, 165, 313
Natarajan, S., 67
Nehru, Jawaharlal, 44, 111, 113, 136, 145, 155, 173, 237; Nehru Plan, 166
Nemade, Bhalchandra, 273
Nimbalkar, Waman, 274, 284, 302, 332
Non-Brahmans, 47, 66, 67; leaders, 37; Non-Brahman movement, 33-47, 99, 100, 101; brokers, 44-46; communication and, 46; grievances understood by both elite and mass, 38
Olcott, Henry, 189
Oturkar, R.V., 9
Padgaonkar, Dileep, 214
Padhye, Bhau, 278
Padmaji, Baba, 45
Padyal, Tukkaram, Tatya, 37
Pagore, Haribhau, 252
Panchbahi, M.D. 255
Pande, Vithoba Raoji Sant, 94
Pandharinath Prabhu, 176
Pandharpur, 10, 11, 13, 24, 26, 44, 56, 93, 128, 244, 245; Bhakti sect, 14
Pantawane, Gangadhar, 218, 268, 269, 271, 274, 277
Panthers, Black, 314; rise of, 179-180
Paranjpey, R.P., 98
Parvati Satyagraha, Pune, 165
Parvati Temple, Pune, entry to, 164, 202
Patel, Sardar, 104, 167, 170
Patel, V.J., 98

Patil, Bhaurao, 37
Patil, Shankar, 273
Patwardhan, W.B., 9
Pawar, Daya, 24, 240, 254, 268, 274,
    278, 279, 281, 282, 283, 285,
    288, 289, 293, 295, 296, 297, 301,
    306, 319, 321, 332
Pawar, J.V., 288, 307
Peasants and Workers' Party, 113;
    Peasants around Pune &
    Ahmednagar (1875), 37
People's Education Society, 71, 137,
    159, 197
Phule, Mahatma Jotiba, 37, 39, 40, 43,
    44, 45, 72, 82, 101, 157, 225, 227,
    271, 324
Poona (Pune), 36, 135, 251; Mahars in,
    10
Poona Pact of (1932), 104, 133, 168,
    169
Prarthana Samaj, 44, 47, 94, 128
Pune (see Poona)
Punjab, 127, 135, 322; 'Ad-Dharm' in,
    57
Radhakrishnan, S, 194
Raidasis (Ravidasis), 56
Rajah, Rao Bahadur M.C., 105, 168
Rajbhoj, P.N., 106, 112, 167
Ramanandi Panth, 93
Ramteke, D.L., 254
Ranade, Mahadeo Govind, 8, 9, 43, 44,
    271
Ranpise, D.P. 252
Ranpise, V.R. 253, 255
Ravidas, 13, 22, 59, 241
Reform movement in Maharashtra, 47;
    social reforms, 204
Reforms Committee (Franchise), 323
Republican-Muslim alliance, 141
Republican Party, 70, 114, 115, 116,
    117, 136, 137, 140-144, 145, 176,
    177, 179, 228, 312
Riddles controversy, 181
Robinson, James Harvey, 80, 84

Round Table Conferences, 67, 94,
    102, 103, 104, 132, 133, 151,
    166, 168, 169
Royal Commission on Indian Currency
    and Finance, 66
Rupavate, Dadasaheb, 179
Sahasarbudhe, G.N., 158
Sakat, K.K., 207
Samyukta Maharashtra Samiti, 115,
    141, 142
Samyukta Socialist Party, 141
Sangarakshita, Ven, 229, 243, 251, 252
Sangari, Bhai, 180
Sankaracharya of Karwar Math, 207
Sankrityayan, Rahul, 190, 208, 237,
    251
Sane Guruji, 13, 272-273
Sapkale, Tryambak, 241, 284, 286, 293,
    296, 332
Sardar, G.B., 9
Sarvajanik Sabha, 44
Sathe, Annabhau, 269, 273, 274
Satya Shodak Samaj, 37, 43, 46; move-
    ment, 39, 271
Savadkar, Subhedar, 36, 68
Savant, S.T., 327
Savata Mali, 22
Scheduled Caste(s), 61, 86, 106, 108,
    109, 110, 111, 112, 114, 116,
    117, 127, 135, 136, 137, 140, 172,
    174, 176, 213, 267, 317, 321; All
    India Scheduled Castes Federa-
    tion, 135; discrimination towards,
    53; political movement 111; Uttar
    Pradesh Conference, 114
Scheduled Caste Federation, 68, 70,
    107, 109, 110, 112, 113, 114, 115,
    116, 117, 126, 135, 137, 140, 141,
    142, 171, 172
Scheduled Tribes, 112, 114, 117, 140,
    173, 174
Servants of Untouchables Society, 169
Shahu Maharaj of Kolhapur, 37, 99,

101
Shende, N.R., 274
Shinde, B.S., 281
Shinde, Gautam, 260
Shinde, Vithal Ramji, 45, 63, 66, 69, 98, 99, 133, 137, 192
Shivaji, Chhatrapati, 43, 44
Shivraj, N, 108
Shivatarkar, S.N., 103
Shotwell, James, 80, 84
Shudras (Sudras), 46, 58, 154, 176, 209, 270
Siddharthnagar, 293-295
Sikhism, 61, 107, 134, 171, 193, 207
Sikhs, 134, 171, 207, 233, 247
Simon Commission, 66, 99, 103, 105, 132, 165; reaction of Depressed Classes to, 101
Singhalese Buddhists, 233
Social reforms, 204; Reform movement, 47
Sontheimer, Gunther, D., 339
Southborough Committee on Franchise, 64, 81, 96, 97, 98, 99, 129, 130, 203, 323
Srinivas, M.N., 139, 205
Srinivasan, Dewan Bahadur R. 102, 132, 168
Srivastava, K.M., 255
Starte Committee, 67
Stowe, Harriet Beecher, 272
Surve, Narayan, 269, 274, 280, 298
Swaraj, 153, 172; Swaraj Constituion, 102
Temple entry struggle, 206; Harijan Temple Entry Bill, 107; Temple entry at Nasik, 170
Temple road Satyagraha, Vaikam, Travancore (1924-25), 103
Temple Satyagrahas, 69, 110
Temples, Hindu, 130, 157, 193
Tendulkar, Vijay, 152, 273, 274, 277
Thailand, 229-230, 232, 243; Thai Budhists (Bhikshus), 229-230, 233,

243
Thakkar, Amritlal B, 168, 169, 176
Thaware, G.M., 113-114
Theravada Buddhism, 236
Thorat, S.K., 254
Tibet, 235; Tibetans, 235, 236; Tobetan Buddhism, 235-236
Tilak, Lokmanya Bal Gangadhar 44, 61
Tipnis, S.G., 99
Tipnis, Surendranath, 68
Traditionalism: Anti-traditionalism, 282-286
Tripartite Labour Conference, 83
Tukaram, 11, 15, 270
United Provinces, 135, 322; "Ad-Dharm" in Punjab and, 57 See Uttar Pradesh
Untouchability, 3, 5, 12, 25, 54, 103, 104, 111, 126, 151, 153, 154, 155 156, 158, 163, 168, 170, 173, 175, 210, 238, 324; All India Anti-Untouchability League, 168, 169; Anti-Untouchability, 202; Anti-Untouchability Sub-Committee, 164; Untouchability Offences Act, 117
Untouchables (Untouchable Castes), 3, 9, 10, 12, 13, 15, 23, 33, 36, 38, 39, 45, 46, 53-73, 81, 82, 88, 89, 91, 93, 94, 97, 98, 99, 100, 101, 102, 103, 105, 107, 126, 129, 130, 131, 132, 133, 134, 139, 140, 142, 150, 151, 152, 153, 155, 156, 157, 159, 160, 162, 164, 165, 166, 169, 170, 171, 172, 173, 175, 176, 177, 180, 191, 192, 193, 194, 197, 198, 199, 200, 206, 207, 210, 213, 223, 226, 239, 240, 246, 251, 267, 271, 272, 276, 287, 298, 313, 314, 317-328; Conversion to Islam, 332; difference between Mahars and, 62-64; in North & South, 58; movements of, 82, 90; of Madras,

33; recognition of religious knowl-
edge and purity of life, 200; right
to religious activities, 200, 202,
204-205
Uttar Pradesh, 116, 127, 142-143, 177;
Uttar Pradesh Scheduled Caste
Conference, 114
Vaikam Satyagraha, 152, 160
Vaisyas, 22, 93, 154
Valmiki, 320-321
Varna system, 176; Law of Varna, 154
Vidyabhushan, Satish Chandra, 190
Viharas, (meeting place for Buddhists)
226-227, 229
Vivekananda, Swami, 154
Vivekananda, Thai Bhikshu, 229
Wagle, N.K., 339
Walangkar, Gopal Baba, 36, 38, 41,

45, 57, 58, 59, 63, 91, 94, 128,
197, 198-201, 211, 271, 325; Pe-
tition of (1894), 198-201, 212
Wankhade, M.N., 268
Warerkar, Mama, 273
Watan system, 58, 107
Wilson, John, 322
Women, 22, 322; Dalit Stri Samwadini
(Dalit Women's Dialogue), 322;
Dalit Women's Literary Confer-
ence, 332
Workers' Civil Liberties Suspension
Act, 107
Worli Buddhist Temple, Bombay, 243
Worli riots of (1974), 289
Yagavkar, Gopal Swami, 128
Yervada Jail, Pune, 104, 132